ONCE TO

*The further pilgrimage of
Friar Felix Fabri*

H. F. M. PRESCOTT

New York 1958
THE MACMILLAN COMPANY

Acknowledgments

I wish to thank all those who have helped me in the preparation of this book, among whom are many of the members of Staff of the Bodleian Library, the Ashmolean Museum and the Griffiths Institute in the University of Oxford, and of these, in particular, Mr. I. Robertson and Mr. A. D. H. Bivar for unfailing kindness and interest in my problems. My thanks are also due to Miss Cecilia Ady, Miss Olga Bickley, Dr. Barbara Reynolds, Miss Frances Williams, Professor Paul Kahle and the late Professor Pope. For their kindness during my visit to Jugoslavia I thank Drs. Fisković and Gracić and Signora Vernazza. I owe very much to Mr. G. W. Murray for his help in the interpretation of Felix Fabri's account of the desert journey, and for permission to use his map as the basis of that on p. 38. My debt to Mrs. D. M. Mack and to Mr. Malcolm Letts is greater than all other; I can only ask them to accept my thanks. Lastly I wish to express my gratitude to my Publishers for their patience, and to Mrs. Millar for much help in connection with the illustrations.

Contents

Chapter		Page
	ACKNOWLEDGMENTS	7

Part One: Jerusalem to Gaza

I	INTRODUCTORY	17
II	THE LAST OF THE HOLY LAND	23

Part Two: Gaza to Mount Sinai

III	THE SCHOOL OF THE DESERT	39
IV	THE DESERT JOURNEY	59

Part Three: Mount Sinai and the Monastery of St. Katherine

V	THE MONKS OF ST. KATHERINE	77
VI	THE MONASTERY, THE MOUNTAINS AND THE SHRINES	84

Part Four: Mount Sinai to Egypt

VII	MORE OF THE DESERT	99

Part Five: Egypt

VIII	THE GARDEN OF BALM	115
IX	AMONG THE MAMLUKS	124
X	SEEING CAIRO	139
XI	CAIRO, THE PASSING SHOW	155
XII	GOING DOWN THE NILE	173
XIII	ALEXANDRIA: "THE PUBLIC MARKET OF BOTH WORLDS"	190

Chapter		Page

Part Six: Alexandria to Venice

XV	ON BOARD THE SPICE SHIPS	221
XVI	WINTER VOYAGE	229
XVII	UP THE ADRIATIC	239

Part Seven: Venice to Ulm

XVIII	VENICE OF THE MERCHANTS	257
XIX	THE WAY HOME	268
XX	VALEDICTORY	277
BIBLIOGRAPHY		287
NOTES		291
INDEX		305

LIST OF ILLUSTRATIONS

Plates

Facing
page

1. PTOLEMY "THE GEOGRAPHER" FROM THE CARVING (1468–1474) BY JORG SYRLIN IN THE CATHEDRAL AT ULM. *Reproduced by permission of the Stadtarchiv at Ulm* *Frontispiece*

2. THE TOMB OF BERNHARD VON BREYDENBACH IN THE CATHEDRAL AT MAINZ. *Reproduced by permission of the Dom-und Diozesanmuseum, Mainz. (Photograph Ludwig Richter)* 64

3. SAINT KATHERINE OF ALEXANDRIA. *Reproduced by permission of the Stadtarchiv at Ulm* 80

4. CAIRO, 1512. (Reception of the Venetian Ambassador at Cairo, 1512. *School of Gentile Bellini.*) *Reproduced by permission of the Caisse Nationale des Monuments Historiques, Paris, from the picture in The Louvre* 160

5. GREECE AND THE AEGEAN IN THE FIFTEENTH CENTURY. *Portolan chart by Nicolo de Pasqualin. (Egerton MSS. 73, 23b.) By permission of the Trustees of the British Museum* 224

6. VENETIANS ENJOYING A SPECTACLE. *Detail from Mansueti's "Miracole della Croce"* 240

7. VENICE, 1500. *From Jacopo Barbari's Map of Venice in the Department of Prints and Drawings at the British Museum. Reproduced by permission of the Trustees* 272

8. VIEW AND PLAN OF ULM IN 1493. *Reproduced by permission of the Stadtarchiv, Ulm* 278

Maps and Illustrations in the text

Page

GAZA TO MOUNT SINAI (map). Based upon Mr. G. W. Murray's map of Felix Fabri's desert journey in the *Geographical Journal*, September 1956, by kind permission of Mr. Murray and the Royal Geographical Society 38

PROFILE OF MOUNT SINAI. From Jacques de Verona's *Liber Peregrinationis*, 1420 88

THE BALSAM PLANT. From *De Planti Aegyptis . . .* by Prosper Alpinus, Venice, 1592 119

11

LIST OF ILLUSTRATIONS

	Page
PLAN OF CAIRO. From the original by Paul Walther, 1492, in the Bayerische State Archives at Neuberg-on-the-Donau. *Reproduced by permission of the Bayerische Stadtarchiv*	144–5
VIEW OF ALEXANDRIA. From Pierre Belon's *Portraits d'Oyseaux, Animaux,* etc. . . . *d'Arabie*, Paris, 1552	198
ALEXANDRIA TO VENICE (map). *Reproduced by permission of Eyre & Spottiswoode Ltd.*	220
VENICE TO ULM (map). *Reproduced by permission of Eyre & Spottiswoode Ltd.*	256

ONCE TO SINAI

Part One

JERUSALEM TO GAZA

CHAPTER I

Introductory

Three times, so Chaucer declared, had his imagined Wife of Bath been at Jerusalem, and by this statement at once gave his contemporaries the horse-power of that remarkable woman. He knew too much to suggest that she had been thrice, or even twice, to Mount Sinai – a further pilgrimage which, if undertaken at all, formed either the prologue or epilogue to the Jerusalem journey – for that would have removed her fictitious but very real character beyond the bounds of credibility. Few among the great number of pilgrims to Jerusalem added Mount Sinai to their catalogue of Holy Places; none of these few went there more than once.

Felix Fabri, the Swiss-born Dominican from Ulm, whose pilgrimages to Jerusalem in 1480 and 1483 are rehearsed in the first part of his vast *Evagatorium in Terram Sanctam* . . . was one of a small number of pilgrims, who in the latter year went on from Jerusalem to the Holy Mount, and it is upon his profuse and lively narrative that the present book, like its predecessor,* is chiefly founded.

Two other pilgrims, who had been in Jerusalem during the summer season of 1483, and shared with Fabri in the pilgrimage to Mount Sinai, also left records of their experiences, though these are neither on the same scale nor of the same quality as that of the Swiss. The chief virtue of the book of Bernhard von Breydenbach lies in the pictures which Erhard Rewich drew for it, though the wealthy lay canon of Mainz earns the credit of having retained the services, throughout the pilgrimage, of such an artist. The narrative, almost as little von Breydenbach's own as the illustrations, though produced in his name, is for the most part a condensation of Fabri's *Evagatorium*. Only now and then the man who paid the piper intervenes, laying his hand, as it were, upon the instrument, to contribute a brief tootle of his own, usually upon the subject of food.

The *Itinerarium* of Friar Paul Walther of Guglingen, a sixty-year-old Franciscan, is on the other hand the personal expression of a man of character, intellect and education, but of one whose inward-turning eye found little to interest it in the desert, and even looked with indifference

* *Jerusalem Journey*, London, 1954.

upon the crowding experiences of Egypt. And yet this difficult and emulous old man will sometimes be seen to soften towards young creatures, for their beauty or for their pitiable misfortune.

In addition to these three narratives of the pilgrimage to Sinai in 1483 other accounts have been used to explain or supplement the picture which they give. The period which these cover stretches from the last decade of the fourteenth century to the first dozen years of the sixteenth. The writer may be knight or merchant or priest; almost all are on pilgrimage; but the knight may combine with this a military reconnaissance of an enemy country,* or a new, Renaissance interest in travel for its own sake; † the merchant may be a passing visitor who eyes with interest the commodities of a strange land,‡ or one who, having been resident there for years, is as friendly with its Moslem as with its Christian inhabitants;§ the priest may be a Venetian patrician by birth, a sea-captain turned Friar, a man who had first known Alexandria when he and other gay sparks from the ships had gone about with sticks at the ready, to beat the devil out of an aggressive Moslem.‖

Besides these there are men whose experiences of the East went far beyond that of any ordinary traveller or merchant. There is Niccolo Conti, tragically unfortunate, who, attempting to pass through Egypt on his way back to Venice after years of trade and travel in the Far East, lost not only the great fortune he had made in India, but wife and children as well. There is Johann Schiltberger, who, taken prisoner at the battle of Nicopolis, served as a slave many royal masters, including the great Timur himself, yet contrived after thirty years to return to the home he had left as a boy.

Only rich men, and priests who drew upon the liberality of the rich for their expenses, could afford the necessary outlay for the Sinai journey. And besides the outlay, the hardships and hazards of this pilgrimage, compared with which that to Jerusalem was "no more than a holiday and diversion"[1], prevented most pilgrims from undertaking it. Pilgrims to Sinai braved the passage of the Tîh Desert on their journey to the Mount; from there, through the defiles of the mountains, they reached the Red Sea, and along its parched shores made their way to Cairo, the capital of the Mamluk empire. From Cairo they sailed down the fabled Nile to Alexandria, and from there took passage back to Venice in the ships of the Venetian spice fleet, which returned from Alexandria every autumn laden with precious cargoes of the Far East, touching on their

---

* Guillebert de Lannoy, Bertrandon de la Broquière.
† Pero Tafur, Arnold von Harff.   ‡ Leonardo Frescobaldi, Simone Sigoli.
§ Emmanuele Piloti.   ‖ Francesco Suriano.

INTRODUCTORY

homeward voyage at ports which belonged either to the colonial empire of Venice, or to her satellites, the Christian Dukes of the Ægean Islands.

The scope of the travellers' experience was, therefore, wide, and their narratives touch and illuminate history at many points. In the almost timeless conditions of the desert a bunch of late medieval pilgrims will seem to approach through the centuries till it moves through the wilderness alongside the caravans of the eighteenth, nineteenth, even of the twentieth centuries, up to the day of motor transport and the jeep. Once they reach Egypt, however, the point of interest is not timelessness, but the very opposite, as we become acutely conscious of the passage of time – of the end of a period. When Felix Fabri and his companions watched the old Sultan Qa'it Bey dispensing justice in his citadel palace at Cairo, the Mamluk Sultanate had only thirty-four more years to run before the conquering Turks hanged its last ruler at one of the gates of the capital. Fourteen years after the pilgrims of 1483 saw the harbour of Alexandria crowded with the merchant galleys of the Mediterranean, the Portuguese discoveries of the Cape route would bye-pass the commanding geographical position of Egypt, and the spice trade begin to leave its ancient course for the new ocean passage. Felix Fabri's narrative brings us home with him to Germany, and here again the end of a period is near, for less than forty years after the Friar knocked at the gate of the Convent at Ulm, Luther was hammering his nails into the door of the church at Wittenberg, and the Protestant reformation was in sight.

Only a score of pilgrims, all, with two exceptions, German, remained in Jerusalem in the late summer of 1483, in order to make the Sinai pilgrimage after the rest of the two hundred or so pilgrims of various nationalities, having completed the usual exhausting fortnight of sightseeing, had returned to the waiting Venetian galleys at Jaffa. During the voyage out, and the set tour of the Holy Land, like had drawn to like, and already these twenty men had fallen naturally into three companies.

The first of these was the most cohesive, formed as it was of neighbours and friends, and cemented by the bond of kinship.* Bernhard von Breydenbach was the man of the greatest importance among these though not of the highest birth, for the first in rank as well as the youngest of all the pilgrims, was John Count of Solms, third son of Count Cuno of Solms Liech;[2] the boy was accompanied upon this fifteenth-century equivalent of the Grand Tour by his tutor Philip von Bicken, and the coats-of-arms of these noble families were later to adorn the title page of

* The Breydenbach and Bicken families had intermarried in 1455 (v. Davies, *Bernhard von Breydenbach*, p. iii).

Breydenbach's sumptuous volume. The three noblemen, as befitted their wealth and rank, travelled in style, with an "accomplished cook" named John, an Italian-speaking interpreter, and the artist Erhard Rewich. Rewich was a man – if his woodcuts of harbour scenes are anything to go by – of a pleasant humour: certainly he was one with a quick eye for the attitude of lounger and loafer, and the craft to reproduce it by a few lines, sometimes in a figure hardly bigger than a grain of wheat. During the pilgrimage, motives of discretion caused him to be classed as an esquire.[3]

The members of the second company were all German but one, and all laymen but two. Of these was the Franciscan Friar, Paul Walther, and with him came one of the lay-brothers from the Franciscan Convent at Jerusalem, a Pole, Thomas of Cracow, a notable linguist who could even speak and understand Arabic. The laymen included five knights, and one servant. The character of one of the knights, Bernhard (or Vernand) von Mernawe, is revealed by one of the descriptive tags which Friar Felix sometimes, but all too rarely, attaches to individuals, as a man who was "everyone's comforter";[4] the rest are mere names to us. As servant they brought along with them a man who may well have been one of the most interesting people among the pilgrims. Conrad Artus had come out to Jerusalem with the same party of Suabian nobles to which Felix Fabri had acted as Chaplain on the journey to Jerusalem. When these, their pilgrimage accomplished, had left for Jaffa with the majority of the pilgrims, Conrad had remained, attaching himself as servant to the knights of the second company, in order, one may suppose, to see more of the world. This gifted rolling-stone served his new employers as cook, caterer and barber, and was, in addition, a most skilful lutanist and performer upon the viol.[5]

In the third company there were six men, two of whom were priests and four knights. Felix Fabri was one of the priests, and with him went Archdeacon John Lazinus, his closest friend among the pilgrims. John Lazinus, Archdeacon of Transylvania, was a Hungarian, "knowing not one word of German," and it was as a result of Fabri's persuasion and encouragement, when the two became acquainted in Venice, that he had decided to undertake the Sinai pilgrimage; coming, as Felix says, "under my safe conduct" (*sub mea confidentia*) he very naturally "stuck to" the Friar throughout the journey. We shall find him sharing the excursions and climbing most of the heights which Fabri's boundless energy drove him to climb, and all with only one recorded protest. A man of good family and varied gifts, with a manner of speech at once gentle and humorous, he had the reputation of an able mathematician, and possessed the accomplishment, immensely admired by his friend, of impromptu Latin versifying.⁶

Among the four knights Heinrich von Schonberg (or Schauenberg) stood highest in Friar Felix's estimation and affection; with his ability and integrity, he was that one to whom the Friar would turn for help in any dangerous predicament.⁷ Caspar von Siculi,* (perhaps "of Sicily"), was Schonberg's friend – a young man, and if the same as that Caspar who is mentioned among the pilgrims as being Marshal to Duke George of Bavaria,⁸ one not unused to Courts. Of Sigismund of Morspach we know nothing beyond his name; but the personality of the sixth member of the party, Peter Velsch, makes itself clear, even though Fabri commits himself to no comment. Versatile, energetic, impatient, no country-bred knight but a native of Strasburg, he was one who would take hardly to the discipline, though he might welcome the dangers, of pilgrimage; when, in almost the final glimpse, we see him leaving the ship at the last port before Venice, decked in a fine gold chain,⁹ and if such a chain, surely in no pilgrim garb, we suspect that he was off on some wild, young man's fling, which should recompense him for self-denials past.

One more personality must be mentioned, though he was not a member of the pilgrim company. As their guide across the desert the pilgrims took with them Elphahallo, the Lesser *Calinus*, a devout and loyal Moslem, who regarding with respect the religion of the Christians, was a man in whose probity the pilgrims might safely confide; with this noble octogenarian they need fear no treachery, nor collusion with the desert Arabs, while his long experience of the desert journey, which he had made no less than forty-eight times,¹⁰ had rendered him familiar with the tracks and wells, as well as with the wild people of the wilderness. It is probable that all the pilgrims liked and trusted him, even though on occasion some few might entertain fantastic suspicions of his probity, and in general the whole party would treat him with the restive, though not unfriendly, insubordination of a crowd of schoolboys. But Felix Fabri's feeling for the old man went far beyond this casual liking; the Friar's warm but not indiscriminating regard was wholly his, and when Fabri speaks of information given by "a certain Saracen with whom I was great friends," we cannot but guess that Elphahallo is spoken of, and picture the two conversing, either side by side on their donkeys in the long burning marches, or during the cool hours after sunset, or perhaps in the night silence when the Christian had read his Office, and the Moslem had prayed according to the prescription of his faith.

All told, and considering the long-continued propinquity and the test-

* "Sienli, Sehelin, or Siculi" (*v.* Davies, p. iv).

ing trials which a desert journey entailed, we learn surprisingly little of the individuals who made up this company of pilgrims. We should not expect to find many personal anecdotes in von Breydenbach's book, nor, except when they relate to the author himself, in that of Friar Paul Walther. But even Felix Fabri, while giving us an abundance of lively and detailed pictures of the small events of the journey, will, with rare exceptions, preserve the anonymity of the actors.

This reticence may be due partly to discretion; it was perhaps safer, certainly more tactful, to conceal the names of those knights whose swords had once among the mountain passes been at their fellows' throats; or of those who joined most often and loudly in the chorus of complaints which went up from the little company of pilgrims as they toiled across the huge emptiness of the desert. Habits which were the subject of joke and laughter on the march might take on a different colour at home; one "valiant knight" was so squeamish that in the regular evening *séance* devoted to de-lousing he would never touch the creatures with his fingers, "but always took two stones and where he saw a louse on his shirt he would put the shirt on a stone, and would slaughter the louse by beating it with another stone."[11] To be teased about this in the desert was one thing; it would be another to be forever twitted with it at home. Yet we would wish to know the name—and why should we not?—of the kind-hearted donor of the pair of new and handsome "blue, or rather grey" boots, in which Friar Felix was to make the ascent of Gebel Katerina in greater comfort than most of his companions.[12] And which of the knights on the voyage home, taking advantage of a day in port, rowed over to visit his friends in another galley, bringing with him sweetmeats in a golden bowl borrowed from the Venetian Captain, and had the ill-luck to drop the costly thing into the sea as he went up from the boat?[13]

Perhaps discretion had less to do with this reticence than the strangely particoloured vesture of the Friar's mind. For Felix Fabri, though all of the new age in so many of his habits of thought, has yet one foot firmly planted in the Middle Ages, and those ages, so careless of the individual's part that the builder of a Cathedral may leave no name, perhaps show here another aspect of their bias towards anonymity. Whatever the cause, the reticence is there; and because of it, while we watch the pilgrims on innumerable occasions, commonplace, laughable, strange or sad, it is for the most part as though we stood just too far off to recognise the individual faces, though the liveliness and variety of the antics of this little company of human beings is never in doubt.

CHAPTER II

The last of the Holy Land

In the small hours of August 24, 1483, the most holy and venerated church in Christendom, the Church of the Sepulchre at Jerusalem, echoed to the footfalls and subdued voices of a small company of pilgrims, as with kisses and tears they took their leave of the Holy Places, which during six weeks' stay in the city had become almost familiar, and which it was unlikely that any of them would see again. At the same time and, as the hours wore on, ever more anxiously, they kept an ear pricked for the sound of the key turning in the lock of the great west door, and for the entrance of the Saracen officials who came to open up the Church and to order them out.

Between these conflicting tensions their minds must have been already sadly distracted when the Upper, or Chief, *Calinus*, that is to say the superior of the two official Moslem dragomans of Jerusalem, unable to enter the church as his charges to leave it, announced to them through the small wicket in the west door that the escort for their journey awaited them. This naturally increased the fret of anxiety and the helpless irritation which is engendered in travellers of all periods by the inexplicable proceedings of officials of other nations, so that those feelings must have overwhelmed any softer or more spiritual emotions. Meanwhile a fresh misgiving, fortunately quite groundless, now assailed the pilgrims; were they—to borrow the phrase of another age and another continent—were they to be framed, and, upon some pretext, kept captive in the hands of the Saracens?[1]

It was close on noon when the pilgrims were allowed to leave the Church of the Holy Sepulchre. They hurried off to their respective lodgings, there to make a hasty dinner, and afterwards to meet at the Franciscan Convent on Mount Sion where the escort waited. Here, in the Chapel of St. Francis below the church, the Friars had allowed them to store the impedimenta which they had been collecting for their journey. The pilgrims had taken this business of provisioning very seriously; already a month ago they had begun it by ordering for each man a new mattress, stuffed with the cotton which the country round Jaffa produced so abundantly.[2] A fortnight later they had paid a visit, and a fee, to the

Gazelus, the official who had the right of issuing licences to Christians who wished to buy wine.³ For the last few days before their departure the pace had quickened, so that the chapel was by now pretty well filled by jars of wine, baskets of eggs, sacks of smoked meat and cheese, cooking utensils, waterskins, candles, medicines and above all by huge quantities of biscuit; of this they had provided far more than they themselves would need, having been instructed already that biscuit was a kind of desert currency, and very useful in mollifying the wild Arab.⁴

In addition to all this, the common stock of each of the three companies, we may be sure that few, if any, among the rich laymen left Jerusalem without providing themselves with a supply not only of holy relics, of whatever authenticity, but also such objects of secular interest as would take the eye of gentlemen with money to spend travelling in a strange country. Even Felix Fabri, a Mendicant Friar, carried with him Syrian silks and carpets for the church at home in Ulm, as well as the basket of pebbles which he had collected with devout enthusiasm from various places in and about Jerusalem, and which he was to take along with him through all the difficulties and discomforts of the journey. Friar Paul, a guest for the last twelve months of his fellow Franciscans of Mount Sion, no doubt stacked with the rest of the luggage the thoughtful subvention of the Prior—"two jars of the best wine, and a big bag with the best fish, smoked meats, cheese, oil, rice, almonds, raisins big and small, vinegar, salt, and a good supply of other necessaries."⁵ When all was piled in one great heap outside the doors of the Convent the camel-men and the two *Calini* expressed themselves as "astounded." Felix himself admitted that "a man would hardly believe that twenty persons could need so much luggage in the desert."⁶

The pilgrims had done their part when they had carried up the stuff from the crypt-chapel. Now it was for the camel-men to load their beasts, while Felix and his companions stood, earnest to watch the operation, and this for two reasons. First "we watched their hands intently lest they should steal . . ." and second in the hope that "we also should learn how to load the camels and manage them." It is not likely that they progressed far in this ambition, but they did learn—and Felix relayed the knowledge to his home-keeping readers—that "the camels' loads must be exactly and delicately weighed so that they are equal." As a result of this passionate pre-occupation of the camel-men it was only after long delay, and "with much labour and many disputes," that the immense pile of the pilgrims' effects was transferred to the backs of the baggage camels.⁷

On this occasion, as was usual in pilgrim caravans, camels were used only as beasts of burden, and the Western travellers rode on donkeys.

Von Harff, it is true, was carried by a camel, and in the same sort of contrivance which was used by women who made the pilgrimage to Mecca, for he sat in "a wooden box covered with a thick pelt," and shaded from the sun's heat by a kind of open canvas tilt, which hung on one side of the camel's hump, and was balanced on the other by "goat skins full of water, wheat, meal, biscuit and other provender."[8] Perhaps the French pilgrims, whose journey is described in the "*Pèlerinage*," used something of the same kind;[9] certainly the sick among Felix Fabri's companions made the journey each in an empty baggage pannier, with provisions and the like on the other flank of the camel to give equipoise.[10] Only rarely among pilgrims will a man of such independence and initiative as the Burgundian, de la Broquière, have learnt the knack of riding a camel in the Eastern way, and become accustomed to that "long stalking pace," which, as Charles Doughty says, bows the rider to the beast's neck fifty times a minute.[11] This unusual accomplishment gave the Burgundian knight the laugh of the rapacious donkey owners of Gaza, who, knowing the pilgrims' usual preference for the donkey as a mount, stepped up their hiring tariff to an absurd figure. But how—de la Broquière asked them, with his usual cheerful and friendly impudence—how could he manage to ride a donkey when he was already riding a camel?[12]

When the loading of the camels had been accomplished the moment had come for the pilgrims to choose among the little crowd of donkeys brought for their inspection. This was an important choice, for whichever beast a man hit on would be his mount not only to Mount Sinai but from there to the frontiers of Egypt, and the realisation of this was responsible for a fresh outbreak of storm and debate, but this time among the pilgrims themselves. Now the lords and knights "ran here and there among the donkeys, trying first this and then that, and quarrelling over them, for sometimes two or three pilgrims would be hanging on to one donkey," while the drivers, "who knew which donkeys were good and which bad," looked on in non-committal silence. Felix Fabri, having withdrawn himself from the turmoil to sit on the top of the steps leading to the Friars' church, also looked on; and thus sitting, he observed among the animals one which was spurned by every disputant, "a big white one, whose ears hung down and whose head seemed to be too heavy for him; an ugly looking beast." The Friar decided that this creature should be his choice, and when the confusion had abated he came down the steps and mounted it. This he says he did "in order to make a joke for the noble lords," and, if we may believe him, altruism here reaped a rich reward. No sooner was he in the saddle than the donkey-men crowded round, laughing and demanding money, and the Friar, at first disconcerted, was made to understand that what was demanded was the tip customarily paid by whichever pilgrim selected the best of the beasts. Once more, as in his first pilgrimage, luck had provided him with an excellent mount, for the big white donkey "was the surest footed beast, untireable and without vice; he never fell with me, never lagged, never took fright, never kicked nor bit, but unflagging, and without a goad, he led or followed." The owner of the animal confided to Felix that he would not part with it for less than 10 ducats, and one wonders whether in fact the Friar had not blundered on a descendent, elderly and therefore reduced in circumstances, of that noble and costly race, Damascus bred, of white asses.[13]

All these transactions had taken up time; it was almost evening before the Western knights and priests, entering into the Church of the Franciscans for the last time, received the pilgrims' blessing and parting kiss of peace from the Father Guardian of Mount Sion, and, having mounted their donkeys, followed the camels down towards the Fish Gate, now the Jaffa Gate. The pilgrims were, says Felix, in tears at this departure from that city which they had so longed to see, and in which the Friar himself had had "most happy days and hours."

But they had little time to indulge such feelings, for as they made their way towards the gate they were mobbed by a crowd of young Moslems, who tugged at the camels' loads, trying to bring them down. In the confusion one of the camels fell, and a jar of wine was smashed. All the wine jars had been carefully swathed in sacking to conceal them from the disapproving or covetous eyes of good Moslems or bad; but now the wine dripped through the sacking, not only a sad waste, but an incitement, so the pilgims feared, to the disorderly rabble which followed them, to smash all the jars. This would have been a disaster of the first magnitude; Felix goes so far as to say that "if we had lost our wine we would not have dared the Sinai pilgrimage; we could not have survived the desert without wine to drink." Fortunately this one jar was the only casualty, and it is an ill wind that blows no one any good. Friar Felix, who could not endure to see good wine go to waste, handed over his donkey to one of the knights, and dismounting, "ran beside the camel. I would let no Saracen come near, and I filled my flask . . . from the drips."[14]

When the pilgrims turned their backs upon Jerusalem, upon the Franciscan House, the Father Guardian and the kindly Friars, they severed the last tenuous thread of the life-line which had so far connected them with their own world and their fellow Christians of the Latin Church. Weeks ago they had lost the sheltering and controlling hand of the great pilgrimage organisation or industry, call it what you will, which the

Venetian merchant princes had built up and maintained, a system which not only supplied its clients with transport from Venice to Jerusalem and back, but, in their dealings with the Moslem officials of the Holy Land, provided them with agents or advocates in the Noble Captains of the Pilgrim Galleys, men who had behind them the military and diplomatic prestige of the Republic.

The last office of this benevolent superintendence had been performed at the negotiation of the contract by which the pilgrims' journey was to be regulated. This had been signed on the very day which saw the withdrawal from Jerusalem of the main body of pilgrims, and therefore before the departure of the pilgrim galleys had weakened the bargaining power of the pilgrims by depriving them of this means of retreat. Its terms were fought out between the chief men among the pilgrims, assisted by the Father Guardian and the two Noble Captains on the one side, and on the other the Moslem Governor of Jerusalem and other Moslems of high rank, together with the two *Calini* officially appointed for the control and guidance of pilgrims. This document, sealed, at a cost of two ducats, with "the seals of the Lord of Jerusalem and the Greater *Calinus*" was in itself the symbol that the pilgrims had passed beyond the ambit of the Venetian tourist agency, and from now on must themselves deal directly with the Moslems. They were not, of course, setting out upon unknown ways. They would cross the desert with the Lesser *Calinus* as their guide, and in Egypt would find a system of official dragomans, hospices, escorts, and safe-conducts. But till they stood once more upon the deck of a ship of Venice in the harbour of Alexandria their only appeal would be from Moslem to Moslem, their only hope that, if not the honesty, then the enlightened self-interest of the Saracen would insure the fulfilment of any bargain. Von Breydenbach breaks through his usual reserve to remark, of the contract drawn up in Jerusalem, that "as usual with the heathen, it was not well kept," but if this contract was broken, the infringement was as nothing compared with those instances of sharp practice from which the pilgrims would suffer while in Egypt.

By the terms of the document, while each pilgrim was to make his own bargain with the owner of the donkey he rode, the Greater *Calinus* engaged to provide transport for all the baggage, exclusive of wine, to procure a water skin for each man, and "three little tents" for the accommodation of the three companies. He also made himself responsible for all tolls as far as Gaza, thus relieving the pilgrims of an annoyance from which they had suffered in Palestine, where they had found toll to be demanded at all sorts of places, and by all sorts of people of whose right to exact it they had often been dubious.[15]

It is possible to compare the terms of this contract, though only approximately, with those given by the author of the *"Pèlerinage,"* earlier in the century, and by von Harff a dozen years later than Felix. At first there seems to be great discrepancy between the three estimates. Against Fabri's total of 23 ducats we have to set the Frenchman's 40 to 43, and von Harff's 14. But Fabri's includes neither the money spent by the pilgrims in Jerusalem upon provisioning, nor the further 3 ducats per head laid out at Gaza,[16] while the very full and detailed list in the *"Pèlerinage"* includes such expenses. If we extract from the Frenchman's list those items which it has in common with the contract made by our pilgrims, we reach a sum of 18 ducats; to this must be added the cost of the keep and expenses of the dragoman who was to be their guide and "speak languages in Italian," estimated at 6 *gros* per day; so that all told, perhaps the amounts were not greatly dissimilar.[17]

Von Harff calculated upon a different basis from either of the other travellers. Starting from Cairo, and in the opposite direction from our pilgrims, he made his agreement direct with his camel driver, and in this may well have had the advice and assistance of his friends among the resident Western merchants in Egypt. What he and his companions, the three pilgrims and two merchants of Genoa, paid their dragoman, he does not say, but for 2 ducats he hired the man and his camel, with its harness and riding pannier, and two goat skins for water.[18] This seems to be a ridiculously low figure, but there is an item in both the Frenchman's and von Harff's budget which we have not yet considered. It is clear that for them tipping along the route was both a necessary and a considerable expense. "Item," says the Frenchman, interrupting his catalogue in order to offer the advice of one who knows, "Item, to travel happily with these cur-dogs, the fellows who bring the donkeys and camels, each man must every day give half a *gros* or a *gros*, or else they will go along yapping and snarling, and being as awkward as they know how." He reckons 2 ducats for this, and another couple to be administered at Mount Sinai, where the dragoman also was to receive a tip of 2 ducats.[19]

Von Harff is equally positive that "anyone who does not give . . . secret presents, which are called in their language courtesies . . . will have to suffer insults and hardships," and to his extremely low estimate of expenses he claps on "10 or 12 ducats . . . as courtesies," and is also prepared to share his provisions with his camel-man.[20] Bearing all this in mind the reader is inclined to suspect that much of the unpleasantness, which, as we shall see, arose between our pilgrims and their camel-men, was due to the fact that they did not personally, or at least only under duress, tip members of their escort, since this should have been done for them, under the terms of the contract, by the *Calinus*.

The distance between Jerusalem and Gaza can be ridden in thirteen and a half hours, but the pilgrims did not reach the outskirts of the town till sunset on August 29, having spent two days sight-seeing around Bethlehem, and, when that delay had brought down upon the haughty Upper *Calinus* a sharp official rebuke, having insisted, much to his indignation, upon the visit to Hebron for which provision had been made in their contract.[21]

Now, in the evening coolness, five days after leaving Jerusalem, they sat down in one of the pleasant groves of fruit trees, almond, palm and fig, which crowded so thick about Gaza as to make it seem a city set in a wood.[22] Here they ate their bread and cheese, adding to these such handfuls of sweet ripe figs that Friar Felix, always as greedy for fruit as any schoolboy, suffered as a result a painful rash about his mouth.

It was almost dark when the *Calinus* led them into the town, and to a hospice all too small for their party. There was a sharp wrangle, after which the *Calinus* went off to look for a more suitable lodging, leaving the pilgrims to a long and anxious wait, "crowded into a narrow street between the camels and the donkeys," so that when he returned and conducted them to a square, walled court, unroofed except for two filthy hovels, and containing a brick kiln, they were glad to make do with what was offered. There was at least a door, and it had a lock; when their baggage had been brought in, they cleared the court of every person but themselves and Elphahallo the Lesser *Calinus*, that gentle mannered and noble hearted old man, whom they counted, alone among all Saracens, as to the uttermost their true friend and ally. Having blocked the door with stones they lit a fire, and prepared their supper, "so that at least we should have something cooked and hot in our bellies, for we had tasted no hot food all day long." Supper over, they lay down to sleep, some in the open court, some in a long trough which ran round the walls, all of them under the stars and exposed to the night dews. And, since this frontier town was situated only a few miles from the coast, "when all was quiet we heard in our courtyard the noise and roar of the sea."[23]

Gaza stood at the meeting place of various lines of communication. From here you might pass direct to Egypt by the frequented coast road; from here pilgrims who were bound for Sinai followed one or other of the routes which would lead them through the lonely and infertile desert. As the last large town of Palestine it was consequently a place where final preparations were always made for the desert journey, and pilgrims would spend a few days, either in Gaza itself, or at Es Zawieh on the border of Egypt. Some waited till they got here to hire their camels, their donkeys, even their guide for the desert,[24] and though our pilgrims had made all these arrangements in Jerusalem they had postponed a certain amount of buying in of stores to be completed at Gaza.

The *Calinus* had not yet provided the tents stipulated for by the contract, and the pilgrims therefore, expecting a stay of three or four days, set themselves to make the open court more habitable by rigging up shelters against the sun's heat and night chills, using for this their own cloaks and mantles. On Sunday, two days after their arrival, they contrived a make-shift altar, surrounding it with carpets and linen cloths hung on cords, and, lighting candles in this home-made chapel, celebrated Mass.

They had secured privacy by locking the gate of the court and setting old Elphahallo on guard; but these precautions were unable to keep out every intruder. Close by, a hole in the mud brick wall was occupied by a colony of wasps of enormous size; if one exit were blocked they broke out by another; vain were all the pilgrims' efforts to contain the enemy, the wasps were irrepressible; yet, Friar Felix records, they stung no one.[25]

Gaza was no unpleasant place for a few days' stay. An unwalled city, bigger than Jerusalem but much less handsomely built, its houses being mostly of mud-baked brick, it yet had some fine mosques, and exceptionally good public baths, while all provisions here were in such plenty and so low in price that the town had the nickname of "the butter ditch." Its population, a medley of races and religions – Ethiopian, Arab, Egyptian, Syrian, "Indian," Eastern Christian, Moslem and Jew, was of a notably friendly and pacific nature. The Western visitors, bearing the pilgrim badge of the red cross on the breast of their gowns and on their hats, went unmolested here; Friar Felix, who wandered alone, according to his custom, far and wide through the town in his white habit, "heard never an ill word," though elsewhere Moslems were frequently resentful of the wearing of white by any but members of their own religion.[26] The Saracen governor, too, when the pilgrims waited on him in order to obtain the necessary licence to move freely about the place upon their lawful occasions, proved no less benevolent; all that they asked "he granted, and very kindly he treated us, although he was a heathen."[27] Theirs was a very different experience from that of von Harff at Gaza fifteen years later; but it seems, from that young man's guarded remarks, that it may have been his own unwise behaviour which got him into a scrape.[28]

Though Gaza might offer all these amenities, the pilgrims did not wish their purses to be drained by an unduly long stay, and therefore, Sunday having passed, they turned their attention to the important duty of sight-seeing. In every direction, in the town and through the countryside beyond, clung memories of Samson, a hero with a chequered history which, in its achievement and in its minatory disaster, appealed to knight and to ecclesiastic. A Saracen guide led the pilgrims first to the ruins of a large building in the midst of which rose "two marble columns, enormous, grey in colour." Here, he told them, had stood the temple of Dagon, in which the Philistines feasted, and it was by laying hold with his arms upon these very columns that Samson had brought down the house upon both the ungodly and upon himself. Friar Paul, and doubtless others of the pilgrims, savoured the experience of setting their own arms about these interesting relics.[29]

The Franciscan and some others fell out before the next part of the expedition, which took the pilgrims through the Eastern gateway of the city, and to the hill-top beyond, whither Samson had carried the gates of Gaza. Felix, never one to miss a view, made the ascent, and looked about at a prospect of sea and mountains, recalling as he gazed at the countryside, every exploit of the hero. The tour terminated at the door of a mosque, which it was said had been a brothel in Samson's day. The aspect of the hero's life which this recalled gave the Friar an opportunity for a fling against women, and a comparison between them and Samson's vanquished lion. "For a woman is an animal insatiable, wrathful, faithless, lustful, quarrelsome, hungry for empty things rather than for solid good." Not every women, the Friar admitted, was so. "Among such a huge multitude who can doubt that there will be found some devout, modest, and saintly women, worthy of the greatest respect." Yet the odds were so heavy against an encounter with these few, that he felt himself driven to recommend that the prudent should avoid all.[30]

Having extracted from the Greater *Calinus* a promise that they should leave Gaza next day, and bearing in mind the nature of the journey which lay before them, the pilgrims next decided to devote some hours to a very pleasurable occupation. While in the Holy Land they had taken as kindly to the habit of using the elaborate bathing establishments of the East as had the barons and merchants *d'Outremer* in the old Kingdom of Jerusalem. This visit to the baths therefore, was by no means their first,[31] but it had a special importance as the last opportunity of enjoying such luxuries until they had accomplished their desert pilgrimage, and come safely to the civilised comforts of Egypt. Besides, the Gaza baths were more than usually well appointed, and Felix spends himself in describing, for the benefit of his friends at home, their beauties and conveniences.

Entering, the visitor found himself in an antechamber surrounded by a covered passage "like a cloister walk" in which were little cells for the bathers, each spread with woven palm-leaf mats, and closed with curtains. "In these, people wishing to bathe undress and dress themselves. Clean linen cloths hang in the cells with which those wishing to go in gird themselves. . . . In the middle of the cloister there is a fountain springing by many jets from a marble column, and all the walls and the pavement outside and inside the hot room are of various kinds of white marble, so polished that anyone crossing it has to take care to go cautiously, lest he should slip, like a man walking upon ice. The hot room itself is foursquare like a tower, and the dome or vault is not covered in but has many round holes, [big] as a man's head, closed with glass of different colours, by which a dim, but sufficient, light is admitted. In the hot room there is no furnace, and you do not feel the heat and smoke of fire, but under one part of the pavement there are (hot) coals which warm the marble, and boiling water running in a channel hollowed in the stone makes the whole place warm. On another side cold water enters. So there is on one side a fine heat and hot water, on the second side coolness and cold water, the third side is empty and quiet, on the fourth is the door, and in the middle is a temperate warmth."[32] You could, in fact, hardly do better in the baths of Egypt, though at Cairo there was a succession of separate rooms of gradually ascending temperatures, and in these some "fine marble vessels" into which the warmed water flowed, and in which the bather could sit, while "domes of glass" above made the interior as bright as the streets outside.[33]

Both in the baths of the capital city, and at Gaza, the attendants practised those arts of manipulation and massage upon which Western visitors looked with the greatest interest and respect. "I saw once," says Felix, "a certain Ethiop who came for treatment to the baths, saying that he had a constriction* of the chest. The bathing attendant laid him on his back on the pavement, sat down on his belly, and so gripped his neck with both hands that the man's face began to swell, since he was altogether prevented from breathing, and held him thus for so long that I was frightened that the man would be strangled, for they had even stopped up his ears with silk. But when at last he let him go, and he came to himself, that man was well content because he said that he would be cured. It was," Felix concludes, "delightful to see these things."

Delightful it may have been; nevertheless the contrast between such cures "of half an hour" and the long and expensive treatments at thermal establishments at home in Germany, caused the Friar some uneasiness.

* Reading *constrictum* for *constructum*.

Comforting himself as best he might, he decided himself to be almost sure that the Moslems used charms to help their skill; the bath attendant "was muttering to himself or into the ears of the patient I don't know what, all the time, and it is their habit in everything to use incantations."[34]

The pilgrims had intended to complete their final purchases for the desert journey, and to be off on the day after their visit to the baths. But their hopes were dashed when there entered Gaza that morning, "in grand style," a contingent of Mamluk troops from Egypt on the march to Northern Syria.

Father Paul must have watched their entry, and his Latin fairly staggers at the impact of the martial glory of that spectacle. They came by in two troops, the first with "eight kettle drums"—instruments for which the Friar could recollect no classical equivalent and therefore left them between Latin and plain German as "octo paucher'"—'two drummers, and four pipers." When the second troop came by there were sixteen kettle drummers, four drummers [if *trumptores* and *drumptores* meant the same to Paul] and eight pipers going in front, with many great and costly banners of various colours, and painted, and all on unusually fine horses, beautiful and costly." That was not all; three hundred and more led chargers, armed and caparisoned, followed, and baggage camels to the tune of close on three hundred beasts.[35]

After this, Friar Paul's only reference to the Mamluk soldiery itself is brief and unflattering. They were, he says, "renegades, and worse and more fell than other Saracens."[36] That verdict would have been endorsed by the residents of Gaza, or indeed of any other city subjected to this plague of human locusts. When Felix, as caterer for his company, attempted to tackle the business of commissariat he found an empty market, and cookshops, butchers' shops and the booths of merchants all shuttered and locked, and learnt on enquiry that this would so continue, as long as the Mamluk soldiery remained in Gaza, because "they come, and whatever they like they grab, and take away without paying, and there is no man who dares deny them." So the commercial life of Gaza went underground, and "the people . . . kept their livestock in their houses, horses, donkeys, sheep and goats, because they would have been carried off by that soldiery."[37]

But though Felix may, in the abstract, have concurred in Friar Paul's verdict upon the cosmopolitan army of ex-slaves, from amongst whom the Mamluk Sultans rose to sovereignty, and upon whom their power rested, in practice the convivial Dominican took a much more lenient view. For in the ranks of this contingent, as among the Mamluk military society which the pilgrims were to encounter at its headquarters in Cairo, there were many men who had turned Moslem to save their lives after capture in some engagement of the endless border warfare that flickered or flared along the eastern marches of Europe, as the Turk pressed on always towards the West. These had denied their faith, but could not deny the call of memory, and of race, and it was not long before Hungarian Mamluks, hearing of the presence in Gaza of a man of their nation, came to seek the Transylvanian Archdeacon, John Lazinus, to ask for news of home. After them came others, Sicilian and Spanish, and all sat down with our pilgrims to eat, and also, but secretly and in the shelter of the tents, to drink.[38] In providing this entertainment the pilgrims were conforming to custom. "You have to feast them," said a French pilgrim, whose visit to Gaza also coincided with that of a Mamluk band, "and give them wine to drink, and then a 'courtesy,' which means money."[39] Clearly he grudged the outlay, but our pilgrims offered their hospitality in the friendliest spirit, and the atmosphere of hilarity and goodwill must have increased the disgust of the two *Calini*, who, true-born Moslems of pure Saracen race, hated the Mamluks, both as renegades and bullies. They were, and expressed themselves, shocked to see the pilgrims consorting with these apostates. "Are you," asked the Greater *Calinus*, the stern and somewhat disagreeable Sabathytanco, "are you Christians indeed? How, for shame, can you eat and drink with those who have, with detestable oaths, forsworn the Christian faith?" Old Elphahallo, who believed that every man would come to heaven who remained loyal to the religion of his childhood, added his gentler rebuke; "to both," says Felix, "we answered as best we could."[40]

Though the Christians might find it difficult to justify themselves in argument, that did not mean that they allowed the reproaches of the two Moslems to influence their conduct. After dinner their new friends paid another call, and some at least of the pilgrims, Friar Felix among them, went blithely off to make an exhaustive tour of the Mamluk camp outside the city, where they viewed everything "with astonishment." They returned to meet very black looks from the two *Calini*; "but little we cared."[41]

Next day the Mamluks departed; Gaza came to life again, and in the afternoon Felix Fabri, accompanied by the knight, Peter Velsch, set out to spend the 18 ducats entrusted to them by the members of their company. In spite of all the provision made at Jerusalem, there was still much to be bought, and Felix, haunted through the whole of this part of his journey, as heavily-laden travellers are wont to be haunted, by a sense of the embarrassing weight and bulk of their possessions, is earnest to justify these to his readers. To provision for a journey across the desert, he points out, was a more anxious business than all the preparations which the pilgrims had made at Venice, for in the sea are islands and ports where you may replenish your stock, "but in the desert there are no ports nor inns, but a huge loneliness, in which not even the animals can find food, as you shall hear."[42]

Consequently he and the other caterers of the pilgrim companies went to work doggedly, even though it were to pile Pelion on Ossa, that Ossa of baggage, which they already recognised as a cause of daily friction between themselves and the camel-men. They bought more sacks of bread and biscuit, more jars of wine, more water skins, and even some water which was guaranteed to remain fresh indefinitely. They bought dried meat by the sackful, cheese, butter, oil, and other foodstuffs, not forgetting such dainties as rice and almonds, "soft drinks" and medicines for sickness. They bought, as well as two baskets of eggs, three more coops of live poultry and "one big white cock standing on the coop, which told us the hours of the night in the desert." But here the reader may check, whether to marvel at the bird's talent, or to wonder whether indeed this cock was one of the pilgrims' purchases, and not rather of the Arab camel-men, and fellow to that which travelled with Charles Doughty's companions of the Mecca Pilgrimage, a white cock, which the Englishman guessed at first "might be a standard of theirs, so gallantly rode Chanticleer aloft, in a chain and pair of golden jesses," but which he came to believe to be "a mystery of religion."[43]

As well as eatables the pilgrims now provided themselves with all sorts of conveniences for travel in the desert: a miscellany of lanterns, boots, oblong baskets of glasses and other table ware; "little baskets with hooks, in which we could keep biscuit and other non-liquid things, hung from the saddles of the donkeys"; big baskets for the spits, gratings, grids, tripods and all the apparatus of cooking. Not for them however that ingenious contraption recommended by a French pilgrim—"spectacles of glass sewn upon linen or leather, which you wear in front of your eyes and mouth as a protection against blowing sand" in the desert.[44]

It was now high time to be leaving Gaza; even the *Calini* had declared themselves ready; but a sudden sickness attacked the pilgrims; both Friar Felix and Paul went down with it, Bernhard von Mernawe was seriously ill, Peter Velsch delirious, and Bernard von Breydenbach was not expected to live. Such a visitation left the pilgrims daunted and shaken. In what came near to panic they began to consider changing all their plans. Some were for returning to Jerusalem, some even would have made for Baruth and homeward-bound galley. Others thought it would be best to go on to Egypt by the coast road and take ship at Alexandria; others talked of attempting the journey to Sinai from Cairo. There were those who wished to wait at Gaza till all were recovered; some, the most resolute of all – and one fancies that Felix, always one for bold measures, was of this number – clung to the idea of starting at once for Sinai, carrying in baskets on camel-back all those who could not ride. It was a time of wrangling, dissension, and suspicion, for the pilgrims managed somehow to persuade themselves,˙ in spite of their own record of events, that the Greater *Calinus* was responsible for keeping them in Gaza.[45]

But as suddenly as their nerve had broken, they recovered their tone. Prayers for the sick at Mass on the Nativity of the Blessed Virgin (September 8) had an immediate and striking effect; quarrels subsided, and the party were of one heart and mind again, and determined upon the pilgrimage to Sinai.[46] But when the Greater *Calinus* appeared, followed by the whole escort prepared for the road, the pilgrims refused to be hurried off; they would spend the day in honouring feast of Her to whom, they believed, they owed their cure. So high did their spirits soar that they imparted this decision to the *Calinus*, a man whom they usually regarded with even more awe than dislike, "somewhat roughly and rudely," and, having dismissed him, betook themselves to their devout junketings.[47]

Part Two
GAZA TO MOUNT SINAI

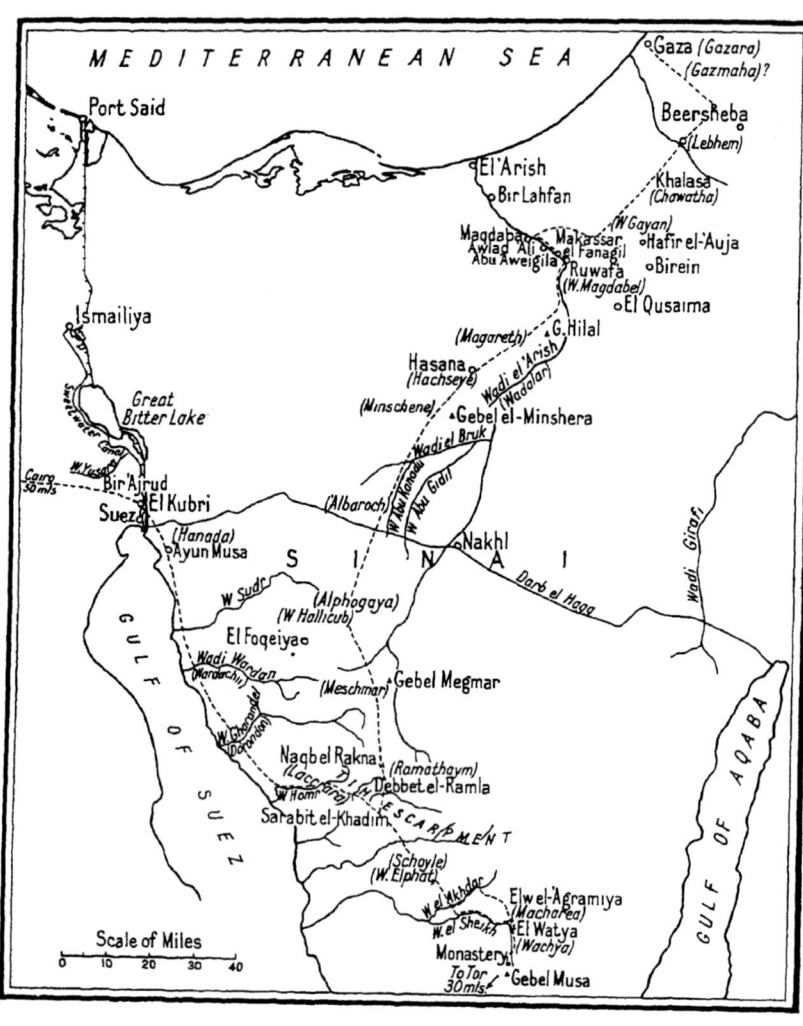

CHAPTER III

The school of the desert

It was not until September 9 that the pilgrims at last started from Gaza.*¹ At noon on that day, after a morning of bustle and strain, they sat down to a cheerful dinner, forgetful of – or at least resigned to – a final piece of unpleasantness; namely the implacable decision of the Greater *Calinus* that their latest additions to their baggage had made it necessary to hire three more camels, for which the pilgrims must pay extra.† When they protested that by the terms of their contract it was his business to provide camels, he did not deny it, but pointed out that if they would leave behind every superfluous article the original number of camels would suffice. As to what constituted a superfluity there could be no agreement between these disputants, for "he thought some things superfluous which we thought very necessary...." For the sake of these necessities the pilgrims resigned themselves to hiring, at their own charges, three more camels.²

As soon as he had reduced them to obedience the *Calinus* departed, to return at noon on horseback and bringing with him the donkeys and donkey-men. Soon after, the camel-men arrived and loaded up the pilgrims' stuff, a big baggage pannier being left empty for the accommodation of each of the two pilgrims as yet insufficiently recovered to ride. The other laymen were now bidden by the *Calinus* to resume those swords, of which, during the whole of their stay in the Holy Land, they had been deprived, but which the uncertainties of desert travel made permissible. As well as swords some of the knights had provided themselves with Saracen bows and even fire-arms, while the donkey- and camel-men had knives, swords or bows.³ The caravan consisted, according to Felix, in addition to the 25 camels and 30 donkeys, of "7 camel-men, 6 donkey-men, two head guides, Arabs, the Lesser *Calinus*, Elphahallo, and a young Ethiopian." With these, for the first day's march, went the Greater

---

* Fabri gives September 9 as the date; Walther (p. 193) says September 8, and continues one day ahead in his reckoning until September 19 (*ibid.*, p. 198). I have followed Fabri's dating, as Walther leaves one day unaccounted for on the journey.

† Fabri and Walther differ again as to the number of camels. Fabri has 22 at the start from Jerusalem, and 25 from Gaza. Walther (pp. 188–9, 193) gives the number at Jerusalem as 13, and at Gaza 23 – an improbably large addition to the caravan.

Calinus and his son "Abre," and Felix contrives to add up these figures to a total of forty men.[4]

The camel-men, hired at Jerusalem, were Moslem country folk from Trans-Jordan, who, dark-skinned as the desert Arabs and habited like them, were accepted by the tribes as kinsmen. The donkey-men were, on the other hand, Christians, fine, upstanding vagrants from the Caspian, but doing their best, during the desert journey, by dress and demeanour to pass themselves off as Moslems. Between them and the camel-men there was ceaseless bickering, which yet, because both parties were orientals, never developed into a fight. The pilgrims, or at least the ecclesiastics among them, considered these Eastern Christians as heretics; experience was to show that there was little to choose, in the matter of thieving, between them and the camel-men.[5]

When all the preparations had been completed the party rode out of Gaza, and down the hill towards the South, perhaps already sinking their teeth into the last of their purchases, ripe and delicious pomegranates, which they had bought "to suck in the desert," sweet or sharp according to each man's taste, and so cheap in the market of Gaza that you got forty or fifty for a medine, "big, and fresh as fresh."[6]

After the stress of preparation and the exhilaration of the start it was a sharp disappointment to the pilgrims when they saw the camel-men turn their beasts off the road into a field, and there, early though it was, begin to unload for the night. It might have helped to soothe their irritation could they have known that 400 years or so later the delayed start and short first stage, against which they so impotently fretted, would still persist, an ineradicable custom among Arab camel-men, and that "Patience," as Mr Baedeker counsels, "is therefore indispensable at starting."

Though they had not gone far on their road, and though they camped among cultivated fields, olive-yards and villages, yet Friar Felix was conscious that in turning their backs on Gaza and their faces to the desert, they had entered upon a new stage of their journey just as effectually as on the day when they sailed from Venice. Faithful to his custom of grounding his readers in the primary facts of a new *milieu* in his travels, he breaks off his narrative in order to impart to his home-keeping readers the information without which, he considers, they will be unable properly to appreciate his narrative. So now he announces: "A consideration of three things before we enter the desert . . . namely of donkeys, camels, and of the waste itself,"[8] and, in fact, also treats briefly of the camel-owners and donkey-men. It will be as well if we follow his example, in an attempt to set the little company of pilgrims against the vast background of the desert, and amongst the conditions of their daily life, before we follow them upon their journey, in this not limiting ourselves to Felix's introductory set-piece, but ranging over his and other travellers' accounts of the desert journey, and deducing from these the constants of desert travel which controlled every day's march. While we do this we shall realise frequently how constant indeed are those conditions, and how unchanging the world of the desert, as we catch, in the accounts of modern travellers, echoes, astonishingly precise, of the experience of the fifteenth century pilgrims.

"In desert travel the dominant factor is the camel.... And the cameldriver is the next...." Such is the pronouncement of a man of our own day,[9] and if Felix does not state the axiom so plainly it is clear that he would have been prepared to endorse it. According to his promise the Friar treats his readers to a short essay on the camel, the material for which is derived partly from books and partly from his own observation. From the old story of St. Jerome's lion and the monastery donkey, and perhaps as well from his experience in the Holy Land,* comes the assertion that a camel caravan goes all the better for having a donkey to lead it; from books too, the belief that the camel's docile subjection to man is due to the peculiar property of its eyes, which magnify fourfold the figure of its master; from books the statement that it is professional jealousy which causes the camel to dislike the horse and mule who compete against him for the burdens which he loves to bear.[10] Such obvious facts as the qualities of the camel which fit it for the desert—its tolerance of thirst, its capacity for carrying heavy loads, as well as its long pace and soft footfall—Felix may have drawn as well from his voluminous reading of travel literature, as from experience. But now that he comes to close quarters with this creature, so very rarely seen in Germany, and "a wonder among us"—now that he sees it moving across the empty desert from dawn till evening, or pasturing in herds about the watering places,[11] he has observations more particular and curious to record. He could not forget, it seems, the shock he experienced when he first heard and saw a camel uttering its raucous cry: "It opens its mouth, stretching its neck far out, and twisting it now this way now that, so that anyone who has not seen it before is startled and alarmed."[12] He watched the ways of the camel-men with their beasts; the driver would strike the animal's knees or, whistling to it, lay a hand on its neck, whereupon the creature would at once couch down, "nor will it move its body, but only its head, with a great roaring while it feels the loads being put on."[13] All this was identical with what Charles Doughty watched, almost exactly 400 years

---

* Gertrude Bell (Letters) saw the Arab camel trains of northern Syria led by a donkey.

later; he also saw the drivers bring the camels down—"The stiff neck of any reluctant brute is gently stricken down with the driving stick, or an hand is imposed upon his heavy halse; any yet resisting is plucked by the beard . . . ."; he also heard "the sudden roaring and ruckling hubbub of the . . . camels grudging to be loaded. . . ."[14] The Englishman, writing in his own tongue, uses words of more force and tension than Fabri had at command in his clod-hopping Latin, but Doughty and the fifteenth-century Friar are speaking here of the same things.

Many other details Felix thought worthy of the attention of his readers at home; he explained to them how the baggage panniers, unlike the saddle of horse or donkey, were attached to no girth, but depended for security upon their equilibrium on either side of the animal's hump. He told them of the song by which the camel-men soothed the beasts while they were loaded; and he must have strained his ears to catch the syllables of the chant which, instead of whip or goad, they used to encourage the animals on the march, a chant which a French pilgrim tersely and uncharitably describes as "so very melodious that dogs or wolves howling could not do worse."[15] "Han na yo yo an no ho ho oyo oho" is Felix's version of the strange sounds,[16] and we wonder whether he also carried home in his head the mournful tune, and rehearsed it for the benefit of his untravelled friends in Germany.

All these particulars of the camel's nature and behaviour were matters of entertainment and interest both for the Friar and his readers, but there were others which gravely affected the comfort of the pilgrims, and which could neither be altered nor ignored. Before even the travellers reached Gaza they had discovered, when tempted to halt for dinner in some pleasant shade of fig trees and olives, that this might not be; camels, once loaded, must go on without pause till the evening camp; till then they must neither be unloaded nor stand under their loads. So the *Calinus* told the pilgrims, "and," says Felix, "it is true." This idiosyncracy condemned travellers of the fifteenth and nineteenth centuries alike to a régime of picnic meals, eaten in the saddle and on the march.[17]

While it is perhaps only to be expected that the habits of the camel should remain unchanged for centuries, it is surprising to find how little the character of Arab camel-men, either from the borders of Egypt or from Syria, has altered between Fabri's day and our own. "Very few camel-men can resist taking toll from food in sacks," says a modern traveller.[18] "They stole our biscuits, eggs, or anything they could steal," cried Felix. "At night they would come by stealth to the sacks of biscuit, and tear holes in them and take out as much as they could." The pilgrims might set a watch to thwart the marauders, but, "however well we watched, in the morning we would find holes made in the sacks, and bread taken out, or eggs stolen from the baskets...." The wretches were most accomplished thieves, and could steal under the nose of the watch: even when detected they were completely without shame.[19]

Yet it was not this propensity, irritating though it might be, which aroused in the pilgrims their hottest ire, but the behaviour of the camel-men at each day's loading up. Our modern traveller also notes that an hour might be wasted at the beginning of a day's march by the squabbles which arose owing to the extreme and irascible jealousy with which the camel-men insisted upon the equal distribution of loads between their beasts. "I learned," he says, "that it is best to make up equal loads oneself, and then let the men have the choice of them."[20]

This was to take a high line, and easy enough for a man who had behind him a couple of centuries of European ascendancy. But our pilgrims must be content to endure this tiresome habit at Jerusalem, at Bethlehem, at Gaza, and at any time through all the desert journey.[21] Nor was delay the only resulting disadvantage. The insistence of the camel-men upon equal shares for all meant that at each loading the luggage of the three companies became hopelessly mixed, for the camel-men took now this, now that, haphazard from the pile of things, so as to make the loads of the camels equal. The result was "most inconvenient" to the pilgrims, since "one camel sometimes carried things belonging to the three companies, and to six or eight pilgrims, and there was muddle, trouble, and running about at the unloading, as each man had to collect his stuff from three or four different places." An attempt was made to persuade the camel-men to reserve certain camels for the exclusive use of each company, but "they would not understand, nor do it."[22]

That the men should have been so obtuse or so disobliging in this matter might have been partially justified by the difficulty of communication between East and West, and by the *finesse* necessary to obtain equilibrium between each pair of panniers. But they played other, and more infuriating, tricks upon the pilgrims, and all, it is clear, as a means of exacting from their employers those "courtesies" or tips, which it would have profited the pilgrims to bestow with at least an appearance of willingness.

On the second day out from Gaza the camel-men staged a go-slow strike; late in starting, they "loaded the camels as though they were bored and unwilling, and left lying many of our things, so that we scolded and abused them a great deal. But as we swore in German at them, and they shouted in Arabic at us, neither they nor we could understand the other. Really," says Felix, "it would weary me to write all their naughtiness

... they would carefully leave behind something, a bed or a basket, or a sack, knowing that we had our eyes on these. And they did this so that the pilgrims to whom belonged whatever was left behind should be obliged to ask them to pick it up." It would be picked up, but of course at a price, either of money or of a dole of the coveted biscuit. Felix would have us believe that when the pilgrims had found their feet in the ways of desert travel they learnt how to deal with such blackmail. "We gave our orders," he declares, "and made them do what we wanted."[23] But it is by no means clear from his narrative that this satisfactory state of things did ever in fact obtain. Meanwhile, for the first part of the journey at least, the loading up every morning was only accomplished after a great expenditure of time and temper, the pilgrims being reduced to such a state of fury that, as Felix remarks, "we could have eaten them alive, as the saying is."[24]

It was not only these Arabs of Trans-Jordan stock, with whom the pilgrims came in contact in their journey, and whose behaviour and customs they were forced to take into account. The Arab of the desert, moving here in his own element, "the lord of all waste spaces," and subject only to the vague suzerainty of a distant Sultan, could not altogether be avoided, and must be treated according to his own code and character. The Arab tribesman of the Middle Ages was even more miserably poor than his descendants of the early twentieth century.[25] "Wretched and like to beasts,"[26] the nomads roved the desert with their flocks of camels and scrawny goats. The pilgrims, torn between pity and disgust, would see these "worst and poorest" of creatures, squatting naked in the waste, "as if they were toads," and even Friar Paul, with his queer tenderness towards children, could only liken the little Arab boys to "apes, sitting in the sand."[27] None but the chiefs wore Saracen dress, the rest went naked except for "a piece of old wool or linen, half in front and half behind down to the middle of the thigh." The women wore a girdle of palm leaves, from which hung "in front and behind, a little bit of goatskin with the hair still on"; only their head-gear showed a trace of anything above savagery; they were veiled with a short piece of linen, and wore their hair braided and bound across the brow,[28] though sometimes a ragged woman with a dirty face would be seen decked out with ornaments of silver and gold.[29]

These wretched folk knew hunger and thirst as well as nakedness. Meat they ate seldom, sometimes killing one of their goats, or hunting the jerboa, the desert rat, which they ate, "as we eat young rabbits."[30] Biscuit, with herbs and roots, and milk from camels and goats, formed their common diet. Bread was scarce among them; it was "a solemn feast" if they baked flat cakes in the ashes, and ate them with meat "still bloody," and cooked, if fuel was lacking, by the sun's heat upon a flat stone. When the French priest, Jean Thenaud, was entertained by an Arab chief, the repast consisted of butter, and dough made into five or six flat cakes and cooked on the sunbaked stones, with two half-ripe apples. Thenaud, who as we shall see had little cause to love any Arab, pokes bitter fun at the whole festivity; the Arab inquired whether "in Christendom we were so comfortable and had such food; then I had to pay him for it, 10 medines. . . . For he believed that we lived on roots and wild fruit like pigs."[31]

Their dwellings were as poor as their diet and apparel. The house of Jean Thenaud's "noble prince of Araby" was such that he must "enter on his knees, and in it remain on his knees. . . ." "It was," says the Frenchman pungently, "no more than a good foxhole,"[32] but he does not make it clear whether the "foxhole" was one of the caves which the Arabs on occasion used as dwelling-places, or one of those tents of leather which, Felix says, gave so much better protection against the sun's rays than the woven tents of the pilgrims; or even a hovel of palm branches such as the nomads would build when they encamped near an oasis.[33]

In spite of his wretched poverty, the desert Arab, then as now, held his head high, and for the same reason. His pride of race reminded Felix of that of the Suabian nobles at home, who, despising the industrious townsman, looked for any increase of income to the precarious profits of the tournament. Just so the Arabs, in their own country, claim, he says, to be "the only true noblemen, who live on plunder and do not swink . . ."[34] and his remark finds its echo, both for content and tone, in the exasperated comment of the nineteenth-century traveller, who describes the Arab as one "who has a constitutional dislike to work, and is entirely unscrupulous as to the means he employs to live without it; these qualities . . . he mistakes for evidence of thorough breeding, and prides himself accordingly on being one of Nature's gentlemen."[35]

The Arabs of the desert, in the fifteenth century, depended for their livelihood, except in so far as it derived from their flocks, upon the toll, or plunder, exacted from passing caravans of merchantmen and pilgrims. Haunting the neighbourhood of wells they would greet their prey with a clamour in which a French pilgrim made out the repeated word "*Pan, pan*," that is to say, he explains, "bread, bread."[36] This was their peaceful approach; if the travellers were in small force they were bolder, mounting their horses, camels and donkeys, and approaching with much shouting and shaking of spears, while the women skirmished on the outskirts, throwing stones.

Usually however a moderately strong and well-armed party of Western travellers was in little danger; only a resolute bearing and prudent generosity were sufficient to avert trouble. Man for man the Arab was certainly no match for such Western pilgrims as the German knights with whom Friar Felix travelled. "... Small... brown in colour, of wretched physique, with voices like a woman"[37] the nomads wore no armour, being not only poor but, as our pilgrims were to learn, fatalists.[38] What weapons they carried were of the weakest: "spears not so stout as darts, with shafts like canes,"[39] for they were in fact armed "not for fighting but for robbery."[40] At close quarters they would lay their brag aside, asking pacifically enough for the payment of a toll; in the fifteenth century, as in modern times, their demands would prove to be almost laughably moderate; a few coins would suffice, and a few biscuits added to these would be a bounty.[41] On the one occasion when an Arab band made something like an attack upon the caravan of our pilgrims of 1483 – though it was only an attack upon the baggage – the sight of the knights with drawn swords standing shoulder to shoulder, "with a look hardy and bold," was too much for the nomads; they sheered off, and the matter was negotiated and settled upon the usual cash basis.[42]

Yet the old and experienced *Calinus*, Elphahallo, was careful to impress on his charges the necessity for patience and prudence in their dealings with the desert men. At this time the Arabs were becoming increasingly insubordinate to the Mamluk rule, and there was always the possibility that if the wild folk were seriously provoked they might gather together such a multitude of their fellows from the desert fastnesses that, even to their tottering courage, violence would appear to involve no risk,[43] since, as Suriano acutely observed, the nomads made sure of "keeping always on the side of the victor."[44]

What Charles Doughty described as the "feline and chameleon nature"[45] of the Arab was capable of the widest variations of behaviour, from cruelty and treachery to loyal hospitality and gentle forbearance, and the pilgrims of three or four centuries earlier had experience of just such variety. Not quite a hundred years before Felix Fabri made his pilgrimage to Sinai, three Florentine merchants, Leonardo Frescobaldi, Simone Sigoli and Giorgio Gucci, took the same journey, but in the reverse direction. Nothing untoward happened till they were within less than a day's march of Gaza. Then the Dragoman began to behave suspiciously; in spite of the remonstrances of his employers he left the caravan to proceed without him, and though he returned that same evening, the sinister and unprecedented sight of many camp fires round about in the desert seemed, when darkness fell, to confirm their fears. It was not, however, till the following afternoon that they had positive confirmation of his treachery. Then they were met in the way by "a troop of men, both on foot and horseback, and armed after their fashion. Amongst them was one man who carried a mace. At once we said to our Dragoman 'You have betrayed us.' "

The Dragoman tried to evade the accusation by telling the Christians that the newcomers intended only to inspect the Sultan's safe-conduct which the pilgrims carried. Whatever the truth, it was unfortunate that Frescobaldi had the safe-conduct packed in one of his saddle-bags alongside "some silver cups, a spoon and other choice articles." The sight of these was too much for the natural rapacity of the Arabs, who at once fell upon the caravan and began to ransack the baggage.

This was too much for Frescobaldi, who, a merchant and elderly, was yet a man of stout heart. At the first sign of trouble he had taken his sword and his glove. Now he rushed at the Dragoman, who stood chatting with "him of the mace," both of them being on foot.

" 'I know,' " cried the Florentine, brandishing his sword, " 'I know that today I shall die a martyr for Christ's sake, but you shall die first.' "

At once "the Dragoman . . . begged me to put up my sword into the sheath and my goods should be safe." But Frescobaldi was not only a bold man, he was also a loyal friend; he replied that he and his party "were comrades, and what went for one, went for all." He did not, in fact, save the purses of his companions, for these, though mostly younger men than himself, had already suffered damage to their goods and had ransomed the rest by a payment of 22 gold ducats. "But of mine," says Frescobaldi with pardonable pride, "and of my servants' stuff, nothing was taken."[46]*

Though the Italian merchant's conception of the qualifications for martyrdom is perhaps not that of everyone, his method of dealing with the Arab was that which travellers of many centuries have found successful. Resolution and a show of force have proved enough to dash the desert men in the nineteenth, as in the fourteenth, century; yet if the balance of strength inclined too far in their favour the Arabs might kill. In 1870 was published a letter from the Orientalist, E. H. Palmer, giving an account of a hold-up by armed Arabs which he had experienced. Threats, stone-throwing, and a declaration of war were part of the demonstration, but in the end "we at last arranged the matter for a

---

* Sigoli (p. 46) makes much less of this incident and seems in no way to blame the Dragoman, whom he calls elsewhere (p. 15) "quite a good fellow for a Saracen."

pecuniary consideration, our late antagonists consenting themselves to act as our guides for the sum of not quite 8 shillings, to be divided amongst them all."[47] Palmer makes a good story out of the episode, and evidently found it amusing, but twelve years later he was murdered in the desert by just such another band of Arab brigands.

Only one of the pilgrims, whose narratives have furnished the material for this book, came within measurable distance of the fate of the nineteenth-century Englishman. This was the French priest, Jean Thenaud, who set out from Cairo for Mount Sinai in 1512, with a hired guide, and who picked up as Dragoman at Suez one of those unhappy and unwilling renegades from Christianity, with whom more than one of our pilgrims became acquainted. Except for this man, who hoped, and eventually succeeded in escaping from Islam, Thenaud's companions in the large caravan were all Moslems, most of them being merchants on their way to Tor.

Thenaud's troubles began when he, his Dragoman, his guide and a small party of Arabs left the main body, and turned off into the labyrinth of mountain gorges by which they would reach Mount Sinai. Then the guide, who had all along shown his ill-will, began to bully the priest unmercifully; worse still, at the first halt he went off, leaving Thenaud with the Arabs and the Dragoman, that is to say with potential enemies and a man whose life depended upon concealment of his religious sentiments. At once the Arabs turned on the Christian pilgrim. " 'Tell the dog and son of a dog' ", they bade the Dragoman, " 'to pay us the *seraph* he owes us' "; when Thenaud denied the debt they took him roughly by the beard and forced him to open the scrip where he kept his food. "But they found nothing there save biscuit, onions, and a cheese so hard and ill-smelling that it would have driven the rats out of doors." Still the fellows demanded *"laet, bait, beidh,"* as the Frenchman rendered the Arabic words for bread, meat and eggs. When Thenaud answered " '*mem phis*'*–that is to say, I haven't any" they returned to the question of money, but though they kicked and beat him he wisely persisted in answering "'*Memphis fluss*' †", "I have no money." Finally, having stripped him naked, they drove him a bow-shot from the camp, where for three hours he lay in the sand, contemplating his predicament and imploring the help of God, while they discussed and decided upon leaving him to die in the desert.

But now the guide returned and his presence seems to have given Thenaud's Dragoman courage. Appealing to their better nature–"the holy

---

* According to the Editor this represents the Arabic *"Ma fich!"*
† Ed. *"foulous" "argent"*

law of Mahomet . . . forbids robbery and the breaking of faith," and to their worldly prudence, – the priest's master, he told them, "who holds him dear, is at Cairo, and speaks daily with the Sultan," he finally persuaded them to spare the Frenchman, and to restore his garments, which, Thenaud notes, were "torn in several places. . . ." It had been a very close call; yet the Arabs, though they continued to bully him, never discovered, nor does Thenaud tell his readers, the secret of the hiding place in which he kept his money.[48]

After these accounts of Western travellers in which the Arab appears as something between a bad child and a gangster, it is right that we should listen to the testimony of two pilgrims, Arnold von Harff and Bertrandon de la Broquière, who found in him loyalty, honesty, and that noble desert hospitality which is as traditional in his race as its predatory habits. Von Harff discovered that his system of tipping liberally, and sharing his provisions with his camel-driver, had secured the man's faithful service; when "the wild Arab charged at us in the wilderness with loud cries, as though they would strike us dead . . . then my mokarii* stood by me faithfully, ready to answer with blows or battle."[49]

The experience of de la Broquière was even more remarkable. The adventurous and fearless Burgundian had gone two days journey into the wilderness on his way to Mount Sinai when he became so gravely ill that his pilgrim companions decided that he must be sent back to Gaza. They therefore mounted the sick man upon a donkey and sent him off with an Arab of the escort and two camels laden with wine and food; probably the provisions which he had laid in for the whole journey.

That evening the sick man found himself riding into a big encampment of the desert folk. Eighty tents and more, pitched orderly in two lines, "like a street," from which ran out several men who greeted de la Broquière's guide as a friend. Then, says the Burgundian, "seeing how ill I was they made me get down from my donkey, and lie on a mattress which I had brought with me, and they doctored me in the way they have, kneading and pinching me with their hands so that for weariness I fell asleep." For six hours he slept after this exhausting massage, and when next day he continued his journey with his sickness alleviated if not cured, he knew, not only that while he lay helpless among the Arabs they had done him no harm, but that these people, whose livelihood lay in robbery, had touched neither the 200 ducats – an enormous sum in their estimation – which he carried on his person, nor had laid finger on the

* A camel- or donkey-owner who accompanies the travellers who have hired his beast.

contents of the camel's panniers. As for the Arab who guided him, "a very good comrade he was to me," says de la Broquière; and adds, with truth, that this "they are not generally to a Christian."[50] But all de la Broquière's relations with Saracen and Arab show that he was one of those Europeans whom the Eastern folk loved.

In their encounters with Arabs Felix Fabri and his companions were to experience something which lay well between the two extremes which are illustrated by the anecdotes of Jean Thenaud and de la Broquière. For the most part they had good reason to dislike both the Arab of the Sinai Desert and the Trans-Jordanian Arab camel-men. Yet we shall see that this history of provocation, misunderstanding and resentment was varied by intervals, brief but pleasant to contemplate, of tentative friendliness, charity and laughter.

The most acute dangers which travellers in the desert had commonly to face did not come from any human agent, but from the desert itself. Sickness and death were there at home. Von Harff, travelling with a large caravan down the coast towards Tor, learnt the merciless rule which experience had laid down: if a man sickened he must be left to die, while the living passed on to reach the water without which they could not survive.[51] In a small cohesive party like that of our pilgrims there was no thought of leaving any man behind; the sick travelled, as we have seen, in the big panniers provided for the stores, but it is significant that throughout the desert journey there were always sick men to be thus carried. None of Felix's companions died in the desert, though one succumbed to dysentery at Alexandria. He was one man out of twenty, but of the three with whom Jean Thenaud had originally intended to make the pilgrimage to Sinai, one died at Tor, and another at Alexandria on the return journey.[52]

When Frescobaldi and his party met a company of young French nobles in the desert, the first question which the young men asked was—how many of the Italian company had died? They themselves, originally a party of twenty, had lost eleven, "and," they said, "have buried them in the sand."[53] Another Italian pilgrim roundly asserted that only those who took with them the "syrops of lemon, the rose and white sugar," which Cairo supplied in greater perfection than any other city, survived the journey; of his fellow pilgrims "died five comely youngsters, men of wealth and nobility in their country."[54]

A worse, because a slower, death than that by sickness might overtake a sound and healthy man if he should once stray so far into the featureless desert as to lose touch with his company. "We could never find that good man," is the brief summary of one such tragedy by another pilgrim writer.[55]

In one of the bad sandstorms which might rage in the desert for days, a whole party could be wiped out as easily as a single traveller. While the storm lasts, "all the surface is shifting, and a man sees nothing but sand, as if it were a cloud, so that you cannot keep your eyes open," and the flying grains sting not only the eyeballs but any uncovered flesh. In a great storm it was hopeless to try to travel against the wind; for a while you might turn and go with it, trusting to the instinct of the camels to know their direction when the storm had blown itself out; but you must, at last, camp, and if the wind held, where you camped, there you might die.[56]

Even a brief sand-storm had its perils. Once, while on the march, our pilgrims had to ride forward into the blowing sand which rushed by them like water; half-blinded, no man could see beyond the head of his own beast; deafened, too, by the noise of the wind, each must press on, dreading always that he had unwittingly turned aside from his companions, and now rode alone into the deadly solitude of the desert.[57]

Apart from any danger, the discomfort caused by such storms was extreme. At supper time the wind would blow the lighted brands from under the cooking pots; at bed-time, after a cheerless cold supper, tents and mattresses would be found full of sand; however tightly the travellers swaddled themselves in their cloaks the sand sifted in; throughout the night the air was full of sand, sky and stars were totally blotted out by sand. And next day, even if the wind had dropped, the caravan would be floundering through drifts of newly deposited sand so deep and soft that "the beasts sank into them as into deep snow."[58]

Almost every pilgrim who journeyed to Sinai and left a record of his experiences would make an effort to capture and express in words the loneliness and desolation of the deserts of the Peninsula. "Neither man, nor beast, nor bird, nor . . . tree, nor bush, nor any sort of wood,' nor anything green. . . ."[59] "No water, tree, greenery, nor anything else that any man might take pleasure in . . ." with soil "for the most part like fine sand, all white."[60] " . . . No village nor town . . . neither house nor dwelling, neither field nor garden, tree or grass, nothing but barren sandy earth, burnt up by the great heat of the sun."[61] So the negatives are piled up in the effort to express the vast emptiness.

Of that last over-ruling fact of desert travel, the sun's heat, not one medieval traveller attempts any description. Such phrases as later generations forged are far beyond the range and temper of mind of the pilgrims of the fifteenth century. "The summer's night at an end," says Charles Doughty, "the sun stands up as a crown of hostile flames. . . . The desert day dawns not little and little, but it is noontide in an hour. The sun entering as a tyrant upon the waste landscape, darts upon us a torment of fiery beams. . . . Grave is that giddy heat upon the crown of the head; the ears tingle with a flickering shrillness, a subtle crepitation it seems, in the glassiness of this sun-stricken nature; the hot sand blink is in our eyes. . . ."[62]

All this we must supply for ourselves in reading even Felix Fabri's voluminous and vital narrative. The Friar takes the burning and dazzling sunshine for granted; he is less likely to mention the heat of the day than to say how cold the pilgrims were on a march that began before dawn, as they plodded on in the teeth of a bitter wind. Only indirectly from his account of the discomforts, sufferings and dangers of the journey, do we arrive at some realisation of the powers of heat and light which governed the waterless, trackless, lifeless waste, where "an hiding place from the wind . . . rivers of water in a dry place . . . the shadow of a great rock in a weary land" were as a gracious deliverance to travellers.

It is not heat itself, not even the thirst which is part of the torment of heat, which Friar Felix describes, but instead the varieties of evil tasting water by which the pilgrims slaked their thirst. At the first desert camp, the donkey-man, sent off for water, made a tardy return as the sun was setting, and when the waiting, thirsty pilgrims put their lips to the water "it was . . . disgusting to us, because it took the colour, a blood-red, of the skins, and caught the salt taste of the leather." Even food cooked in the water tasted of the newly tanned skins, and soon the same flavour was transmitted to the pilgrims' own flasks and bottles. "But all the same," says Felix, "we often got so thirsty we would put our mouths to the empty skins, and think it delicious to suck the tainted water from the stinking leather."[63]

No sooner had the pilgrims acquired a taste for this peculiar flavour than, having now entered upon the limestone district of the Tîh Plateau, they were presented with a new variety of water, "whitish and thick" which looked like milk.* Felix, always with a lively appetite for information, ascertained from the Lesser *Calinus* that while the whitish water was injurious, that tinged with red was not only not bad but medicinal and very beneficial.[64]

Throughout the long days in the saddle the pilgrims found the changing surface of the desert a thing of practical and often painful interest. Some-

---

* E. H. Palmer (*The Desert of the Exodus*, II. 287) speaks of water of the Tîh, the sediment of which, when it had had time to settle, became a solid cake of mud.

times the burrows of little "desert rat" or jerboa lay below a deceptively sound crust.* When a donkey stepped on this the burrow caved in, and as like as not the pilgrim went over the donkey's head.[65] Even if sound, the desert floor frequently made very bad going. There were tracts, says Felix, where the heat of the sun had drawn up the underlying salt, which showed white as frost, and stood up "like sharp spear-points" which would tear even the strong boots which had come from Germany.[66] The white, dried-up beds of the winter water-courses might be split by fissures dangerous to the animals' legs,[67] or there would be drifts of sharp flints to cross,[68] or slabs of stone, flat as a pavement though no man had laid them, and scoured so smooth by the action of wind and blowing sand that even the donkeys went fearfully.[69]

It was, in fact, the desert sand, of a grain so fine, as Felix notes, that it was the best of all for hour-glasses,[70] which, as the pilgrims crossed the Tîh Plateau, took on for them almost the importance of a new element. There were "no sure roads" in the desert, for wind and sand together might change its face in a night, removing or piling up hills, filling valleys, muffling in sand a bare rock face.[71] Those familiar with the wilderness would take bearings upon certain hills which they know, as it were, with their eyes shut, as a good pilot at sea knows hidden rocks."[72]

The daily routine of desert travel soon clamped itself down upon the pilgrims, a routine differing little from that of travellers for centuries before and centuries after their time. The day began at latest with the dawn; often the camp was astir and the pilgrims rousing unwillingly from their mattresses soon after midnight. Always the loading up would be accompanied by brawl and clamour, and to the din of human voices, the camels, according to their habit, would contribute their bellowing roar. Then came the start, and after that nothing but the silent tread of the beasts over the floor of the desert, and the song of the camel-drivers as the caravan moved slowly through the wide and empty land.[73]

Since there must be no mid-day halt, the pilgrims' meal, eaten in the saddle, consisted of cheese, cold meat, either cooked or salt, cooked the previous night, and hard biscuit dipped in the tepid wine or water from the flasks which hung jogging from the saddle beside the rider's knee; one evil day, to the pilgrims' great chagrin, it was discovered that the morning heat had caused the meat to putrify.[74]

In the scanty animal and vegetable life of the Tîh Desert there was little to distract the traveller's attention from his discomforts, but the chroniclers of this pilgrimage of 1483 are strangely silent concerning those

* Felix believed the tunnels to be the work of the snakes which harboured there, but it appears that these would have supplanted the real owners.

beasts which they did see. Not even Friar Felix does more than mention the many gazelles:[75] the little jerboa is passed over in silence, though a French pilgrim saw so many of these "that in some places the ground seemed to be covered with them"; they were, says the Frenchman, "as big as young rabbits and their head was like that of a rabbit, their fur grey, their front legs bent and very delicate, their hind legs a foot in length."[76] Friar Felix records that there were plenty of snakes, mostly small; one day an Arab camel-driver killed "a big long snake," wounding it first with an arrow and then cutting it in two; Felix was interested to notice that, having done this, the fellow contrived that the caravan should pass between the severed parts, "so that they should not re-unite." The Friar, usually scornful of Arab superstitions, was here interested by the fact that he had seen the same ritual observed in Germany.[77] Though the pilgrims grew familiar with the appearance of the tracks of ostriches in the sand, they had to wait till they reached Cairo for a sight of these interesting birds.[78]

At this season of the year, except in a few deep wadis, there was as little vegetable as animal life to be observed, apart from the various prickly bushes on which the camels pastured. But one day the pilgrims came upon a most refreshing sight. They had been struggling through deep, soft sand, the surface of which a strong wind had raised in clouds so that "we were drenched (in it), a drenching which was much more disagreeable than the heaviest rain storm," when, reaching a part of the wadi where rock took the place of sand, they came upon plants and shrubs, and among these "one which put forth many small branches from the root, not tall, but trailing out along the ground about the root, and on them hung much fine fruit, of green mingled with yellow, about the size of two fists, and spherical." The pilgrims flung themselves from their saddles and began to gather the attractive-looking objects; the escort, however, rode on laughing; they knew too well the property of the green and golden globes, medicinal[79] indeed, but far from pleasant. And the pilgrims themselves had hardly to do more than bring the fruit to their lips for the coloquinth to make its astringent bitterness known; Felix's mouth, he says, kept the taste for hours; the tang clung to the hands of the pilgrims, and to the knives with which they had cut the fruit; no amount of washing or scrubbing would get rid of the flavour. Felix, considering that though uneatable the "apples" were worth taking home among his souvenirs, put a couple "in my basket where I had meat, biscuit and cheese, but these things so caught the bitter taste that I could by no means bring myself to eat them, and I had to turn out meat, bread and cheese with the coloquinth." Even then the basket kept a lingering reminiscence of the taste, and imparted it, he was convinced, to anything which was put inside.[80]

In thirst, weariness and monotony the long day's march would wear on till the happy moment when the *Calinus* gave the signal to halt for the night. It was still some considerable time before sunset, for there was much to be done. The camels were first unloaded, the tents pitched and the donkey-men sent off to the nearest well or water-hole.[81] The pilgrims also had their domestic duty, from which, Felix is careful to inform his readers, not one was excused. All must set to work to collect firewood for the night's cooking, and "ordained priests, counts, barons and knights rushed about the plain" pulling up by the roots the dry and prickly bushes of that arid land, which, however, gave forth a most sweet and aromatic perfume when burning.[82] On occasion desert travellers would find that even this fuel failed. Two Jesuit fathers of the nineteenth century have feelingly described the absorbing interest of the search for its customary substitute–dried camel dung–and the sensation of "gentle joy, one of those sudden emotions which create a transient happiness," which is felt when the searcher discovers a piece of this stuff "commendable for its size and dryness." We may take it for granted that, *mutatis mutandis*, in the Tîh instead of the Gobi Desert, Felix and his companions experienced the same elation.[83]

When supper had been cooked and eaten, and the next day's picnic meal prepared and dealt out, together with a ration of wine, "equally ... to each," the wise man betook himself to the disgusting but necessary business of ridding himself of the vermin, whose rate of reproduction was a standing marvel to Felix. "If you rid yourself this evening, tomorrow you find as many and as large as if you had not searched your shirt for a month."[84]

The arrangement of the camp was determined by unalterable rule. In the midst were the tents of the pilgrims, and their baggage; round about, but with a prudent space between, lay the servants, with the tethered beasts. Not very long after sunset the whole caravan would settle down for the night, but during the hours of darkness one man among the pilgrims must always be on guard, chiefly in the endeavour to restrain the pilferings of the thievish escort, but also to be ready to deal with any prowling Arab of the desert who might approach, whether to beg or to steal.[85]

The initiation of the travellers into this item of desert routine took place on the evening of the very day they set out from Gaza, and Felix's first watch provided him with some unforgettable experiences. He had been roused at midnight, and had begun to go the rounds of the camp, staff in hand, and repeating the Psalms of the Night Office, when "suddenly began a loud and terrible wailing. ... I could only suppose," he says, "that they were human voices," and he suggests some startling and picturesque explanations of the blood-curdling noise, among them the surmise that it was caused by "satyrs and other monsters of the desert" who objected to the passage of the pilgrims. Later he was to be told that he must have heard the howling of wolves, but he would have none of that. " ... What it was," he concludes obstinately, "to this day I do not know," and we realise that he did not wish to know. Wolves indeed! He would have found the, probably correct, explanation, that the noise was caused by a jackal pack, even more insipid.[86]

The noise had died away and the Friar had resumed his beat, when he came upon the Greater *Calinus*, prostrated in the ritual of Moslem prayer. Sabathytanco, always a strict disciplinarian, interrupted his devotions to ascertain whether the Friar had adequate reason for being about at this time of night. Once satisfied on this point the austere man, who usually kept his distance from the pilgrims, seems to have softened, perhaps because this was his last night in charge of the party which, as Felix says, "from Jaffa till now he had guided and governed in all our ways," since on the morrow he and his son would start upon their return journey to Jerusalem. As the two men stood together in the now silent night, and under the multitude of stars, "he turned towards the desert and the south, and showed me a very bright star, newly risen, and told me that it was called Saint Katherine's star, and, 'Look,' said he, 'beneath that star is Mount Sinai.' " Felix marked it well; night after night when they marched in the darkness he was to see it shine before them, and know that their guide set his course by it. "Yes, and even when we had left Mount Sinai I used to look back at that star; I saw it when we were in Egypt, and while we stayed at Alexandria, and for a long time at sea; but at last after we had left Cyprus ... I could see it no longer."[87] Thus, with his own brand of sincere and endearing sentimentality, the Friar commemorates that first night of the desert journey, a bright star, and the whole of his Sinai pilgrimage, very much in the spirit of–"*Ah! les beaux temps quand nous étions si malheureux.*"

For, in spite of the extreme of discomfort and weariness which the pilgrims must endure while upon their desert journey, those were indeed "good days" for Felix Fabri, calling up in him the vigorous and eager response which a man will give when he has suddenly discovered his own bent. In the Holy Land, though he had been keenly aware of the fascination of Syria as a foreign country, the overwhelming Christian memories of the land, and the burden of thought and emotion which these imposed upon a man of such genuine religious feeling as the cheerful Friar, had inevitably made him, before anything else, a pilgrim, one with mind and heart tuned to the solemn organ-notes of his religion. But this new pilgrimage was a different matter. Between Gaza and Mount Sinai, and again between Sinai and Egypt, lay many miles of desert, which, except for recollections of the wanderings of Israel, were empty of religious associations as of green things growing. In this, as it were, spiritual vacuum, the traveller who shared the Friar's skin with the pilgrim, came suddenly and completely into his own, so that the same man who so faithfully reflects the traditional piety of medieval Christendom is revealed also as a child of that generation of voyagers, which, after so long a period of slow and fumbling approaches, was soon, in the Portuguese and Spanish discoveries, to set wide the gates of the seaways about the world.

In the age that was passing, trade, pilgrimage, warfare or missionary zeal had sent medieval man upon his journeys. In the new age trade was to be the master motive of those who went down to the sea in ships, or pushed out beyond the known horizons of the continents. The profit motive is neither better nor worse in whatever period it operates, but at this time, when men caught glimpses and heard rumours of lands which had long been fabulous, there was a thrill and tremor of excitement to be found, not only for us in distant retrospect, but by contemporaries, in the process of mercantile self-seeking, and the humdrum actualities of trade were as intermingled with wonder as the story of Dick Whittington.

Pilgrims gazing westward from the top of Gebel Katerina saw ships of strange build and rig upon the Red Sea, and knew that these were merchantmen from India or even the more distant East. Looking down the mountain defiles towards Tor, the little port at which were discharged "spices, pearls, jewels, the treasure of the East."[88] they became aware of India as a place no longer fabulous; it was real, though still immensely distant; from that land where there were "mountains of gold, real ones"[89] came the very spices which they would see on sale at Cairo, or spilt about the quays at Alexandria, or in their bulging sacks filling the holds of the ships in which they took passage back to Europe.

Friar Felix felt all this, but he felt something more besides. During his journey through the Sinai peninsula he discovered in the desert itself an attraction which, though it may have been experienced by other medieval pilgrims, finds its expression in him alone. Like Doughty, Burton and Lawrence, Felix Fabri fell in love with the cruel wilderness. "I declare," he exclaims, "that I took a greater delight in the immensity of the desert, in its barrenness, its terror, than I ever felt at the fertility, the comely and pleasant loveliness of Egypt."⁹⁰ Here as in no other part of his narrative he records particulars of the landscape, and that not only when the pilgrims had reached the savage splendours of the mountains in the south of the peninsula, but even while they were crossing the comparatively monotonous limestone plateau of the Tîh. Now he notes how they passed between rocks white as snow on the one hand, and red as blood on the other; now the sand and stones were black under foot, "as if fire had just now burnt up everything combustible on these plains"; now the caravan moved below white hills "so rounded that they might have been turned upon a wheel."⁹¹ He is careful to assure his readers of the exactitude of all these observations, explaining how when made they were at once recorded, and how he had written down while "sitting in the saddle, the appearance and character of the country on wax tablets which I carried at my belt. . . . Very often I got down from the donkey, and described the route, the mountains and the valleys, for it would have been impossible to keep every particular in mind, without thus being at it all the time."⁹²

Conscious as he was of the power of this passion it is obvious that he felt the need of accounting for an emotion so irrational. And so, having searched his own mind, he attempts to explain in what, for him, lay the inexhaustible interest of this arduous and painful journey. "It is," he puts on record, "principally this, that every day, indeed every hour, you come into new country, of a different nature, with different conditions of atmosphere and soil, with hills of a different build and colour, so that you are amazed at what you see and long for what you will see next. All the time something new comes along, which ravishes you with wonder, either at the marvellous structure of the mountains, or at the colour of the ground, the variety of rocks and pebbles . . . all of which delight the inquisitive."⁹³

After reading that we may well ask ourselves whether Felix Fabri, as well as being one of the great line of desert lovers and desert travellers, was not also a geologist *manqué*.

CHAPTER IV

The desert journey

The loving scrupulosity of Felix's account of the desert journey goes so far as to include a carefully kept list of names–the names of notable hills, of plains or wadis through which the pilgrims passed, and the name of every place where they camped. He tells us how he learnt these; no sooner were the tents pitched in the evening than he sought out old Elphahallo, the Lesser *Calinus*, inquired what the place was called, and at once wrote down the answer[1]–Lebhem, Chawatha, Gayan, Wadalar, and so on–outlandish sounds, but Felix had entire confidence in his own ability to hear and correctly reproduce the Arabic names which they represented. He claims to have made proof of this in conversations with "a certain Saracen," probably Elphahallo himself. Though the old man, who spoke Italian "and bad pidgin German which he had learnt from the pilgrims,"[2] found insuperable difficulty in repeating the German words which Felix tried to teach him:–"he simply could not pronounce (them); no, not if it had been to save his life,"–"on the other hand," the Friar boldly asserts, " . . . all *his* words I pronounced without difficulty."[3]

Once indeed the *Calinus* played a trick on Felix. Just a week after the pilgrims had left Gaza, and immediately the evening business of pitching the tents had been completed, the Friar came to him with his usual inquiry–What was the name of the wadi in which they camped and the desert through which they had that day passed? The old man "thought for a moment, and then said with a laugh, 'The name of the place is Albaroch.' Whereupon the rest of the Arabs and Moslems standing round about laughed too, and made signs to me that I should write 'Albaroch.' I had in my hand pen, ink and parchment, and I wrote as they said, 'Albaroch,' before their eyes, and as they saw me write, and read it, they laughed still more." It was only later that Felix found out that the *Calinus*, with friendly malice, had fobbed him off with the name of Mahomet's fabulous steed.[4]*

---

* The place-names given by Felix Fabri in his desert itinerary have only recently received serious consideration, and as a result Mr. G. W. Murray has identified from

It is to be noticed that these pilgrims of 1483 followed a route different from the one usually taken across the desert of the Tîh.[5] That reached the same pass of Umm Rakna by which Fabri and his company descended from the plateau, but reached it by way of Nakhl, where, upon the ancient Hajj road between Egypt and Akaba, was a great well, known as the Well of the Sultan, because here, during the season of the Mecca pilgrimage, the Sultan retained a man who–as a Frenchman observed– "does nothing but draw up water from this well, by means of two camels, and a machinery of wheels like a mill."[6]

Not only did our pilgrims avoid this place, but during the whole of the desert journey the *Calinus*, with hardly an exception, deliberately refrained from camping at the wells and water-holes which are mentioned by other travellers. In every case the reason was the same; he shunned those places where Arabs were likely to be found.[7] The experienced guide in fact showed himself conscious of those worsening relations with the Arab tribesmen, which in a few years would cause pilgrims to abandon the direct approach from Gaza to Sinai, and to prefer to reach the Mount by the coastal route from Egypt.[8]*

Felix had had his first experience as a night-watchman on the first night out from Gaza, when the caravan was still in a land of villages and

---

them, and from the Friar's descriptions of the physical features of the country, the unusual route followed by the pilgrims on this occasion (*v.* G. W. Murray, *Journal of the Royal Geographical Society*, Vol. CXXII, Part 3, Sept. 1956, pp. 335–342.

Neither Aubrey Stewart, in his translation of the *Evagatorium* (*The Wanderings of Felix Fabri*, Palestine Pilgrims' Text Society, 1892–7) nor M. Sollweck, the editor of Paul Walther's *Itinerarium* (Bibliothek des Litterarischen Vereins CXCII. Stuttgart, 1892) attempted any identification. Aubrey Stewart reproduced without comment, both in his text and maps, the names as Felix gives them, and so far as it is possible to tell, arrived quite arbitrarily at the route shown upon the map. Herr Sollweck explicitly denied any value to the names which Felix gives, dismissing them as hopelessly corrupt, and citing in confirmation of this the above incident. (Walther, p. 195 n.). But the episode can be interpreted in an opposite sense. Not only is it clear that Felix distinguished the joke from the usually serious information which he received from the *Calinus*, but if we may suppose that the pilgrims had that day been passing through the Wadi al Bruk, and that the old man was merely perpetrating a pun, the story is at once an example of a successful attempt on the part of Felix to reproduce an Arabic name, and a further point identified in the route taken by the pilgrims.

While the difficulty of ascertaining place-names from the information given by ordinary dragomen is stressed by modern travellers (e.g. E. H. Palmer, *The Desert of Exodus*, Vol. 1, p. 12) it must be remembered that the *Calinus*, unlike the ignorant hireling of whom Palmer spoke, was a man of education and experience who knew the desert well.

* Suriano (p. 186) antedates the closure of the route across the plateau, asserting that "since 1480 the pilgrims have abandoned it."

cultivated fields. It was only the third day's march which brought the pilgrims into the desert proper. They had camped for the two nights that lay between, first, in a village with a mosque and well; and second, beyond the line of cultivation in the midst of a country where "there was only sandy soil burnt up by the sun's heat." Yet the land had not always been sterile; their tents were pitched in the midst of traces of bye-gone habitation and industry. Felix observed with interest the twelve great walled cisterns, the broken bits of tile and of earthen vessels, the iron shards of a forge which lay about, and other remains of the life which had departed. He wrote the name of the place *Chawatha*; it was almost certainly Khalasa, the Arabic name for one of the deserted Byzantine cities of this once prosperous district.[9]*

It was about noon on September 12 that the pilgrims reached the real desert, "the region itself of immense desolation, in which certainly no man lived nor could live," and it was on this day that they had their first experience of those chance encounters with other travellers which, in the wilderness, were always occasions for anxiety. They had climbed up into a country of craggy mountains and hills of sand intersected by stony wadis when they saw coming towards them another caravan. The pilgrims, who had been primed with terrible tales of what they might expect to suffer in the desert at the hands of man, were "greatly alarmed." But this sentiment seemed to be shared by the strangers; the two caravans met and passed in complete silence.[10]

Not long after this, in a narrow gulley, they saw before them the tents and booths of an Arab encampment. This was far worse: as the pilgrims approached they saw "the black men" stand at the tent doors armed with spears, and they prepared themselves to endure whatever trouble might be in store for them. But once more there was fear on either side; the Arabs made no attempt to intercept the caravan: "they watched us, and spoke not a word. So, quickly and in silence, we went by, glad of their forbearance as they of ours."[11]

Unnerved by these two scares the pilgrims were in a condition to take fright easily; when far away across a wide plain they detected, as they thought, the smoke of many camp-fires, they jumped to the conclusion that they were about to stumble upon a very large Arab band. The *Calinus* was able to comfort them; what they saw were merely sand whirls. Yet that evening, at sunset, he saw to it that the cooking fires were completely extinguished, "lest some spark or glowing ember should shine in the dark"; the pilgrims were also warned to keep good watch

* I have followed Mr. G. W. Murray's identification of the place-names in the pilgrims' itinerary.

for it was "a dangerous place and misliked because of many Arab raids."[12]

They were approaching, and next day entered, the region of the dunes, with all their possibilities of discomfort and danger, soft surfaces and sand-storms. For a while, during that day's march they escaped from these into the sheltered and rock-faced Wadi el Arish, where among the stony floor of the torrent bed there were green things growing which rested the eye, even if much of the show was provided by the deceptive coloquinth. But by the time they camped they were again in the region of sand, and when a gale blew up from the north-west sleep became impossible, not only by reason of a thunderstorm which accompanied it, but also because of the sand which penetrated everything, and they could only lie awake, listening to the storm and watching the lightning flashes in the sky over towards the sea. When, during the night, the pilgrim on watch announced the arrival of two strange Arabs, Felix, as bursar of his company, had to bestir himself. The *Calinus*, experienced in desert custom, and essentially a peaceful man, had been careful to coach the pilgrims in the correct procedure to adopt with such stray visitors, who might attach themselves to a caravan by day or night, sometimes continuing as hangers-on for several days. Felix therefore knew the etiquette; he hastened to open a sack of biscuit, and fill a water jar for these two; the prescribed dole given, however, a warning equally customary was delivered; they must sleep beyond the laager of the pilgrims or expect to be driven off by sticks and stones.[13]

For Felix the next day, September 14, was to be unforgettable. The company was roused before daylight; there was the usual heat and commotion, and a fresh explosion of indignation among the pilgrims at the discovery of further pilfering from the sacks. When the day's march began it led them through the gorge of El-Dha'iqa and along the flank of Gebel Hilal where the rock faces were so scoured by the endless friction of wind and sand that they shone in the sun; it ended probably at some point to the south of the mountain, and they camped in a sandy place among the foot-hills of the higher range. They had come perhaps 25 kilometres of not easy travelling, but when the tents had been set up, and the usual duty of wooding finished, Friar Felix, with energy still to spare, set out on a solitary expedition.

Not far off he had observed "a hill round and high, standing by itself and easy to climb; on the summit there was something that looked like a building." Those who have reached this point in the Friar's narrative will feel no surprise when they hear that he "longed to climb that hill, to see what was on the top, and to look round over the desert." Nor will they think it strange that he despaired of persuading one of his companions to join him. He did not relish setting off by himself, but was not to be balked. "I took heart, left the company as if I was going to pray alone..." and set off among the sand dunes.

It took him an hour to reach the foot of the hill which had seemed so near; and now that he saw it at close quarters he realised that it was altogether more formidable than he had supposed. But he was not one to give in easily. Up he went among crags of rock and over sharp stones, till tired and sweating he reached the top, only to find that what had appeared to be an interesting ruin was no more than a large cairn of stones.

There was still, however, the view; for a time he gazed about at the empty desert, "a confusion of mountains, hills and torrent beds, untenanted by beast, bird or man." Some of the hills were white; some black, but nowhere was there any trace of living green, only the empty land, in which he could not even discern the camp from which he had set out.

One thing remained to be done. The cairn, which, as he explained to his readers at home, was in the nature of those sailing-marks which are set up along the coasts to guide ship-men, was garnished, after the superstitious fashion of the Moslem, with scraps torn from their garments. Felix, full of righteous zeal, and perhaps a little out of temper owing to the unrewarding results of his excursion, set about clearing away all the rags, and in their place set up a cross, made, he says, "of cane." He trimmed the whole heap, here and there with smaller crosses, and scratched with sharp stones other crosses on flat slabs. By all this decoration he would at one and the same time honour the day's Feast, which was that of the Exaltation of the Holy Cross, and record the ascent of the hill by a Christian traveller.

When this was accomplished it was full time to think of returning, but first he must orientate himself by marking the direction in which the camp lay. He gazed round. No sign of the camp was to be seen, not even a drift of smoke from the cooking fires. A spasm of fear seized him, but he kept his head. If he could follow back along the track of his footsteps in the sandy plain all would be well. He hurried down the hillside, and found at the base the marks of his feet, by now half-obliterated by wind and blowing sand. For some time he was able to guide himself by these impressions, then, on more exposed ground, lost all trace of them, and again fear caught up with him, for now the sun was near to setting and he began to dread that his rash adventure might indeed have a terrible ending.

Habit, and the aptness of the words, brought to his lips one of the penitential psalms. As he wandered at a venture, desperately searching for his tracks he repeated it again and again—"Hear my prayer oh Lord ... my spirit is overwhelmed ... I stretch forth my hands unto thee ... hear me speedily ... cause me to know the way wherein I should walk...."

At last on a hill of sand he found a footmark, "and I could have kissed it for joy." Yet after a moment a doubt assailed him and again his heart failed him. Was the mark in the sand, after all, made by the foot of some Arab? He looked closely and saw that the print was that of a shod foot. He pressed on; he saw in the distance white objects, which at first he took for three white clothed figures, therefore Moslems and to be feared; but when he came closer he knew that he saw the tents of the pilgrims, and going down on his knees gave thanks to God.

His return to camp was unspectacular. He found two of his companions still eating in the tents: they chid him for being so late; they had waited supper a long time for him, they complained. "I said, I had been busy."[14]

After the wear and tear, both physical and mental, of such an adventure the Friar perhaps deserved, and certainly must have needed, a long night's rest. But he was not to get it. Before midnight an alarm went round the camp; two of the donkeys had been stolen, so it was rumoured. It was a false alarm; the pilgrims, in bed once more, but awake and chatting after the disturbance, heard the donkey-men come back, reporting the animals found; the beasts had merely slipped their tethers and wandered off. At that, "though," as Felix says morosely, "it was still very early, that is to say midnight," the *Calinus* roused all up for the start.[15]

And it was the start of a bad day. They set out in the dark and bitter cold; when the sun rose they found themselves riding blind into a sand-storm, so that by the time the wind dropped about noon Felix saw that his black tunic was so covered with sand that you could not tell its colour.[16] For a while, indeed, they found shelter from wind and blowing sand in a wide torrent bed where the going was suddenly good, even, Felix says, "delightful." They had, in fact, after making a short cut, re-entered the great Wadi El Arish, which they had left two days earlier, and were in the direct route for the "Well of the Sultan" at Nakhl.

But now the *Calinus* called together his clutch of pilgrims and made them a speech in which he put before them a harsh choice. If, he told them, they made for the well, they might proceed for three days by the Wadi el Arish, "at ease and without storms"; but on the way there would be no water for man nor beast, neither in wells nor surface seepages. Or, if they chose, they might cross from this wadi to another, "and there, perhaps, we shall find a well with water: 'I know indeed,' said he, 'that there is a well, but whether there is water there now, I do not know. And

2. THE TOMB OF BERNHARD VON BREYDENBACH IN THE CATHEDRAL AT MAINZ

if there is water I fear it will be set about with Arabs, and they will refuse us water, and, as well as that, molest us.' "[17]

That was the choice: and they must make their decision in the knowledge that already the water was low in the water-skins. The pilgrims did not take long to decide. They chose to make for the nearest well, fearing thirst even more than they feared the Arabs, and hoping that these might be persuaded to trade water either for biscuit or money.

So, having left the Wadi el Arish and crossed a barren and windswept upland, they found themselves at last looking down upon "many booths and tents pitched side by side as if it were a town," and among these the cooking fires, and the desert men moving about, who, when they saw the little company of pilgrims on the hillside, caught up their spears and took their stand at the doors of the tents. In the midst of the encampment was the water-hole.

Apprehensive, yet resolved, the pilgrims came on till they were within a stone's throw of the camp, when they halted and busied themselves with setting up their own tents, while the servants began to unload the beasts. They had not finished before a few of the naked and sunblackened Arab children came stealing up. "At once we gave them biscuit, which they accepted with glee and went back to their own booths." These pioneers were followed by others, first more children, then women with babies at the breast, and to all the coveted biscuit was given.

The result exceeded the pilgrims highest hopes. This dole "softened the hearts of those Arabs, and they told us to help ourselves to the water, for us and our beasts, and quite contrary to our expectations, we filled our jars and water-skins without the least difficulty."

That did not see the end of the *rapprochement*. During the time which the pilgrims spent at the water holes, "such comradeship as we could have with those Arabs, that we had. For our young knights and their young men competed together, leaping and running and lifting heavy stones, striving against each other in all friendliness." The episode closed in equal harmony. The pilgrims, resolved not to outstay their welcome, struck camp after a stay of three hours or so. When they were ready to start they called the Arab chief, and presented him with a gold ducat, as a reward for his fair and friendly dealing. The gift made a great impression; the Arab declared that "if we wished, he would be willing to come with us and be our safe-guard...."

Pilgrims were generally of the opinion that the briefer the intercourse with the Arab tribesmen, the better, and though you could not refuse to toss them the biscuit they begged for, it was wiser not to linger after you had fed them.[18] Our party had taken a bold course; now they preferred caution; they refused the offer politely, and having dismissed the Arab chief, "left . . . moving off in haste."[19]

They camped that night under the white limestone heights of Gebel Minshera, but were on the march again long before dawn. It was the same next day; they started, says Felix, "in the middle of the night." By now, just a week out of Gaza, with all the novelty of the desert routine worn away, this harsh régime pressed heavily on all, but especially on the sick men. Felix, inexhaustibly entertained by the changing desert scene, yet found in himself a sneaking sympathy for the Israelites, whose grumbling, during their forty years of desert wanderings, was so strongly reprobated by Holy Writ, and had drawn down on them such prompt and sharp punishment. Yet, as he listened to the groans and curses of his companions, the Friar was seriously perturbed; would retribution descend also upon this caravan; and would that flood of complaints obliterate all the merit which should have been earned by the pilgrimage?[20]

The *Calinus* continued to push on fast. On September 17 there was the same early start, for though yesterday the Arabs had promised water, none had been found. And today, when at the sight of bushes growing in a wadi, the pilgrims' hopes had risen, they had found on thrusting in among the shrubs that no water now remained, while one of their number, trying to slake his thirst from the dew upon the leaves, got only the bitter taste of salt on his tongue. Even the stinking water in the skins was again running short; when the thirsty pilgrims decided to open the jars of water bought at Gaza for just such an emergency, on a guarantee that if kept airtight the water would remain fresh, it was discovered that this also was undrinkable; not even the donkeys would touch it; as the pilgrims poured it out upon the ground they reflected with disgust, not only on the "special price" they had paid for it, but also upon the trouble they had had with the camel-men over the loading of the heavy jars.[21]

So once more, finding their thirst intolerable, they insisted that they must be led in the direction of the nearest well, and once more the *Calinus* bore away to the westward of their proper course. As a result there occurred one of those desert meetings with another caravan, which one way or another were sure to make an impression on the pilgrims.

They had reached, and were about to cross, the wide track of the Darb el Hajj, the road of the Mecca pilgrimage, when they saw approaching "a company of Arab merchantmen bringing a cargo of spices from the Red Sea." Apprehension and distrust were usually the emotions raised by such encounters, but this time distress broke down the barriers of race and religion. The Arab merchants were in ill case; approaching the *Calinus* they told him they had gone short of water for days, and "begged earnestly that we should give, if but to one among them, a drink of water, for they were almost at the point of death." And, says Felix simply, "we gave them the rest of our water because we should reach the seepage before evening."²²* It was well done; pity had shown its human face.

But when, not long after, the pilgrims' southward march brought them to a second Hajj track leading to Suez by way of 'Ain Sudr, and they met another merchant caravan, this time coming "from the further parts of the East," the two companies passed each other in silence and with scowling looks, for so, "ordinarily," says Felix, "men of East and West gaze askance at each other, since by nature there is enmity between them."²³

The sun still shone with scorching heat when the pilgrims after a trying march reached Wadi el Foqeia and halted on the edge of a wadi, called by Fabri, Hallicub (perhaps Wadi Khallal), so profound and shut in between such steep cliffs, that they were at first daunted, especially as, peering down into the shadowed gully, they could detect no sight nor sound of water, although, as so often, it was quite obvious that the bed of the wadi formed, in its season, a watercourse. Goaded by their raging thirst they turned angrily upon the *Calinus*, but he, mild man that he was, gave back a soft answer: let them but dismount and climb down and they would find not indeed any running water at this time of the year, but instead, pools among the rocks.

The pilgrims stayed no longer but scrambled down the cliff-side to the bottom of the wadi, where they found indeed what the *Calinus* promised – water left behind in the caves and fissures of the rocks by the rains of several months before. Water it was, but "warm, and of the foulest smell, thick with a sediment of clay, green and full of worms." Thirst made them, for the moment, oblivious of all this; they flung themselves down on their bellies and drank; only when their sharpest thirst was slaked did they pause, see the horrid liquid as it was, and realise that "we had drunk it, worms and all." When they began to strain the water into their jars and waterskins through pieces of stuff, and examined what was left in the

---

* The episode, incidentally, goes to confirm the route which Fabri's place-names suggest as that followed by our pilgrims. If this eastward-bound caravan were so far from Nakhl that they needed to beg for water in order to reach the well, our pilgrims must have been considerably to the west of the usual route. Fabri's words suggest that the merchants had come from Tor; if so it would seem that they had been prevented by unfriendly Arab bands from watering at el Foqeya or 'Ain Sudr. (*v.* G. W. Murray, *loc. cit.*)

filter, their disgust grew, and with it an unpleasant apprehension, as they "fearfully awaited the dismal operation of that inhuman draught," while with respect and some envy they watched how the animals drank, softly laying their lips to the water and, by sucking in from the surface only, avoiding the undesirable substances below. Yet, as Felix notes, by the mercy of God, none of the pilgrims suffered any inconvenience from what they had so indiscreetly swallowed.[24]

Nor was the recollection of that one noisome draught to set the tone for their memories of the evening which they spent at the water-hole. When they had brought the sick men down they found much to enjoy. "For the valley was deep, and shaded by overhanging rocks and jutting blocks of stone, and there were bushes and willows and delightful caverns in the rocks in which we sat." They bathed, too, in the pools, and washed their clothes, and Felix found time, in those hours of delicious coolness and relaxation, to copy into a small book the notes which he had made upon his tablets of "almost the whole journey from Gaza to here,"* and to clean the tablets "so that I could write other things later."

The evening drew on and the pilgrims, having eaten a very merry supper, began to look about among the rocks for comfortable places to sleep. But when the *Calinus* saw what they were up to, he descended upon them: "not for anything would he let us sleep there, but forced us to go up to the baggage." So they climbed up regretfully from the water-hole, a place of which Felix writes—"Never in this journey did we enjoy ourselves as much as we did there." Friar Paul remarks, concerning the same place, only that "the water was not good,"[25] and the contrast is a measure of the difference between the temper of the two men.

Their next day's march, that of September 18, was remarkable chiefly for its difficulty; the pilgrims found themselves negotiating the worst surface they had yet encountered, in a wadi the floor of which consisted of tenacious white clay which had dried and hardened into wide and deep cracks into which the soft-footed camels, the donkeys, and the pilgrims must descend and again climb out. Only Felix, perhaps, found some compensation in the bizarre tints of the hills on either side, black below as if burnt, and white like snow above. Certainly only Felix had sufficient resilience that evening after supper to leave the camp at Megmar and go exploring: it was a brief jaunt compared with his excursion of

* "Almost" but not quite. It seems that Fabri did not record the events of this day and that when he next brought his journal up to date his memory of September 17 and 18 had become confused, so that he had transposed the events of these two days, placing the crossing of the Darb el Hajj and the pleasant interlude in the Wadi el Foqeia after the arrival at Megmar. (See G. W. Murray, *loc. cit.*) I have adopted Mr. Murray's dating.

four nights ago, yet fruitful of interest, and it was conducted with a great deal more caution. Not far from the camp rose a great white hill; the Friar made for this and, poking about among the lower slopes, found there ancient mine workings, which he might have penetrated but for the fear of snakes. Close to the mouth of these caverns he discovered the old slag heaps, and tumbled out upon them fragments of dross, the residue, he was convinced,* "not of iron or any other metal but only of the finest gold of Arabia." Felix had as keen an eye as most pilgrims for souvenirs; he collected a number of these fragments, and found, when he showed them to his companions, that several of the knights were eager to buy.[26]

Wakened as usual next morning long before day-break the pilgrims had no idea that the eleventh day of their march from Gaza was to bring them to the end of the first and worst stage of their desert journey. They rode for a while by moonlight through a ravine so narrow and deep that the moon shone only on the heights above them. This gave place, about sunrise, to a high and bleak plain where rocks and pebbles shone red, across which they made their way southwards for an hour in the teeth of a bitterly cold wind.

Suddenly, after an hour of this they found themselves at the edge of the southern escarpment of the Tîh Plateau. For a moment or two their attention was focussed upon the steep plunge of the cliffs immediately below them; then they realised that the donkey- and camel-men were pointing, with smiling faces, towards the south. The *Calinus* interpreted this gesture. Far away among the tremendous company of mountains which rose "dark as it were with distance," on the further side of the plain below, rose one mountain "having two peaks like two heads"; the *Calinus* told them that this was Mount Horeb, the object and term of their pilgrimage.[27] At this the pilgrims went down upon their knees, as they had done months ago at the first sight of Jerusalem.

When, having said a prayer, they rose to their feet, they were at liberty to appreciate a magnificent view; to their right was the Red Sea, seeming, in the clear air, to be close; but the *Calinus* corrected that misapprehension; it was, he told them, three long days' march away. Before them were the mountains of the great Sinai massif; below lay the wide parched depression known as the Debbet-el-Ramla, which Felix called Ramathaym; and, at their feet the precipitous cliff-side by which the pass, the Naqb Rakna, zigzagged down to the plain.

When, some hours later, they stood in that plain, looking back at the height which they had descended, they could not trace the route by

* But mistakenly (*v.* G. W. Murray, *loc. cit.*).

which they had come, so devious had it been; with some pride Felix declares that the knights "who knew much of the world," said they had never known a worse place. The descent had been a slow and anxious business. The camels, trembling with fear, would take only one step at a time, with long pauses between.* More than one fell; about half-way a camel, having stepped down upon a rock with its forefeet, hesitated just too long before it brought its hind-quarters from the rock above, and in that pause harness and panniers slid forward over neck and head, and went bounding and rolling down among the rocks of the cliff-side. It was a regrettable accident, for the pilgrims' communal medicine chest—or rather basket—was in one of the panniers, and bottles and phials were smashed and scattered far and wide, though after diligent search it was possible to salvage some part of the precious medicines. But the catastrophe would have been much worse had the other pannier contained, as it usually did, "one of the noblest of the pilgrims." Felix, who, the reader will by now have realised, enjoyed a highly spiced episode, assures us that "if that sick nobleman had stayed in his basket he would have been dashed into a thousand pieces, and if he had had a thousand necks they would have been broken." This fate the sick man had narrowly avoided, having been persuaded, much against his will, to make the descent on foot; from this experience Felix deduces that it is not good for an invalid to be allowed his own way.[28]

That glimpse of the holy mountain, caught from the head of the pass, tugged at the hearts of those pilgrims who still kept their health and energy; they would have been glad to push on to the enormous rampart of mountains which faced them across the sandy expanse of the plain; yet for the sake of the sick men a halt was made for the rest of the day. At that low altitude, and at the foot of the escarpment of the Tîh, the heat of the tents would have been intolerable; but they found shade in some caves, and were compensated for the delay by the discovery, as they strolled about in the cool of the evening, that the sandy soil was "full of the prettiest pebbles, transparent and shining, of all colours, black, white, green, red, grey, blue and yellow." From this profuse supply of souvenirs they made a selection.[29]

Next day they entered the stupendous and magnificent mountain group which barred the approaches to the monastery of St. Katherine. For descriptions of that grandeur we must go to more modern travellers,

* Felix says that the descent took nearly five hours, Paul Walther, three. Doughty (*Arabia Deserta*, I, p. 90) describing another such place, explains that there the Mecca pilgrims took the precaution of alighting from their "cradle-litters," since "Camels at a descent, with so unwieldy fore-limbs, are wooden riding; the lumpish brutes let themselves plumb down, with stiff joints to every lower step."

who have both the eye and the vocabulary for æsthetic appreciation which our fifteenth-century pilgrims lacked.

"The desert cliffs and crags," says one of these, "when lit by a bright sun, glow with rich and exquisite hues such as are to be seen in few other parts of the world," and he suggests that it is "the effects of light and air . . . a brilliant sunlight, a sky generally cloudless and an atmosphere of surpassing transparency," which endow with beauty the naked rock.[30] The colours of the mountains are wonderfully varied; sandstone glows warm brown, gneissic rocks show "pale brown or myrtle green streaked with dykes of purple, black, dark red. . . . In the granite districts, red, brown, white, rose and grey are the chief colours . . . the glaring whites and greys of cretaceous and tertiary strata . . . being often streaked with brilliant clays of lilac, maroon and crimson. . . ."[31] Among these walls and crags of rock the wadis, "grand and picturesque . . . sweep in bold reaches between lofty hill ranges, or at times break through them by narrow crooked defiles of surpassing beauty. . . . The cliffs, pressing closely in, tower to vast heights. Here and there you pass the mouths of branch valleys, discovering endless vistas of mountains. . . . The natural wonders are, moreover, heightened in effect by a deathlike silence and stillness."[32]

We cannot hope for any such picture of their surroundings from our pilgrims. Friar Paul's one relevant remark suggests, indeed, a slight feeling of repulsion at the austere grandeur of the scene. The mountains, he says, were "awful and barren," and he does not mention them again, but dwells instead upon the discomforts of that day's march, "the heat, toil and hunger," which, he announces with his usual gloomy pride, fell with especial severity upon himself and his fellow Franciscan, both of whom were observing a two-day fast.[33]

Friar Felix, on the other hand, whether fasting or not, was clearly in a state of elevated delight. The wadi* by which that morning they penetrated the mountain mass, wound between "very high rocks, red, and seeming as if anointed with oil, so did they shine in places where the sun touched the stone." The effect was so curious and striking that the Friar could not be content till he had ridden up to the cliff and learnt "by touching them with my hand that there was no moisture there."[34]

In spite of the strong fascination which the empty wastes of the Tîh had exercised upon him, this sudden change from arid desert to a country where grass and bushes grew, affected him strongly, so that the first sight of a shepherd pasturing his flock was a matter for joy and wonder.[35] Another pilgrim found that in these valleys "the air of a morning is so

---

* Almost certainly the Wadi Khamila (*v.* Murray, *loc. cit.*).

sweet-smelling that I thought I was in a perfume shop";[36] and the Friar and his companions on their first day's ride among the mountains came upon "tall thorny trees* which were just then in bloom, and filled the valley with their fragrance."[37] The pilgrims broke off some flowering branches and carried these with them;[38] "I think," says Felix, fresh from the scentless pure air of the desert, "I think I never smelt a flower that breathed a sweeter scent."[39]

A different but equally gratifying sensation was caused by the appearance, upon a rock high above them, of a strange animal. The pilgrims at first took it for a camel; but did wild camels, they asked each other, inhabit these solitudes? Their conjectures were interrupted by the *Calinus* who overtook them to announce that the creature was "a rhinoceros or unicorn." The second of this odd conjunction of alternatives draws from Felix a recapitulation of all the literary associations of that fabled creature, not omitting that which "they affirm who write about the nature of things," how it can only be caught if "a virgin girl is set before it." "So then," he concludes, "it is a large animal, the colour of boxwood, with the body of a horse, the feet of an elephant, the tail of a sow, has a terrible roar, fights with the elephant . . . and, as has been said, respects virgins to a remarkable degree." The pilgrims, regretting that the animal was no nearer, gazed up at it for a long time; since it also remained looking down at them, they fancied that their interest and admiration were perhaps reciprocated.[40]

All that day their way led them among the high mountains. At one point they were alarmed at the discovery of the site of an Arab encampment so lately abandoned that the fires still smouldered,[41] and it was perhaps in an effort to avoid an encounter with this band that, during the next day's march, the *Calinus* turned out of the broad Wadi el Sheikh, the usual and most direct way to the Monastery of St. Katherine, and took instead the winding Wadi el-Akhdar. If that were the reason for this digression the attempt was made in vain. It was in this wadi that the pilgrims had their only serious brush with an Arab band, and found that the sight of their drawn swords, backed by the mild persuasion of the offer of a very moderate sum of money, soon quelled the Arabs' show of violence.[42]

The deviation from the usual route had however a more unfortunate result. So tortuous was the path which the pilgrims now followed that at times they believed themselves to be moving away from their destination. A feeling of anxiety began to spread. Some at last declared that they were being deliberately led astray. Others denied this. The argument ranged

* Probably acacia (*v.* H. S. Palmer, *Sinai*, p. 46).

more widely as old grudges were raked up, and the old division between the first two companies of pilgrims and the third, to which Felix belonged, began to re-open. To high words–"We are not going to be bullied by you. . . ." "Nor shall you ride rough-shod over us,"–succeeded blows; two of the knights flung themselves off their donkeys and went to it with swords, while Father Paul exhorted to peace "in a loud and lamentable voice." But it was the unarmed Arab camel-men who ran in, regardless of the steel, and brought the unhappy squabble to an end.[43]*

The close of that day's march restored the pilgrims' confidence in the *Calinus*. They camped in a plain surrounded by mountains, and close under the lee of a small solitary hill which stood in the midst of the plain. Upon that hill their guide showed them, as the Arabs still show, the very rock upon which Moses had been used to sit when he pastured the flocks of Jethro[44] "in the backside of the desert," and they knew that they were not a day's march from the Mountain of the Law. That evening the pilgrims must have sat at ease after the long day, as Charles Doughty sat with his Arab companions, when "the crackling and sweet-smelling watchfire made a pleasant bower of light about us, seated on the pure sand and breathing the mountain air, among dim crags and desert accacias, the heaven . . . a deep blue, glistering with stars. . . ."[45]

Next morning, as the pilgrims began their march by both moon- and star-light, the star of St. Katherine seemed, to Felix at least, to "stand close to us," and when they had passed through the narrow defile of el Watia, which to his excited vision seemed to be barely wide enough to let the loaded camels through,† they came, in the green and pleasant plain beyond, upon another reminder of God's Chosen People, finding here for the first time that gum, which, in the late summer, exudes from the young branches of the tamarisk,[46] to form "greyish white pillules of a viscid substance."[47]

Such, to the cool gaze of modern observation, is that substance which for the pilgrims was no other than manna itself, the miraculous food by which wandering Israel had been sustained in this very place, though they admitted that in their own later age the thing had changed its habits, and no longer lay broadcast upon the ground. Nor was it only the biblical associations of the stuff which impressed them. Generations of pilgrims relished it as a sweet-meat; an Italian had "never tasted anything so sweet, pleasing and medicinal";[48] Friar Felix, we are not surprised to hear, ate

---

* The accounts of Fabri and Walther differ. In the first only the argument and the duel between individuals is mentioned. In the second the quarrel is reported as arising between the different companies.

† According to H. S. Palmer, *Sinai*, p. 18, the width of the pass is "no more than thirty yards in places."

"a lot of it,"[49] and the rich Canon of Mainz makes one of his rare personal incursions into the bald, borrowed narrative which bears his name, in order to put it on record that manna "tasted sweet as honey, and stuck to your teeth when you ate it."[50] The pilgrims were to have many opportunities of enjoying this delicacy, after their first sampling of the toothsome stuff, for it was obtainable at the Monastery of St. Katherine, the monks selling phials of it, which cost a pretty penny,[51] and the Arabs also trading something they called manna, which, however, Friar Felix condemned as "faked and not at all genuine."[52]

As they rode on, now once more in the Wadi el Sheikh, they penetrated by another narrow cleft the red granite mountain walls. Suddenly, as the defile widened, "behold! we saw buildings, dwelling-places, and human habitations, and a long church: it was the Monastery of St. Katherine . . . at the foot of the most holy Mount of Sinai."[53] They had made their landfall.

Part Three

MOUNT SINAI AND THE MONASTERY OF ST. KATHERINE

CHAPTER V

The monks of St. Katherine

The monastery of St. Katherine of Alexandria, the mountains at the foot of which it stands, and the shrines and places of religious associations upon and around these, form an immensely ancient complex of sites, some though not all of which are venerated by the believers of three great religions. Jews, Christians and Moslems all revere the traditional spot in the monastic church where the Bush burned with the presence of the Angel of God and was not consumed; various places upon Mount Horeb from early times till this day have been regarded by pilgrims as sanctified by the dread converse of the Patriarch Moses with his Creator; the Medieval Christian Church has added traditions of the Blessed Virgin and of the Saint Katherine of Alexandria, both in the monastic church and upon the mountain known by the name of the martyred Saint. In the desert wadis round about, associations with God's Chosen People, uncritically enjoyed by pilgrims of the Middle Ages, and no less enjoyably debated by modern scholars, are common, almost, as blackberries. And in addition to all this, the whole has perhaps undergone as little change as any frequented locality in the whole world.

Even the youngest of all the ancient things here, the monastery itself, though it has suffered destruction by earthquake, as well as the inevitable decay and alteration of the centuries, is still surrounded in part by the walls which Justinian built, and the monks still worship in the Emperor's own Church of the Transfiguration; within the church the relics of St. Katherine are still preserved in the same stone chest in the same chapel where the fifteenth-century pilgrims knelt before them: modern pilgrims climb Mount Sinai by the same steps up which Felix Fabri toiled. From the summit of Gebel Musa, and from the yet loftier crest of Gebel Katerina to which the Alexandrian martyr has given her name, travellers of any century have looked out over the same stupendous spectacle of mountain, desert and sea.

Here also, in matters unconnected with steadfast religious tradition, there are factors which enduring through the centuries produce, if not a constant, at least a repeating pattern. Thus, the desert which has insulated the life of the monks from many of the mutations of the outside world the wild tribes of the desert, set monks and dwellers in the waste face to face ard alone in the wide and lonely wilderness. Whether the convent had a Christian patron at Constantinople, or a Moslem overlord in Cairo, these, though benevolent, have been far away, while the Arabs were always at the gates.

Relations between the two parties to this neighbourhood varied with the changing equilibrium of power in the Eastern Mediterranean. When Felix Fabri stayed at the monastery, he and his companions were disquieted by the spectacle of an Arab sheikh and his tribesmen within the precincts, encamped round about the Church; the nomads behaved with complete decorum, their design being in no wise directed against the monks but only against the purses of the pilgrims.[1] But the latter years of the century saw a worsening of the monks' situation. When, in 1484, Francesco Suriano, the nobly born Venetian, once merchant and sea-captain, now Prior of the Franciscans at Jerusalem, reached the Convent, he found a small company of monks weeping over the body of their dead Abbot, murdered by the Arabs.[2] The brethren, unnerved by the tragedy, cowered within their walls; had it not been for these, the whole place would have been sacked; and though the tribesmen were unable to force their way in, Suriano during his stay watched how they terrorised and bullied the monks, "like starved dogs" making "such an uproar that it seems like Hell," and keeping all the brethren busy through the whole of every morning, satisfying their demands.[3]

Two years later, when Von Harff visited the monastery, things were quieter, but he noted the strength of the defences at the entrance; there were no less than "three small and low doors covered with iron plates, so that one has to creep through."[4] By the time Jean Thenaud arrived, only five years before the Mamluk Empire fell, these precautions had ceased to be sufficient, and entrance was made in the bizarre fashion which persisted even into the nineteenth century. When a visitor knocked, Thenaud explained, "a rope is let down from the top of the wall, into the loop of which you put your feet and keep them there, and with one turn you are pulled up."[5]

In such an atmosphere of uncertainty and danger, the monks, as might be expected, did what they could to make friends of any Mammon of unrighteousness, beginning with the Moslem Sultan at Cairo. Every year they sent to him a gift of fruit from their gardens, and in return received his protective firmans, of which carefully preserved documents no less than 100 are still in existence among the archives of the monastery.[6]

The monks judged it worth while to make sure of the Sultan's goodwill, but they probably put more confidence in a direct arrangement with the

Arabs; certainly in order to placate their dangerous neighbours they continued for centuries to provide a number of these with a daily dole of food. At least eighty had the right, says Fabri, to be fed with bread and pottage, "and generally," he adds, "a hundred come."[7] As might be expected, no intermission in the custom was permitted by the Arabs who tyrannised over the brothers at the time of Suriano's visit, but in those days, since the monks naturally refused to allow even a single tribesman into the monastery the dole was lowered over the wall at the end of a rope.[8] The custom of the daily dole still survived into the second half of last century, when, however, an Englishman remarked that the bread was of a quality "which no decently brought up ostrich could swallow without endangering his digestion."[9]

Such a liability must have been a drain on the economy of the Convent, and was all the more serious in that the growing arrogance of the Beduin tribes was at the same time so adding to the perils of the desert journey, that the flow of pilgrims, and consequently of their offerings at the shrine of St. Katherine at one period, almost entirely dried up.[10] This source of income, though never perhaps of great importance, was certainly not negligible. After Felix Fabri and his fellow pilgrims had been granted a view of the bones of St. Katherine the sacrist must have gathered up a pretty penny from the coffin, since the Friar preens himself upon the fact that hardly any of the party had dropped into it less than a ducat, while the lords and knights had offered their two or three or four ducats apiece.[11] Even such a waif of a pilgrim as Jean Thenaud, when after all his persecutions at the hands of his escort he reached the monastery, offered his ducat at the shrine,[12] a ducat which, during all the tempestuous happenings of the journey, must have lain concealed in some most ingenious hiding-place.

But the monks possessed sources of income more dependable than the offertory of pilgrims. Subventions were made by the Greek Churches of Crete, Cyprus, Rhodes and Corfu.[13] They owned a large grove of date-palms at Tor, and had a right to a share in the very lucrative customs taken at that port.[14] Benefactions to a place of so great a sanctity came not only from the East but also from Europe. The unhappy Charles VI of France bestowed on the monastery a magnificent chalice of silver-gilt which it still preserves.[15] Even though, about half-way through the fifteenth century, the monks repudiated their age-old recognition of the Roman pontiff,[16] the grandson of the same Charles, Louis XI, a strong believer in the wisdom of taking out religious insurance policies in all directions, promised a princely gift in the shape of an annuity of 2,000 ducats.[17]

But royal gifts, however splendid, had no effect upon the life of poverty, almost of squalor, to which the monks of St. Basil had dedicated themselves. The cells they lived in seemed to the Latin pilgrims no better than "shepherds' huts or garden sheds," built of reeds and plastered with mud, and huddled together anyhow so that those on the side below the overhanging cliff of the mountain reminded Felix of swallows' nests.[18]

That uniformity of monastic dress which the west observed was nothing to these monks; Felix saw among them "different sorts of tunic, one of this sort, and one of that...." He noted too that there was "none of fine colour or good stuff," but that all were "wretched and shabby." Entering one day the cell of an aged monk, and doubtless looking about him with lively curiosity, he could see there "nothing that did not speak of dire poverty."[19]

In their food they seemed to their visitors to fare hardly better than the desert folk. Their Rule forbade them to eat meat, and even the salt fish which they got in plenty from the Red Sea[20] was prohibited in Lent. The grain for their bread came by camel from Cairo,* and this, "with rice and peas which they make into a mess... is their food...," washed down by water,[21] though, as we shall see, they were allowed wine at the greater feasts.[22]

So sparse a diet made necessary a good supply of vegetables and fruit, and this the monks had, for they possessed within the monastery enclosure at least one unfailing well of pure water, and the desert soil needed only water to make it blossom as the rose. The well lying to the east of the Church, and traditionally that from which Moses drew up for the daughters of Jethro,† was sufficient to supply the domestic needs of the monks and their guests;[23] the water of the other, led by channels in the rock and carefully disposed pipes down through the sloping garden, made that a fertile and pleasant place, with grass and vegetable plots, rows of salad herbs, and the shade of many fruit trees—apple and pear, grape-vines, oranges, figs and almonds, as well as so great a number of olive trees that, together with those in a more distant garden, they produced enough oil for the culinary use of the monastery, and for the multitude of lamps which hung in their Church.[24] It was no wonder that the monks were such assiduous cultivators as to cause one of their visitors to remark that they spent in their garden all the hours not devoted to prayer[25] following thus that same ancient and simple pattern which the Rule of St. Benedict had imposed upon the first ages of western monasticism.

* Pococke (I, p. 152) says that they had corn from Cairo and ground it at the mill within the monastery.
† Two wells are regularly mentioned by later travellers. Baedeker (*Lower Egypt*, p. 262) says that the well here referred to has the better water.

3. SAINT KATHERINE OF ALEXANDRIA

A fifteenth-century fresco in the cathedral at Ulm. Mount Sinai and St. Katherine's Mount appear in the background

Here, in fact, as at the monastery of St. Saba in the Holy Land, Felix Fabri was brought face to face with a cloistered life, austere ascetic and uncompromisingly primitive. Deeply engaged as his own hopes were in the reform of German monasticism this should have been an experience to gladden his heart, but instead his account of the days spent in the monastery of St. Katherine is the saddest and sourest part of his cheerful and kindly-tempered book. He admired, but admiration kindled no warmth, and did nothing to sweeten the bitterness with which the Latin Christian regarded his brother of the Orthodox Church, or of any other Asiatic Christian body, whom he came across. To him, good monks as they were, the monks of St. Basil were heretics, and thus–Felix spoke for the Deity with confidence–their virtues were as nothing in the eyes of God.[26] The whole tragedy of Latin intolerance is seen here in little, as we realise that for the Friar the division between two Christian Churches brimmed with more resentment, petty grudge and suspicion than the chasm which separated Christian from Moslem.

It is difficult to ascertain, from the accounts of western visitors, how far these feelings were either deserved or reciprocated. Friar Felix maintains that in their dealings with their pilgrim guests the monks were actuated, not by charitable sentiment but by greed of gain. Every time one of the visitors passed the door of the ancient church he must pay; and this must certainly have borne hardly on Felix, who loved to haunt any holy place near which he stayed. He complains also that the pilgrims paid for the hire of the staves with which the monks accommodated them for the climb up Mount Sinai; those of the knights whose shoes were so worn as to be quite unfit for the rough scramble up the mountain found that it was impossible to borrow any substitute from the monks; when the pilgrims came to fill the water skins for the first march of their return journey they learned that even the water from the great well had its price.[27] Yet all these pin-pricks, and they were no more, for there is no complaint of exorbitant demand, seem but the efforts of an indigent community to make some inconsiderable profit out of their visitors.

More regrettable to modern sentiment was the common but galling experience of Latin priests that they were not allowed to celebrate Mass in the monks' Church, while a Latin pilgrim would be refused burial in the monks' graveyard. Finally, Latins believed that their hosts harboured such hatred against the Roman Church that they would spend the pilgrims' offerings on supplying food to their Arab parasites, yet would have died of hunger rather than make use of the money for their own sustenance.[28] Yet it needed perhaps only the pressure of danger and loneliness to restore the consciousness of Christian brotherhood. Suriano, coming on the heels of tragedy, found himself welcomed, "with great love and charity."[29] Von Harff considered himself very well received by the monks who told him that he was the first pilgrim to enter the monastery for ten years.[30]

Even Felix Fabri's account allows some gleams of amity to show through the obscuring cloud of his ill-will. Brother Nicholas, the sacristan, who shared the pilgrim expeditions up the holy mountain, shared also the festal supper which took place when they returned to the monastery.[31] Friar Felix himself, finding among the monks "many grave and sober-minded old men," seems to have held some converse with them, and goes out of his way to say a few words in praise of the abbot, the same who was to meet his death at the hands of the Arabs eleven years later,[32] but now "a youngish man, strong and wise."[33] The monks for their part, as well as supplementing, with assorted *friandises*, the meal by which the pilgrims celebrated their solemn visit to St. Katherine's shrine[34] gave them as a parting gift a lamb and a kid. Perhaps Friar Felix would have been more grateful for this pleasant addition to the commissariat if the pilgrims' two first camps after leaving the monastery had not been so waterless that cooking was almost impossible; but it is regrettable that he did not trouble to record the monks' generosity.

Apart from such exceptional gifts, the hospitality which the pilgrims of 1483 received was of the simplest, being merely the use of unfurnished rooms, as in the *khans* to which they had become accustomed while in Syria. Here they were forced to continue the monotonous diet of salt and smoked meat from their own stores, obtaining from the monks only firing, and the water from the deep, cold and copious well of the monastery.[35]

Pilgrims of an earlier period, when still Latin and Greek felt the fraternal tie of their common faith, had received daily from the monks two leaves apiece, and were allowed the run of their teeth in the fruitful orchards of the monastery.[36] Even when the breach had been made, exceptional circumstances would prompt the monks to show their old accustomed hospitality to a western pilgrim.

When Jean Thenaud reached the monastery, alone and practically destitute, the monks not only housed but fed him, not only provided him with a meal in his own lodging—fresh barley bread, olives, dates, water and vinegar, neatly served on a reed mat which unfortunately when unrolled proved to be occupied by a dozen or so scorpions—but also invited him to their own evening collation, thus making him the richer by an experience which, could Fabri have known of it, he would vehemently have envied. For it happened that Thenaud had arrived upon the Feast of St. John the Baptist, a major festival upon which, after

Collation each monk was allowed two mouthfuls of wine. This wine their guest, when his turn came, found to be "so delicious and perfumed, of a strange flavour, like manna, that it far surpassed piment and hippocras." The abbot must have divined the Frenchman's enthusiasm, for, making a pretext of a gift of nuts and pears, he followed him to his quarters, and opened up a conversation by inquiring how he liked "the *nebith*, that is to say the wine." When Thenaud declared that if the saintly desert Fathers had drunk it, they were lucky, the abbot at once gave him to understand that the monks would have no objection to a customer. Thenaud was penniless except for the offering which he would make to the Saint; that must not be broken into even for the sake of the wonderful wine, but "the irresistible longing I had to drink of it made me exchange an Irish cloak with which I had covered myself in the desert . . . for two jars of wine." The candid confession of human gluttony disarms criticism; no reader but will be glad to hear that Thenaud found the fruits of his improvidence well worth while. "I think I never kept such a Feast of St. John, both for the spiritual joys which I experienced in that very holy place . . . and for the delicious wine which made me forget all my past sufferings."[37]

CHAPTER VI

The monastery, the mountains and the shrines

The first glimpse of the monastery of St. Katherine caught by approaching pilgrims was less that of a holy place than of a fortification. "Like a castle, square and strong..."[1] "shut in by high walls, like a stronghold..."[2] "wide and thick walls... having a roundway on top..."[3] such remarks record their first impressions of the convent as they saw it stand, so close under one of the huge perpendicular rock faces of Gebel Musa, the Mount of the Law, that "when one stands in the monastery and looks upwards, it seems as if the mountains would fall on it."[4]

The pilgrims had come within sight of the monastery early in the morning; it was not yet noon when they knocked at the gate, were admitted, and with the brethren hospitably helping to carry their baggage, were brought to the rooms reserved for pilgrims. They unpacked; they heard Mass; they dined. But after this for a while not even Felix stirred out; the hours were spent in what must have been, after all the toils of their journey, a very grateful repose.

As soon as they had recovered from their fatigue they set out upon a tour of the monastery. The range of guest rooms which they occupied, each of the three companies having its own chamber, was situated probably not far from the entrance gateway.[5] Conveniently close stood the chapel, known as St. Katherine of the Franks,[6*] which, after the break with Rome, the monks provided for the use of Western pilgrims. A small building of mud brick, its walls were hung with woven palm leaf mats of varied colours.[7]

Within the walls of the monastery the unevenness of the site, which slopes upwards towards the towering cliff above, prevented any of that regularity of conventual plan to which western visitors were accustomed. Instead the pilgrims found the buildings grouped round a series of small courtyards connected by flights of steps.[8] From the guest rooms they descended by some of these to the courtyard in which stood, in strange juxtaposition to the Church of Justinian, a Saracen mosque. They would not stay for this upon their first evening, but once later on they did look in: however, ignoring or failing to notice the beautiful wood-carving of the mimbar and doors, they decided that there was nothing there worthy of their attention.[9]

From the court in which the mosque stood, another flight of steps led down to the portico and magnificent carved west doors of the basilica. Within the church much has been changed since the fifteenth century, by accident, by violence, or by reason of alterations in taste, yet still much survives of the fabric which our pilgrims saw that evening. A single mosaic in the apse behind the high altar is all that remains of those which Suriano admired;[10] the floor is no longer "paved with exquisite little marble stones joined together, adorned with ancient histories,"[11] and the columns of the granite nave which reminded those pilgrims who were familiar with the Holy Land of the beautiful pillars in the Church of the Nativity at Bethlehem, are now covered by a coat of green and white paint.[12] But, then as now, the church abounded in lamps hanging in the many chapels and in front of every monk's stall.[13] "I never saw so many in any church," said an Italian;[14] the pilgrims described them as "countless"; in our more methodical days the number has been reckoned by Mr. Baedeker as 100. As well as the crowd of lamps it seems that the object in the church which most delighted Felix continues in use, though its form has been modified. The Friar noted a strange contraption which took the place of bells;—a thick rod of iron "from which hang brazen rings which chime when the sacrist strikes them with mallets in a certain order and measure, the notes of which are so sweet that you could dance to the tune."[15] Still, on Saturdays, the monks strike on an iron bar, known as the Symandra, as a call to prayer,[16] though the dangling rings which rang so sweetly are no more.

The normal procedure for pilgrims, to which ours also adhered, was to undertake a two-day expedition to the summits of Gebel Musa, the Mount of the Law, and Gebel Katerina, the height which medieval tradition claimed to have been hallowed by the presence of the body of St. Katherine of Alexandria, miraculously conveyed there by angels, and watched by them upon the mountain top for 300, some said for 500, years.

Felix and his companions therefore, having delayed for one whole day in order to give the sick men of the party a chance to recover, arranged to make their ascent of Gebel Musa on the second morning after their arrival. Before that time came, the Friar had had a stroke of luck.

" 'Look, Friar Felix,' said one of the sick knights, 'I bought these shoes to go up the mountain in them; but as I can't go up I beg you to accept them and so give me a share in the footsteps which you will tread.' " The motive for the gift, between the altruistic and the sentimental, was engaging; the shoes of grey, or grey-blue leather, bought in Jerusalem, were an excellent fit. Next day the Friar left his own shoes "old and almost falling to bits, in the room" (a piece of information almost as evocative as Van Gogh's portrait of his old boots), and, we may be sure, stepped stoutly forward in the fine new pair.[17]

Three hours before dawn all those who hoped to make the ascent of the mountain paraded before the Sacrist, Brother Nicodemus, who was to be their guide, but his first action was to weed out all those whom he considered insufficiently robust for the climb. Though the healthy and well-nourished modern traveller may agree with the guide-book that the ascent of Gebel Musa "presents no difficulty" it was otherwise with a fever-stricken and exhausted medieval pilgrim. The little Italian notary, Nicolò Martoni, found his shins "so heavy that they seemed like beams of wood, and several times I said to myself,–'Turn back! You see! You can't keep up with the other pilgrims.'"[18] Martoni's faith and determination had carried him up the mountain, but Brother Nicodemus upon this later occasion was taking no chances, and it was a diminished party which he led off in the direction of the more arduous of the two routes in use today. He and his selected band climbed the rough stone steps, the number of which Felix raises high above the more sober reckoning of the modern age, but the Friar's statistics tend to be emotional rather than mathematical; they passed under the two archways which still span the narrow cleft through which the path ascends; on the way they halted at various chapels, both to acquire the prescribed indulgence and to hear the stories traditionally connected with them. Here they were reminded of the Blessed Virgin, St. Marina, the Prophets Elijah and Elisha; but when they neared the summit it was the story of Moses which overwhelmed all other associations. They came to the "clift in the rock" where the Patriarch had hidden his face from the Glory as It had passed by. So tangible a memorial was just the thing to engage the special interest of the pilgrims. One and all they wriggled themselves into the fissure as far as their middles, no further, however, for that would have meant being pulled out by the heels, since as Felix remarks, a man cannot move backwards like a crab.[19]

Climbing the last steep ascent, among granite jags fantastically speckled and splashed with red, grey, green and yellow, the pilgrims reached the summit. Here a chapel and a cave must be visited; the chapel covered the very spot, they learned, where the Angel of the Lord delivered to Moses the Tables of the Law; in the cave the Prophet had lodged for the forty days of his communion with God upon the mountain. The associations were overwhelmingly august; in the chapel the pilgrims, finding the appropriate place in their "Processionals"–those little books of prayers compiled for use during pilgrimage–were moved "with enormous joy and devotion." But in the cave Felix found time to let a thought stray towards a practical consideration. It struck him that the cavern, "big and wide, with no light except that which came through the opening, would be a rather convenient dwelling for a contemplative monk,"[20] and we cannot but imagine that for a few moments the Friar fancied himself at home in it.

Their devotions were now completed. The mosque did not concern them, though by it, and by the presence of some Moslem pilgrims sitting with their backs to the wall, Felix was reminded that men of three religions held this spot holy; he obviously found it satisfactory that of these only Jews should be prohibited from honouring the Patriarch in this holy place.[21] There remained for the pilgrims only to stroll about the mountain top, admiring the view, to eat the food they had brought with them, and then, after an hour's repose, to begin the descent.

They were not yet, however, to return to the monastery of St. Katherine. Pilgrims of all periods have found that the best starting point for the ascent of Gebel Katerina is the small fortified monastery of the Forty Saints, a dependent cell of St. Katherine's in the Wadi Leja. Here were living quarters for a few monks, and rooms for guests; here also lay that garden, of greater extent and more beautiful than that of the mother house, upon the produce of which the monks largely depended for food and oil; from it came also the fruit which, bottled and crated, was sent every year to the Sultan, and which this autumn would go down to Egypt in the caravan of our pilgrims.[22] The garden, except when locusts abounded at the time of blossom, or when rain failed, or Arabs marauded, was a place of marvellous fertility, only a stone's throw in width, but a mile in length, and full of all manner of fruit, " . . . figs, almonds, oranges, olives, apricots, pomegranates . . . very good to eat."[23] Amongst the trees water ran in paved channels from pool to pool, drawn from the three great rain-water cisterns which the monks had hollowed out in the mountain-side above the garden. This garden, which an Italian said would have stood comparison with those of Sorrento or Salerno,[24] this "paradise in the desert" was tended always by a couple of brethren from St. Katherine's monastery.[25]

The ascent of Gebel Musa is generally reckoned to take three hours, and, as a result of their early start, the pilgrims reached the monastery of the Forty Saints before noon. The monks at once set before them a meal of dates, dried figs and pure water, and it was while they sat at ease enjoying this refreshment that one among them–could it have been

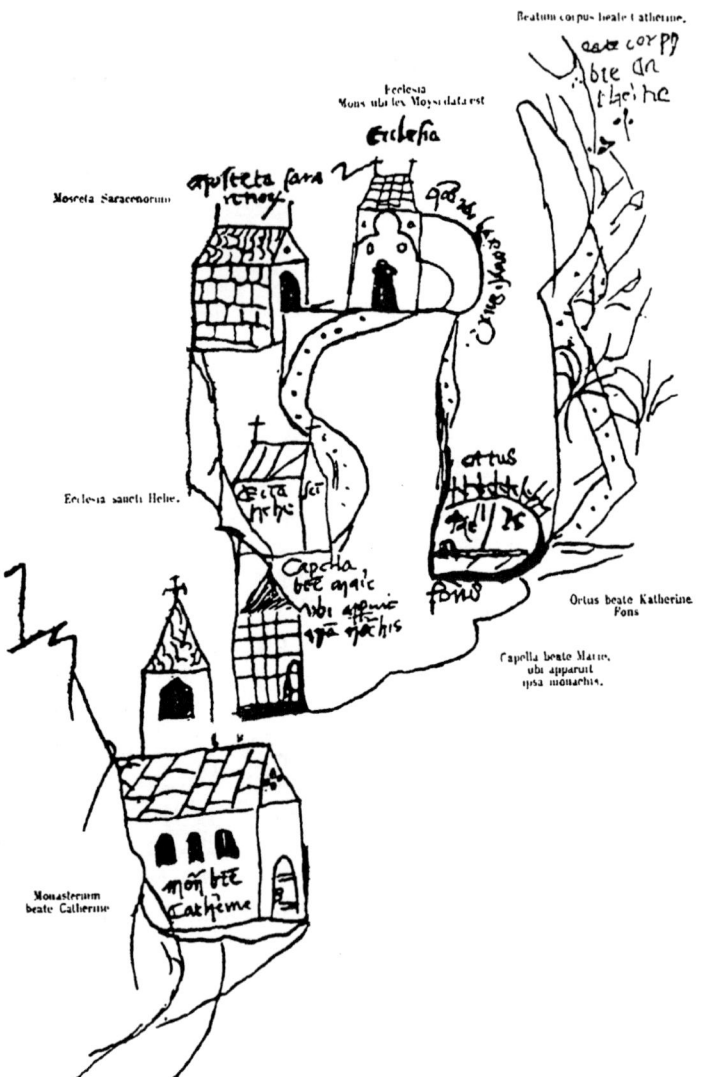

Profile of Mount Sinai, from Jacques de Verona's *Liber Peregrinationis*, 1420.

Saracens' mosque	Church Mount where the Law was given to Moses	The blessed body of the blessed Katherine
Church of the holy Elijah		Garden of the Blessed Katherine Well
Monastery of the blessed		Chapel of the blessed Mary where she herself appeared to the monks

Felix?—posed the question: why should they wait till next day to attempt the climb up Gebel Katerina?

The noon sun stood high above, and it was clear that the less robust among the pilgrims could not attempt the climb except in the cool of the morning. But the stouter hearts agreed that it would be unendurable to spend the rest of the day in idleness; "so ten hardy pilgrims rose up ready to make the ascent even in the fiercest of the heat."[26] Four of them were knights, Felix's admired von Schonberg and his friend Caspar von Siculi, Sigismund of Morspach, and the boy Count; two were servants, Count John's cook, and Conrad the barber-musician; four were ecclesiastics, the two Franciscan Friars, Archdeacon John Lazinus, and Friar Felix. Brother Nicodemus presumably, and certainly some of the donkey-men and Arab hangers-on, were also of the company.

A climb "hardly," as Baedeker mildly puts it, "suitable for ladies," it was too much, in the tremendous heat, for one of the knights, who threw in his hand and, "sitting down on a blazing hot slope, could go no further." They were half-way to the top but he had had enough, and only begged to be left where he was till their return. The pilgrims tried encouragement, then gentle compulsion; at last with someone hauling on a napkin tied to his belt, two pulling him by the arms, and others pushing him from behind, they brought him along. "A terrible business," says Felix, "we had with that pilgrim."[27]

Upon the tiny level plateau which forms the summit of Gebel Katerina there is the long depression in the rock which is still pointed out as having been miraculously caused by the pressure of the Saint's body. In the fifteenth century two other hollows, one on each side, were presumed to have been made – though it is clear that Felix Fabri found it an awkward presumption – by the posteriors of the attendant Angels.[28] At that time the whole stood open to the sky, though nowadays it is covered by a small chapel, and some pilgrims noted, as a token and assurance of the holiness of the spot, that birds, though uninhibited in their behaviour in other parts of the small plateau, treated this particular spot with respect.[29]

The pilgrims, and most specially Felix, inspected the place with feelings of lively devotion, but these were at last obliterated by the pangs of hunger. Unfortunately, in the *élan* of their start, almost all the pilgrims had forgotten to bring their bottles, and all but one their scrips.

Friar Felix was that solitary exception. "I do not know," he says, "by what providence it happened that I alone had a basket with biscuit, hard-boiled eggs, smoked meat, cheese and wine." These the good man, with something of a flourish, invited his companions to share, in the name and honour of the Saint. For, as he explained to them, he considered

St. Katherine as his "most sweet spouse in God," seeing that on her feast he had begun his noviciate, and on her feast had entered Religion. Joyfully, and with a somewhat surprising levity and familiarity, he emptied out the contents of his basket into the depression which had been caused by the Saint's head, and the whole party, including donkey-men and Arabs, fell to. What would have been a square meal for one must have been slender provision for so many. Soon not a fragment – not a crumb – remained. "Never in all my pilgrimage was my basket so empty and so thoroughly cleaned out as here."[30]

When the sun began to sink low over the mountains the Arabs urged the advisability of prompt return, and the pilgrims accordingly pelted down the mountain-side at such a rate that Friar Paul took a nasty tumble; only the direct intervention of St. Katherine and God prevented this being fatal. They had made the difficult descent none too soon; it was already dusk when they rejoined the rest of the party in the pleasant garden of the Monastery of the Forty Saints.[31]

Next day the official expedition took place. Three hours before dawn those who were to make the ascent rose from the floor upon which they had dossed down for the night, and prepared for the start. "Most of those who had already climbed the mountain stayed quiet," but Felix and the two Franciscans had the energy and resolution to repeat yesterday's excursion.[32] That had been a wild escapade; today's would be a far less dashing affair, and its discomforts, though no less severe, would be of a nature entirely opposite.

Brother Nicodemus led the way, setting a slow pace for the sake of the less hale among the pilgrims, and this time a proper supply of picnic baskets and water and wine bottles were carried by the servants. Having left the monastery garden behind, the party climbed an open hill-side in brilliant moonlight, but, once entered within the great rock walls of the mountain, their way was dark and the going very rough. Here, where Felix and his companions had yesterday sweltered in the burning heat, the pilgrims this morning suffered from a biting cold which grew more intense as they mounted. Yesterday, on the way up, the pilgrims had found the only alleviation to their labours in the two springs of deliciously cool and pure water. Today when they halted it was to make a fire at which to warm themselves. The pilgrims carried no tinder box with them, but the Arabs chafed dried grass, and after, kindled it by striking stones sharply together, a process which Felix watched with fascinated attention.[33] When they moved on some of the pilgrims carried smouldering brands with them for the sake of the warmth, and their climb was later interrupted by a pause to make a second fire.

THE MONASTERY, THE MOUNTAINS AND THE SHRINES 91

From the first part of the ascent they emerged at dawn upon the steep but smooth and grassy slope from which rise three peaks,* with Gebel Katerina among them, not the highest, "but incomparably the most imposing, consisting of one huge, rugged block of porphyry."[34] The last climb, up that precipitous mass of rock, was the worst: "faint hearts or dizzy heads were of no use here . . . they went up like ants crawling up a tree,"[35] the stronger hauling the less able-bodied after them, till at last they reached the summit. But here they met a wind which blew so strong and cold that for a while they could think of nothing but their bodily discomfort; "we could neither pray nor do anything proper, till we had a fire"; when a great fire had been kindled they could only stand about it, till, the sun rising higher, the wind dropped, and, warm at last, they took out their "Processionals", and joyfully sang and devoutly prayed before turning their attention to more secular matters.

The first of these to engage their attention was the view. Perambulating the narrow platform, prudently furnished with a low containing wall to safeguard preoccupied visitors from the danger of a false step,[36] they gazed out upon a stupendous panorama. Friar Felix, so ardent in achieving and recording the delights of a fine prospect, drank it all in and wrote it all down, embellishing his description with a profuse display of geographical and classical learning. In fact he overdid it, so that the view is lost under the weight of references to St. Jerome, derivations of the name "Persia," a fleeting allusion to the Ganges, and another–by no means fleeting–to Babylon and Nineveh. It is better to borrow from the accounts of modern travellers sufficent matter to enable us to realise the majestic sight which was spread out before the eyes of our pilgrims.

Away to the north lie the heights of the Tîh desert, all round the savage, sterile but superb peaks of the Sinai *massif,* where "the tints are those of sunlight on the coloured stone, the outlines the natural contours of the rocks." Below, and close to, the green summit of Gebel Musa seems almost insignificant in height.[37]

From that high altitude and in that pellucid air, two seas are visible, the Gulf of Arabia to the east, of Suez to the west, each a part of the high way, as the pilgrims knew, by which the spice cargoes of India and the Far East were carried to the little port of Tor which lay to the southwestward two days' journey away down the mountain defiles. Some pilgrims could tell their readers that they saw ships upon the waters;[38] some on this occasion of their first glimpse of the famous Red Sea, assured their untravelled friends at home that the waters of the Red Sea are not red,

* Abu Rumail, Gebel Zebir and Gebel Katerina. Felix speaks only of the last.

but take this colour from the sand and rocks below their surface, these being of the colour of cinnabar.[39]

The meal, to which the pilgrims next addressed themselves, was more plentiful than the scanty picnic of yesterday, and certainly no less gay. For each man among the pilgrims was conscious that standing upon this airy height he stood also upon the watershed of his pilgrimage. Once they moved from here they would no longer be going forward but returning. When therefore they began the descent, they took it in holiday mood, and went "not walking but tumbling downwards, because we knew that we were beginning to go home."[40]

As at Jerusalem, so here, in the neighbourhood of Mount Sinai, all sorts of sacred and historical associations had been attracted, as if by a centripetal force, into the vicinity of the original tradition, so that the pilgrims, on their way back to St. Katherine's monastery, were presented by their guide with a conspectus of the Forty Years' Wandering of Israel. They were shown not only such possible sites as the rock from which Moses dashed down the first divinely written Tables of the Law, but also, regardless of credibility, the plain where Korah, Dathan and Abiram perished, and the rock from which the rod of Moses struck forth water; this last identification, indeed, did strain the credulity of ecclesiastics who knew their Scriptures. ". . . Whether it was," Friar Paul remarks, "I leave to others. . . ."[41]

When the ascent of the two mountain peaks had been accomplished, there remained the ceremonial visit to the relics of St. Katherine, and to the most holy spot where Moses had stood before the bush which burnt unconsumed, where he had received his commission from God, and learnt the awful Name.

Early in the morning of September 26 the pilgrims and the Christian donkey-men mustered at the doors of the basilica. Joined there by the abbot and monks they moved on in procession, each man bearing a lighted candle, till they reached the tomb of the Saint, a small marble sarcophagus, carved "with figures and small plants and leaves," which stood, a man's height from the ground, under an arch on the right hand side of the choir.[42]

Drawn up in line on either side, the pilgrims now waited while Brother Nicodemus brought the key, and struggled with a stiff and rusty lock. Meanwhile the monks sang an antiphon in which western pilgrims were sometimes able to catch here and there a familiar word; Friar Felix distinguished "apostles" and "martyrs,"[43] an Italian merchant the word "Kyrie."[44] This last was hardly to be wondered at if, as a later traveller remarked, the Kyrie was sung "forty times over," though, in order to shorten the long service, the monks would take it on a single breath.[45]

When the lock had yielded, and the tomb was open, the Abbot and monks one by one approached, reverently bent, and devoutly kissed the relics. Now came the turn of the visitors, first to salute the Saint with reverence, then to lay any jewels they might have in contact with the sacred bones; lastly, to drop their offerings into the coffin. All the while this was going on the Abbot stood close. Felix, though naturally without jewels of his own, had with him a considerable amount which had been entrusted to him by friends for just such a purpose, and as he lingered at the side of the coffin he noted that the eyes of the Greek monk never left his hands.[46] The Friar had no evil intentions, but there was good reason for the Abbot's vigilance, for many of the devout considered the theft of relics no sin–centuries of such pilfering and earlier generous presentations by the monks,[47] had left little of the Saint's skeleton. In the coffin pilgrims saw a few ribs and leg bones, the skull, "a fairly big head without jaws," adorned with a diadem of gold,[48] and the bones of the left hand "white as milk... the fingers... long, and covered with rings," set thick with jewels.[49]

Of greater sanctity even than the body of the Saint was the Chapel of the Bush, and when the pilgrims had entered the Chapel of St. John, by which this was entered, they were told that they must now go barefoot. Passing through a small door they found themselves in a chapel with marble encrusted walls and many lamps, in which, stepping upon costly rugs, they approached the altar, where "a thin plate of copper" was set in the pavement "engraved with the similitude of the Burning Bush, and Moses sitting down and taking off his shoes."[50]*

It was the custom for pilgrims when they reached this chapel to soak, in the oil of the lamps here, the small snippets of silk which had been dealt out to them from the coffin of St. Katherine; Felix Fabri went one better, and contrived to bring away with him a little glass phial of the oil. It proved to have useful curative qualities, but must have seemed to him a poor substitute for the oil which he had read about as being brought away by pilgrims of old time, for that had been miraculously sweated by the bones of the Saint after friction had been applied.[51]

With the visit to the relics of St. Katherine and the Chapel of the Bush the chief, though by no means the only, holy places in the Church had been honoured. The pilgrims now perambulated the rest of the building, paying their devotions to a variety of saints, both familiar and unknown,

---

* Now, as already in the seventeenth century, the spot is marked by a slab of marble. (Pococke, p. 150; Rabino, p. 31.)

till the procession arrived once more at St. Katherine's tomb where the tour was concluded.[52]

This day was to be the last of the pilgrims' stay in the monastery, and departing visitors had certain customary duties to fulfil. Well-born secular pilgrims were in the habit of leaving, instead of their names in a "Visitors' Book," a representation of their armorial bearings carved upon the walls, or doors, or even upon the refectory table of their hosts.[53] If, on the other hand, any pilgrim happened to have a literary *flair*, he was expected to write, and attach to the hanging mats in the little Latin Chapel, a poetical tribute to St. Katherine. The pilgrims of 1483 included in their number the Archdeacon, John Lazinus, a fluent and erudite versifier. He produced, as his contribution to the collection of these devotional bread and butter letters, a poetic trophy celebrating in flattering terms not only the Saint, but each of his fellows of the famous third company. His intention had been to deal similarly with the members of the other two companies, but, in all the haste and stress of that morning, there proved to be no further opportunity for writing poetry.[54]

No longer, as in the earlier part of the century, did the monks keep up the custom of giving to each noble visitor "the device of St. Catherine, which is a wheel with teeth of gold,"[55] nor did they now supply the pilgrims with the meal of bread and fish, and half a glass of wine apiece which Frescobaldi and his friends enjoyed after their ceremonial visit to the Church.[56] But as our pilgrims sat down to a meal of their own salt and smoked food they were visited by a couple of monks, bearing, as a gift from the Abbot, trays of twisted, spiced loaves, and fruit of various kinds; dates, figs, raisins, and bunches of fresh grapes.[57]

Dinner over the pilgrims wasted no time in turning to the business which was now closest to their hearts. They sought out the *Calinus*, and begged "that he should no longer delay here, but lead us on our way to Egypt." The old man declared himself ready to start at any moment, but privately, to Felix, he expressed a misgiving. "I fear," said he, "that we shall not leave this place unmolested, for the monastery is full of Arabs who have come on our account."[58]

Travellers of the later years of the nineteenth century discovered to their cost that two very ancient customs were still operative at the monastery of St. Katherine at Mount Sinai. By the first of these the monks were pledged to give the Arabs of the neighbourhood notice of the arrival of visitors by leaving footmarks round about a near-by well; by the second, every Arab who came in answer to that signal had the right to exact a fee from the strangers.[59] Felix does not mention either of these usages, and very possibly never heard of them, yet the experience of our pilgrims of 1483 seems to suggest that both may already have been well established.

During the time which the pilgrims had spent at St. Katherine's monastery they had been uneasily conscious of the arrival, day by day, of more and more Arabs. Some of these, and among them the Sheikh himself, camped in the courtyard below the pilgrims' lodgings, "nor could we come at the well to draw water without passing through the midst of them. They did nothing to us, neither good nor ill, nor shouted at us, but all the same their waiting there irked us."[60]

The misgivings of pilgrims and *Calinus* were only too well founded, and their start from the monastery was not to be accomplished without tribulation, endured at the hands of the Arabs of the neighbourhood, of the pilgrims' own camel-men, and of both of these working in collusion. That they were also to find themselves in hot water with the Abbot of St. Katherine's was another matter, and not undeserved.

Trouble began directly the pilgrims' preparations for departure were noted by the Arabs within the monastery, the Sheikh sending a haughty message to the effect that they should not hope to leave before their dues had been paid. After long argument a few ducats changed hands, and the pilgrims believed that they had now franked their way out. They were never more mistaken. As they waited for the beasts to be brought, and as nothing happened, they learned first that the camels, and later that the donkeys, were being held up by armed bands of Arabs, and must be bailed out.[61]

It was at this point that the pilgrims received a message from the Abbot. "A piece of the tomb of St. Katherine had been broken off by an iron instrument; if we delayed to restore it, the Arabs, into whose hands he would put the matter, would see that we did so without delay."

Irresponsible relic-hunting on the part of individual pilgrims was always liable to land a party in just such a position of acute embarrassment and inconvenience, and those among the pilgrims who were innocent at once made an effort to discover the thief, "each one looking at another, and all cursing the man who had done it; we asked each other that the guilty party should not be ashamed to confess and give back the broken piece, and we would all share in the blame, and pay whatever was to be paid; but there was no man who would own up, till our *Calinus* said that the thief should secretly hand over to him the bit of stone, and in secrecy he would smooth the business over. And thus it was done; but," says Felix, and, we fancy, regretfully, "who among us was guilty to this day I do not know."[62]

When this matter had been satisfactorily concluded the pilgrims decided that it would be wise to avert any further trouble from the concourse of Arabs by arranging with the Sheikh to provide an escort during the first two or three marches, and meeting him in solemn conclave in the mosque they were able to make this arrangement.

All this had taken time; the heat of the day was upon them when the loading up began, and the camel-men took their turn in the game of baiting Christians. "They threw down our waterskins which we had filled, and when we put them back again, again they threw them down. Short of blows we treated them as roughly as we could, using the most furious gestures. At last some Arabs came up who made an agreement by which we should give the camel-men more money to carry those waterskins. And if," Felix sagely remarks, "we had consented to do this at the beginning we should have had no trouble."

At last the camels were loaded, the travellers mounted their donkeys, and the whole caravan began to move. Now the pilgrims must have thought that the malicious teasing of the wild men was at an end. But no. Even as they began to go down from the gate of the monastery "an Arab came running after us, carrying a bed and a basket which our camel-men had left behind on purpose, and so the owner of the bed, if he wanted to keep it, must buy it from the Arab, and when he had got his bed the camel-man would not put it up on the camel unless he got some more coppers."[63]

Part Four

MOUNT SINAI TO EGYPT

CHAPTER VII

More of the desert

When in the heat of the September afternoon the little company of German pilgrims, donkey-men, Moslem desert-folk, slow-striding camels and daintily stepping donkeys began to go down from the gate of the Monastery of St. Katherine, the travellers must again submit themselves to the now familiar routine and the equally familiar discomfort and weariness of desert travel. They must also, for the next two and a half days, suffer, except during one brief digression, the tedium of retracing their own steps. The *Calinus*, having chosen the more northerly of the two routes to the coast,[1] would bring them once more almost to the foot of the Tîh plateau before turning aside to enter the defiles of the western mountain group, and passing through these to the coastal plain, reach the common route of merchant caravans between Cairo and the port of Tor.

The one digression from their previous line of march, in which in fact they reverted to the usual route, instead of the exceptional course by Wadi el Akhdar and Wadi Hargus which they had taken on September 21,* was made early in the morning of the first full day's march. It brought them through the great grove of tamarisks known as Tarfet el-Gidarein,† where, in the first cool hours after sunrise, the dew still lay upon the foliage of the trees, dew with which the pilgrims eagerly quenched their thirst, and found it honey-sweet.[2]

There were other gleams of interest during these arduous days which Friar Felix savoured, and did not omit to record. The pilgrims had the good fortune to get a close view of the handsome wild ass of the mountain country, concerning which "naturalists say many things"; of these Felix reports a few, and among them the striking statement that the animal brays twenty-four times in the twenty-four hours, "and by this means the inhabitants tell the time in the night."[3]

Another spectacle, which however made less impression upon the pilgrims that their view of the wild ass, was offered next day when, as

---

* See above, p. 72.
† As before I have followed Mr. G. W. Murray in the route suggested for the pilgrims.

they passed along the flank of Serabit el-Khadim, the Arab camel-men brought them to a cave in which, draped about with scraps of worshippers' clothing, stood "an idol in the shape of an Ethiop boy." The camel-men, after their custom, contributed a few more rags, and invited the pilgrims to leave an offering of money—an invitation which they, not unnaturally, ignored.[4]*

But on the whole the journey, with its long and wearisome marches, was painful to the pilgrims; and still more so when, on the third evening, after a day spent in toiling over ground that was "not of sand, for that would have been tolerable, but of dust . . . and ashes," they found themselves without water to spare for cooking. They were still among the mountains, and the scenery about them might, one would have thought, have consoled at least Friar Felix, for it must have been sensational enough. These "great stony mountains" were such that another pilgrim said he had "never seen before in all my journeys. The face of the rock was of many colours, yellow, red, black and other colours, three roods broad and striped from top to bottom."[5] Surprisingly, however, it is von Breydenbach among the pilgrims who recalled the beauty of the wadis through which the pilgrims were passing.[6] In their camp that night it is likely that none of the German party gave a thought to their majestic surroundings. As they champed their dry biscuit and sipped the warm and scanty water their thoughts were of how differently folk at home would be spending this same evening. For there tonight all would be keeping the Michaelmas Feast; there fires would blaze, kitchen tables be loaded with huge provision of wildfowl, of farmyard poultry, of the geese for which Ulm is still famous; in imagination the hungry pilgrims saw "the spits of roasting meat, the baskets of fish, the cauldrons of broth," and, like Israel in these very deserts, they yearned for the fleshpots.[7]

Next morning, after several hours' march, daylight found them once more upon the sandy plain into which they had descended from the plateau of Tîh, and in sight of the pass by which they had made their descent. It was at this point that the *Calinus* diverged from their previous route, and took the way by Wadi Homr which would bring them to the coast.

By now the pilgrims cared little which way they went, so long as it led them to water, for they had found no well nor water-hole since they

---

* The Arabic name of the mountain means "the Heights of the Servant"—the word Khadim signifying "a male slave," and when E. H. Palmer passed this way in 1870 his Arabs told him that the name was given by reason of a black statue of a "servant or slave," which had stood here until " 'removed by the French' during their occupation of Egypt." (E. H. Palmer, *Desert of the Exodus*, Vol. I, p. 233.)

left St. Katherine's Monastery,[8] and the skins and bottles were almost empty. Water, they told the *Calinus*, they must have, and soon.

Whether the kindly and gentle old man would have yielded to their importunity we do not know, for an Arab intervened, a stranger, one of those wanderers who would join a caravan and go along with it for a few days. He knew, he said, a place where there were many water-holes, and would bring the pilgrims to them. His offer was accepted, and while the *Calinus* and the camel-men continued on their way the pilgrims, led by the Arab, turned away to the right, into a deep and stony wadi, shut in by threatening walls of rock. Even as they went the pilgrims wondered at themselves, "that for the sake of water we should part from all our possessions on the camels, and the donkey- and camel-men, and cleave to a man who was altogether a stranger, and follow him through these pathless places. However, we all thought that the Arab was a good fellow." He was, at least, quick-witted, sensitive to the atmosphere of doubt, and did his best to dispel it, going before the party with a smiling face, and by his gestures seeming to point out—as mere matters of pleasant interest—"the height of the rocks and the desolation of the wadi."

And soon, sure enough, he led the way down through bushes of the thorny, flowering acacia to a sandy bottom where there were footprints of men and their beasts, and, among yet more stunted trees, a number of shallow pits. The Arab had brought with him a leather bucket, and now let it down into one of these. But when he drew it up the water proved to be so salt that not even the donkeys would drink it.

Here was a sad blow. All the pilgrims' doubts returned and they looked askance at the guide who had so cheated them. He, however, unabashed, persuaded them to try the other pits; but in these they found nothing to the purpose for themselves, though there was water good enough for the beasts. To the western travellers this must have appeared as the extinction of their last hope, but they were now to learn a lesson in the craft of the desert. The Arab began to dig a hole with his hands, casting out the sand; when the pilgrims followed his example, to their astonishment, in the shallow pit "water began to bubble up, muddy indeed, but not salt, and we filled our bottles and our bellies, caring nothing for how muddy it was."[9]

It was well that they drank their fill while they might, for their camp that night, in a wadi of white rocks and white dust which drenched them like the flying flour of a mill, was waterless, and the water in their bottles was bitter now with salt. Fortunately in this discomfort they found grateful shade and coolness under the lee of an overhanging cliff.[10]

This was their last day among the mountains. In the morning they emerged on the limestone coastal plain, which stretches, "a long narrow slip," from Thor to Suez, "smooth level desert sloping gradually towards the sea."[11] It was a dreary, sun-smitten landscape, yet their first day's march was to bring them a poignant and pleasurable experience. Since a few miles south of Gaza they had passed through a land where "there was neither street nor road"; in which travellers must use "the stars for guide as is done at sea."[12] Now once more the pilgrims came upon a road—it was *"via regia,"* "the king's highway," by which the camel trains brought the spices of the furthest East from the port of Tor to the markets of Egypt. No wonder that, as Felix says, "we rejoiced above measure at finding the road, and felt that we had come back into the world."[13]

That evening they camped, at some little distance from the road, and upon ground which swarmed with those insects, "as big as almonds,"[14] known to pilgrims as "Pharaoh's lice." The pilgrims were thoroughly disgusted with the site of the camp, but not only, nor perhaps chiefly, because of the prevalence of vermin. Only with difficulty and after the deployment of many cogent reasons, had the *Calinus* prevented them from halting some miles back at the very place where, so all pilgrims believed, the Israelites had camped, at that "Elim, where were twelve wells of water, and three score and ten palm trees." The arithmetic of these features was not now quite correct; Friar Paul could only count three wells; Friar Felix admitted that there were "not exactly twelve" and passed off the discrepancy with the remark that "there are many springs of water running down from a hill-side in every direction." The number of trees could not be made to tally either; "there are not seventy palms but many more"; however, Felix stoutly declares, "it is the same place."[15]

Quite apart from its Biblical associations the runnels of water were irresistibly attractive to the pilgrims after their experience of the desert, and, though forbidden to camp there, no sooner were the tents pitched and the firing collected than they were off to the springs, in company with the donkey-men. When the servants returned with the full waterskins the pilgrims remained, drinking, washing and bathing "for in that sweet place ... we found abundant water, clear and slightly warm."

Every circumstance assisted the pilgrims to realise that they had indeed "come back into the world." Beyond the trees and bushes beside the waters there was a village, and about the village a grove of palms. A goat-herd came by, and they chaffered, though unsuccessfully, for one of the kids of the flock for their supper. Some girls, rather pretty ones too, brought their flocks down to the springs; they stared at the strangers and laughed; they spoke, seeming to beg for something. The more discreet and sober-minded among the pilgrims ignored these advances, but could hardly restrain some of the younger knights from making beckoning and friendly gestures. It was probably fortunate that at this point the *Calinus*, impatient at their long absence, sent to recall his charges to camp, and to a supper which, after such refreshment and relaxation, was an unusually merry meal.[16]

No greater contrast could have been experienced by the pilgrims than that presented by the gaiety of this evening and the discomfort of the next, though the two camping places were separated only by a short day's march. Starting late, owing to the delay caused by two straying camels, the pilgrims had been forced to halt early, since this day, October 2, was the eve of the first day of Ramadan, the month during which good Moslems might eat only during the hours of darkness, and it was therefore necessary to give the Arab camel-men a chance to sleep before they rose, in the small hours, to prepare a meal.*

Everything conspired to increase the impatience and discontent of the pilgrims. That morning they had been caught up and passed upon the road by a wealthy Mamluk and his retinue, mounted upon the swift *theluls*, or riding-camels, which easily outdistanced the slowly pacing baggage animals of the pilgrims. The Mamluk, "a portly and personable man," who was at first inclined to take exception to the fact that the pilgrims carried swords, had, before parting, accepted the Frankish kinghts as fellow fighting men; if every one were as bold as they, said he, there would be no trouble with the Arab tribes. In the friendliest spirit, though quite untruly, he informed them that the spice caravans from Tor had already reached Egypt, and that the Venetian ships, in which the pilgrims must sail or spend all winter in Egypt, were in port at Alexandria, and soon to leave.[17] With good reason therefore the Christian travellers were in a fret to be moving, and found their forced inactivity hard to bear.

But besides this natural impatience and anxiety they were suffering considerable physical discomfort. They had camped upon one of those plains where the sand "white, and fine, and soft as silk"[18] gave no hold for the few tent pegs which still remained after the wear and tear of the journey. They therefore sat in the full blaze of the afternoon sun, and, to make matters worse, could see between the "little hills of white soft sand" the blue waters of the Gulf of Suez, apparently less than a couple of miles away.

* Presumably because Fabri took for granted that the Moslem and Christian calendars must coincide he cooked his dates in writing up his notes, and put the eve of Ramadan back to September 30 (*Evag.* II, p. 517). But in 1483 the Feast began upon October 3 (Ibn Iyas, p. 226).

Though all may well have experienced the attraction offered by those gleams of blue, it was the Strasburg knight, Peter Velsch, who succumbed to it, and who played the part of Temptress Eve to his fellows of the third company. "Why," he suddenly asked, "should they sit melting in the sun, when there, so near, lay the sea, and they had yet hours of daylight before them? What I say is come down and get cool, and enjoy yourselves."

When no one answered he called them "a poor sort of friend, who daren't come, to please me and yourselves as well. I am ready to fight for you, and none of you are willing to come and bathe with me. What are you frightened of?"

They replied, reasonably, that the *Calinus* would not hear of them going off without the rest of the party, but he only grew angry, and "laughing us to scorn threw in our teeth that we were disloyal and cowardly." That was too much. As one man the third company rose to its feet, mounted the donkeys, and started off towards the coast.

The debate must have been over-heard by the rest of the pilgrims, for as the third company moved off John, the Count of Solms' cook, deserting the fire which he had lit, hurried after them, hastily explaining to his master that he only wanted "to go and get cool and would be back in no time to cook the supper." On the other hand the *Calinus*, seeing what was on foot, "shouted after us, telling us to come back; the Arabs, the camel- and donkey-men all called out, begging us not to go; but we pretended not to hear."

None knew better than old Elphahallo the risks of such an expedition. When the rash and insubordinate members of the party had passed out of ear-shot he told their companions, as a cautionary tale, of another occasion when, equally without fault on his side, a couple of pilgrims had strayed from the caravan in his charge. For three days they had been missing, and it was two crazed and dying men who were led back to their friends by some Arabs who had found them wandering in the desert.[19] Recalling this tragedy and the undeserved official reprimands which it had brought down upon him, the *Calinus* called the remaining pilgrims to witness that if the wilful bathing party lost their way and became "children of death" he was guiltless; nor was he satisfied until their companions had promised him a written quit-claim of his responsibility should the truants not return by nightfall.

Meanwhile Felix and his comrades, soon losing sight of the camp among the dunes, rode forward lightheartedly, confident that a short ride would bring them to the sea.

But time passed: the sea still lay before them, but still seemed to be no nearer. Angry, daunted, yet refusing to give in, they pushed forward. It was not till three hours after leaving the camp that they reached the shore; and by this time the sun had set.

They were really frightened now, but having come so far they would at least take their dip. They rode down towards the water, only to find the donkeys sinking to the girths in a broad stretch of mud. They struggled out, tied up the beasts and tried again on foot. This time they were able to wade out to the water. They stood for a few moments, washed their hands, and waded back to the shore. The delightful bathe which they had promised themselves amounted to just that.

Yet they had spirit enough left before they turned their backs upon the sea, to collect from the shore "some enormous oyster shells," which should prove that at least they had reached the coast; then "not washed but dirty, not refreshed but alarmed, not happy but wretched," they began their journey back.

At first they could find their way by following in reverse the slot of the beasts. But soon it grew dark, and then it was necessary to dismount and feel with their hands for the marks of the hoofs. They halted, and discussed what were best to do; some said; stay and wait for morning; others said, that was death, for the rest of the caravan would break camp long before daylight, and, at the best, they could not hope to overtake it till the evening, which would mean thirty-six hours without food or water for man and beast.

Most of them, in fact, agreed that it was best to go on, but there was no agreement as to which direction they should take; "so dark was the night that we could see nothing of our tracks, nor of the hills, and hardly even the sea behind, though that of its nature gleams in the dark with a sort of radiance,"[20] They therefore proceeded for a while by fits and starts, according as one opinion or another prevailed, but always stopping from time to time to listen for sounds of the camp and to shout, careless if by so doing they brought down robbers upon themselves, being now obsessed by a far greater fear.

Suddenly, "We saw before us a flame spring up; it blazed higher, and we rejoiced, thinking that our friends had lit a fire on our account; but when we joyfully followed the light we saw that we were deceived, for it was a star which in its rising had cast its beams over the crest of a hill."[21]

At this point that admirable person, Heinrich von Schomberg, "a wise man with a reflective mind," pointed to a particular star, and told his companions that if they made in that direction they would find the caravan. "How he arrived at this," interjects the admiring Felix, "I do not know; but I know that if we had taken his advice we should have come straight back to camp." Unfortunately by this time fear and distress had inflamed tempers; a bitter argument sprang up, and Felix fearing that "our two chief knights" would be at each other's throats, pushed himself and his wise old donkey between the angry pair, thus averting, he believed, not only possible bloodshed, but also the fatal mistake of any separation of the party. Peace being re-established a compromise was arrived at. The pilgrims agreed to climb to the top of one of the higher of the many sand-dunes among which they were wandering, and there, having unsaddled, to rest, though not, in their perturbation of mind, to sleep; rather they must remain vigilant for any sound which would lead them back to camp.

It might have been thought that all those who had undergone such physical toil and mental stress would have been content to repose. But not so Felix. With an energy which the reader must find admirable, and a kindness of heart which is endearing, the Friar, rising to say his Hours, took it into his head to go off down the hill towards a shadow which, in the darkness, seemed to be a group of bushes; intending to gather some green branches "to give to my donkey, who was fasting along with me." But the patch of shade proved to be only a clump of dried thorn, so the Friar rambled further; he climbed a hill, hoping perhaps his ears might be blessed by some sound from the main party. The reader guesses what is about to happen. When he tried to return, the hill upon which he expected to find his friends proved to be empty and silent; he was now doubly lost.

The shock of dread which he must have experienced could not have been pleasant, but the upshot was comedy rather than tragedy. Raising his voice he began to call on the name of "the bravest, noblest, most loyal knight, and my special friend . . . Schonberg." From far off came the answer "Felix! Felix!" The Friar hurried towards the sound, climbed another hill, and again found no one. "So again I cried 'Ho! Ho!' and 'Where are you? Please to answer me till I reach you.'" By this means he came safe again to his companions, and got what he deserved – a good scolding, "for I had gone much further away from them than I had thought."

But by now midnight was far past, and the time drew near when, if ever, they might hear the sound of the breaking of camp. "In perfect silence therefore we sat, longing to hear the roaring of the camels. And when we had for some time sat thus – there! the camels did begin to lift their voices and to roar. And . . . that terrible noise . . . was sweeter to us than any sound of music."

In a moment they were tumbling down the hill-side on their donkeys and racing in the direction of the sound; they arrived in camp to find the *Calinus* justifiably enraged, and a couple of camels already loaded with food and water and two Arabs told off to act as search party. Their adventure had reached a happy end, but the past night, Felix reckoned, was the worst he had ever spent.[22]

Fortunately the events of the day which was now about to dawn were of a nature to compose and refresh the jaded members of the third company. The rest of the pilgrims, though they had disapproved of the illicit expedition, were not going to let slip an opportunity of officially sponsored sea-bathing. The *Calinus* provided a guide (he himself would continue along the road with the camels), and, the course of the march having now brought the caravan much nearer to the coast, it was not long before all the pilgrims, including the chastened Felix and his companions, reached it at the very place, so the Friar believed, where the Israelites had come to land after the miraculous passage of the sea, and where, instead of last night's mud, was firm clean sand and clear water. The party bathed; like other pilgrims on this shore they piously and cheerfully baptised each other "after the fashion of the Fathers, in the sea."[23] They rambled along the beach, and again like other pilgrims, picked up shells and pieces of white coral "and other kinds of gems."[24] For here were to be found stones pretty enough to be set in rings, and crystals,[25] mother-of-pearl shells,[26] shells with strange names—"Venus shell, wild ducks, gudgeons, bulimus, and numberless other like kinds which were a source of joy and surprise."[27]* At last, sitting at ease upon the beach they "ate and drank happily" the usual picnic meal of mid-day.[28]

Even when they decided that this pleasant dalliance must cease, and that they must hasten after the camels, their way was cheered by the unwonted hilarity of the Arab guides. These, who had probably been enjoying themselves almost as much as the pilgrims, now ran alongside the donkeys, goading them with their spear-points till the beasts fled at the pace of a horse. But it was the fleet-foot Arabs themselves that caught Felix's imagination that day. "I never," he says, "saw men run so fast as these run, with their lean, hard shanks, and neither shod nor girded," and he surmised that their turn of speed was due to their hard living, while, conversely, "daily over-eating" accounted for the comparative shortness of breath of Germans.

So, with laughter and fooling, the donkeys galloping, the Arabs now

---

* According to Baedeker (*Lower Egypt*, 1895, p. 246) pilgrims of more sophisticated ages are still accustomed to follow this ancient and engaging custom, but his reference to our pilgrims is incorrect, as he is speaking of a stretch of coast much further south.

running effortlessly alongside, now forging ahead to spar together with their lances, the party proceeded in the highest spirits. "I never laughed so much," the cheerful Friar declared, "in all this pilgrimage, as I did going up from the Red Sea. . . . There was among the rest a strange Arab whom I had never seen before, who did the most absurd things, so that I thought that I should not be able to stay on my donkey for laughing."[29]

The gaiety and good-fellowship of that morning were, as we know, exceptional in the intercourse between the Christians and their servants, and the day-long fast of Ramadan increased the tension between the members of the two religions. The pilgrims, who every evening saw the Moslems of the escort sit round, silent, glum and drooping, as they waited for sundown to release them from the fast, considered themselves entitled to a feeling of irritation[30] which was heightened to vigorous resentment when, just as they themselves were settling down to sleep, the Moslems began their nightly junketings. After enduring the disturbance for a while, one or other of the pilgrims, exasperated beyond endurance by the sounds of carousal, "would leave the tents, and rush over to them, silencing them with threats; yet," the Friar adds, "yet, sometimes when they were cooking their bread under the ashes, we stayed with them watching their foolishness."[31]

This spectacle of desert cookery was not new to Felix, nor was the quality of the finished product unknown. From the earliest days of the journey he had watched the Arabs making their bread, noting how they spread out a sheepskin on the ground, poured the flour out upon it, and then mixed this to a paste with water. "When the dough is ready, and shaped into broad, flat cakes, they move the ashes from the place where the fire was, and put the paste in the hot place there, and cover it with ashes and charcoal, and so it is cooked. . . ." When cooked and taken hot from the embers it was, Felix knew, "a very tasty bread,"[32] and it is hard to imagine him going back to his bed after one of these minatory excursions without a handful of the delicacy.

Apart from the hardships or inconveniences of Ramadan, as they affected Moslem or Christian, these last days of the desert journey were painful and arduous for all alike. After leaving the clear springs of the Wadi Gharandel they were following that route along which other travellers saw scattered the dead and sun-dried bodies of men and camels horribly mutilated by carrion beasts and birds.[33] Though here and there the ground was "marshy and full of waters, which, breaking forth run down to the Red Sea,"[34] the springs were warm, and so saline as to be only fit for beasts to drink. The water of the famous and venerated "Well of Moses" (*Ayun Musa*), in quantity "nothing much," was in quality, at least when the well had been nearly drained by a large caravan, "so foul," even if filtered, "that you have to hold your nose in order to drink it."[35] That its usual condition was not much better we may guess from the action of a company of pilgrims, merchants of Florence, who, finding the well sullied by all manner of filth, stripped themselves to their shirts, and barefooted set to work, with very practical piety, to scour the stone curb and clean out the well.[36]

Even the "Well of the Sultan" beyond Suez, which our pilgrims passed on October 4, and which like the well at Nakhl was officially maintained for the use of the Mecca pilgrims, was little better. For all the "great and noble tank," the water-wheels worked by oxen, the stone well-head, the spouts, the water of the well was "abominable . . . being salty, and warm with the sun, and red in colour."[37]

A few hours before they reached this well Felix Fabri enjoyed one of those moments of illumination which he is so happy to share with his readers. They had followed the coast from the Wadi Gharandel; now they came to "a mountain, to whose feet extends an arm of the Red Sea, and here it ends." When the termination of the long gulf was visible and unmistakable, "a great puzzle" which had perplexed the Friar throughout his journey was resolved. In spite of, perhaps even because of, all his readings in geographers ancient and modern, he had confusedly believed that the Red Sea and Mediterranean met hereabouts, and that, like the Israelites, he and his companions would have to cross the Red Sea in order to reach Egypt, though "how we should get across . . . I could not think."[38] Now he knew better; "a wide space (and) many mountains" separated the two seas, and there was nothing to prevent the pilgrims from reaching Cairo dry-shod.

It was in the light of this new understanding that the Friar was able to appreciate the significance of his next experience. For in this very place, "in the mountains where the Red Sea comes to an end, we saw the mighty works of the ancient kings of Egypt, who tried to bring the Red Sea to the Nile, and to this end began to dig through the mountains and split in two the hills, cleave rocks and stones asunder, and make a canal. . . ." The Friar, looking at the now broken channel choked with sand, saw through the windows of his imagination wide seas and the traffic of nations, for this canal should have been "a way for the merchants of the world to trade everywhere. And indeed," he exclaims, "it would have been a grand thing if they had finished the work. For then from Venice, aye, and from Flanders and Ireland they would have sailed to Egypt . . . and reached the land of cinnamon, and thence they would have come to wealthiest India."³⁹ The pilgrims stood a while gazing at the Gulf before they turned their faces towards Egypt and continued on their way.

For Felix that new acquisition of geographical fact and that vision of world trade were not to be the only memorable experiences of the day. Not long after they had left the Red Sea behind them they came upon, and now took, the wide trodden track, which was the road of the Mecca pilgrims between Aqaba and Cairo, and which, some days' journey to the east, they had crossed in their southward march across the desert. Now, as they followed it in the direction of Cairo, they began to meet large companies of pilgrims, sometimes with as many as fifty baggage camels, as well as finely harnessed horses, for these "were magnificent folk, rich Saracens, going on pilgrimage." This was the season when the Hajj set out in great state "with horses and mules, camels and footmen"⁴⁰ upon its forty days' journey under the command of an Emir appointed by the Sultan,⁴¹ and men would take wives and children, to ride two or three together in the hooded litters which von Harff tried to represent and Piloti to describe.⁴²

The Friar watched the riders go by. These people would pass through Arabia Felix; they were bound for Mecca, where not only was there held a great and famous market "for sweet-smelling spices, pepper, cloves and ginger,⁴³ but where also the tomb of the Prophet hung unsupported in air, presenting to Felix a problem even more tantalising than that which had been raised for him by the cross of the penitent thief in Cyprus.

He had learnt, possibly in conversation with the old *Calinus*, that a Christian would be permitted, even encouraged, to go along with the Moslems in their pilgrimage, and now, having almost reached the last day's march of the toilsome desert journey, the thought of a new enterprise tugged at him with the pull of a magnet. "Often," he cried, "I have been tempted to visit . . . that accursed sepulchre, and if I had had but one to go with me, hardly could I have refrained."⁴⁴

That night the pilgrims spent in great discomfort, at a place which Felix calls "Choas." Unable to set up the tents because the pegs were dragged from the deep soft sand by a high wind, they had to sleep in the open, half suffocated by the blowing sand, and in the course of the night the weather drove in upon their camp some of those Arab waifs to whose approach they were by now accustomed. These men, "as they seemed to be humble and well-behaved," were received without suspicion, and given the usual dole of bread.

But upon the next day's march it appeared that the pilgrims might be made to regret their charity. They had been upon the road for some time, but the sun had only just risen, when von Breydenbach, "the splendid and high-born" Canon of Mainz, announced that he had lost a large sum in gold ducats, which he carried for safety sewn into a belt. Von Breydenbach, a sick man for the whole of the desert journey, was still carried on camel-back in one of the big baggage panniers. Some time before daylight he had dismounted, had walked for a while, and only when back again in the pannier, had discovered his loss.

At once the whole caravan halted. The pilgrims themselves traced Breydenbach's footsteps back through the desert, and taking care to keep off the Arab strangers and both camel- and donkey-men, searched all round the place where he had dismounted, "turning over the sand with our hands," but in vain. It was clear to them that someone must have found and appropriated the money, and almost transported with rage they were prepared to go to any lengths of physical violence to recover it. Turning upon the unhappy *Calinus* they declared that every man of the escort should be stripped and searched, and the servants' baggage also ransacked. Old Elphahallo tried to mediate between the two parties, but his appeal to the escort, and the pilgrims' own offer of a reward produced no result. The six knights then drew their swords, the search of the baggage was begun, while the Arab servants, Christian and Moslem, cowed by the fierce bearing of the Latins, looked on trembling and even weeping.

As suddenly as the excitement had arisen it was quelled. One of the stranger Arabs approached the *Calinus*, and handed over the money. The Arabs of the escort hastened to vouch for the fellow's excellent character, and since the pilgrims themselves considered that "he had a simple look and an honest face" the restitution was taken in good part. Von Breydenbach with alacrity bestowed a ducat as a reward, knowing that he might well have had to pay ten times that sum if the Arab had stood out for it, and the caravan, having tidied up its disarray, in good spirits and in harmony once more, proceeded on its way.[45]

Their camp that night, at a fork in the Hajj road,* was perhaps the worst and most cheerless of all the journey. Once more a high wind left them without the shelter of the tents; but now they lacked even the means of cooking supper. At Choas, believing this to be their last camp, and finding no firing in the desolate sands, they had recklessly built their fire of anything they could lay their hands on, using "the wooden jars out of which we had emptied our wine and water; the egg-baskets, and hen coops."[46] Tonight nothing was left. Even when they lay down to

---

* Felix calls the place Maffrach, von Harff, Maffra—Mafraq means "a fork" (*v.* G. W. Murray, *loc. cit.*).

rest they knew that they must sleep with one eye open, for the *Calinus* had warned them that this place, being close to the borders of Egypt, was frequented by outlaws and desperate men who had fled from justice. So, "weary and exhausted by the toil and hardship of the desert," says Felix, "we lay down under the sky, with no other solace than this, that we knew the end of our labours and the boundary of the desert to be close. Not for all the world's wealth would we have endured another fortnight in the wilderness...."[47]

Once more, as so often on their journey, they rose long before daylight, and were on their way soon after midnight, travelling over "parched sands." With the first light a cold wind drove a spitting shower in their faces, but at dawn it dropped, and they were able to go on between the new and loosely piled drifts of sand, among the grains of which the low sun picked out metallic gleams as of gold.[48] A dreary plain succeeded the dunes; impatient for the time when they would see the last of the desert, they pushed on at a smart pace.

Without warning the hoped-for moment arrived. From the edge of a plateau "we looked down to where, over against us, far below, lay a country of a different kind ... from ... our barren and enormous waste. For we looked down upon a part of Egypt, a kindly land.... And seeing it we were seized with both joy and amazement: with joy because we saw the end of the dreadful wilderness, men's dwellings, plentiful water, and many other things we had lacked in the desert. Yet amazement too, because we looked at a strange land. For we saw a great gathering of waters, as if it had been the sea, and high above those waters grew groves of tall palms, and other fruitful trees, and towers and other lofty buildings rose from the waters, towns and villages stood wonderfully in the midst of the waters.... For it was the time of the rising of the Nile, which river, leaving his bed, enriches and irrigates the whole of Egypt."[49]

Part Five

EGYPT

CHAPTER VIII

The Garden of Balm

From the hillside, with its astonishing view, the pilgrims came down to the plain. For a while yet they followed the Hajj road, but eventually, having left the town of Khanka on the right, they turned off to the left hand, and reached, at one and the same time, a village and the uttermost of the desert, for "the waste ended at the hedges and walls of the village; outside all was dry and barren, but within fertile and like to paradise."[1]

"Like to paradise" the village of Matariya may well have seemed to men fresh from the parched loneliness of the desert, for here rose that famous and holy spring, known to Christians as the Well of the Virgin, whose waters, not only abundant and perennial but also sweet, were almost unique among the brackish springs of Egypt.

This well, and the beauty and fruitfulness which it brought with it, made the village a place of resort for such rich Mamluks as the Emir Yashback, who built "a domed house" here, in which from time to time he entertained his master and friend, the old Qa'it Bey. The Sultan himself would also on occasion spend the equivalent of an English weekend under canvas, among the gardens of Matariya, regaling his guests with sumptuous banquets,[2] and doubtless recreating himself and them in the bathing establishment which stood close to the spring, an imposing building, large enough, Felix believed, to accommodate three hundred bathers, with handsome, painted rooms, and belvederes that gave wide views over the flat country.[3]

But there was another and more important reason for the fame of Matariya. To Christian and Moslem both, the place was known for its Garden of Balm, the precious product of whose bushes was all the Sultan's own, and a very considerable asset; while for Christians, and to a lesser degree even for Moslems,[4] the association of both well and garden with the Holy Family during the Flight into Egypt, made the place one of the venerated sites of Egypt.

The ancient Christian legends which accounted for the existence at Matariya of the well of pure waters, and of the Garden of Balm which these irrigated, are among the most gentle and touching of all medieval traditions. The Holy Family, so the story went, paused outside the village of Matariya, forwearied in their flight from Herod. Laying the Child down upon the ground the Blessed Virgin went on to beg in the village for water, which, however, the villagers had not to give her. But while she was away the Baby, as babies will, drummed upon the ground with his heels, and the mother, returning, found that where he had kicked a spring now ran. Thus the well was made, at once miraculous and homely. But another marvel was to follow. Our Lady took advantage of the water to wash not only the Child, but also his little shirts, and when she hung these out to dry, "from the water that dripped from them as they dried, for every drop there sprung a little bush, and these bushes produced the Balm."[5]

It is true that other legends, confused or even contradictory, co-existed with these. Friar Felix credited the Blessed Virgin with the origin of the well, but inclined to believe that the bushes of balm, brought from India by the Queen of Sheba on her visit to King Solomon, had flourished in the Holy Land till rooted up and transplanted to Matariya by Augustus Caesar; alternatively Cleopatra might have been responsible for their introduction into Egypt; but the Friar was confident of one thing: that the plants never did well until the visit of the Holy Family.[6]

The *Calinus* led the pilgrims through the village to a walled enclosure which apparently formed part of the cluster of buildings attached to the Sultan's bath-house. The gates, hastily closed at their approach, were quickly opened again in answer to the unmistakeable and persuasive gesture, on the part of the visitors, of hands going to purses; the pilgrims were led in and across a courtyard in which, surrounded by a green cane brake, was the life-giving and holy well itself–a large basin with a curb of white marble from which a wheel worked by oxen drew up water for the irrigation of the garden.[7]

In the range of buildings beyond the Well Courtyard they were allotted a cool delightful solar or dining-parlour, whose windows looked out towards the Garden of Balm; though this lay beyond an intermediate garden, and within its own high walls and gate, the air of the room was fragrant with the scent of the bushes.[8]

Hardly were they settled in their new quarters, than the Arab camel-men came asking for their discharge. In the old days, before the prestige of the West had been undermined by so long a succession of Turkish victories, the official Interpreter or Dragoman of Cairo had been used to wait upon Christian pilgrims at Matariya, and there conduct an enquiry into the behaviour of the Arabs during the desert journey, before these were allowed to depart; should any Christian lay a complaint against an

Arab the man would get a drubbing with a thong of "well-dried oxhides."[9] Times had changed, and no one would punish them now for the sake of a Christian, yet the desert men were still uneasy in the vicinity of Cairo; they flatly refused to stay and earn an extra fee by carrying the baggage into the city, and without further delay took their departure. Though the pilgrims had tried to retain their services, yet their reaction to the knowledge that they had seen the last of those exasperating servants was "not grief, but great relief, as though we had been delivered from a great load and a heavy burden."[10]

One more piece of business must be transacted before the travellers could abandon themselves to the enjoyment of leisure in agreeable surroundings: Taghribirdi, the Chief Dragoman of the Sultan,* must be informed of their arrival. A message was sent, in reply to which the Interpreter came promptly, prepared to escort the party into the city. The pilgrims met him, not as a stranger but almost as a friend, for they had encountered him already in Jerusalem, had found him all politeness and very prolific of promises, and had enjoyed a pleasant musical evening in his company.[11] Assured therefore of his complaisance they now met him with a request to leave them at Matariya for the night and return for them the next day. With unimpaired affability he consented, making only one condition; himself a skilled practitioner upon lute and viol, he remembered the quality of Conrad Artus's performance on these two instruments, and asked that the musician might be lent to him for this night.[12] The lords of the second company, for whom Conrad acted as cook, agreed, and the matter was thus arranged with satisfaction on both sides.

The pilgrims now prepared to enjoy themselves. Dinner today was to be no snack of cold meat, cheese and hard biscuit, eaten in the saddle and washed down by warmish wine and foul-tasting water. Country folk had already come in with their produce, those delicious eatables which Friar Felix loves to record:—"fresh bread, eggs and fruit," all cheap "except the wine," and when the pilgrims sat down to dine, what lay before them was a spread which lingered pleasantly in the memory even of the austere Paul Walther.[13]

The rest of the day was spent as enjoyably, either resting in "the pleasant shady solar room," or bathing in the pool, whose waters the Saracens themselves believed to be holy and medicinal.[14] That night, instead of being ordered by the *Calinus* into the crowded and stuffy tents, "every man slept where he chose." The place chosen by Felix and "a

---

* I have used the word dragoman in spite of its modern associations. As will be seen, the Chief Dragoman Taghribirdi was a person of considerable importance.

friend," whom we may well suppose to have been the Hungarian Archdeacon, was the brink of the holy spring where, "beautifully sheltered by a thick cane-brake ... we slept sweetly and safely" in the soft Egyptian air, so different from the bitter night temperature of the desert.[15]

The Chief Dragoman did not return to lead the pilgrims into Cairo until noon next day. But as time passed so pleasantly at Matariya they felt no impatience to be gone, and when he did arrive, accompanied by Conrad the lutanist, a number of servants, ten camels and their drivers, they suggested a further delay in order that he might show them the Garden of Balm before their departure.[16]

The Dragoman looked grave; to arrange this, he said, he must first confer with the keepers of the garden. The pilgrims did not yet know their man; when he came back and announced that entrance to the garden would cost them 6 ducats, apart from tips, they made no question, and at once clubbed together and produced the fee. But it was not long before their hands must go to their purses again. As they approached the gate of the garden a small mob of gardeners, gate-keepers and their wives made haste to assist at the opening. When this ceremony was completed the pilgrims were free to enter the outer garden which lay between their lodgings and the Garden of Balm itself.

Though the bushes of opobalsamum were the chief object of visitors there was here another sight which no Christian would miss. An immense and ancient fig-tree grew close to the gate; in its hollow trunk, as in a tiny chapel, two lamps hung, for by Christian tradition the tree had once opened to provide refuge for the Blessed Virgin. Such a hollow, and of such holy associations, was not to be passed by until each pilgrim had inserted himself into the cavity. The Dragoman also distributed twigs broken from the branches, said to be of medicinal value, and the pilgrims ate some of the figs, which "were large and good," but did this—we have Felix's word for it—"more to do the Virgin honour than because we needed, or because we liked them."[17]

From the fig tree they passed on among trees of strange habit of growth, and, as they were to discover during their stay in Egypt, of the most dulcet and delicious fruit, till they reached a small gate, barred and locked, which led into the inner garden. Here, when they had satisfied the importunities of a crowd of women and children, wives and families of the gardeners, the Dragoman delivered to them instructions and a warning. Five only at a time* were to enter the garden: the rest must wait their turn outside. And none must "pinch or nip off leaves or twigs to take away."

---

* Walther (p. 220) says six. He went in with the second batch.

The door was opened; the first detachment stepped inside, accompanied by the Dragoman, and several servants whose duty it was to see that the visitors neither pinched nor nipped;[18] then the door was shut and locked again. "See," Taghribirdi announced impressively, "See, these shrubs are the bushes of balm. Look! Touch! Smell!"

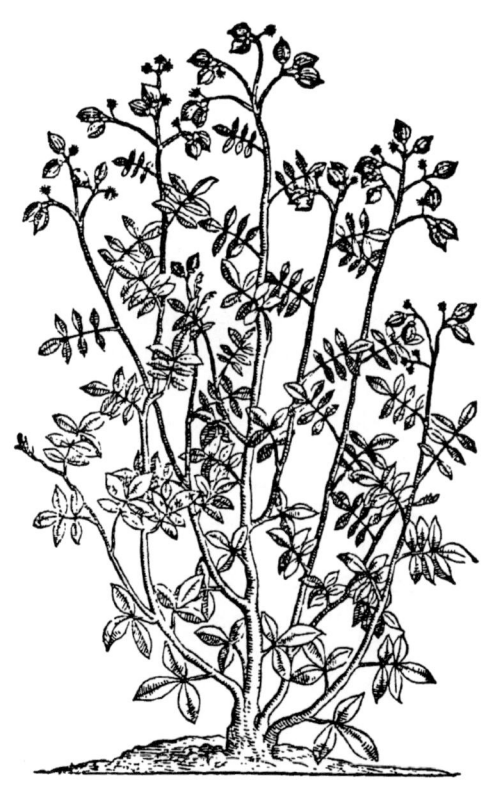

The balsam plant, from *De Plantis Aegypti* . . .
by Prosper Alpinus, Venice, 1592.

When medieval travellers try to describe the shrub, known to Felix as "Opobalsamum" and to modern science as "Commiphora Opobalsamum" (L.) Eng:,"* they use various comparisons by way of illustration. The bushes, say one pilgrim, are like small bramble bushes,[19] another suggests birches,[20] but most agree in comparing them with vines.[21]

* A native of South West Arabia and Somaliland. I am indebted to Mrs. A. Arber, F.R.S. for these particulars.

Their leaves reminded Felix Fabri of those of rue, but he noted that the stalks of the balm bush were white;[22] to an Italian the leaves recalled the leaves of sweet-basil.[23]

In their accounts of the cultivation of the balm all Christians seem to have agreed upon two points; consequent no doubt upon the holy origin of the plants they must be watered only from the Virgin's Well, and must be tended only by Christian gardeners.[24] Annual pruning was necessary, and one pilgrim speaks of the necessity of covering the bushes with tow in the winter.[25]

Every part, and every product of the plant, was of value. A confection called "syrup of balm" was made from the tips of the branches, cut off at the time of flowering, which occurred in August; this was esteemed for many curative properties, while even the bare twigs after the extraction of the balm and the fall of the leaf were bought up by apothecaries.[26]

The balm itself was, naturally, more valuable still, but of the three grades of this the first, and purest, never came within the ordinary range of commerce, or figured in the lists of Egyptian exports. Of the other two, the better was extracted from the fruit of the bush; the inferior by boiling the branches, after the true and most costly opobalsamum had been drawn from them.[27] Even these less honourable products, the carpobalsamum and xylobalsamum of the merchants, were desirable commodities; benificent and holy, used medicinally they had curative properties, or, mixed with other oils, would impart a special sanctity to the sacramental chrism.[28]

If inferior kinds possessed healing powers, far greater was the range of benefits to be expected from the opobalsamum itself: Moslems recommended it for use in nasal trouble, lumbago or pain in the knee,[29] Christians, in a still wider selection of diseases, included the stone, toothache, poisoning and snake-bite.[30] When pilgrim writers begin to describe the method of producing the pure opobalsamum, contradictions multiply, and no wonder, since the precious balm being a monopoly of the Sultan the process of extraction may well have been something in the nature of a state secret.

Our pilgrim writers cannot even agree as to the colour of the oil. It was green at first, changing to red; it was "white like the milk of figs"; it was the colour of wine; it was yellow.[31]* Again, there is considerable difference of opinion as to how, and at what season, it was extracted. Piloti, who should have had means of ascertaining the truth, reports that in August and September† the leaves were torn from the plant "in such

---

* Dr. Arber describes the colour as waxen yellow.
† Von Harff (p. 126) says May; Tafur (p. 77) October; Fabri (III, p. 16) December.

a way that the branches sweat, and drop the sweat, and the Christian gardeners squeeze the branches with their hands, and collecting the moisture put it into phials of ivory."³²* An Italian pilgrim who claims to have been an eye-witness of the process, speaks like Piloti of the tearing off of the leaves from the stem, and the consequent oozing out of moisture, which was wiped from the plant by bits of cotton, which were afterwards wrung out into little phials."³³ Friar Felix as usual launches out boldly into a voluminous account of the process of collecting the balm; a slit is made in the branches, and for this purpose no steel must be used, only knives of stone or bone; a small glass pot is then hung below the incision, and into this the balm slowly distils, to be emptied later into vessels of gold.³⁴† But this is one of the occasions when we happen to know that he is drawing only upon his books for information. Friar Paul lets the cat out of the bag: "How the balm is extracted," says he, "I do not know, for we were not told."³⁵

Whenever and however extracted the balm must next be subjected to another process, which though in itself only a simple matter of cookery, was, at least in the earlier part of the century, erected into a religious ritual. In the Coptic month of "Bashans" (i.e. May-June) at the Sultan's castle, and in his presence, the two Christian patriarchs, the Caliph with other Moslem "wise men," and some high court officials, came together. Now "the balm is put on the fire, and boiled a little, and while it is on the fire the Caliph and his bishops on the one hand say prayers, and the two Christian patriarchs on the other . . . say their Office according to the Christian faith, unitl it has been long enough cooking."³⁶ The function is a curious instance of the genuine though superficial respect felt by Moslems for the Christian religion, which Piloti noticed, and commented on to a friendly Moslem when he saw him bathe, as Christians bathed for the sake of its miraculous powers, in the waters of the Virgin's Well at Matariya.³⁷

As a recognition of their part in the process the Sultan was accustomed to give the two Christian prelates a portion of the oil, so that when de Lannoy was in Egypt the Patriarch of the Jacobites was able to present to him "as Ambassador of the King of France, a phial of the pure balm."³⁸ Another part of the product went in ceremonial gifts made by the Sultan to other potentates,³⁹ part was customarily sent to hospitals,⁴⁰ and favoured Mamluks were said to receive small quantities,⁴¹ though by

---

* Reading "*ampoules*" for "*amoules.*" The editor accepts "*amoules*" and, as a translation suggests, "*boites d'ivoire, moules, formes.*"

† Von Harff also speaks of little pots of glass, but in his version the balm exudes from cuttings from the trees which are put in these.

some it was thought that the Sultan was more ready to sell than to give, and that he drove a good trade in the balm among his courtiers.[42] Upon whatever terms the Mamluks of the court may have obtained the coveted oil, certainly it was from them that Christian pilgrims hoped to obtain the genuine and unadulterated article.[43]

That Western travellers should wish to obtain it was as natural as that their eagerness should invite exploitation. The price asked was such that only men of substance could hope to buy, and the Moslems themselves raised their eyebrows at the fantastic sums which these were prepared to pay.[44] The rich men among our pilgrims were no exception: they bought, but Friar Paul was sceptical as to the success of their deal; "they spent a lot of money," he says sourly, "so as to get it pure, but they were cheated." His personal opinion was that no Christian had a chance of acquiring any of the unadulterated product.[45]

With a restricted supply* and a large demand it was not surprising that there was a good deal of faked or adulterated opobalsamum on the market. The credulous might be fobbed off with another oil, such as terebinth, or a mixture of nard and terebinth; or the true balm might be adulterated by various other sweet-smelling oils of which Friar Felix gives an impressive list: "oil of roses of Cyprus, of mastic, of terebinth, often of myrtle . . ." and so on. The thought of so many varieties of imposture available to the wily oriental caused the Friar's heart to fail for a moment, and he was driven to comfort himself with the thought that, at any rate, "in heaven . . . it will be pure."[46]

The intending purchaser, conscious of such risks, defended himself as best he might. Most of our writers rehearse a series of tests by which true and pure balm can be distinguished from the false, or the adulterated. Take, says one, a living coal—a drop of the true balm will quench the fire; take a white cloth—a drop of the true balm will leave no stain upon it.[47] Take, says another, a silver goblet of goats' milk, stir quickly, add a drop of balm, and the milk will curdle; expose a little balm to the heat of the sun . . . put a little on a knife close to a hot fire . . .[48]—and so on. One much-quoted pilgrim writer, a man of almost inexhaustible credulity, even assures us that true balm may be known because a drop put upon a man's hand will pass right through it and drip down below.[49] How effective any of these tests were we do not know. Friar Felix, except in that one instant of despair, believed in them and consequently believed that at least some of the balm which went back to Europe in the baggage of the pilgrims was the real Mackay. The Sultan's Mamluks, from whom

* Tafur (p. 77) says, "There is so little that it does not reach half an *azumbre* of our measure." An *azumbre* is an eighth part of an *arroba*.

it was bought, had subjected it, in the presence of the purchasers and their friends, to a number of these trials, and when the pilgrims were home once more the same tests were applied, "publicly and before all . . . in the presence of the Archduke Sigismund at Innsbruck, and of the Archbishop at Mainz, and of the lady . . . widow of Charles Duke of Burgundy," and demonstration made that here was indeed the true and pure balm, costly and holy, fit to be mingled in the sacring oil of kings.[50]

All this was in the future. Now, as the pilgrims stood among the bushes of balm the Chief Dragoman took a bone knife and with delicate precision cut a slit in one of the branches. From this, as the pilgrims watched, a clear thick oil slowly oozed, of which oil the Moslem smeared a little upon each man's hand, and bade him put it to his nose. The perfume, which a modern will describe as "a penetrating odour," or, at best, "a pleasant smell," Felix rapturously declared to be "incomparable," and so clinging that this small quantity rubbed on the skin "so drenched a man in the scent that for several days he could smell nothing but balm."[51] Except for that lingering perfume Friar Felix, it appears, brought nothing away with him from the Garden of Balm. It is Friar Paul who announces with some pride that he contrived surreptitiously to break off a piece of one of the bushes and to smuggle it out with him.[52]

CHAPTER IX

Among the Mamluks

Not until evening was closing in did the pilgrims begin their ride to Cairo, the Chief Dragoman being now their official conductor, though their old friend Elphahallo had not yet taken his leave of them.[1] Night fell as they left behind them the last of the desert, and entered upon a road which at first led between closes of fruit trees and gardens, divided everywhere by the flooded water channels; long before they entered Cairo itself, however, they were among great houses which stood up like castles "in one continuous city." For two hours, according to Felix's reckoning, they rode through the streets, thronged, since it was Ramadan, by old and young, so that the pilgrims were subjected to the usual attentions of unlicked Moslem youth, and must scurry along in undignified haste to avoid the showers of dirt with which they were pelted.

Yet it was not this unpleasantness which formed the most vivid recollection of their entry into the city, but rather the impression they received of great crowds and many lights, for "there was so much noise and such a concourse of people that it is beyond expression, so many lamps and candles . . . as if the whole world made holiday, and this not in one place only, but in every street."[2]

At last they reached the house of the Chief Dragoman; his servants ran out and the guests were brought into "a great handsome paved hall, painted, and adorned with polished marble, but without beds, hangings or benches." As their baggage had been stacked for the night in the courtyard outside the pilgrims were forced to get what sleep they could sitting on the bare floor with their backs to the wall, and sadly disturbed by the noise of the Moslem revellers "capering about in the court," till the first morning light brought with it once more the torpor of day-time Ramadan.[3]

At this period the right to provide lodgings for Christian pilgrims in Cairo, with all the opportunities of profit which this afforded, appertained to the Chief Dragoman of the Sultan.* Sometimes the Christian visitor

---

* This appears to have been the rule also at the end of the previous century (Sigoli, p. 17). An apparent exception is to be noted about twenty years later; the author of the *Pèlerinage* was quartered upon a kindly Christian, Master Lucca, who welcomed the Frenchman with a regale of fruit, meat and good wine (*Pèlerinage*, pp. 98–9).

was fortunate in his host; Pero Tafur, travelling alone, was received by the Dragoman, a vigorous ancient of ninety years whose youngest child was born during the Spaniard's visit, with as much good will "as if I had been his son, and he allowed me to mix with his wives and children," a degree of hospitality which the guest understood to be quite out of the ordinary.[4]

The experience of other pilgrims was less happy. Frescobaldi and his companions found that they paid through the nose for their lodging while in Cairo,[5] and the pilgrims of 1483 were to discover that Taghribirdi the Dragoman was a very different person from their affable and obliging acquaintance of Jerusalem. They received the first shock of disillusionment no later than the morning after their arrival in Cairo. They had wakened long before the weary Moslems, and it was in the quiet pause before the household was astir that they were visited by a resident Christian merchant, a goldsmith and jeweller of Mechlin in Brabant, by name Francis. He announced that having seen them arrive on the previous evening, he had now come to do them a service by warning them against their host, a man, he told them, of crooked dealing, an extortioner, whose air of mildness was no more than a mask assumed "in order, in the event, to drain our purses." They would be wise not to remain here; he himself, so he told them, would find other and better lodgings for them in a Christian house. The pilgrims gave him grateful thanks and accepted his kindly offer.

It was, however, one thing to decide to leave the Dragoman's house, another to put the decision into practice. When Taghribirdi arrived accompanied by servants, to make arrangements for the greater comfort of his paying-guests, and was informed of their intention, he flew into an hysterical rage. The pilgrims, he declared, were his, and their safety in his hands. "If I will, I can keep you here by force, and put you in irons." Changing his tune he told them suddenly to go, and take the consequences; then curbing his anger spoke softly, asking what was wrong with their quarters. "See, they are spacious, roomy and pleasant; you will not find the like among your Christians. My house is your house, my servants your servants. If you will, stay here and be safe; if you will, go elsewhere, and see to your own safety."[6] The pilgrims, daunted, and unsure of their position, decided to remain.

The first day of their residence in Cairo they spent settling into their new quarters, while the bursars of each company set off upon a shopping expedition, since by custom only lodging was provided at the house of the Dragoman, and for the rest they must shift for themselves.[7] On the second day Taghribirdi took them upon a conducted tour of his residence, acting the showman to his own opulent establishment;[8] the pilgrims having knuckled under to him, he chose for the time being to show his pleasant side. On the third day old Elphahallo came to take his leave; he was about to set out on his return journey as guide to "some African Saracens," who were bound for Jerusalem. The parting was sorrowful; when the old man had gone the pilgrims felt as though they had been left fatherless.[9]

It was perhaps to cheer themselves up after this wrench that they made their first combined expedition. Now that they were once more in a great city they were moved to consider their appearance. Inquiries for a Christian barber were made in vain of the Dragoman's servants; fortunately the friendly goldsmith arrived, and hearing what they wanted promptly led them to the house which was occupied by the Venetian Consul when he came up from Alexandria to the capital on business. Here, at the hands of the great man's own barber, the pilgrims' hair was washed and tidied; Friar Felix, whose "tonsure... was almost hidden" had his shaven crown restored to him; all issued from the barber's ministrations spruce and clean, although of course retaining their pilgrim beards. In this condition they were pleased to accept an invitation to wait upon the Consul, who, from an upper window, had observed the arrival of their travel-worn and dishevelled party.

Andrea Cabriel,* as Consul of the Venetian merchants at Alexandria, was the representative of the great Republic in Egypt. The pilgrims while in Cairo were to become familiar with the sight of this small, spare man, bald-headed, but with a long and full beard which Friar Felix much admired, riding about the city upon a mule with silken harness, stately and handsome in his long gown of crimson damask. Gifted with the eloquence which meant so much to an age in which the bulk of the world's business was conducted *viva voce*, and possessed of all the dignity of his patrician blood, the Consul had also the grace of manner which goes with a gentle and generous nature. He welcomed the pilgrims with the kiss which was the customary greeting among Italians, listened to their account of their pilgrimage with flattering attention, and made the priests among them free of his chapel and its golden altar vessels. When they put to him the question which had been so much upon their minds—had they arrived in time to take their passage home in the ships of the Venetian spice fleet?—he was able to give them reassuring answer; the ships lay

---

* Fabri does not mention him by name. Walther (p. 249) calls him Capriel. Another member of the Cabriel family was governor of Modon in 1500. (Miller, *Latins in the Levant*, p 496.)

still in the port of Alexandria, and he himself was waiting to travel back to Venice in one of them.[10]

From the august memories of Mount Sinai, the tender and gracious associations of the Garden of Balm, the pilgrims had now reached the centre of one of the two great Moslem empires of the Levant. Egypt, the river-built land between desert and desert, Cairo itself, the vast city with its wealth and teeming population of alien race and religion – these were strange enough to Western visitors, yet in all they saw there was nothing more strange than the very structure of society and government, in which there was imposed upon the native peoples of Egypt the rule of a military caste, which, consisting exclusively of ex-slaves, spurned those two principles fundamental to the social and political structures of Europe: free personal status and hereditary succession.

There were in fact two populations in Egypt. That which was native, whether Coptic or Saracen, peasant or townsman, was gentle and unwarlike, and excelled in the arts of peace. Piloti, the Cretan-born Italian who had lived among them for so long, loved them, and looked forward to a time when, Egypt having been once more conquered by Christian Crusaders, there would be nothing to do "but to sing the *Te Deum*, praising God, and to hear always the sound of minstrels, harps or lutes, to be always joyful and of good cheer, and to be good friends with the Saracens." For the merchant was convinced that though pagans these were "by nature innocent and without malice," accepting Islam, so he argued, "until God shall send them the light of the truth." Indeed he went so far as to claim that they might be called "bastard Christians" since in their lives they showed more justice and charity than the true heirs of the Kingdom.[11]

It was this endearing gentleness which had been the cause of their subjection. When it came to fighting, Piloti admitted, "you can count them as women," and de Lannoy, the man of courts and camps, wrote them down as "too cowardly and of too weak a fibre to keep their country safe."[12] The militant Mamluk Sultanate did that for them, and they paid in the sufferings imposed by an unbridled alien tyranny, for the Sultan's soldiery lorded it over them with an arrogance which would have been more suitable in a victorious army of occupation. No civilian dared to protest, even a look of resentment was dangerous, when the Mamluk bullies flogged their way through the crowded streets of Cairo with the heavy sticks they always carried, "caring less how they injured men," said Felix Fabri, "than one of us would in going through a herd of swine."[13] Such, and worse, tyrannies were of every day; on the occasions when Mamluk bands fought among themselves private houses were sacked, the Jews pillaged, and the ex-slave soldier, a "tough fighter" against foreign enemies, showed himself "a devil unleashed."[14] As a result of such disorders, and of the Sultan's exactions, wealth in Egypt literally went to ground; here, said Piloti, "there is more gold hidden under the earth than in any country in the world," and a rich man would try to conceal his good fortune by dressing in the poorest clothes.[15]

The Mamluk Sultanate, triumphant in arms abroad, cruel and oppressive at home, had lasted for just over two hundred and thirty years when Felix Fabri and his companions were in Cairo, and was to continue for another thirty-four. In 1249 Jean de Joinville had seen the egg out of which was to hatch this cockatrice. The decisive charge which broke the Christian chivalry at Damietta in Saint Louis' disastrous Crusade, was made by the Sultan's Guard, and de Joinville, a man of equal bravery and candour, explained to his readers that this Guard consisted of slaves. The Sultan, says he, "for horsemen has mostly men of foreign nations, whom the merchants bring to foreign countries for sale, and gladly he buys them and a high price he pays."[16]

When these same slaves had been metamorphosed into Sultans they continued, as eagerly as their predecessors of the legitimate line, to buy slaves and train them to arms; so too did the great Emirs who had shared their captivity,[17] so that from top to bottom of this military society slavery was an experience common to all, and the enfranchised Mamluk trooper of today might be the Emir of next year and the Sultan of the year after.

This common experience, proclaimed in the very name by which Sultan, Emir, and soldier were known,* dictated both social relations and the structure of the State. Torn from his place in the world, and with every family tie severed, the Mamluk soldier gave his loyalty, first to that man, whether Sultan or Emir, who had bought, trained and enfranchised him; secondly to those with whom he had shared the shames and fears of slavery.[18] And more and more as time went on, those able and ambitious men who had risen to the rank of Emir combined to close the way to advancement against anyone who had not, like themselves, passed through the slave market. Just as few sons of Mamluks were allowed to rise to high office of state,[19] so it was only rarely that the son of a Mamluk Sultan contrived to establish himself upon his father's throne. Deposition or death was commonly the penalty for an attempt to do so, and after the removal of the heir the rival Emirs fought it out through the streets of Cairo, till the strongest, ablest or most ruthless prevailed.

* The meaning of the word *mamluk* is "that which is owned."

The task of one who came to power by such a road was likely to be hard. "This lordship," remarked de Lannoy with justice, "is very perilous and very unstable."[20] Against the factious Emirs from among whom he had come to the throne the Sultan must always be upon his guard; a vigilant eye, and the application of punishment both prompt and sharp, were essential; few Emirs but suffered at some time or other the result of the Sultan's anger or suspicion; it was counted worthy of remark that Qa'it Bey "from the time he was appointed to the Sultan's Guard until his own accession . . . was never exiled, nor put in chains, nor imprisoned."[21]

As well as repression of ambitious rivals, the Sultan used a profuse generosity to attract and attach friends. A ruler without a jot of hereditary right, he must go always "with gold in his hand, and then he will do well."[22] His largesse took different forms. If, three times a day, he discarded, never to wear again, a suit of sumptuous garments, this was not of pure extravagance, for "he gives all to his lords and his closest friends." When a provincial governor's lavish present reached the Sultan as he took his pastime in the hunt, he might make the episode an opportunity for a display of generosity, so that in an hour the whole rich burden of a hundred camels, "gold and silver coin, and silks woven with gold and silver," would have been unpacked and distributed among his companions and attendants.[23]

Yet severity, however timely, and liberality, however prodigal, were neither the only nor yet the chief means by which a Mamluk Sultan maintained himself upon the throne. His chief strength lay in the Guard of highly trained soldiers with which he surrounded himself.

In the Sultan's interest a high-ranking Mamluk official with various assistants under him[24] kept an eye upon the slave-markets, being always on the look-out for likely lads between the ages of ten and twenty,[25] whether these had been taken in slaving raids, or sold to dealers by necessitous parents.[26] Sultan Qa'it Bey, a Circassian by birth, had been bought "among a lot of young slaves at 50 dinars each," by one Sultan;[27] he became the property of his successor,[28] and was, in due course, set free, with the usual endowment of horse and arms, and the usual place in the Sultan's Guard. Between these landmarks in his career the lad, following the routine which produced the trained and hardened fighters of the Sultan's Mamluks, was "enrolled in the school of the lads of the Guard."[29]

This school, the results of whose training so nearly concerned the Sultan's interests, was situated within the precincts of his castle-palace at Cairo. The large building, four storeys high, housed five to six hundred lads, under the care of a staff of eunuchs; the pupils were divided into classes of twenty-five, each class having its own separate room, suitably and hygienically spread with reed mats.[30] Taught at once the Moslem religion and the practice of arms, their training in the latter was thorough and severe. Riding and archery were the chief studies, as in the Sultan's slave-guard of de Joinville's day,[31] for the short Tartar bow was always the weapon of the Mamluk army.

Every year, during the festivities which took place at the flooding of the Nile, the boys gave a display of their proficiency. Drawn up in formation, and "taking their turn as if in a dance," they were drilled in the presence of the Sultan. The function, as well as a display, partook also of the nature of a "passing out exam:" for three ancient Emirs stood by to watch, and chose from the performers those of best attainment, as fit to be entered among the Sultan's Guard. After this promotion the young Guardsman was provided by the Sultan with arms, a horse and a horse-boy, and might now set up for himself in lodgings in the city. In addition to his pay he received a daily ration of bread and meat, and barley for his horse, and Western pilgrims who passed near the Citadel at a certain hour in the day might see the swarm of "young blackamoors who all belonged to the Mamluks . . . going to the palace with sacks and boxes . . ."[32] to collect this provision.

The young soldier was still bound to appear upon the parade ground below the Citadel for drill and warlike exercises three days a week, and these attracted the keen professional interest of those pilgrims who were also fighting men. Sometimes there was little of interest for them to watch, only the spectacle of "the handsome lads, fair and ruddy, like sons of noblemen at home,"[33] "standing by a wall with outstretched arms as if to climb it on hands and feet," a posture which was intended to supple their limbs.[34] At other times the young Mamluks would be seen shooting with the bow, lifting weights, throwing stones, or contending on foot and horse "without breast plate, gorget or helm, though indeed they carry targes and shields." This neglect of heavy protective armour seemed strange to men of western Europe, but it suited the traditional oriental reliance upon those mounted archers who even in battle wore only a mail shirt covered with silk and a round head-piece.[35] In the rough and dangerous mimic warfare under the walls of the Citadel, where the lads were seasoned and salted into a first-class fighting force, wounds and death were often incurred, but, says Felix, "here they care less for the slaughter of a man than if a hen had been killed."[36] In addition to this note of humanitarian disapproval he recorded with distress and resentment his observation that instead of "the shapes of lions, bears, dogs, donkeys or other beasts" of western heraldry, all these young warriors bore upon their shields a golden cup on a blue field. This device he believed to have been adopted as a calculated blasphemy against the chalice of the Eucharist;[37] in fact it merely and innocuously represented the cup which their master Qa'it Bey bore as his coat-armour, in memory of the time when he himself had held the office of cupbearer to another Sultan.[38]

No doubt those who came young into the slave-market after a time acclimatised themselves to their new life and new religion. But there were others whose fate was more harsh, and it was with these, with the knights and men-at-arms of Christian nations who, in their maturity, had been taken prisoner in some battle against the Turks, and bought for the Sultan or one of his Emirs, that our pilgrims had associated at Gaza, and were to associate in Cairo.

Their intercourse with these men in both places was to a great extent of a cheerful and convivial nature, but for the Christian priests among the pilgrims it had its more serious side. In Cairo, as at Gaza, many of the Mamluks whom the pilgrims encountered were Hungarians, and Archdeacon John Lazinus, amiable, eloquent and earnest, at once seized upon the opportunity offered by the contact with these apostate countryman, to strike a blow for the salvation of their souls. He was able to do so with more effect, owing to the assistance of one of their number, a man of handsome appearance and great stature, a member of the Sultan's Guard, and high in his favour. This man had a remarkable history. Captured in battle by the Turks after such a heroic resistance that they judged him, as "a giant and wonder," to be a fit gift for the Ottoman Sultan, the Hungarian had later been presented by his first royal owner to Qa'it Bey. Since the best efforts and worst threats of both these masters had failed to move the noble slave to abjure Christianity, he was allowed, in Egypt, to pass for a Mamluk while still retaining his faith.* So highly indeed did the old Sultan prize him, that with the cognizance of a few of the great officers of State, he had supplied the Hungarian with letters which should serve as a passport out of Egypt when death removed his protector.[39] It was at the house of this man, that with all due secrecy, the Archdeacon preached to the other Hungarian Mamluks, reasoning with them, re-marrying such of them as wished for the Christian rite,

* Cf. Tafur (pp. 96-9) where a Spanish corsair serves the Sultan, without renouncing Christianity. The pilgrims of 1483 found "the son of the King of Sicily" (actually Alonso, the bastard son of Ferrante of Naples) resident in Cairo, and appearing as a Mamluk at the Sultan's court, though without abjuring his faith (*Evag.* III, p. 33), but the ten years' residence of Alonso in Egypt was a matter of high politics (see Hill, *A History of Cyprus*, II, pp. 609, 700-1).

even baptizing some of their children. This last would have been a greater triumph had the pilgrims not suspected the purity of the parents' motives; firmly convinced, however, as Felix and his friends were, that to have been a Christian was an essential qualification for becoming a Mamluk,* they could not but fear that the baptism was valued as the first step in the career of a young renegade.⁴⁰

While the Hungarian Archdeacon laboured to reclaim his own countrymen, Friars Felix and Paul concentrated upon the German Mamluks. From one of these Felix, after long persuasion, received an assurance that he would be glad to renounce Islam. Friar Paul reports a more elaborate and gratifying anecdote; the same man, expressing to the Franciscan, as a great secret, his hope "soon to be in Venice, like you," asked for a letter of recommendation to the Franciscan Prior at Jerusalem, which would be of use if he could put in practice his plan of escaping by way of Beirut.⁴¹†

To judge by words, "almost all Mamluks," the pilgrims concluded, were restless and unhappy in their new religion, and longed to return to Christendom.⁴² While many, moved by a desire to please in Christian company, may have exaggerated this state of mind, yet it was one not improbable in these men who had suffered the deep derangement inevitable in their experience of slavery, and the compulsory acceptance of another faith. Though few, perhaps, ever tried to put into practice the aspiration of escape, and fewer still succeeded, yet there were some who did both. Piloti, a merchant, but a man of some daring, was responsible for smuggling out of Egypt "several Christians who had denied the faith against their will."⁴³ Jean Thenaud crowned his perilous desert pilgrimage by bringing safe to Rhodes his Mamluk dragoman, who was there received once more into the company of Christian men.⁴⁴ Our pilgrims found in the house of Taghribirdi itself two would-be fugitives, a German and a Spaniard, of whom the latter wept with joy at the sight of a Christian face, and kissed the crosses which the pilgrims wore.⁴⁵ Still more notable than these anonymous persons, were two who left accounts of their life and misfortunes, the tragic Nicolo Conti, and Johann Schiltberger.

* Perhaps this belief arose from a knowledge of the Islamic precept that Moslem should not enslave Moslem (*Encyclopaedia of Islam*, ed. 1954, s.v. Abd, p. 32), and that therefore no Mamluk should have been Moslem by origin. (Ayalon, *L'Esclavage Mamlouk*, p. 24).

† Walther calls this man Seefogel; Fabri gives no name but talks of a German Mamluk from Basle. Von Harff, rather more than a dozen years later, travelled to Jerusalem with a dragoman of 60 years called Conrad of Basel (Von Harff, pp. 182–3). We can only speculate as to whether this was the same man, and if so, whether Friar Paul's letter at last came in useful.

But as well as the Mamluks who under pressure, and with greater or less conscientious scruple, had accepted Mahomet and denied Christ, there were other men of more dubious character who had turned their religious coat for the sake of a career. Of such was the German engineer from Oppenheim, who altered and added to the castle of Alexandria for Sultan Qa'it Bey, and who, having accumulated "a great treasure," at last returned to the country and faith of his childhood.[46] Of such, too, was the Chief Dragoman, Taghribirdi, the host of our pilgrims of 1483.

A renegade Christian of European birth was peculiarly suited for the office of Chief Dragoman, Interpreter, or Orator, of the Sultan,[47] comprising as it did, relations with pilgrims of Western nations, and the duties of interpreter at Court. It is therefore not surprising that we hear of more than one of such voluntarily deracinated persons occupying the position. Almost exactly a hundred years before Friar Felix's sojourn in Egypt the Chief Dragoman at Alexandria was a Frenchman "with a Christian wife born in paynimry, and between the two of them," remarked a pilgrim tartly, "they have much less than one ration of faith."[48] In Cairo at the same period a Venetian renegade had succeeded his Florentine father-in-law in the same office, "and his wife ... one of our Florentine women, a renegade, both she and her father."[49]

It is with surprising exactitude that such men as these, and Taghribirdi himself, inhabitants alike of the strange and sinister territory of doubt or scepticism or half-hearted apostasy which lay between Christianity and Islam, echo the restless discontent of the pilgrims' Mamluk acquaintances. "If the Sultan sends me to Alexandria," Frescobaldi's host told him, "and I can in any honest manner return to the West, I will do it."[50] Friar Paul overheard "that accursed man," Taghribirdi, declare that "he would not for the whole world be forced to remain an infidel, but with God's help he would shortly deliver himself and his wife."[51] It is likely, however, that Frescobaldi's acute comment meets the case of both these cosmopolitan adventurers, and of the Mamluks besides. It would be a hard thing, the Italian merchant remarked, for the renegade Dragoman "to leave his two wives, and children, and wealth and position."[52]

The French, and Florentine and Venetian Dragomans of Frescobaldi's day are not even names to us, and, but for this brief glimpse, we know nothing of their history. It is very different with Taghribirdi, for the career of this man of great ability and ambition, and of conveniently few scruples, can be traced at intervals for many years, both in pilgrim narratives and in the State Papers of the Venetian Republic.

A Jew of Sicily,* and a Rabbi, he forsook the faith of his race and became a Christian, studied theology in the schools,[53] and was made deacon.[54] But now occurred a crisis at the cause of which we can only guess. He fled from Italy to Egypt, says Felix, and became a Moslem;[55] he fled, says Friar Paul, with a well-dowered Christian wife.[56] If this second statement is true, we may ask ourselves whether the heart of this astute and scheming Jew had not for once got the better of his head, since to be a deacon meant to be celibate, and whether the flight from Italy was not in fact an elopement. However that may be, the Sicilian, at first in Alexandria, later in Cairo, tried to find a market for his talents, but it was by means of his wife that opportunity came to him. She, perhaps like Taghribirdi a Jew by birth, and like many Jewesses[57] a highly skilled worker in silk, was patronised by Qa'it Bey's wife, and was thus able to recommend her husband to the Sultan.

Once established at Court, the Sicilian, now under the Turkish name of Taghribirdi, with his command of languages, his suave approach and subtle brain, began to make his own way. He procured the office of Chief Dragoman, by cash purchase Friar Felix understood; by that and a trick of the devil Friar Paul believed.[58] However acquired, the office was to remain his, with at most a few interruptions, until 1512.

In 1483 Taghribirdi, with the Chief Dragoman's right to a fee of 5 ducats a head from each of the pilgrim lodgers, and 2 ducats from every Western merchant visiting Cairo,[59] was a rich man, living in ample style. He was also in favour at Court, and here, for such a man, there were further opportunities of profit. In 1488 he was taking bribes from Venice, and acting on behalf of the Republic as *agent provocateur* with regard to the opponents of Venetian policy in Cyprus. In the next year the Signory considered that this "man of authority, astute and experienced," was worth attaching by "secret gifts, promises and attentions."[60] When, in 1490, Venice finally took over the sovereignty of Cyprus, Taghribirdi, as Qa'it Bey's Chief Dragoman and *Alto Spadier*, was present at the meeting where this matter was regulated between the Sultan and the Signory.[61]

Suriano, at Cairo in 1494, found Taghribirdi still in office,[62] but if we may identify him with the Taghribirdi Ilbay of Ibn Iyas's narrative,† he

---

* According to Fabri (*Evag*. III, 20) and Walther (221-2). According to a later pilgrim "out of Spain" (Georgii Gemnicensis, *Ephemeris*, p. 482), but this might well be understood at this period to include Sicily. Von Harff, almost certainly speaking of Taghribirdi, calls him a Genoese.

† Ibn Iyas mentions three persons bearing the name of Taghribirdi, but of these only one could possibly be our Chief Dragoman, as the other two died during his known life-time (Ibn Iyas, pp. 67, 284). Taghribirdi Ilbay was major domo to the

had already fallen out of favour at Court.⁶³ If, again, in 1497 he still continued as Chief Interpreter fresh adversity overtook him during the riots which followed the death of the old Sultan, for pilgrims staying in Cairo soon after at the Dragoman's house found themselves in surroundings very different from the elegant establishment which the pilgrims of 1483 had known; von Harff complained that what the Dragoman offered was "holes like pig-styes, and nothing inside but bare earth."⁶⁴ But the wily official had contrived to hide away his best stuff during the late disturbances.⁶⁵

To whatever degree the Jew had suffered a reverse of fortune in the last years of the century, the period of his eclipse was not long. In 1501 it was at his house that the ambassador of Ferdinand and Isabella, the Catholic monarchs of Spain, stayed while in Cairo; it is no less a sign of Taghribirdi's importance that a Venetian envoy, receiving his instructions from the Signory, had it impressed upon him that his dealings with the Sultan must be "*solus cum solo,*" and without the knowledge of the Chief Dragoman, who was by now the declared enemy of the Republic.⁶⁶

Whatever were the feelings of the Venetian Signory towards its erstwhile friend, he was a man impossible to ignore or evade. In 1507 he landed at Venice as envoy of the Sultan; his arrival was celebrated with great solemnity, his departure with many gifts. In spite of all this diplomatic cordiality, he was later to repay his hosts by blowing the gaff with regard to a most delicate and secret part of the negotiations in which he had been engaged, a piece of malice "which," remarked the lords of the Signory, "may God pardon the Chief Dragoman...."⁶⁷

We are privileged to be able to assist at the rejoicings and festivities which attended Taghribirdi's return to Egypt, through the narrative of the Carthusian Prior George of Chemnitz, who sailed with him from Venice to Alexandria and watched it all. The arrival of the Chief Dragoman at Alexandria was greeted by a salute of guns; he was received by the Governor of the city and the Venetian Consul, while "all the youth of Alexandria poured out to see him and fought to do him honour."⁶⁸ His journey from the port to Cairo was accomplished in an equally high style. He, together with the brace of wives who accompanied him, and their luggage, filled one Nile boat, his Mamluks another. The Prior and his party shared a third with a mixed crowd of Jews and Egyptians.

On the way up the river the craft in which the great man travelled was

---

Sultan, and on one occasion took advantage of his position to recommend for office an individual whom the chronicler considered unsuitable (Ibn Iyas, p. 198), a piece of manipulation which we could well believe of the pilgrims' Taghribirdi.

dressed every night with lamps, rigged out pyramid-wise, and many little bells were attached to the sails to chime and tinkle sweetly in the cool soft wind. At Cairo he stepped ashore magnificent in the golden tunic which had been one of the gifts of the Venetian Signory; met and escorted home in great state by a number of notables, he there sat down to eat with them upon carpets spread in the courtyard. The festivities were watched from above by his harem of no less than thirty-five;[69] that impressive number, compared with the modest total of two which our pilgrims of 1483 record, gives an indication of the degree to which the Chief Dragoman had gone up in the world.

Yet neither the passage of years, nor the improvement in his circumstances, had caused the leopard to change his spots, and the warning which Francis the goldsmith gave to the pilgrims would have been of value to the German Carthusian and his companions. Introduced at Alexandria to this influential personage, and finding him gracious and friendly, the little company of strangers had thought it well, "in order that we should, under the shelter of his patronage, make our pilgrimage with the more security," to offer him a present of 50 gold pieces. "But when he had swallowed our money . . . he looked askance at us, and lost interest in us."[70]

The embassy to Venice marked, perhaps, the summit of Taghribirdi's career. Three years later he was in prison. It may be that this was the end, and that he had shot his bolt. He must have been an old man by now, but the last news we have of him shows him still running true to form; in his captivity he is employed in forging letters designed to procure his release and re-habilitation.[71]

Two more members of this curious *demi-monde* of religion became known to the pilgrims of 1483, in the persons of Taghribirdi's wives; and of the elder of these Friar Paul and Friar Felix each paint an equally striking, though strongly contrasting, picture. To Friar Paul she was a woman wronged; after all that she had done for her husband, he, once turned Moslem, had used the latitude allowed by his new religion to take a second wife, buying from a brothel keeper a girl, hardly more than a child, by birth a Greek Christian.* Soon, all his affection was set upon the fair young creature, and the two of them would make mock of the older, Italian wife. To the Franciscan the injured woman confided her jealousy and unhappiness. "Would that I were in Christendom!" she would cry.

If Paul's account of the lady sounds a tragic note, that of Felix is pure

---

* Fabri (*Evag.* III. p. 25) says that the pilgrims were told that the elder wife had been bought in an Alexandrian brothel, the younger in Greece.

comedy. Though he did not attempt to deny her comeliness, he found this "large masculine and eloquent woman," a totally unsympathetic character. From the first he had cause to disapprove. On the second morning after their arrival, the pilgrims had rigged up a make-shift altar in the upper room inhabited by the second company, and were in the midst of a celebration of Mass when "Lo! Satan entered;" that is to say they were invaded by "the wives of Taghribirdi, bedizened, whore-like, in the style of noble ladies, with an extraordinary high adornment on their heads, set about with jewels and gold;" at their heels their men and maids crowded the doorway. The officiating priest stopped, and there was an embarrassed pause while the pilgrims "muttered together, not knowing what to do," since no one felt bold enough, having regard to the temper of the husband, to turn the ladies out.

The pilgrims' embarrassment was not shared by their visitors. Before anyone else could speak, the elder wife took the floor; she deprecated their perturbation, claimed that she and her fellow-wife were loyal to the Christian faith, "which we have never denied nor ever will deny;" gave a short account of herself and her companion, "unwilling bedfellows of one who had denied Christ," and of the rest of the party, "bought waiting- and serving-maids; these slaves are our eunuchs;" and concluded her oration with the announcement that the two of them wished to attend Mass. "Would it were lawful for us to take eat, and communicate."

The feelings of resentment caused by this intrusion had not time to die away before the second encounter took place between Friar Felix and Taghribirdi's Italian wife. That very morning, the Chief Dragoman, after showing the pilgrims over his "palace," led them, un-shod after the Saracen fashion, into the circular upper chamber where his two ladies sat among their maids.

The elegancies and splendours of Taghribirdi's establishment had greatly impressed the visitors; here was an apartment more sumptuous still, with its windows of coloured glass, marble pavement, and costly rugs spread upon the floor and hung about the walls. The sight was too much for Friar Felix, still, we must suppose, smarting from the late discomfiture of Christian males by such a woman as the Dragoman's chief wife.

"See," he broke out, addressing his host in Latin, "See, here you have your paradise. But what, I ask you, will you receive in the next life?"

It was not Taghribirdi who answered that searching question, but his Italian wife, who, "being of a ready tongue, lifted up her voice."

" 'Truly,' said she, 'both here and there we shall enjoy paradise.' "

At no time would Friar Felix have considered it seemly for a woman to enter into an argument with men; today, after this woman's profession of loyalty to the Christian faith, he found it outrageous that she should make such a claim for the followers of Mahomet, and he told her curtly that what she said was impossible. "She answered back. But," says Felix with hauteur, "I scorned to reply to her volubility."

Shortly before the departure of the pilgrims they were favoured by another visit of Taghribirdi's ladies, the Italian wife having received permission from her friend Friar Paul for herself and the young Greek wife to attend their Mass. So, to pass the word over to Friar Felix, "there came in three Goddesses, Venus, Pallas and Juno, that is to say the two wives of Taghribirdi and a waiting woman got up in superb style. . . ." Friar Paul was gratified by the devotion which the Italian exhibited during the Office, and believed that it was also "to the satisfaction of all the pilgrims," but it is clear that he did not speak for Friar Felix.

It is the Franciscan who writes the postscript to the story of this commanding female personality. Whether impelled by Christian ardour or by jealousy and rancour, the elder wife of Taghribirdi did what the pilgrims had heard so many renegade Christians vow that they would do. Waiting until the absence of her husband gave her the opportunity, she broke into his money chest, helped herself to a thousand ducats, "and secretly and in haste went down the Nile with one maid-servant, and came to Alexandria, and at last with speed sailed for Christendom and . . . was received into the bosom of the Church, and so was saved from the jaws of the devil and of that wicked man."[72]

Note.—The whole question of the Mamluks is full of obscurities and contradictions. Ayalon (*L'Esclavage Mamelouk*, p. 24) gives, as one of the necessary qualifications for becoming a Mamluk ". . . avoir été acheté en bas age." But it seems clear that as a general rule the Mamluks with whom the Western pilgrims became acquainted had been grown men captured in battle by the Turks and sent as slaves to Egypt that they might not escape again to their homes (*Evag.* III, 34–5. Von Harff, 121, 122. Cf. Lane Poole, *Art of the Saracens*, p. 21). Fabri (*loc. cit.*) and Breydenbach (115a), in their account of the Hungarian Mamluk taken prisoner, enslaved and enrolled among the Mamluks, yet allowed to remain a concealed Christian (see above, p. 131 and n.), clearly consider that it was this last fact alone which made him an exception among his companions.

Until the reign of Barqūq, the first of the Circassian Mamluk Sultans, Turkish Mamluks had predominated among a mixed company of nations, and even at the close of Barqūq's reign it was considered good policy by some to keep the army from being swamped by Circassians (Ayalon, *Circassians*, p. 141), so that in 1422 de Lannoy (p. 118) could say that the Mamluks came from " . . . Tartary, Turkey, Bulgaria, Slavonia, Wallachia, Russia, as many from Christian lands as others." (Lannoy, p. 118.) But the process which Barqūq had initiated, of filling the Mamluk ranks from the largely Christian Circassian tribes (Ayalon, *Circassians*, p. 135, 136–7, 139, 140) continued and was accelerated, so that later in the fifteenth century the statement made by so many Christian pilgrims (e.g. *Evag.* III, 92–3; Piloti, 331; Tafur, 74; Suriano, 191; Harff, 92, 121) to the effect that "all Mamluks are renegade Christians," was roughly true.

CHAPTER X

Seeing Cairo

On the morning of October 11, four days after their arrival in Cairo, the pilgrims found the courtyard of Taghribirdi's house crowded with a company of Mamluks in their long white gowns and tall, fringed, red *zamt* hats, each with a stave in hand and curved eastern sword at his side.[1] Among them were men of Sicily and of Spain; there was a German with whose high-born relatives Felix Fabri was well acquainted, and whom the Friar had actually met once in Basel.[2] But, as at Gaza, the majority of the visitors were Hungarians, and these "handsome and dignified men"[3] gravitated naturally to their countryman, the Archdeacon, so that it was the third company among the pilgrims who saw most of the Mamluks.

Next day, when the visitors called again, bringing this time a present of "dates and spiced bread, bunches of grapes and other things of this kind," the Archdeacon and his comrades were just sitting down to dinner. They cordially welcomed in the unexpected guests, and hastened to produce whatever they could for their entertainment, even setting before them their last precious reserve of wine. Then, behind locked doors, the whole party sat down to an hilarious meal, during which the visitors, as they knocked back the forbidden wine, "blasphemed against Mahomet, abused the Saracens, and confessed Christ the Lord..." to the delight of their hosts. Before the party broke up it was arranged that the Mamluks should call next day and take the third company upon a tour of the city.[4]

This was the first of the three conducted expeditions in which Felix Fabri participated during the eleven days which he spent in Cairo; it differed from the others in that it was peculiar to the third company of pilgrims, being a special jaunt for which their Mamluk friends were responsible; the other two excursions were shared by the rest of the party, and both were arranged and one was accompanied by the Chief Dragoman. Unfortunately, the Friar, contrary to his practice in his narratives of sight-seeing in Jerusalem, makes no attempt to relate separately the experiences of this first expedition, but confessedly throws them into his account of "the general perambulation of everything," which took place on the following day,* with the result that on this occasion the whole party of pilgrims is credited with such a feat of sustained touristry as would not disgrace the slickest of modern globe-trotters.

Of only one of the tourist sights of Cairo can we be sure that it was visited during the first expedition by the members of the third company. At this period the Pyramids were out of bounds for pilgrims,† but, as Friar Felix proudly explains, "by the special favour of the Hungarian Mamluks we were taken over the river" and thus were able to see at close quarters those "marvellous ... sepulchral monuments of the ancient Kings of Egypt," the distant view of which from Mount Moqattam must suffice the rest of the pilgrims.[5]

To Friar Felix this near approach was precious. Peering into the low and dark entrance passage, he decided that but for this tunnel "each (pyramid) is a solid mass" and is thus in a position to refute the belief popularised in the pilgrims' "little books," and held even by such an educated man as Friar Paul, that these huge edifices had been designed to hold the prudent hoard of corn which Joseph had counselled his master to prepare against the lean years of famine;[6] this, the view commonly accepted by pilgrims of the Middle Ages, is sometimes embellished by a description of a circular stairway within the building, by which the laden beasts should ascend and through the windows in the walls of which the sacks were emptied, until the granary was full "to the top."[7]

Nearly a hundred years before the visit of Felix Fabri, when there was no embargo upon visits to the Pyramids, the knight Ogier d'Anglure rode out from Cairo in a select party of four, all mounted upon the admired Egyptian donkeys, "clipped, fine and fat," to visit the great monuments. There were, he explains, many pyramids up and down the banks of the Nile, "but where we were, only three, which were pretty near to each other," and these, which we may take to have been the three at Ghizeh, were in the opinion of the Frenchman, "the most marvellous thing which we had yet seen in all our journey." Writing for a public which photography and the printed book had not familiarised with the remarkable appearance of the buildings, he describes the shape as "after the fashion of the point of a diamond, that is to say very wide below, and very sharp above." He not only measured the base of the largest, reckoning each side as "900 paces and more," but tried to give an impression of the monstrous size of the whole mass: when seen from the ground a man standing on top looked no bigger than a cornel berry.

* The accounts of Fabri, Walther and Breydenbach differ both as to the dates of their excursions and the places seen. I have followed Fabri except where otherwise stated.

† As also for Nicolò Martoni in 1394-5, when Sultan Barqūq being absent on his campaign against Timur, there was danger from the Arabs (Martoni, p. 602).

The Frenchman also noted with admiration the construction of the mighty monument, the "huge, big stones well cut . . . " the mere assembling of which was a thing to wonder at;[8] a later visitor remarked, too, how these "hard thick flag-stones" were joined "with marvellous art, without lime,"[9] while Friar Felix recorded the existence upon them of carved inscriptions, "in writing to us unknown," a testimony which is supported by that of other medieval writers, although no trace of the inscriptions now survives.[10]

Von Harff was another visitor who not only measured the base, and estimated the size of the great stone blocks – 6 or 7 feet long, he says – but also picnicked on the top. The ascent took him and his guide three hours,[11] a very generous allowance of time, seeing that the decadent modern is advised that thirty minutes spent on the ascent will be amply sufficient, and will enable him to avoid "the discomfort of arriving breathless and heated at the summit."[12]

Already for a long time the process of despoiling the pyramids of their facing of dressed stone had been proceeding. As Anglure and his party approached the Great Pyramid they heard a sound of masons' mallets at work; then, upon the flank of the pyramid above "we saw the huge stones come down like wine barrels."[13] The stone for the great works of the Mamluk builders was, in fact, largely supplied from these magnificent and royal quarries.[14]

Anglure and his party, at the end of the fourteenth century, and Francesco Suriano a hundred years later, were among those who actually penetrated into the interior of one of the pyramids, and the modern reader may experience one of those pleasurable mental jolts which the conjunctions of history will sometimes produce, at the thought of these contemporaries of Chaucer, or of Henry VII, groping among the remains of that most ancient civilisation, remains with which we have become so familiar, but which were for them all but unheard of, and totally unexplained.

The Frenchman, indeed, did not penetrate far in that visit to the interior, concerning which the modern guide book throws in the curt parenthetical warning ("not recommended"). He entered "a hole right down on the ground* and it is not the height of a man;" it was also "very dark and ill-smelling from the beasts that lived there;"[15] at the end of the nineteenth century the height above ground of the entrance to the Great Pyramid was 48 feet, but the dark tunnel and the strong smell of bats were still the same. Anglure and his friends, discouraged by these conditions, turned

---

* This may have been the entry made by Arab treasure seekers (v. Baedeker, *Lower Egypt*, 1895, p. 146).

about and came out again upon the sunshine of the Egyptian November day.

It is Suriano, the high-born Venetian, once merchant-captain later mendicant friar, who penetrated furthest into the darkness and silence of the Great Pyramid. "You can enter the side," he says, "... by a small door, and then further on there is another door which with difficulty can be entered and (sic) with a light. Then there is a passage that leads to a tomb ... marvellously worked of fine marble ... it stands in a room encased in the finest marble of ancient work, with inscriptions all round. You can go around the tomb." Suriano did not stop at this notable piece of exploration, but entered another pyramid in which he reports "a tomb so stupendous and precious that it amazes the one who sees it both for its work and preciousness and also for the ingenuity and marvellous work of the artificers."[16] He had perhaps penetrated the pyramid and tomb chamber of Menkaura, and, if so, it seems possible that the lid, missing from the stone sarcophagus when the tomb was opened in the nineteenth century, had already been removed, and that the fifteenth-century Venetian gazed upon the gilded and painted coffin crowded with the images of its ancient gods.[17]

When Felix Fabri and his companions turned their backs on the Great Pyramid they came shortly after upon the columnar figure of a woman, prone in the sand. Felix diagnosed it as a representation of the Goddess Isis,[18] and, if he was right, it is likely that the party now stood among the ruins of her shrine, to the south-east of the Great Pyramid, and if so not far from the Sphinx. "... Near to the image of Isis," he continues, "lies a certain formless stone, which they say once bore the likeness of a bull and was an image of Osiris or Apis." This effigy, he explains, was a thing so huge that even the Romans, with their craze for filling Rome with idols of alien gods, found it "unsuitable to take so far across the sea."[19] That is all; and we are left wondering whether Felix Fabri had seen, and been more than ordinarily baffled by the mystery of the Sphinx, or whether he here describes some other ancient relic. Certainly to Suriano the colossal recumbent statue was known as "a wonder of the world," and he described it as "a head of fine marble of such a size that it amazes the looker; it is 60 braccia high; its ears are five braccia long and the eagles build their nests in them...."[20] About twenty years later another Italian saw this enormous head of a woman and remarked that "the nose has fallen off because of age."[21]

Upon the day which followed the expedition of the third company with their Hungarian friends, the Chief Dragoman left his house in the first light of dawn, and returned soon after with two Mamluks, of whom the German Seefogel was one, and a sufficient number of donkeys for the party; these were handsome beasts and gaily harnessed,[22] not impossibly in the same fashion as the "excellent asses" upon which nineteenth-century Cairenes would ride, with the stuffed saddle covered in front with red leather, and behind "with a kind of soft woollen lace ... of red, yellow and other colours."[23]*

It was still early when the pilgrims set out upon this "complete circuit of the city"[24] with the German Mamluk at the head and the other at the rear of the procession. The cavalcade started off in a roughly northerly direction,[25] at first among crowded streets, and through one of those gates "of iron, huge and very old," which divided the various quarters of Cairo. After passing through the Tartar slave-market the party reached an old stone bridge across what Felix calls "a branch of the Nile which cuts through the middle of the town," probably the "Khalig" (Canal) of Cairo. Here, obeying the common human inclination to halt upon bridges and look down at the water, the pilgrims paused awhile, and it was during this pause that Friar Felix experienced one of those moments of illumination peculiar to the historically-minded tourist. Some wretched-looking fellows were busy mixing the sticky Nile mud with straw, and fashioning it into the bricks of which all the buildings in Cairo, with the exception of such great edifices as mosques, palaces and the like, were constructed. There was, however, no thought of fifteenth-century Cairo in the Friar's mind as he watched; rather he was "delighted to see those poor men stand thus at work," because just so, and to produce just such bricks, had the Children of Israel laboured for Pharaoh.[26]

From the bridge the pilgrims passed through a new suburb, which, their guides told them, had taken the place of an ill-famed neighbourhood, an area of swamp and scrub. Though all this was gone something of the unchancy character of the place remained in a "large and beautiful house" on the bank of the Nile, inhabited, so the pilgrims heard, by "the lady Nymphs" who resorted there by night and were somewhat rowdy tenants, though they had the merit of paying their rent regularly.[27]†

Soon the pilgrims found themselves at one of the busy quays on the

* Though we have three accounts of this excursion, and, in addition, one of those sketch maps (see over) which Friar Paul provides for his readers (Walther, pp. 228-9) the route taken by the pilgrims is difficult to identify, as, until that part of their tour which brought them to the Coptic settlement of Babylon, or Old Cairo, none of the pilgrims mention by name any landmarks, other than the Tartar slave-market and the river. The account of this expedition is drawn from the *Evagatorium*, III, 37-42 and 49-70 unless otherwise indicated.

† In the Friar's German version of his book his description of this house suggests the presence of a fifteenth-century poltergeist.

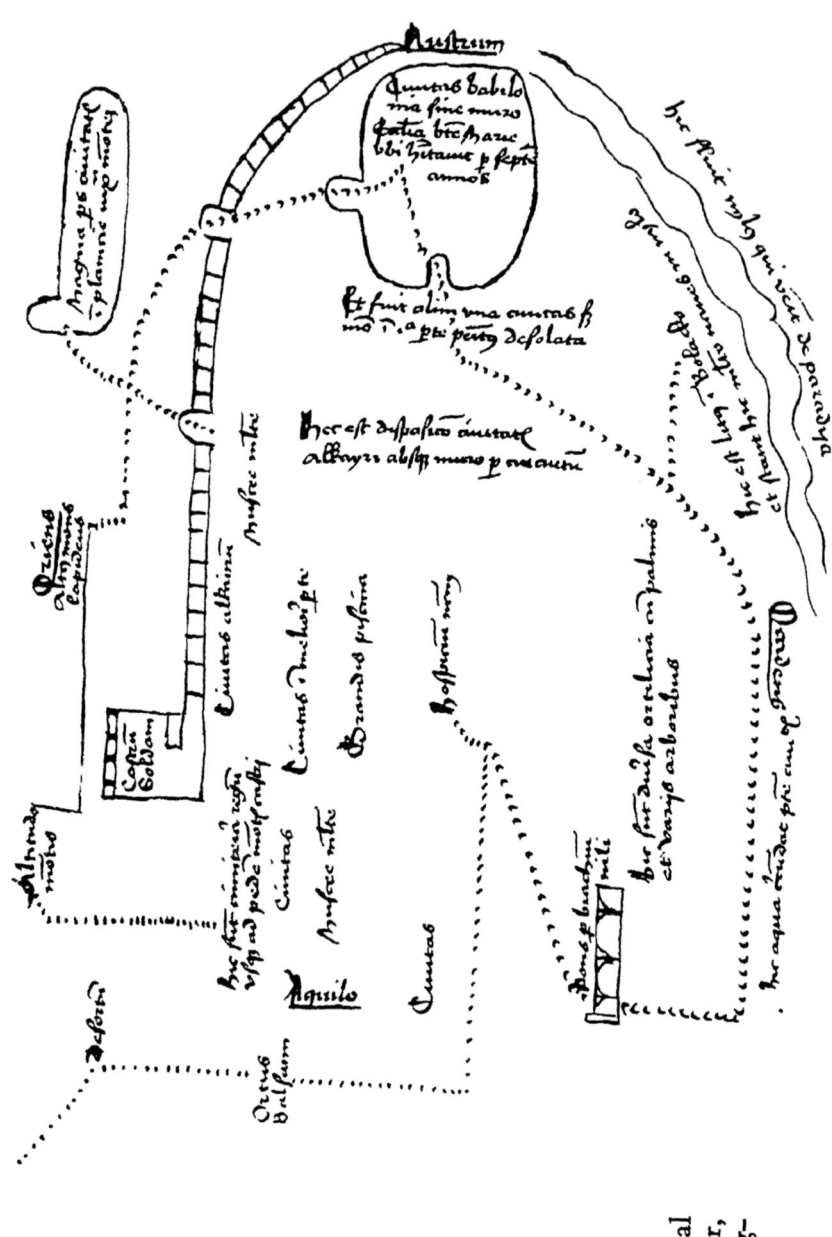

Plan of Cairo, from the original by Paul Walther, 1492, at Neuberg-on-the-Donau.

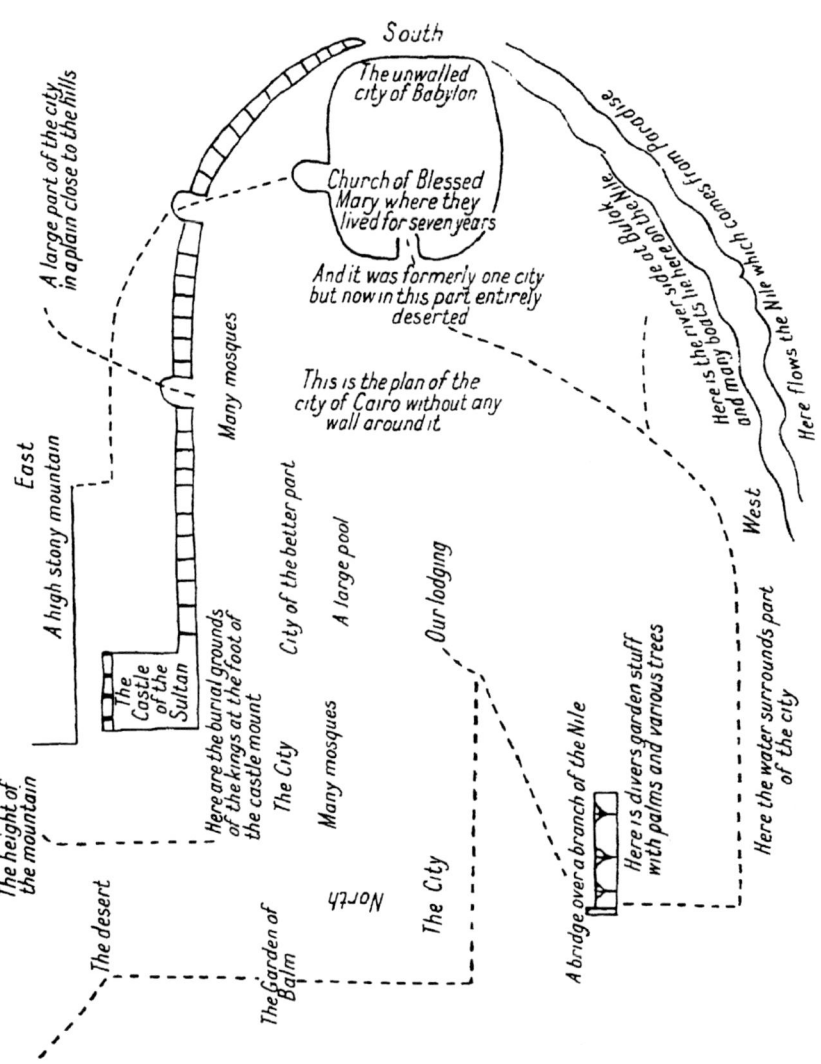

Nile. Big boats, from as far down the river as Alexandria,[28] here discharged their lading of food or other merchandise for the capital. The vessels lay crowded close together, painted with coloured patterns, their long high prows jutting inland over the edge of the quay,[29] very likely much the same in appearance as those which had moored along the quays of ancient Egypt, and those too which, in the 1830's, Laborde saw at Suez, with their long prows and high poops curving up from the waterline.[30]

The riverside wharf was full of bustle and interest for the pilgrims. Trains of camels came and went, bearing the big waterskins for the sprinkling of the dusty Cairo streets; a crowd of men was bargaining close to the boats; here, or a little further up the river, there was a market for corn, fruit and poultry, and the visitors saw for the first time one of those prodigious flocks of hens which in Egypt were driven along "as if they were geese, six hundred at a time."[31]

The whole business of the production and management of domestic poultry in Egypt ran the pyramids themselves close in the fascination it possessed for western visitors. The pilgrims were at this moment making for the village of New Babylon which lay to the south of the city and a little inland from the river. Here the fortifications of a Roman castle sheltered a population of Coptic Christians, and the pilgrims, for the first time since leaving Jerusalem, were intending to visit a round of churches. But on the way to New Babylon[32] there was one of those establishments where the people of the land "with marvellous art" incubated eggs without the assistance of a broody hen, and the pilgrims demanded that they should take this in passing. They were, however, out of luck. In any case it was too late in the season for the "chicken ovens" to be at work, and as the party approached the "long low building" it was met by an old Moslem who announced that his master was away and that therefore nothing could be seen.[33]*

But whether western writers saw with their own eyes the incubators at work, or drew their information from books, few omit to describe the amazing phenomenon. During the early summer months country-women would bring their eggs to the ovens "as they take their dough to

---

* With regard to the incubators there is a discrepancy between the accounts of Fabri and Walther. The first (*Evag.* III, pp. 57–8) speaks as if the pilgrims actually saw one of these, and places the visit after his description of the Roman column (see below, p. 149). It is possible that he had, in fact, visited a chicken oven with the Hungarian Mamluks, and that the members of the third company were "those among our company who, ranging round the city," did, according to Breydenbach (f. 118a), see this interesting sight; but part of his description of the process is confessedly drawn from Vincent of Beauvais, and he echoes, without acknowledgment, Ludolf von Suchem's "*domus dimisse et basse*" with "*domus bassa et dimissa.*" I have therefore followed Paul Walther's more circumstantial account.

the bake-house," says Friar Felix;[34] "good eggs" Friar Paul interjects;[35] eggs "as fresh as they can find in all the land," Piloti, the merchant, insists.[36] The oven was a construction of two storeys; in the upper the eggs were deposited "in little holes like round cups," and covered well with dung; according to some, with straw. On the ground-floor was the furnace, in which "a gentle and regulated fire" was maintained, "so that the fire, the hot dung, and the hot air of the country working together, turn the eggs into chickens. . . ." Such was the process according to most of the pilgrim accounts,[37] and it is much the same as that described by Lane in the nineteenth century. Emmanuele Piloti, however, so long a resident in the country that he if any must have seen what he described, records what was perhaps a variant of this method. Having compared the construction of the chicken oven to "our furnaces where we bake jars and bowls and earthenware pots" he goes on to say that dung is placed both over the eggs and in the chamber below, "in the place where we put the fire." This was closed by a small iron door, pierced by one round hole; through this hole a lance was thrust, "and all the time they keep on stirring the dung both day and night and never rest."[38] At the end of a period, estimated variously at anything between twelve days and three weeks, the chickens hatched out, and at once, if we are to believe the parson of Suchem, the chicks were handed over to the care of an old woman who "nurses and cherishes them in her bosom;" or, if we prefer the more sober narrative of Piloti, "then they cry on high, all round about 'A hatchery of chicks is ready and will be emptied tomorrow.'"[39]

Their unusual entry into the world was not the only thing by which the Egyptian hen engaged the earnest interest of Western pilgrims. The whole conduct of her life provided matter for wonder. The sale of young birds was a thing worthy of remark, since the quantity was assessed neither by weight nor number but by volume. The birds, says von Harff, were crammed into a measure, "the merchant . . . pressing them in with both hands as if he were selling wheat, one had its head in the air, another a leg, another two legs, another a wing, so that one [buyer] got twenty for his measure and another twenty-four."[40] The measure "which is like half-a-bushel," had no bottom; when it "is full of chicks they lift it, and the chicks remain."[41]

So successful was the Egyptian method of incubation that hens were "like the sands of the sea for number," and in the country they could be seen grazing in flocks like sheep.[42] They were brought to market in the same huge throngs; Paul Walther had guessed six hundred as the number of those the pilgrims saw at the riverside; Ludolph of Suchem multiplied his figure by ten, and added to the moving tide of poultry a camel with panniers to take the eggs which were laid on the way to market.⁴³ Such migrations were remarkable enough along country roads, but Emmanuele Piloti describes the passage of the hens through the busy streets of Cairo where "there will be, on a sudden, a great crowd of men and beasts, and the hen-herd will loose all the [birds], and see not one left; yet the said herd does not move till the crowd has passed by, and then he finds the hens at the road-side, and they all go back to the middle of the road, where they were at first, in such a manner and fashion that he does not lose one." This display of road-sense, the observer justly remarks, "is a pretty thing," and one of which in all his years of residence in Egypt he did not tire. "I, for my pleasure," he says, "have often gone to watch the said herds when they are going by."⁴⁴

It is left to Friar Felix to cap all these stories. The Egyptian chicks, he observes, hatched out by man's device, learn to follow man as an ordinary brood will follow the hen. Therefore the hen-herd will precede his flock, bearing in his hand a long feather broom, with which he sweeps the dust of the road," and as the dust is stirred, up run the hens and the cocks, the little and the big, looking for corn, and so they follow him . . ." Felix is careful to add that "though this may sound like a story, nevertheless thus it is done."⁴⁵

Arrived at New Babylon the pilgrims visited first that church, the crypt of which was traditionally occupied by the Holy Family while in Egypt.* It came almost as a surprise to them, says Felix, to find themselves once more in a Christian church, among the "altars, paintings and pictures with representations of the Passion of Christ and of the Blessed Virgin, with crosses and a baptistry as well. . . ." They took out their Processionals and made a tour of the building, visiting the crypt, and noticing near the altar in the upper church, "a great deep hole, like a big tomb, full of water," – the well, in fact, still existing in the church, from which they were told St. Joseph drew water "for washing the Child Jesus, for cooking and for drinking."⁴⁶

Babylon in fact was full of churches, great and small. Not all were open, but the pilgrims were able to investigate three, "note-worthy and fair," and each containing the carved marble tomb of a Saint. It was regrettable that the Eastern Christians "do not know how to pronounce Latin well, but speak in an extraordinary swallowing fashion" (*mirabili stomachatione loquuntur*) so that the pilgrims could not always be sure to

---

* Felix says (*Evag.* III, pp. 49–51) that the Church was dedicated to the Blessed Virgin. Baedeker (*Lower Egypt*, 1895, p. 83) gives Abu Sargia (St. Sergius) as the patron saint of the church thus connected with the Holy Family.

whom they paid their respects, though they believed that they caught the names of St. Anne, St. Barbara, St. Katherine and St. George.[47] In the church dedicated to the last of these Saints Christian pilgrims of family were customarily knighted by its "Bishop". This dignitary being absent the knights gave each other the accolade while the Mamluk guides looked on;[48] such superimposed knighthoods as that received here, in Cyprus and at Jerusalem constituted part of the *cachet* of a gentleman's pilgrimage.

But this oasis of Christianity was of small extent, and was surrounded by the overwhelming relics of paganism and antiquity. The pilgrims had passed into Babylon beneath the gateway arch "faced with polished marble, high, great and ancient,"[49] of the Roman fortress within whose walls the houses and tiny churches of the Copts now sheltered. When the pilgrims left Babylon behind them they made their way among ruins of "most ancient and massive walls of carved and squared stone," to which now clung the wretched habitations of the poor. They were probably passing through the sites of the first splendid Arab capital, Misr-el-Fustat, the Town of the Tent; but in a courtyard they came upon another relic of the Roman Empire. A circular monolithic column "of prodigious height and amazing size" rose above the surrounding slums; a small distance away stood a similar monument. Down the whole length of the column were carved "large Latin letters in such a way", Friar Felix explains, "that one letter stood on the head of another, and the first stood under the Capital of the column, and the second under that . . ." a laboured description which Friar Paul effectively avoids by giving a diagram. Owing to their age the letters were difficult to read, but "it seemed to us that their meaning was 'Jovinianus Augustus.'" This ability to interpret the inscription moved the tactful guides to astonishment and admiration; "never," they exclaimed, "had they met a man who understood them."

Before the party moved on the Mamluks told a number of stories, vouched for by the inevitably gathering crowd of locals, of a mysterious tremor which affected one of the columns; of a tomb chamber, inaccessible to the boldest climber, on top; of a subterranean passage; of buried treasure. All these Friar Felix retails with the covering remark, "whether they are true I do not know," and warns his readers that Eastern peoples are prone to credulity. He has repeated the tales, he declares, in order to amuse the Brethren at home, and having thus asserted his own immunity, he proceeds to revel in stories of tremulous or weeping pillars, giants, caverns and hidden gold. All of these he admits belong to the world of fantasy, yet—and he suddenly abandons his pretence of superiority—yet these ruins of old time do exist, and where such mighty monuments remain something marvellous may well lie underground; his own guess is a labyrinth.[50] We may smile at his childishness, but the little crowd of hot and hairy Germans who gazed up at the column stood in the sunshine and upon the soil of Egypt of the Pharaohs, where, if anywhere on earth, stories of buried treasure came by legitimate descent from a truth greater and more astonishing than any tale of their Mamluk guides.

Through the tumbled ruins of earlier Arab suburbs the pilgrims continued in a north-easterly direction; passing under the arches of the aqueduct, traditionally the work of Saladin, and still supplying the Sultan's castle, they took advantage of a trickle of water which flowed through a joint in the masonry to have a drink; sight-seeing in the heat is thirsty work and Friar Felix found this grateful draught worthy of record.[51]

Beyond the aqueduct they were faced by the walls and towers of the castle and the stately palaces which the walls enclosed, all seen across the wide space of the Mamluk parade ground. Here the attention of the pilgrims was drawn not only to the manoeuvres of a detachment of horse and foot, but also to the Sultan's pigeon cotes, where the birds of the official pigeon post were housed.* Friar Felix, like most pilgrim writers, was keenly interested in this ingenious means of communication, the use of which was the prerogative of the Sultan, who never set out on journey, campaign, or even hunting expedition, without carrying with him a supply of these trained messengers.[62] Unfortunately the Friar aims, in his treatment of the subject, less at imparting information than at a display of erudition; he quotes from this or that author, running through the history of the birds—dove or pigeon is all one to him—connected with Venus, Mahomet and Semiramis, and concludes with the assertion that "such was not that dove which descended upon Christ at baptism."[53]

It is Schiltberger, the escaped slave, who with better opportunities than the tourist-pilgrims, and no classical learning to display, tells us how the postal pigeons were trained. The first step was to put in a cage together a cock and hen, and to add sugar to their food. After a suitable period the cock was removed, marked with its home address and caged separately. But not only was it thus segregated from female society; its sugar ration was also stopped, in order that, under the compulsion of two strong instincts, the bird "may wish to return as soon as possible to the place where he was before, and where he was trained."[54]

The pilgrims were not, on this day's excursion, to visit the Castle of the Sultan, but leaving it on their left hand addressed themselves to the

* Casanova (*Histoire . . . de la Citadelle du Caire*, p. 595) says that the pigeons were kept in towers within the citadel.

steep climb up the side of Mount Moqattam, which is still *de rigueur* for tourists, and from which every visitor still sees as our pilgrims saw, "the whole great city of Cairo . . . and the course of the river Nile, the land of Upper and Lower Egypt and the Sultan's Citadel," with the Pyramids and the Western Desert beyond.[55] Unfortunately this superb prospect was suddenly obscured by one of the unpleasant dust-storms of Cairo, which still blew in their teeth during their descent of the hill by a path so steep that even the sure-footed donkeys must be led by the bridle.

The long morning of sight-seeing was concluded by a visit to the *medresa* or college of Qa'it Bey, and his tomb-mosque, which had been completed about fifteen years before in preparation for the death of the still-reigning Sultan. There was, says Felix, "a great court . . . a large and rich mosque with a high tower, and beside it an oblong building with separate cells, as though it were a monastery for Religious. . . . We saw through the doorway of the mosque many hanging lamps burning and very beautiful buildings after their fashion." That is all which he has to say, while Paul Walther and Breydenbach are completely silent* concerning this magnificent product of the accomplished and intricate art of Mamluk Cairo. Here is no word of the carvings in ebony and ivory, the inlay of mother-of-pearl, the vessels of brass, copper or bronze inlaid with silver, nor even of those "plants, roses and flowers" which graced the serene spaces of the mosques of Islam.[56] Perhaps the art was too strange, or the religious associations too inimical for any conscious aesthetic enjoyment. Felix himself was disturbed in mind by the presence of those "priests" who lived in the *medresa*, "day and night hymning and singing in the mosque and howling in the towers. They howled unusually loudly while we were there, praising Mahomet, and perhaps cursing us." Yet what the pilgrims saw held them long enough to draw upon them the unfavourable attention of "a very old and angry mosque official," who rebuked the accompanying Mamluks for introducing unbelievers into the mosque, though a small gratuity pacified the venerable purist.[57]

The return through the crowded streets was an occasion of great discomfort and some risk to certain of the pilgrims. While the Mamluk guides in front clove a path through the throng by dint of blows, the justly irritated passers-by took it out of those at the tail of the procession. What with the long morning's sight-seeing, and this last trial of nerve and temper, it was a weary party which reached their lodging to "recuperate ourselves with food, drink and repose."[58]

The pilgrims of 1483 were not in the way of getting so much as a

---

* Perhaps because this visit actually took place upon the expedition peculiar to the third company.

glimpse of the daily life of the Mamluk Court or even of its public shows and pageantry. The hawking and hunting days of the old Sultan, when with a huge concourse of horsemen he went out with his falcons and hunting leopards, were over; the annual season for polo would have ended several months before with its usual banquet;[59] the royal parties of pleasure at the pyramids, with flags flying above, and music and banqueting at the foot of the ancient tombs,[60] were quite beyond the experience of a company of unimportant Western visitors.

Some of our pilgrim writers did indeed penetrate the palaces which lay within the walls of the Citadel, and met the ruling Sultan face to face. Tafur, employed by Janus III of Cyprus to bring the yearly tribute of the Kingdom to Bars Bey, had been received with the pomp proper for such a ceremony. Having entered the Citadel he was led to the large and sumptuous tent where the Sultan would dine. After a suitable interval a door opened and the Sultan rode into the courtyard. His black horse was shod with gold and trapped with white damask bordered with pearls, the bridle and saddle shone with gold, and in the saddle-bow was a ruby "which looked as large as a good-sized orange." According to custom the Spaniard received, on leaving, the ceremonial gift of a robe "of olive green and red, worked with gold and lined with ermine,"—a handsome garment, and presumably one of the carefully graded "robes of honour" customarily bestowed by the Sultan, but it was "an emblem of vassel-age."[61]

Even when the Mamluk Sultan received an embassy from rulers who were not, like the later kings of Cyprus, his tributaries, forms of great abasement were demanded of the envoys. The French ambassadors of 1512 approached the audience chamber through two courtyards; in the first 500 Mamluks were drawn up in rank, in long white robes and turbans of green and black; in the second stood 1,000 more of higher degree and richer garb.[62] Before the presence was reached the envoys must halt before seven successive curtains, and while these were drawn aside must bow and kiss the ground;* face to face with the Sultan in his jewelled robes the ambassadors must kneel and kiss his hand, but the Moslem potentate would protect this from the touch of Christian lips by withdrawing it into his sleeve.[63]

Of the beauties of the palaces and gardens within the fortifications of the Citadel, even those few of our pilgrims who entered them have little to say. Von Harff, having been commanded to appear before the son of Qa'it Bey, and having expended during the audience a good deal of tact

---

* Bars Bey permitted that the ground should be touched by a hand, which was then kissed. (Schiltberger, M.191-2.)

and some hard lying in order to produce acceptable answers to questions upon European politics, was shown a number of the palace apartments,[64] but of the "marble and gilded mosaics," the "panelling illuminated by a thousand colours," the ceilings "picked out with gold and azure," the windows "of Cyprus glass coloured like the precious stones set in the vaulting"[65] he says nothing at all; even the private chamber of the Sultan he dismisses in two words, as "exquisitely adorned."

It is perhaps only to be expected that the fullest description of the mingled delicacy and opulence of the oriental palace comes to us from a Venetian, that is to say one born in a city whose art had many and close affiliations with that of the East. Trevisano, at Cairo in 1512, could appreciate the carved, gilded and inlaid ceilings, the costly rugs which lay upon the pavements, the intricate mosaics of marble, porphyry and serpentine, more beautiful, he considered, than those in the Hall of Audience at Venice. The rooms thus decorated looked out, through grilles of bronze instead of iron, upon small delicious gardens. One was planted with orange trees; in another stood "an open kiosk raised upon columns and covered with green plants," while from every column hung a cage containing a singing bird, and rich hangings gave shade from the sun's heat. Even the State Apartments opened upon delightful prospects of cool waters and green leaves; the spray of a fountain outside fell almost to the windows, and the basin, with its many jets of water, was surrounded by orange trees which pleasantly tempered the light in the room within.[66]

Though Felix Fabri and his companions could hope for no such admission to the palace they were determined to get a sight of Mamluk Sultan. During their excursion round about the city they had tried to persuade the German Mamluk, Seefogel, and his companion, to take them to the Citadel, but the two had refused, and continued to refuse even when the mention of ducats crept into the conversation; Qa'it Bey did not, they said, "love the Franks as his predecessor had done."[67] Yet when the pilgrims took up the matter with the Chief Dragoman he consented to bring them into the Sultan's presence.

On the day following their extended tour of the city,[68] Taghribirdi therefore led them to the palace, not indeed to have speech with the Sultan; perhaps only to attend one of the regular sessions of justice which were customarily held two or three times a week in one of the courts of the Citadel.[69] The pilgrims, having passed through a succession of iron-bound gates, found themselves standing in a crowd, while the Chief Dragoman left them to approach more nearly the high dais, covered with fine carpets and shaded by a tent of rare and costly materials. Here, cross-legged, sat the Sultan, an unusually tall old man of seventy-three, white-gowned, his slightly yellow-complexioned face of the Arab type, with a profile of "distinguished delicacy,"[70] surrounded by a group of dignified officials. Our pilgrims were allowed to drink in the spectacle for close on an hour before Taghribirdi came to lead them away. Fatigued as they still found themselves by their efforts of the previous day, they halted on the way back to Taghribirdi's house only to watch some Mamluks bargaining for horses in the market just outside the Citadel. Dinner, a visit to the hot baths and some shop-gazing filled agreeably the remainder of the day.[71]

CHAPTER XI

Cairo, the passing show

Though these three excursions represented the sum total of the pilgrims' regular sight-seeing in Cairo, they furnished by no means the whole, and perhaps not even the greater part of their impressions of the city, for the daily life of the great capital was in itself as a continuous spectacle. To this part of their common experience the reaction of our two priestly Chroniclers, Felix Fabri and Paul Walther, provides a significant contrast. The outlook of the Franciscan upon Cairo and all it contained was one of obdurate disapproval; he was, emphatically, not amused by the sight of the teeming alien life around him. If, with a few companions, he went abroad in the streets to do some shopping, he saw "nothing rare;" if he stayed indoors "nothing new, nothing marvellous, worthy (of note)" offered itself to his jaundiced eye during the long day.[1]

For Felix Fabri it was otherwise. With regard to the manifestations of Moslem religion, disgust and unwilling admiration, reprobation and respect flickered across his mind in rapid alternation. He records, incorrectly, the various calls of the muezzin, the different types of Moslem priest and their duties; he has a word to say about Moslem saints, "for they have their saints as we do," but, he is careful to point out, Christians must realise that it is the power of the devil which enables these infidels to achieve their all too impressive austerities.[2] He speaks with high praise of Moslem women, who, he thinks, must follow the precepts of their saints, commending their great decorum and propriety in dress, and their habit of going veiled; they are, he sums up, "in all externals so modest that our women cannot be compared to them."[3] And if on occasion he gibes at Moslem superstition, and even at Moslem devotion, he tells one anecdote in which there is nothing acid, nothing ungenerous, but only the recognition, by one man of good will, of the light of sanctity in the face of another. When the pilgrims were travelling down the Nile from Cairo to Alexandria, Felix noted a certain Saracen who like themselves had gone on board at Cairo. He guessed the man to be "a *Czamutlar*,* a holy man who keeps perpetual silence:" he knew him at first sight for

---

* Fabri's attempt to render the Arabic word samit-lar, the silent people. I am indebted to Professor Kahle for this translation.

one "of so great, and if it is not wrong to say it, of so spiritual a discipline as could nowhere be found among the Religious of Christendom, and it was as if the holiness of the man shone in his countenance. I would," the Friar adds, "have been glad to speak with him if I had known his language."⁴ Like Emmanuele Piloti, Friar Felix could discern that Christian and Saracen, "we are all God's creatures."⁵

Among all others one overwhelming impression was made by Cairo upon every Western visitor – the impression of size. "The biggest city of our time," says one, "in all the world ... two German miles long ... and in breadth three Italian miles,"⁶* and this was after the reduction in size resulting from one of its great plagues. Before that disaster another pilgrim was told by Christian merchants that the city stretched for fifteen miles one way, and five the other.⁷ Von Harff recorded a different estimate; he heard that the circumference of the city measured thirty-six Italian miles.⁸ Friar Felix, true to his habit of putting down whatever information came his way, and leaving the reader to sort it out, gives a variety of measurements. The city, as it stood, covered, with its buildings and open spaces, an area three German miles long by one and a half wide, and this included neither the Mamluk tombs nor the Castle of the Sultan, which in themselves he reckons to be equal in extent to almost the whole town of Ulm. Or he attacks the problem from a mathematical angle. If, as he had read in a book at Cologne, Cairo is seven times the size of Paris, and if Paris is three times the size of Cologne, and Cologne three, if not four, times the size of Ulm, then eighty-four Ulms could stand within the walls of Cairo, if, he adds, Cairo had walls. Or, coming down to the homely and familiar, he tells his readers that the length of the city was as great as the distance from Ulm to Memmingen along the Iller valley.⁹

De Lannoy, the soldier, made no attempt to play at this game of astonishing his readers. Clearly and succinctly as always, he remarks that this, "the master city of Egypt," comprised not only the original city, but had spread out to, and now included, the villages of Bulak and Babylon (or old Cairo), about three miles off.¹⁰ Occasionally a pilgrim with an unusually inquiring mind would attempt his own assessment. One of the German knights among Felix's companions sent a servant with orders to pace out the length and breadth of the city; the result, which was disappointingly small,† caused Paul Walther to look with suspicion upon the inflated figures commonly given.¹¹ Friar Paul himself, with something of the same spirit of cold inquiry, had, when on Mount

---

* That is, rather more than eight miles long, and about three-and-a-half miles in breadth.
† 16,000 paces by 864.

Moqattam, "silently counted to myself the towers of the mosques" and had not apparently reached anything like the commonly reported total of sixty thousand.[12]

Estimates of the population of Cairo offered a field for computations of almost astronomical magnitude and elaboration. A common method, not so much of assessment as of suggestion, was to mention the phenomenal number dead in the last plague. This figure, very variously given, was said to have alarmed the Sultan, but he, like the pilgrim writers, was easily persuaded that the number of survivors was far greater.[13] The sum could also be stated in more cheerful terms. "I have given you," a pilgrim reminds his readers, "the certain number of persons who can be counted, such as 24,000 cooks, 48,000 bread bakers, and 30,000 who bring water ... daily for the people to drink. Now reckon how many people there must be to eat and drink all this, and yet," he adds, "this total will not include the Mamluks and their servants."[14] Retreating from such high altitudes of calculation we may fall back upon the startled exclamation of a Frenchman, who found the city "marvellously populated by Saracens, and there are so many people that no one who had not seen could believe it,"[15] or on Breydenbach's remark that Cairo was as crowded as Rome in a Jubilee Year,[16] or simpler still, and perhaps more expressive than any, another Frenchman's statement: that one can hardly go four steps in the roads without knocking against someone."[17]

An ecclesiastic might believe and roundly state that this vast capital of a military Empire was "without any walls at all,"[18] but a soldier's practised eye noted that there were walls in certain places, but that "in the greater part you see neither gates nor walls, for joining onto the walls there are everywhere houses and buildings, and in the ditches and elsewhere, like faubourgs, so that it does not seem to be walled; yet there is no way right into the city but by the gates, and these are shut at night."[19] Our pilgrims, if they failed to notice these outer gates, were impressed by those which divided quarter from quarter within the city, a prodigious number of them, Felix Fabri heard, "with bars, locks and chains," and these also were shut at night, whether to control the people, or, with more probability, "in case of disturbance from Mamluks."[20]

Even medieval European visitors considered, and even the inhabitants of Cairo admitted, that the multitudinous streets of the city—by pilgrim tradition they numbered 24,000—were excessively narrow.[21] On each side rose the tall houses, rarely of stone, commonly of mud brick in the lower storey, with those constructions of mud and wattle above which to Western visitors gave the buildings a look of poverty.[22] This use of Nile mud might have been disastrous, Friar Felix thought, for, "if it happened to rain in Cairo for two days as it goes on sometimes for six with us, the whole city would melt like wax, and become a heap of mud . . . ;"[23] as, however, according to modern statistics the annual rainfall of Cairo is 1 inch, the danger was not great. Flat roofed, so that they looked, Friar Paul thought, as if ruined and roofless,[24] the oriental houses turned a blank face upon the street, and kept their comforts and their beauties for those who entered.* Open upon the upper storeys to admit air, shaded from the sun by high wooden shutters† or awnings from noon to sunset, supplied with ingenious contrivances above the roof to induce into the house a current of air from the wind which blew for ten months in the year, the Cairene house was cool even in the summer heat,[25] and the flat roofs which Paul Walther despised provided a place where members of the household slept at night.[26]

Our pilgrims of 1483, though they must have known the interior of other houses, describe only that of Taghribirdi, which, in conformity with the usual oriental plan, was built about a central courtyard. Like almost every house of any pretensions the rooms were decorated with mosaic of marble "of all colours mixed together and worked with histories and flowers, so that," said von Harff, who stayed there a dozen years or so later than our pilgrims "you can see yourself reflected in the pavement."[27] Paintings, marbles and polished plaster adorned the large chamber where Felix Fabri and his companions spent their first night in Cairo, and the living apartments of the master were more splendid still. The harem, according to universal Moslem custom, was upon an upper floor, and here the pilgrims were presented to Taghribirdi's two wives as they sat at their needlework, in a room lit from every side by windows of coloured glass; this introduction of male strangers into the women's quarters was, of course, flat against the custom of the East, but natural enough considering the history of the Chief Dragoman and his family. Friar Felix explicitly calls the apartment "a bed-chamber,"[28] but whether this implies that the Dragoman retained the western habit of sleeping in a bed we do not know; in the ordinary Cairene house men slept at night, as during the daytime they sat cross-legged, upon those "exquisite carpets or cloths worked with silk," the number of which at

---

* Few among the pilgrims praised the architecture of Cairo; Ogier d'Anglure (pp. 59–60) admired the "very large and fine houses . . . well built in wood, stone or some material like plaster" and rated the city as "better built than any other we saw anywhere. . . ." He also noticed the grandeur of the mosque doorways. Nicolò Martoni (p. 595) was charmed by the river-side houses, with their gazebos, glass windows and pleasant gardens, as attractive, he considered, as the houses on the sea front at Naples, though not so large.

† Perhaps not unlike the latticed *meshrebiyas* which survived in old Cairene houses into the nineteenth century (Lane Poole, *Cairo, Sketches*, p. 130).

bedtime was indicative of what modern officialdom terms "the income group" of the owner, for "the richer a man is the more he has under him."[29]

Above the roof-level of Taghribirdi's house rose the round tower in which the harem was situated, terminating in a cupola of lead and topped with the Crescent of Islam. Elsewhere at roof-level there was some sort of gazebo,* such as those which Martoni admired, giving a fine view over the city. To this point of vantage Taghribirdi led his guests one night soon after their arrival, so that they might look out over Cairo, astir with all the animated life of a night in Ramadan,[30] when every cook-shop stood open through the hours of darkness and at intervals the "priest" (actually one of the *Musahhirs*) would go through the crowded streets, beating his little drum.[31] It was not, however, all this noise and stir which chiefly engaged the pilgrims' attention, but "the multitude of lamps burning in the towers, which made the city seem one flame." From the topmost storey of each tall minaret of all the mosques of Cairo rods were thrust out, and from these hung lamps, "cunningly devised with a cover on top lest the wind should put out the light," so that high above every mosque as many as twenty, forty, even sixty lamps were burning,[32] while below not only the interior of the mosques, but also the streets shone with lamp- and torch-light,[33] for every fourth or fifth house would have a lantern hanging out above the doorway.[34] Even indoors lights burnt all night,[35] and this profusion of lamps, and the consequent expenditure of oil and wax, for no animal fat was used,[36] was a matter of standing amazement to the Western pilgrims, so that a Frenchman reckoned that "as much oil is burnt as they drink wine at Orleans," and it was the declared opinion of "experienced Christians who saw it" that "no king in Christendom whether of here or there, could pay out of his revenue for the oil which in this city is burned in the lamps!"[37] The nightly illumination, so extraordinary to men of Western Europe, had an irresistible fascination for Felix Fabri, and again and again after this first visit he would climb to the gazebo, to hear the cry of the *muezzin*, to see the great crowd moving about in the streets, and to stare, with a delightful shudder, "at the sight of those too many lamps."[38]

During the daytime, still without going beyond the house, there was much to interest and amuse the visitors. Tame doves "which are as white as snow and whiter, if it could be so, with red beaks and feet," built their nests and hatched their young in the windows of Cairene houses, "and really," an Italian exclaimed, "they are a charming sight."[39]

* Fabri calls this an "*altana.*" Martoni speaks of houses "*cum gaysis*" (Ed. "*ancien mot napolitain qui signifie loggia ou balcon.*") Cf. *Oxford English Dictionary*, s.v. gazebo.

But as well as these pretty visitants every great establishment in Cairo included other animals of greater value and rarity. Taghribirdi's stable contained upwards of fifty superb horses, whose saddlery was overlaid with plates of silver-gilt, and their bridles and head-stalls studded with silver. In and around the courtyard the Chief Dragoman kept, after the contemporary Egyptian fashion, a selection of birds and animals, tame or savage.[40] In one corner a fierce leopard was chained up, "a dreadful animal to look at" with a head and throat like a lion and reddish hair with black spots...."[41] There was a caged civet cat, and the Dragoman, not, one feels, without intention, demonstrated to the German knights the method of extracting that substance "of the sweetest scent, like musk, but more precious than musk," being in fact worth its weight in gold, and at once had them clamouring to buy.[42] In a railed enclosure there were three ostriches, creatures whose footmarks in the desert were well known to all the pilgrims, and their natural history to the learned among the party. Felix corrected Vincent of Beauvais' estimate of their size; the body of the bird might be as big as that of a sheep, but hardly as that of a donkey. He was ready, however, to accept Master Vincent's word for its habits— how raising those little wings with "feathers like wool," it would run more swiftly than any horse, at the same time contriving to cast stones backwards at its pursuers"; how it would lay its eggs only when "raising its eyes to the ... stars," it could see the Pleiades; how these eggs were incubated by the heat of the sun; or even, perhaps, by the bird's concentrated and powerful stare alone.[43] In a number of pendent cages the Dragoman kept a fine collection of "the most beautiful parrots ... from the coasts of India, green all over except for their scarlet necks."[44]

If the pilgrims tired of Taghribirdi's menagerie they would still find amusement in the antics of strange beasts which extraneous showmen brought to the courtyard. A performing lion was led in, and put through his tricks by a young Egyptian; three men playing on pipes and horns brought a bear upon which rode a piping monkey; a party of four Saracens accompanied a beast which, though devoid of accomplishments, was in itself of a form so remarkable that no pilgrim ever omitted it from his account of the strange creatures to be seen in Egypt, but lavished upon it a wealth of adjectives expended upon no other. The "Seraph" or Giraffe is "an astonishing and beautiful creature"; "it is a proud and vainglorious animal and beautiful to behold.... One feels an incredible pleasure in looking at it;" it is "a lovely and gentle beast." Friar Felix, among the rest, labours to describe its appearance, its head, its tongue, its hide, "red with white spots like stars," its disproportionately long front legs, which effectively preserved it from having to bear the burdens imposed on other

4. CAIRO, 1512

An artist's impression at a time when very large turbans were in fashion. (*Reception of the Venetian Ambassador*—School of *Gentile Bellini*.)

beasts by man, the astonishing height at which it carried the small and harmless horned head.⁴⁵

All these things, to Felix, were food for curiosity and enjoyment, only exceeded in interest by what he saw when he went beyond the door of Taghribirdi's house, to move about in the midst of a great, ancient and capital city, inhabited by a swarming population of alien faith and strange customs, whose daily life was controlled by the remarkable geographical and climatic conditions of Egypt, so vastly different from those which produced the woods, the rivers, and the green pastures of Germany.

In Egypt, a country with "the softest air in the world, and the best for man's health,"⁴⁶ a great deal of the life of the inhabitants was spent in the open air. At night, "for one Saracen who sleeps indoors," Piloti reckoned, "fifteen or twenty will sleep outside the doors on the benches of that house," and there were thousands of homeless poor–Felix believed that they were as numerous as the whole population of Venice–who lived and slept in the open spaces of the great city.⁴⁷ In the daytime the streets were thronged by a crowd which consisted of many races, religions and degrees of men. Poor men would go by, naked except for a loin-cloth, chained captives begging for charity,⁴⁸ women in white cotton gowns, muffled to the eyes in their black veils. The experienced could detect a man's religion from his turban; Saracen Moslems wore white, Arabs white too, but with a piece of the material drawn across under the chin; the turbans of Eastern Christians were blue, those of the Jews yellow, while Turks wore long pointed hats wound round with a white scarf.⁴⁹ The press in the streets was increased by the great numbers of donkeys, horses, mules and camels. None but the poorest went on foot, "for it is a serious and perilous thing to walk here because of the overcrowding... so that everywhere at street corners stand donkey-boys with harnessed donkeys or horses, handsomely saddled and bridled with stirrups and harness of silk, and whoever wants a good beast well caparisoned can have one, but it is best," Felix adds, "to take one for yourself or you may be given a poor countrybred nag."⁵⁰

Among the throng countless hucksters offered their wares, sellers of fruit or bread, sweetmeats or firewood, and of many other commodities. Water was one of the most important of these; all of it came from the Nile, and was carried up to the city on camels or donkeys for sale to householders for domestic use, or on the shoulders of thousands of humble water-sellers, who would pour out for a customer from the water-skin by a brass funnel into "a pretty cup of inlaid brass" either for washing or drinking. The price, according to Felix, was not quite so much as the thirtieth part of an Ulm penny.⁵¹ Devout persons, in order to fulfil the

Moslem duty of charity, would sometimes carry a water-skin, and out of it give as much as any man asked;[52] others, at once pious and wealthy, set up in squares and streets "great vessels . . . which they keep full of water, from which Christians, Jews and heathens can drink;"[53] childless people would bequeath water "for the love of God" in their wills.[54] Besides all this traffic in water there was an official service by which camels carried it around the city, morning and evening, for the sprinkling of the streets, in order to lay the dust which rose so chokingly in the narrow alleys.[55] Besides those who sold there were others who practised their craft in the streets; barbers were to be recognised by the little mirror worn on the breast; they were assisted by little negro boys who "go about calling 'Who will be shaved?'"[56] But to the pilgrims the most interesting of all these itinerant tradesmen were the itinerant cooks. For, in addition to the public cook-shops, as marvellously clean here as in Jerusalem, there were "other little poor cooks, without houses or kitchens;* these have a square fire-box† coated inside with clay, which they fill with charcoal, and on this they put little cooking pots and gridirons, with meat boiling or roasting, then they take up the iron thing thus made ready, and carrying it on their heads, go about the lanes, crying out what they have cooking, whether meat, or little fishes or milk dishes. Then men in their houses, hearing this, look out of their windows, and if they like what is cooked they buy. But strangers, or poor folk who are content with little, meet them in the street, and go off to some corner, and there sit down and eat. The cook carries with him his little dishes and everything he needs. There are," Felix concludes, and we feel he relinquishes this fascinating subject with regret, "There are in that city many thousands of these cooks."[57]

As, according to custom, pilgrims who lodged with the Chief Dragoman had to cater for themselves,[58] the bursars of the three companies very soon became acquainted with the food supplies of Cairo. On the morning after their arrival three pilgrims, of whom Felix was one, set off to market attended by one of Taghribirdi's servants. They returned with their purchases and with the knowledge that all goods were to be had cheap but two—wood for firing, and wine. Wood you actually bought by the pound, and the price was horrifying, even worse than at Ulm, and no wonder, for there was no wood in Egypt but that of the wild date palm which was cut down annually.[59] But there were substitutes: cow-

* Thenaud, p. 47, remarks "that these cooked so dirtily that we were horrified at them."
† "*Ferula.*" Prometheus carried fire, according to the legend, in the pith of the giant-fennel (*v.* Lewis and Short, Latin Dictionary, *s.v.*). Felix Fabri is showing off his knowledge of the classics.

dung mixed with straw, pulverised camel-dung sold in flat cakes, even, says one pilgrim, "earth made into bricks which burns better than wood; it does not smoke and has no flame, but it reddens like hot iron and remains red from morning to evening...."[60] The lack of wine was a more serious matter, for by now, of the store which the pilgrims had brought from Syria, only a small quantity remained, which it would be wise to conserve in case of illness. Here again there was a choice of alternatives. Tafur's indulgent host had offered him wine, but the Spaniard had chosen to drink water,[61] and, living as he did with the family, he was able to sample the pleasant and medicinal drinks of the Moslems, especially that so beneficial when taken as an *apéritif* in the hot weather, consisting of water "specially treated, and in it were certain seeds, like hemp."[62] There were besides a variety of "syrops of sugar and other confections, more delicate than anywhere else in the world."[63] which were sold in "jars of glass or wood very pleasingly carved."[64] Nor indeed was it impossible for those who knew the ropes to obtain wine, for there was a regular import from Crete for Mamluk customers of wine in "little barrels covered with linen cloth," but as these must be bought surreptitiously, the price was 14 ducats apiece.[65] Yet, even if you drank nothing but Nile water, and at Cairo there was no other that was not saline, you drank, as Felix admitted, "the sweetest water of all the world and the healthiest," and no wonder, since as everyone knew it flowed to Egypt from the Earthly Paradise. Even at its worst it was harmless, Friar Felix assures us, for "I often," says he, "drank with a burning thirst the thick and muddy water, and never took any harm."[66] Properly treated it became perfectly clear and positively beneficial to the digestion and appetite, and for this needed only to be allowed to stand for twenty-four hours in a large, covered eathernware vessel, during which time the sediment settled to the bottom; it was also possible to clear it more quickly by the addition of milk of almonds.[67] But the Friar and his companions, while yielding to none in their respect for the waters of the great river, were no Rechabites. "You may be sure," he says, "that Rhine wine would have suited us better than any water of paradise."[68]*

Except for water and wood there was no lack in Cairo. An Italian remarked that there were more ships on the Nile at Cairo "than ever I saw in the port of Genoa or of Venice or of Ancona,"[69] and from these were landed, every day and all day, food and provisions of all sorts at the quays along the river. From the fertile district of Gharbiyeh came

* De Joinville (p. 80) mentions the Egyptian habit, imitated by the Crusaders, of hanging water "in pots of white clay which they make in the country, to the cords of our tents; the water becomes in the heat of the day as cold as well water." None of our pilgrim writers mention this practice.

sugar, "white as snow and solid as a rock";[70] sesame seeds for oil, since olive oil must be imported from Syria; rice, corn, beans, lentils, cucumbers and other vegetables.[71] Egyptian bread, made "like buns, bought at 3 a soldo," was very white, but the pilgrims disapproved of the way it was cooked.[72] The Nile itself produced a bountiful supply of fish and there was meat in plenty, of oxen, buffaloes or goats; a great deal of mutton was eaten and von Harff tasted and relished some camel meat which he bought from one of the itinerant cooks.[73] Geese were brought to the capital from the Island of Gharbiyeh, while fowls, boiled and roast, were as common a food as they are to this day in the Levant.[74] A tenth-century visitor to Egypt had seen in the markets of Cairo in December "red roses, lilies, narcissi, bitter and sweet oranges, lemons, apples, jasmine, melons, *dastbuyas*, bananas, olives, dates, grapes, sugar cane, mad-apples, gourds," as well as the humble onion, garlic, carrot and beetroot.[75] The profusion and variety of fruit, all of it "very mellow,"[76] delighted our pilgrims. Much of it they had tasted already in Syria; even the date-palm grew there, but, Felix explains, by reason of the fertilising waters of the Nile the palms in Egypt "grow taller and more plentifully than elsewhere; for you can see in Egypt groves of palms growing. And the palm is a noble and remarkable tree, of lasting beauty and strength, always green, keeping its leaves without fall, summer and winter, slender in the stem and hairy and of great height. . . . The trunk is strong and of close texture . . . but it is not of wood like other trees, for the trunk can be reduced by hand to nothing by pulling off the fibres, for the whole trunk is like a bundle (*compaginatio*) of hemp."[77] Having noted that these fibres are used for making ropes, and the leaves for baskets, the Friar reaches the crown of the tree and the climax of his subject in "that most excellent fruit, the date, so rich in sweetness that it might have lain in honey . . . and the country-folk pick them, throw away the stones which lie in the midst, press them into lumps like bread, as they do also with figs, and eat and sell them like that."[78] And still after nearly five centuries they continue to do so.

But there was one fruit which was new even to experienced travellers such as our pilgrims, and which they describe with eager particularity. Even Paul Walther allows himself to become enthusiastic about this "fairly big tree, not woody but green all over in colour . . . with very green leaves eight feet long by two feet wide" and with a fruit "when it is ripe most sweet as sugar" (*sic*), and besides sweet, "very wholesome, green in colour."[79] Friar Felix tunes his instrument to a higher pitch still, though at the start he warns his readers that this tree, "this surely marvellous tree," is so different from others, and so unusual in growth "that I cannot describe it properly." He follows up this warning by a description positively breathless. "... It grows from the earth like a cane, not that it is a cane nor of the cane family, but like a cane it is without branches but has leaves all round the stem.... But it is a great stem and it has huge leaves..."-huge indeed, for he doubles the length given by Paul Walther and adds half as much again to the width-"And the fruits are long fruits... and round, not very thick or fat.... But the fruit does not grow each one by itself but twenty or more grow in one bunch like many grapes in one. They are pale gold in colour." From all this description emerges a picture of the *musa sapientium*, that is to say the banana.* The reader, who by now knows Felix Fabri well, is not surprised to hear that, "of this fruit I ate to satiety." He remarks also that it is served cut up into thin slices, "as radishes are with us," and eaten with salt to temper the sweetness.[80]

The bursars must also have become proficient in that subject always so anxious and engrossing for the traveller-the currency of a strange country. Venetian ducats were accepted in Egypt, but no German money. If the gold coinage did not much concern them, being in value beyond their daily needs, they must accustom themselves to the silver money, the medine, and the little *asper*; the medine had the Sultan's name upon it, and was "not so broad as our *kreutzer*, but better, and of pure silver" and was reckoned at 25 to the ducat.† The *asper* had a very little silver in it, and was worth very little. Even the silver coinage, however, was less useful in household shopping than copper, so cheap was "bread or cheese, or a drink of water or anything small." The copper coins which were used for this sort of purchase were known to the pilgrims as "fluss,"‡ and were of all sorts, sizes and denominations. The money-changers kept great basketfuls of them, and having first tested a proffered silver coin by biting it, "having the art" of thus detecting false money, instead of counting out the copper in change, would lay this in the pan against weights of lead or iron, or "a stone of known weight," and the pilgrims found that they got a whole purseful of copper for one medine.[81]

But as well as the markets, with their abundance of foodstuffs, there were in Cairo a multitude of small shops[82] which were crammed with the delicate and sumptuous goods proper to a capital city, and one,

* Fabri (*Evag.*, III, pp. 5-6) appears greatly to exaggerate the circumference of the fruit when he says that it is "not so thick or fat that when a man takes it in his hand he touches finger with finger about it."

† von Harff, p. 112, gives 26 to the ducat. The asper, originally struck in the Empire of Trebizond, was very widely used in the East (W. Wroth, *Brit. Museum Cat: Vandals* etc. London, 1911. Intro., p. lxxvii ff.)

‡ This is clearly the same as Thenaud's "flux" which his editor corrects to "foulous" by which he understands "money" (Thenaud, p. 66).

moreover, which, as Piloti said, was "made of gold, for all the fat of the land settles there."[83] These commodities came from every direction, and western merchants would sail up the river to Cairo[84] to sell there not only the raw materials which Egypt lacked, but those manufactured goods of fine quality in the production of which Italy, Flanders and even Germany now competed with the skilled craftsmen of the East.

It was naturally however, the exotic products of India, Persia or the Far East which captured the attention of the western pilgrims, and opened the purses of the rich men among them, as they passed through the bazaars, from the street of the gold and silver smiths to that of the sellers of silks or linens, of drugs, carpets or perfumes,[85] or sought out the jewellers' shops near to the Sultan's castle, kept for the most part by Jews or Persians, where the purchaser could make his choice between "emeralds, rubies, balases, turquoises . . ." and "great pearls."[86] Perfumes were to be had in great variety, musk and civet, ambergris and frankincense.[87] Aloes wood was almost a product of Egypt, for it came floating down the Nile from, as it was said, the Earthly Paradise; this cheap method of transport did not, however, lower the price; but though they might grumble merchants would buy, and Felix Fabri saw "a great trunk of this wood in an apothecary's at Venice."[88] By no means all of these perfumes were for re-export; a Cretan resident in Cairo told the Florentine, Simone Sigoli, that "the men and women of the city . . . spend daily on flowers and roses which they wear at their breast, and musk and rose-water and other sweet scents . . . three thousand gold bezants, and," adds Sigoli, with the precision of the merchant, "the bezant is worth one and a quarter florins; and that is spent every day."[89]

It was for the inhabitants of Cairo, and especially for the Mamluk Sultan and Emirs, that the watered silks, the embroidered Persian vests, the exquisite cottons and linens, whether imported, or manufactured not far from Cairo, and in Alexandria, were shown in the bazaars.[90] Western merchants remarked especially the white muslins and lawns, fine and soft as silk, "the prettiest stuff in the world, all bright and thin and shining," in which men and women of substance commonly dressed, the men in long gowns with long wide sleeves like those of a priest, their heads wound with the white turban, and carrying on their heads or on their shoulders little scarves of coloured lawn embroidered at each end. Women wore a gown short to the knee and with short wide sleeves, and below the gown the white lawn or linen trousers, sewn at the ankle with silk or gold, jewels or pearls, according to the condition of the wearer's purse; many painted their hands, and almost all, their nails; a fashion dies hard in the East.[91]

A recital of the rarities and luxuries which from East and West were brought to the markets of Cairo, recalls that other catalogue of sumptuous goods which the writer of the Apocalypse rehearses in his indictment of Imperial Rome. To Rome, the Elder's Babylon, as to Cairo, the Babylon of Mediaeval Christendom, came "merchandise of gold and silver and precious stones, and of pearls, and fine linen, and purple and silk, and scarlet, and thyine wood, and all vessels of ivory, and all manner of vessels of most precious wood, and of brass, and iron and marble. And cinnamon and odours and ointments and frankincense, and wine and oil, and fine flour, and wheat and beasts and sheep and horses and chariots...." And to Cairo as to Rome, came, and were sold, "... slaves and souls of men."

Slavery was as fundamental to Moslem domestic life as it was to the edifice of the Mamluk state, and quite early in their stay the pilgrims were brought face to face with the trade in action. One afternoon the young Count of Solms set off upon a shopping expedition; two knights, von Schonberg and Peter Velsch, were with him, Friar Felix, and a Mamluk servant from the house to act as guide. In their progress they came upon one of the slave-markets, where were displayed for sale "men, young women and children of both sexes, both black and white." As the little group of pilgrims stood watching, with their Moslem guide, a rich man rode up, looked them over, and offered to buy the lot. Taghribirdi's servant played up to the suggestion, expressing the traditional unwillingness of the seller: these sound and healthy specimens would fetch a good price in Alexandria or abroad. The intending buyer persisted, and taking 10 ducats from his purse, tendered them in the presence of the little crowd, as usual assembled to witness the conclusion of a bargain, and was only enlightened as to his mistake by the cheerful merriment of the supposed slaves. The pilgrims continued on their way; another slave-market was visited, where only black folk were on sale, and here the young Count wished to buy an Ethiopian boy; as, however, no Moslem slave-dealer could be persuaded to sell to a Christian, the young nobleman had to be content with the purchase of a monkey, some rich silks, and various Saracen garments.[92]

The pilgrims had, of course, encountered slavery in Moslem Syria, but they had seen there nothing to compare with the slave-markets of Cairo, and though a lad like Solms might think that it would be amusing to buy a slave, and though Felix was ready to laugh at the comedy of finding himself and his companions regarded as saleable, he and the older men among the pilgrims were fully conscious of the tragedy they had witnessed. Felix, watching the brisk business a-foot in the market for Tartar slaves in Alexandria, could see in these grotesque and stumpy little figures, with their large eyes, half-hidden by thick lashes, broad, all-but hairless faces, and strangely shaved heads, not only the ugliest people he had ever beheld, but "the most precious merchandise... rational creatures of God, made in God's image, offered for sale at a wretched price."[93] The whole procedure filled him with a fascinated horror; he marked the cold, calculating survey, in which an eye as searching and experienced as any doctor's passed over the goods, a survey which was followed by the separation from the rest of any slave likely to please, for the purpose of a yet more narrow examination. In this the slave was made to speak; eyesight and hearing were tested; finally the piece of merchandise was stripped naked, looked over once more, driven hither and thither, and, at the crack of a whip, made to run, to walk, to leap. After this the contracting parties might begin the tactics of bargaining; if 15 ducats was the seller's price the buyer would perhaps offer 5. They haggled over the human being "as we do," says Felix, "over a horse."[94]

But when the bargain was concluded there was worse to come, for, as the new purchase was led away, "a great cry and weeping rises among the crowd that was for sale, since perhaps he that was sold has his mother or his brother waiting there to be bought," and children must watch the sale of parents, and husbands of wives. Human nature appears to be able to endure and adapt itself to almost any conditions, and those who had already passed through the slave-dealer's hands learnt to assume a complaisant demeanour, in the hope that this might win them a good master. Such masters there must have been, yet slavery, with its essential defencelessness, was a state abhorred and wretched, and the slave might well choose the dire alternatives which flight offered—on the one hand the cruel penalties imposed upon a re-captured slave, on the other a wretched existence of near-starvation on the fringes of the desert.[95]

If the pilgrims felt distress and compunction at the sight of Tartars and negroes sold as slaves, still more poignant for them was the spectacle, with which they were to be faced at Alexandria, of a group of captured Christian seamen led bound through a jubilant Moslem crowd to the slave-market, there to pass into what might well be a lifelong and hopeless servitude.[96]

Sometimes such stories would have a happy ending, and the pilgrims themselves were to be witnesses of one of these. To the house of Taghribirdi came a Christian merchant and his brother, to find whom he had travelled to Egypt, and whom he had redeemed from slavery. But one night the Christians were made aware of the past sufferings, whether mental or physical, of the rescued man, when he roused all by his screams, as he endured again in a nightmare the miseries and fears of a slave.[97]

Yet Christian merchants, and in particular those of Venice and Genoa, had for a long time competed with Moslems in the lucrative trade, in spite of exhortations from the Pope and consequent prohibitions by their various governments; and some enterprising individuals had recently broken new ground by approaching the Emperor Frederick III, and from him obtaining licences to sell slaves in Germany.[98] In Italy, in spite of all the Pope or the City States might say, there were many slaves; Fabri, with his liking for round numbers, estimated that there were in Venice alone, besides Slavs, 3,000 Tartar and Ethiopian slaves.[99] Nor were they only in the hands of nobles, but a pastry-cook would find the services of a slave of use in his business,[100] or a German merchant, resident in Italy, own a couple, though he might be moved to set them free in his will.[101] Though it was not usual for these slaves to be Christian, it was not unheard of that a rich man should buy, at a high price, a comely Russian girl,[102] and the most terrible and poignant story of slavery which Felix Fabri tells is of a Christian slave in the hands of Christian owners.

At the Catalan Fondacho in Alexandria, where the pilgrims themselves stayed while waiting to go on board for their return voyage, there was a female Ethiopian slave. "This Ethiopian woman, reproved one day by her mistress, resented the rebuke and resisted the correction of the lady, who ordered her to be beaten. But she continued still so contumacious that the slave who beat her seized a staff and flogged her with all his might, as though he were beating a donkey, and throwing her down on the ground he kicked her. Yet for all that she resisted fiercely, striking, spitting, putting out her tongue, till her tormentor was almost worn out. At last, when with difficulty she had been mastered and tied up with ropes, she began horribly to attack herself, bellowing like a bull, tearing at herself with her teeth, beating her head upon the walls and ground and ... by all means endeavouring to do herself to death." When at last she desisted, it was to rail not only against her master and mistress, but against the God whom she and they alike worshipped.[103] If, as Felix believed, the Moslems, with their "inordinate appetite to possess their own bought slave," brought into their house along with that same slave the curse of God,[104] what may we suppose of the Christian? But upon this question Felix is silent.

In addition to all the other extraordinary sights recorded by visitors to Egypt, there was one, simple, single and fundamental to the very existence of the whole country, the Nile itself. The great river, its source unknown, its annual and most precious flood unexplained, had fascinated geographers from the time of the Greeks, so that when Friar Felix sets out to consider the subject his native shrewdness is all but extinguished under the accumulated load of his authorities. Only here and there do we catch a flicker of that untrammelled glance of inquiry which the Friar had directed upon the empty spaces of the desert. Having grafted on to the common medieval belief that the Nile rose in the Earthly Paradise the theory that it shared, with the three other rivers of Paradise–the Ganges, Euphrates, and Tigris–a common source in a lake, or "abyss," he suddenly turns from his ancient writers to an example homely but apposite, for if the Nile rises "out of an abyss" so too "in its own fashion, the little river Blau breaks forth from a very deep hole." On the one hand the great and storied Nile, on the other the little Blau rising in the tiny, crystal clear, cornflower-blue lake at Blauburen "coloured like the bright sky," and wandering down its gentle valley to meet the Danube in the fishermen's quarter of Ulm.[105]

It is the same when he comes to inquire into the causes of the momentous flood, and to account for the curious fact that it took place in summertime, when rivers naturally run low. He arrays with pride his battery of learning, quoting Eupolemus who wrote about Moses; Thales; "one of the Seven Sages"; Anaxagoras; Herodotus and the rest. He refutes "a certain Memphitan," who had suggested that the irregularity was accounted for by the fact that the river rose in the "opposite zone," where seasons went contrary to ours; no river, says Felix, could reach us from the opposite side of the globe "since the earth is made round, and it would be necessary for the water to run uphill."[106] But it is to his own real and known world that he appeals when, having admitted that rains in Ethiopia might well be the cause of the flood, he offers as a parallel fact that "our river Rhine floods more in summer than in winter, because of the melting snow of the Alps."[107] Yet it is not Friar Felix but de Lannoy who goes straight to the heart of the matter. "I understood," says the soldier, "from the opinion of several people, that the reason why (the river) rises thus every year, is because of the very heavy rains that there are ... about 100 days' journey above Cairo...."[108]

Whatever the cause of the inundation it was the central fact of Egyptian life. "They do not pray in that country for rain nor shine, but for the ... inundation of the Nile."[109] and in the nineteenth century at least the fear of a failure in the flood would bring Moslems, Christians and Jews together in prayer at the venerable "Old Mosque" of Amr in Cairo.[110]

The first sight of the flooded country had filled the pilgrims with wonder, for with the ancient system of irrigation there was a total, though controlled, flood, and the villages, built up on their mounds of earth,[111] each "with a trench about, larger than the moat of a city," in which the precious water would be conserved,[112] lay like islands in the waste of the beneficent waters.[113]

For this inundation, so different from the raging, scouring floods of the Rhine, the Danube, the Iller, and even the little Blau, which "tore out the entrails" of fertile fields and gardens, did its work according to the farmer's pleasure, since "the water, with its gentle flow is easily controlled by small dykes," so that "the loveliest view of Egypt is thought to be that when the Nile has covered the fields."[114] The country folk, forced to go about their business in boats while the flood held,[115] were "the more rejoiced the less they saw of their land,"[116] knowing that now they needed only to wait till the muddy waters had receded to sow their crops in the sodden fields "and without fail ... receive twenty or twenty-five fold" of their sowing.[117]

Even before the modern system of irrigation the flow of the waters was under careful official control. Mamluk guards were posted along the river bank, who opened the sluices when the flood had reached its height; and keeping in touch with the other posts by means of fire-signals at night, closed them when the waters had covered all the fields.[118] In Cairo itself the government kept an equally close watch upon the gradual, but irregular, rise of the water. In a low building on the shore of the Island of Rôda, the foundations of which lay deep below the surface of the river, stood a "tall thick column of crimson or purple marble,"[119] upon which "certain lines and ancient letters" were carved, by which the height of the flood was measured;[120] this, the famous Nileometer, was under constant observation.

In the nineteenth century, from July 3 onwards, the "Cryer of the Nile" used to go about the streets of Cairo attended by a boy; the two would halt outside various houses upon their route, and recite antiphonally a pious dialogue including an announcement of the latest reading of the Nileometer, embedded among polite blessings upon the household within, much in the manner, and with the same motive, of the Christmas wassail—

God bless the master of this house. . . .

and so on.[121] In the days when Cairo was the capital of the Mamluk Sultan a similar announcement was made every morning, but with far greater pomp, horsemen with banners riding down to the Nileometer to read the flood-marks on the pillar and returning through the city crying that "the river has risen last night so many marks."[122]

The "Completion" or "Abundance of the Nile," still celebrated within living memory, though with sadly diminished show, was a popular occasion, ancient even in the fifteenth century, when it was marked by "a great festival, and a great procession of rowing boats and barks on the river." This was the day, usually in the second or third weeks of August, of the breaking of the earthen dam, which had barred the entry of the flood waters into the Khalig, the canal which, leaving the river opposite the Island of Rôda, penetrated the city in a more or less northerly direction. When Emmanuel Piloti watched the ceremony it was the Sultan himself who gave the signal,[123] though sometimes one of the great Emirs would act for him.[124] Dismounting from his horse, says Piloti, "he strikes, with a golden whip, the earth which closes the mouth of the canal, and remounts; then there are innumerable people with as many whips, and they clear away the earth . . . and at once the river flows in among the city, and the tall houses on one side and the other . . . , and a number of barks therein, and they sing and make merry after their fashion."*[125] What that fashion was Piloti does not say, but we may learn it, since such a tradition changes little with the years, from an Elizabethan traveller. The canal once open, "there are innumerable barks rowing to and fro, laden with gallant girles and beautiful dames, which with singing, eating, drinking and feasting, take their solace,"[126] until, doubtless, the lights lit in the tall houses on either side of the canal, cast a bright and broken reflection—like golden dinars, the Moslem poet said—upon the dark water.[127]

* Lane, *Modern Egypt*, p. 503, describes the nineteenth-century ceremony which the Governor attended, but in which he took no active part. S. L. Poole, *Art of the Saracens*, p. 243, quotes an eleventh-century account in which the Khalif carried "a valuable whip in his hand." Suriano, p. 194, who watched the Emir Ysbech deputise for the Sultan, saw him "give the signal with his hoe." Lane, *loc. cit.*, says that the earth of the dam is cut "with a kind of hoe."

CHAPTER XII

Going down the Nile

On October 16 the pilgrims received news which put out of their heads all the strange sights and interesting experiences of Cairo, for, as once before, upon the road from Tor, and again prematurely, they were told by "certain Christians . . . that the ships were loading at Alexandria, and that we should make haste to be gone." Once again their only thought was of dispatch, and they demanded that the Dragoman should make instant arrangements for their journey to the port.

Taghribirdi made no demur, but he painted for them a gloomy picture of the inconveniences which they would be likely to suffer if they came before the Customs officials of Alexandria without a letter from the Sultan's Chancery. He could get this for them, he said, and it would cost so much. The pilgrims, considering that the money would be well spent, commissioned him to obtain the letter.

When two days passed and no letter had appeared they began to think it time to meet guile with guile. As unostentatiously as possible they hired a couple of Moslem donkey-men and ordered them to come to the Dragoman's house in the afternoon. Meanwhile they had chosen one of the knights, a member of Fabri's own party, to be their harbinger; he was to go down the Nile in company with, probably, the same Christian merchants who had brought the news, and at Alexandria he should secure passages for himself and the rest in the Venetian ships.

The donkeys and their owners arrived and were admitted into the courtyard; the knight brought down his baggage; the beasts were loaded. But now it was discovered that the gate had been shut and locked, and there was not a servant to be seen, for the slaves had all taken pains to hide themselves. Then the knight rushed about the house shouting and yelling, but they pretended not to hear.

Not until an hour later did a slave appear and then only to reproach the knight for trying to leave with debts unpaid. The accusation was false, but denial was vain. In order to gain his freedom the knight consented to accompany the Moslem about the town, in search of a Jew who would consent to play the part of creditor; but one Jew was honest, and the other could not be found, so that after a long search the knight was allowed to return to the Dragoman's house.

"Meanwhile," says Felix, "Taghribirdi, whom we knew to be at home, lay hid. . . . And that slave and other house-servants teased the pilgrim-knight unmercifully. After much teasing he gave the servants no small sum in medines for a vail . . . and set off, well-chastened." Yet he was the fortunate one of the company, for at least he was quit of the Chief Dragoman. "He reached the port on the Nile and went on board with the others, and sailed down the Nile in great peace."[1] When, two days later, his companions followed him, their journey was to be far from peaceful, and before that time came they were fated to suffer a considerable amount of mental stress, including at least one very disturbed night. On October 15 their rest had been broken by the loud and untuneful lamentations with which the Moslems had greeted a total eclipse of the moon.[2] On October 17 they had been kept awake by the hooting of an owl which took up its position close to their windows, causing them not only loss of sleep but a superstitious anxiety, which a later unhappy event seemed to justify. And now, on the night following their companion's departure, they were roused, after the usual nocturnal stir of Ramadan had subsided, by a disturbance indoors; the Chief Dragoman having occasion to chastise one of his wives, the sobs and cries of the lady, and the sounds of altercation broke the stillness and disturbed the pilgrims' sleep.[3]

Even without these annoyances the mounting anxiety of the travellers might well have been enough to impair their rest. For Taghribirdi had still not produced the promised letter. On the 17th they approached him upon the subject, and found him in a very bad temper after the unpleasantness with his womenfolk. He did, however, promise to make an effort, and having ridden off to the Sultan's Castle, returned with "the precious letter."

The pilgrims, in possession of this and of the Dragoman's promise that he would set them on their journey next day, congratulated themselves upon a double success. Their minds would have been less serene had they known that Taghribirdi had written a second letter, this one to the Dragoman of Alexandria, in which he reported the pilgrims as rich and liberal.[4] Such a description, though in itself flattering, dwelt upon just those qualities which in the circumstances their owners would have preferred to remain unstressed.

The greater part of that Saturday night Friar Felix spent "sleepless, writing up by lamplight all that was to go down in the *Evagatorium*, for our departure was at hand."[5] Next morning the pilgrims had just finished

Mass when the Dragoman arrived with his reckoning"–6 ducats each for his fee, 4 for the Sultan's letter, 24 ducats for a boat to go down the Nile to Lower Egypt. Then he commended his wives to us and his servants, saying that they had all been eager in our service; that was in order that we should give them a vail. On top of this he asked 6 ducats for the donkeys and donkey-man who were to take us to the Nile."

The pilgrims made their usual whip-round for this communal expense, and handed over a sum which not only covered all the items of the bill, but allowed something extra. They were then told to make ready.

Yet, when all their preparations had been made, and they waited for the arrival of the donkeys, they saw Taghribirdi roving idly about the court and house, letting it be seen "by his expression and demeanour, that he was angry with us, and pretending not to know that we were waiting." The anxious pilgrims could only have patience. "We were in his claws, and could not get away without suffering for it."

At last, towards sunset, they called the house-steward and inquired of him the reason for the delay. "He answered shortly, 'If you want to have the master in a good temper, and wish to get away in peace, open your purses, pour out your money, and promptly and cheerfully offer more than was asked for lodging, vails for the ladies, and tips and *pourboires* for every one of the household officers.'"

The pilgrims, with smiling lips and hearts full of rage and distress, took this advice. At once Taghribirdi cheered up, called upon his servants to assist the pilgrims, and when all was ready mounted his horse and led them out upon their last ride through the crowded streets. That ride was not only their last, but their worst. At the head of the procession Taghribirdi cleared the way with blows of his stick; at the rear the pilgrims had to endure reprisals at the hands of the justly indignant passers-by, who jolted one pilgrim from his saddle and gave him a beating which he felt for days after.[6]

But at last Bulak was reached, and, having pointed out among the throng of shipping the boat which he had hired for them, the Chief Dragoman handed them over to "a certain Mamluk called Halliu," took his leave and departed, leaving the pilgrims to experience a sober thankfulness in that they had at least "got away from that rogue with whole skins, though with light pouches."

While the less resilient among the party went on board at once, "to have some peace," others, and among them Felix, rushed off to the nearest cook-shop to buy food for the journey. It was dark when they came back, dark enough at any rate for the Moslem crew to be sitting down to their supper, and the pilgrims followed their example. When the meal was finished the sailors cast off, and the voyage down the river began.[7]

The pilgrims had escaped out of the hands of the Chief Dragoman at Cairo, but they were to find his deputy almost as unacceptable. This man, Taghribirdi's underling, had not, it is true, the Dragoman's ingenious malice, but his indifference and inertia left his employers in the lurch in a succession of tight places. Even before experience revealed these qualities, Friar Felix, so he assures us, took an intuitive dislike to the fellow, as one "pale and sly, altogether contrary to my humour." The antipathy was mutual. "I did not fail to cross him by word and action . . . he did not spare me."[8]

In the fourteenth century and the earlier part of the fifteenth it had been possible to make the whole journey by water, since Nasir Mahomet's canal, which left the Nile a little way below Fua, brought travellers to within a couple of miles of the port. By now, however, this canal had ceased to be navigable[9] and since Christians were forbidden to approach the naval port at the mouth of the Rosetta branch of the river,[10] it had become the practice of pilgrims, as it was also that of many Moslem merchants, to disembark at Rosetta and there to hire beasts for the forty miles odd which lay between them and Alexandria;[11] so frequented was this route that the mules and donkeys of Rosetta were said to follow it without needing any guidance from their riders.[12]

The journey down the river was slow, because, though they went with the current, the North wind was against them, and the sailors had to work at the oars in order to make headway. But there was plenty around them to interest and divert. The river was full of the lateen or square-rigged Nile craft,[13] and they moved among a crowd of other boats laden deep with spices, going down-stream, for it was now the season of the great spice market at Alexandria when "all the country is moved as if to go to a fair."[14] These vessels, like their own, were almost wind-bound, but other craft on the way up river went by at such a rate that it seemed "as if they flew"; not only had these the wind behind them but also they were towed by horses, just as at home, the Germans noted, barges were towed up the Rhine above Cologne.[15]

During this day of leisurely progress the pilgrims were also entertained by the sight of a country which amazed them by its wonderful fertility; every few miles they would pass a small village where the houses, "domed like bake-ovens" and plastered with Nile mud, Felix at first mistook for "little mosques, because they are built prettily with vaulting." Round about each village were "most lovely gardens, fields and groves of fruit trees."[16] These gardens Felix and his companions saw only in passing, but another party of pilgrims, marooned on one of the islands in the Nile as the result of a collision, enjoyed a delicious experience, sleeping in the shade of the trees, eating their fill of the fruit, and listening the while to the sound of water, which, raised from the river by a wheel worked by oxen, "ran ever through the said gardens, to our great delight."[17] But as so often, where every prospect pleased, man was vile. Upon the river bank pilgrims would see many boys and girls "naked and black as coal," shamelessly begging from passing boats.[18]

So the long day passed; the fasting and sleepy Moslem sailors went heavily about their tasks, and the pilgrims did not even land to buy food, but ate what was left of that which they had brought at Bulak, and drank the muddy water of the river, knowing well by now that this would do them no harm.

At sundown the crew began to perk up, "to sing, howl and eat," with the result that some of the pilgrims, and Felix among them, gave up all attempt to sleep and instead sat up on deck, watching the bank slowly sliding by; it was during this enforced vigil that the Friar got his first sight of that savage and dangerous beast, which finds a place in every medieval pilgrim's account of Egypt, and in every bestiary, namely the crocodile.

Hatched from an egg, no bigger than that of a goose, and in this stage of its existence "hardly a palm in length," the creature grew to be "as big as a mastiff and half a lance in length," said one pilgrim; fifteen to sixteen feet long, said another. In shape like a lizard "or dragon" the crocodile had a head as big as a horse, with face "most hideous," the jaw as broad as the forehead, its eyes were bright and set in deep sockets, its teeth "as sharp as a steel saw," the upper and the lower fitting so closely into each other than when the animal seized its prey it could not easily let go. The hide was "of a grey colour; at the sides it changes to yellow," that of the back, "covered with thick coarse scales," being so hard that not even a cross-bow bolt would pierce it. The skin of the belly, however, was soft, and fishermen would kill the animal by a blow here from a sort of barbed harpoon. The crocodile's proper diet was fish, but it would seize any beast-ass, mule or camel-which came unwarily down to the river to drink; one pilgrim writer actually saw a big buffalo dragged under. During the daytime it would lie up on the bank or the warm sand; the night it spent in the river, and in the moonlight Felix and his companions saw one creature swimming round, and heard him "groaning and belching under the water."[19]

The crocodile, though inedible, was reputed to supply certain useful by-products. Felix quotes from Albertus Magnus the assertion that from the animal's droppings a face-cream was made, which women used to eliminate wrinkles and improve the complexion; to little purpose, the Friar adds, for the wrinkles would return, and worse than ever.[20] The creature's skin was put to various uses and highly prized. Pedro Tafur was commissioned to procure one for King Janus of Cyprus, and the Spaniard approached for this purpose the Governor of Damietta, who was able to offer him a skin, "but it smelled very rank...." "I would rather," remarks the usually grave Spaniard, "have carried away the Governor's pretty daughter...."[21] Experienced pilgrims were amused on their return to Europe to see the skin displayed to the ignorant as the skin of a dragon by merchants or pedlars* or by the guide in a church in Venice.[22] The tough hide of the back was put to practical use in reinforcing the doors of castles and strongholds.[23]

Even after this wakeful night Friar Felix rose at dawn to say his Hours, and was thus in time to perceive, with growing alarm, the wild course taken by the boat, which swung this way and that while the steersman dozed with his head upon the tiller. "But after a little while, when I was not noticing so much, the boat ran its bows hard aground, so that everyone who was asleep started up, and all were very frightened." The soft mud of the bank however prevented damage, and Nile craft being built with just such accidents in view,[24] it was floated off again without much trouble.[25]

The slow course of yesterday was resumed, and again among country of such luxuriant growth that it was "as if we sailed through paradise." A large island in the river was pointed out by the sailors, who said that by custom it formed part of the dowry of the Sultan's chief wife, and, because so rich, fruitful and lovely, was known as "the golden island."† The pilgrims could see as they passed the imposing edifice of the Queen's house, built like a castle, but half hidden in groves of fruit-trees of all kinds. The Friar, whose profession inclined him towards an unfavourable view of the married state, reflected upon the judgment displayed by the Sultan, who had the sense to keep his wives in different places, and thus avoid the bickering which must arise if more than one were together in the household.[26]

The island lay opposite the busy town of Fua, and, it being now noon, the sailors anchored, and the pilgrims at once went ashore to buy, cook and eat in a pleasant spot between the river and the town wall a picnic

---

* *Gyrovagi*, perhaps wandering monks as in earlier Middle Ages (v. *Oxford English Dictionary* s.v. Waddell, *Wandering Scholars*, pp. 163, 267.

† Fabri says (*Evag.* III, p. 109) that the name of the island is "Delta." von Harff, (p. 100 and note) speaks of "an island of gold the name of which is Getzera de Heppe." (Ed.: Gezeret ed Debub.)

meal of "bread, chickens, eggs and fruit." By the time they sat down to this "almost the whole population of the town, especially the youngsters, had come out to look at us strangers, just as we do when the Gypsies come to our part of the world." There had been a difference of opinion between the pilgrims and the Moslem spectators as to the theologically correct method of killing poultry, which had almost resulted in the pilgrims' dinner being thrown into the river. Other pilgrims discovered that such an infringement of the Moslem law in this matter might put a Christian in danger at least of "fifty golden florins or more, according to the friends you have,"[27] but here the sailors decided that the pilgrims had the right to prepare their dinner as they chose, and the inhabitants of Fua seem to have borne no grudge; they watched the pilgrims eating their improperly slaughtered fowls, and some among them turned the occasion to account by offering for sale articles calculated to appeal to western travellers. One man exhibited in his hand a young crocodile, so small—no more than "two spans long"—that the pilgrims were amazed; a lad offered an "Egyptian mouse," or "Pharaoh's mouse," a creature "as big as a six-months' kitten.* The "young dragon or crocodile" was bought by von Rappelstein; Nicholas Mallengart bought the mouse, "but it did not live long after."[28]

As the sailors made no move to leave, the pilgrims spent the afternoon bathing in the river, keeping to the shallows for fear of the crocodiles. They bathed, Felix claims, less from necessity than piety, bearing in mind the while that they took their dip in the holy waters of Paradise.[29]

The sun was setting when they went on board again to continue their journey; as before, the sailors, "who had slept all day, now wakened, and sang and ate," while Felix and some of the other pilgrims sat on deck, sleepless, but enthralled by the beauty of the scene, for as they dropped softly down the river, "it was strange and lovely to see by night those parts which were inhabited, for everywhere lights burned on the towers of the mosques, and their flame was seen from far off in the darkness."[30] About midnight the sailors hove to and tied up to a mooring post, for they were only a little way from Rosetta, and now in the stillness those on board "could hear all round huge crocodiles knocking against the boat. Most people," says Felix, "went to sleep, but I could not rest for the bumping of the crocodiles, so I sat and looked into the water wondering at the motion of the huge beasts," and wondering also at the strange mentality of "the ancients who had dedicated temples to them."[31] †

---

* Walther estimated the length of the crocodile as 1½ feet, and says that the mouse was the size of a large cat.

† De Lannoy, p. 135, says that crocodiles abounded near Rosetta.

Up to this point their journey had been without incident, but soon their troubles were to begin, so that the rest of Felix's account of the journey to Alexandria is in the nature of a miniature and comic Odyssey. For when, with the morning light, the vessel was brought to the landing place and the pilgrims made to carry their baggage on shore, to their astonishment and chagrin the sailors demanded payment for the hire of the boat. The pilgrims replied that they had already paid the Chief Dragoman; but at this the sailors merely laughed, "saying that he had given nothing to them."

In the squabble which followed the pilgrims were at odds among themselves; some were for being "tough" (duri), even to the point of going back to Cairo, there to lay their case before the Sultan, and it was with difficulty that these were prevailed upon to join with the more prudent majority, and pay their share of the imposition. At last, however, the money was collected and handed over, and the pilgrims landed and sat down to wait for the gates of Rosetta to open, when they would be able to hire beasts for the rest of their journey.[32]*

As soon as possible, therefore, the pilgrims saw the gates open, they sent off Halliu into the town to make the necessary arrangements. He returned with dire news. Instead of the usual plentiful supply of beasts "there was not one camel, donkey or horse" left in Rosetta; all had been hired already by merchants to carry "the merchandise of the Indies" to Alexandria.[33] The animals would be back in three days; all that Halliu would suggest was that the pilgrims should wait for their return.

This was a disaster, and it was made no easier to bear by the glimpses which the pilgrims caught of the sharp-peaked lateen sails of craft going up and down the Nile, "and did we not," says Felix, "wish that we were in one of those boats." But when they suggested to Halliu the daring expedient of continuing the voyage by way of Rosetta and the sea, he would have none of it; though in this he probably judged wisely, "that bad man" consistently refused to put himself out in any way on behalf of his employers.

Left to themselves the pilgrims, "with bitter feelings and panting to be on our way... rambled round the place, and strolled about among those who had come out of the city to stare at us." In the crowd they found

---

* Livio Sanuto in the sixteenth century (v. Thenaud. p. 29 n.) describes Rosetta as having no walls. He speaks however of a mosque, one gate of which opened upon the quay at which the cargo boats for Cairo loaded up, and it is possible that Fabri mistook this gate for a gate in a town wall. On the other hand Pococke (I, p. 15) in 1638 speaks of a castle at Rosetta about 2 miles from the river mouth which was said to be built by "Keych" (presumably Q'ait) Bey, and Fabri might be referring to this.

one who spoke Italian, and entering into conversation with him, the pilgrims, full of their woes, spoke of their need for a boat. Could he, they inquired, find one for them? They would be ready to pay for it, "a round sum, a very round sum."

Their new acquaintance was prepared to help them; he went off, to return shortly with a boatman; in the negotiations that followed the pilgrims suspected, though they could not understand what was said, that Halliu was trying to sabotage their arrangements; certainly he warned them "that if we ran into danger we should not blame him, nor did he choose to get into trouble with us." Disregarding his advice, and dispensing, for the moment, with his services, the pilgrims came to an agreement with the master of the boat, and without delay got themselves and their luggage on board.

But now they were to suffer another check. Before the boat could push off, the owner of the boat was hailed from the quay and forbidden to sail. This gave Felix and his companions a bad fright, since they took it that the prohibition was on their account. Though this proved not to be so, the result was bad enough; once more they must lay hold of their stuff, and painfully, "for we had a lot of heavy luggage," carry it back on shore.

At last they were accommodated with a boat whose owner volunteered to take them wherever they would, and at a fair price. The offer was not to be refused; the pilgrims went on board, regretting only that "it was a rather small boat for so much stuff and for so many men, but the poor man, the owner, had nothing bigger. . . . We sat down, close together and very crowded, but we much preferred to endure the close quarters than three wearisome days." So they judged, believing that they would reach Alexandria by evening;[34] but they did not yet know what lay before them.

From the first they met unexpected difficulties. The channel which they must take branched off only about four miles above Rosetta,* but

---

* Which was this channel by which the pilgrims eventually reached the sea at a place which Fabri (*Evag.* III, p. 139) calls "Canopus"? I would suggest that it can be seen in the early sixteenth-century reproduction by Piri Reis (*Kitabi Bahriye*, Istanbul, 1935), which includes, as well as the coasts of the Mediterranean, the course of the Nile as far as Cairo. In this map a branch is shown as leaving the Nile below Fua, and after broadening out during part of its course into a lake or swamp, entering the sea east of Abukir. See also Livio Sanuto's *Geographia* of 1588 (Africa Tabula VII), where, on a smaller scale a similar branch appears passing through the "*Bocchirus Lacus*" (Lake of Abukir), the sea mouth of which is shown close to what is now the western promontory of the Bay of Abukir, and which seems to include the area which is now covered by the lakes of Abukir and Edku. There is further evidence of the existence of this outlet. In 1512 Jean Thenaud (p. 29 and n.) going from Alexandria to Rosetta crossed a branch of the Nile (ed. "du Maadieh") after leaving Abukir. In 1638 Pococke (p. 13), following the same route, crossed "the Medea or

their transit took two hours, and to make it the master and his crew must haul the boat along by a tow-rope. Even when they reached the new channel and hoped to make better progress they were disappointed, for the same wind that had baffled them on the way down to Rosetta blew once more in their teeth, "with such a blast that it beat back the waters of the river so that they seemed to run backwards, and we could not see their natural flow." Towing must continue, and if it was bad for the pilgrims it was worse for the sailors, who stumbled on through mud "up to their knees, up to their haunches; sometimes they fell in waist-deep, sometimes they had to swim." The passengers, cramped and uncomfortable though they were, "felt most truly sorry for those wretched Moors."[35]

The slow pace of the boat and its proximity to the bank laid the pilgrims open to inconveniences of an entirely different nature. At one point they were waylaid by a single rider who came down to the edge of the river "through the thick mud and the reeds, shaking his lance ... (and) demanding toll in the name of the lord Sultan, a *medine* for every man." While the sailors declared that they had never heard of such a toll Halliu, "that good-for-nothing infidel, would have us pay. He would not have cared if we had been left without a penny. So we gave the man a medine each, and went slowly creeping on."[36]

The next encounter was more alarming. About an hour later seeing on the bank a crowd of men, women and children, and beyond the tents of an Arab encampment, the pilgrims at once "knew that we should not get by without trouble, and our sailors were afraid of them too, and much more than we were."

As the boat drew slowly near, an easy prey, the Arabs, armed with lance and sword, rushed down to the river, snatched the tow-rope from the hands of the crew, and dragged the boat inshore "so that the prow ran hard aground." Then from the high banks the young men jumped down among the pilgrims sitting tightly packed in the crowded boat, and at once began to tear open sacks and baskets, while their victims, fending off the attack as best they could, appealed to the elders upon the bank above: Why did they allow such violence to be done to travellers who were ready to pay whatever was asked?

The older men saw reason in this, and cried to their juniors to desist,

---

ferry, about a league" from Abukir, and close to the sea. "The passage," he says, "is over the outlet of a lake that is supposed to have been the lower part of the Canopic branch of the Nile...." Baedeker (*Lower Egypt*, 1895, p. 224) mentions El Maadiyeh, a station on the Alexandria-Rosetta Railway, 6 miles east of Abukir, as being near the former Canopic mouth of the Nile. If this identification is correct (cf. Walther, p. 239) the flooded area in which the sailors lost the channel is well accounted for by the lake. (Cf. Heyd II, p. 429 and n.)

but without result. At this, the pilgrims, goaded beyond discretion, "rose up against them, and threw them roughly out of the boat, though," Friar Felix admits, "we should never have dared to do it if we had not understood that the older men were in favour of it."

When the young men had been ejected the affair was not over. Assisted by the women and boys of the tribe the youths hurled down mud and earth, "for," luckily, "there are no stones there," while even the elders began to differ among themselves, "some wanting to pick us clean, the others saying no."

At last the latter opinion prevailed, the hubbub died down, the pilgrims paid a ducat, gave the usual present of biscuit to the women and children, and were allowed to proceed. When a little further on they saw others of the tribe upon the bank they forestalled trouble by throwing biscuit also to them.[37]

That was the last that they saw of the Arabs, but now the elements were to conspire to plague them. While the wind continued to rise, "we came to a very wide place where the Nile, overflowing his channels on every side, filled the whole plain with water, except where humps and mounds stood up above it here and there. . . . In this wide place our sailors could no longer tow the boat because the water was too deep, but came on board with us. So we drifted haphazard on the water, hither and thither, and could not advance because of the contrary wind. In this wandering course we left the real current and course of the Nile, and lost it, for the water was as muddy as it was broken, the wind high and the waves rough; we could see no bottom, and thus we sailed on over fields and flats."

It was a matter of time and chance alone how long this aimless drifting should continue. Twice the boat ran aground, and twice the crew stripped, went overboard, and somehow hauled and heaved her off. After the second occasion, as they tried, wading or swimming, to bring her back to the channel, "there came a great outrageous blast of wind which tore the boat from the sailors' hands and drove her with huge force upon a place where the water was very shallow and there she stuck so fast in the mud that there was no hope of moving her." Notwithstanding, the crew laboured valiantly once more to drag her off.

Hopelessly aground the pilgrims could now look about them. There were many boats to be seen in the wide expanse of flood water. Those coming up from the sea, though they too might have lost the true channel, sped swiftly by with the wind in their sails; even when they chanced upon a shoal, "borne by the wind they ploughed through mud and water," and continued on their course.

It was otherwise with the vessels which were going in the opposite direction, heavy with cargo, and forced to beat their way against the wind. No less than six deep-laden merchant craft lay grounded in the mud round about that of the pilgrims; but Felix and his friends could draw no comfortable sense of comradeship from this. For when the crews, which had laboured till evening to haul their vessels off, gave up this hopeless attempt and clambered on board again, there was a good deal of hailing from one to another, and inquiries as to who were the passengers; as soon as they were known to be Christian curses were hurled at them as bringers of ill-luck.[38]

The night came on, and Friar Felix judged it the worst night of all his journey, with the exception of that which he and his companions had spent lost in the desert. For their supper there was nothing but hard biscuit—and not much of that, for the sacks were under all the other luggage at the bottom of the boat—and water from their flasks. When twilight had faded, black dark fell, "without light, without fire, but," says Felix, "with plenty of water," for it stretched away on every side. The hours seemed interminable. Crowded together and unable almost to move, they slept, but uneasily, or talked a little, or prayed. Friar Felix, by request, obliged his neighbour with a brief summary of the lives of a few of the Patriarchs, and with his views upon the source of the Nile.

With the dawn, deliverance came. The wind swung round to the south; when the sail was bent the boat came quickly from the mud-bank; soon the channel was regained, and "with speed and smiling faces" the pilgrims were borne on their way. When, in the first rays of the sun, they caught a glimpse of the sea, some of them, but prematurely, wept for joy.

It was still early when they cast anchor among a great throng of merchant vessels, close to a landing-place alongside which boats were lying, and where there was "a great crowd of the heathen, with many camels, donkeys and horses, unloading from the ships the sweet-smelling spices." The pilgrims watched this busy scene and listened to the babel of voices with considerable, and well-founded, apprehension; it was unusual for Christian pilgrims to use this branch of the Nile; they judged therefore that the less conspicuous they were, and the sooner landed, the better for them.

But when they asked to be put ashore the sailors stood further off, "lest we should jump out," while the captain, seizing part of the ponderous baggage of the knights, declared that though they had paid their passage money at Rosetta, they yet owed for transport of their stuff. Against such a demand there was no redress. With rage at heart the pilgrims paid; the boat was laid alongside the wharf, and they thankfully got themselves and their baggage ashore. Here they hastened to find "a place apart among the reeds, and there we sat down together, and gnawed a biscuit and cheese and drank Nile water"—a poor meal enough, for they had eaten no cooked food since their dinner at Fua two days ago. Meanwhile they became disagreeably conscious of the scowling looks and unfriendly gestures directed against them by the merchants.

Their need now was to hire camels for their stuff, and donkeys for themselves, for the miles which still lay between them and Alexandria,* but they soon realised that if they tried to do this they would find themselves in competition with the merchants, already heatedly disputing amongst themselves for precedence in disembarking their goods and loading them upon the camels. Once more Halliu, sent off to procure transport, showed his ineptitude; he returned "saying that we could not possibly hire beasts that day, what with all the merchandise and the impatience of the merchants." Once more the pilgrims took matters into their own hands, and once more what seemed a triumphant success proved to be illusory.

For they found it no trouble at all to engage camels; the owners were only too pleased to engage to carry, instead of the heavy spice sacks which paid a low tariff, the lighter effects of the pilgrims for which they could charge at a higher rate. But when five camels had been hired and the usual brawling confusion of loading up began, this mild domestic disagreement was overwhelmed by another far more embittered, as the merchants fell upon the unlucky camel owner and his men, and tore the pilgrims' baggage from the camels' backs; when other camel-men dared to approach the pilgrims they were hustled and beaten; at last "the poor country folk with the camels sat themselves down complaining with tears that they were unjustly beaten, to which the merchants retorted that they had what they deserved for wanting to attend to the Christian dogs and rascal Franks before Saracens, and they threatened them with more of the same if they served us before them." The pilgrims "sat sadly down, and," says Felix, "we gave up hope of being able to leave ... while one sack remained on the river bank."[40]

For an hour, says Friar Paul, for two or three says Friar Felix, they sat apart and despaired. But now there came to them no gentle Egyptian countryman, but "a Moor, a rough fellow from Mauretania, asking if

---

* Modern El Maadiyeh is 20 miles from Alexandria. Felix gives the distance between their landing-place and the city as "not less than three long German miles; ("*non minus quam tria non parva milliaria allemanica*") i.e. about 12 miles English, but he adds that "they seemed to me five because of the fatigue of the journey." He does not often underestimate, but here his impression seems to have been more nearly correct than his information.

we would like to go along with him. . . ." The pilgrims were overjoyed; the Moor brought his camels; when the merchants tried to intervene they found they had one to deal with who could give as good as he got. And if he saw to it that the pilgrims paid a steep price, at least it was not long before the camels were loaded and they were free to start.

But now another difficulty presented itself. They had hired camels for the baggage, and donkeys for their own riding, but when, encumbered with what we may call their hand-luggage, they mounted the donkeys and began to ride away, the merchants pursued, hauling the pilgrims from the saddle, and beating the donkey-men. After a furious altercation carried on in German and Arabic, throughout which Halliu preserved a perfect neutrality, although a few of the knights contrived to retain their mounts, a number of the pilgrims, and among them the two Friars, gave up the struggle and, on foot, set themselves to catch up with the departing camels.

The pilgrims were, by any reckoning, twelve miles from Alexandria; the sun was now high in the sky; the ground was of fine, deep, soft sand, burning hot to the feet; they were hungry, and above all thirsty, "nor had we one drop of wine or water left to drink." Even the stout-hearted Felix began to think he would die of heat, hunger and thirst. But he was a man of resource. "Therefore I approached a camel-man and asked him by signs to let me, for a few medines, get up on a camel as far as Alexandria. He took my medines, and made the camel crouch, and me sit on top. So I sat on top of the baggage, and, saved from the labour of going on foot, I took heart again." Though he does not say so he probably enjoyed the experience of what seems to have been his first ride upon a camel.[41]

Paul Walther was not so fortunate. Though the kind-hearted Fernand von Mernawe paid a camel-man to give him a lift, the wily Arab, hanging back till the knight had gone forward beyond call, then demanded more money, and when Paul could not pay, promptly brought his camel down and turned the Friar off.[42] The march which followed must have been a gruelling experience for a man of sixty odd years.

For all, however, even for the weariest, the toilsome journey along the sands of the sea coast at last come to an end. As the day drew towards evening they turned inland across a plain which was in fact all one rich salt pan, whitened as if with frost by the salt. A sunk road led between low hills; now they threaded their way among "the ruins of huge and most ancient walls," probably the remains of the Augustan suburb of Nicopolis, and at last came in sight of "the glorious city of Alexandria, girt by the sea for the most part, and surrounded on the other by the most beautiful gardens and orchards, in which grow palms, so many and so tall that it is like a pine wood."

The city wall was before them; there was a gate in the wall, and it stood open. But before the pilgrims were allowed to approach they were rudely pulled off their mounts by their Moslem companions who declared that it was unseemly that Christians should enter a town otherwise than on foot.

This was a common practice, to which the pilgrims had grown accustomed in Syria, but here at the gate of Alexandria they were to experience a worse rebuff. At sight of them "the guards, shutting the gate behind them, rushed at us, waving sticks and staves and crying that this gate was open for the people of Alexandria, and known Moslems and servants of Mahomet, but certainly not for dogs of Christians." These, the pilgrims learnt, must go further along the walls, to a gate "where foreigners are examined and tested to see whether they were fit to be let in or not," and where, in fact, the customs officials conducted their inquisitions.*

On, therefore, the pilgrims trudged, but, unfortunately, not unaccompanied. For, "some Saracen boys who were playing together at their childish games outside the first gate, seeing us, left their play, and ran after us, shouting and jeering and throwing stones." When the pilgrims retaliated, the young rascals took to using slings, and, safely out of range, kept up their attack. Meanwhile, "some men ran along the walls, shouting at us and throwing stones. Never," says Felix plaintively, "were we so ill-received as at Alexandria." This was not to be wondered at, for the people of Alexandria had not forgotten the terrible storm, sack and massacre perpetrated by the Western adventurers under King Peter of Cyprus, little more than a hundred years earlier, which had scattered silks and gems from the wealthy city throughout Europe and as far as distant England,[43] filled the streets with dead, and initiated a period of decline from which medieval Alexandria never recovered.[44]

At last the wretched pilgrims, "in great weariness, and so weak and spent with hunger and manifold tribulations that we could hardly walk," reached the gate to which they had been directed, "large, high, wonderfully defended by turrets and ramparts, with iron bars, and a fourfold

* The pilgrims, coming from Abukir along the coast, must have approached the ancient "Sun Gate" or "Canopic Gate," later the "Rosetta Gate." De Lannoy (p. 108) says that Christians were not admitted by a gate on this side, and supposes that the reason for this was the proximity of one of the two "Mounts" or fortified posts within the city; this was probably the ancient artificial mound called Kom ed-Dik. (Baedeker, *Lower Egypt*, 1895, pp. 16 and 11.) The gate to which the pilgrims were sent must have been that known as the Gate of the Column (*ibid.*, p. 15. See Pococke, Plan, Vol. I, p. 2; Kahle, *Mélanges Maspero*, p. 143). The Bab ez Zuhri (Kahle, *loc. cit.*) would have been closer to the Kom ed-Dik, but neither de Lannoy nor Pococke mention this gate.

entrance from gate to gate... and there was a drawbridge over the ditch between the two gates." So Felix describes the elaborate and impressive barbican connecting the inner and outer walls of the city, which were, like the houses of Alexandria, of white stone.[45]

At the outer gate stood one of the customs officials; but when the pilgrims approached he exacted only a trifling duty on the beasts. At this most unexpected moderation–for the Alexandrian customs examination was the bogey of every pilgrim's waking dreams–their spirits soared; they began to think that they had "escaped from the hands of the tax collectors by the first payment," that late as it was these officials had gone home for the night, and that it would be possible to slip into the town unobserved and un-examined.

A Saracen guard met them at the first gate and admitted them in silence, only ordering them, once inside, to halt; "when all our company had come in they shut the door, and told us to move on."

Beyond the inner gate of this first tower of the barbican the pilgrims found themselves in a "twisting (*curva*) road between very high walls and towers,* which led to the inner gate of iron...."[46] Hopefully pressing forward to this gate, which stood open, they were sharply pulled up by a considerable armed guard, which, with sticks and cudgels, warned them to go no further. These guards then withdrew into the city, locking the gate behind them, and telling the pilgrims that they would have to pass the customs next morning.

"So then," says Felix, "we stood hemmed in by gates of iron, and bolts and iron chains and great high walls." Halliu had been admitted with them, but the camels, with all their baggage, remained outside. They were still fasting, and though they had some biscuit with them, this was practically uneatable unless soaked in water. In this desperate condition they acted *sans façon;* each man took up a stone from the roadway and began to beat upon the gate which led into the city. At that up rushed Halliu, "and sternly scolded us for making such a noise, but we took no notice of him, trusting in the humanity of the people of Alexandria, that they would not let us perish, as we were like to do."

Roused by the clatter, some neighbouring members of that population came hurrying to the gate to ask what it was all about. The pilgrims explained their need, and since at the foot of the gate there was a considerable gap between the iron-bound timbers and the ground, they were able to push money through, and even water-jars and flasks. Away went the townsmen, to return with "bread, but hot, and just out of the oven,

---

* Martoni (p. 587) nearly a hundred years earlier, speaks of "a sort of vault curving back (*revolvens*) towards the second gate."

and jars of water, and a basket of fruit of the date-palm. So we sat down, and each had a little of what had been brought, and felt better for it, but by no means satisfied, for we were as hungry as dogs, and thirsty as the hart, and what we ate rather sharpened than satisfied our appetites; but we were grateful all the same for the kindness of the heathen."[47]

They were grateful, too, for another thing; though penned in like sheep, they knew that no one could get in to molest them. With good cheer they disposed themselves for the sleep of which they were so much in need. Yet before Friar Felix lay down that night he had carried out one of his solitary tours of investigation. On the right hand side of the inner gate he found "a small door left open by which there was a way through into the space between the high inner wall of the city and the outer wall which rises from the edge of the moat." It was possible to go a long way in this space between the walls; it was also possible "to climb up the outer wall to the ramparts, and into several towers, and this," says the Friar, that indefatigable climber of every commanding height, "this I did."[45]*

* For a description of this double line of fortifications in the seventeenth century see Pococke, I, pp. 3-4.

CHAPTER XIII

Alexandria: "The public market of both worlds"

"Whoever is lord of Cairo," said the merchant Piloti, "may call himself lord and master of Christendom . . . and . . . of all the islands and places where the spices grow, since of necessity all merchandise of spicery from whatever direction can come and be sold only in the land of the Sultan . . . this," he explains, and Friar Felix, who had seen the land-barrier which lay between the Mediterranean and the Gulf of Suez, would have taken his point, "this, is because Cairo is built between two seas."[1]

The strategic mercantile position of Egypt had been accepted as a disagreeable but ineluctable fact by the maritime powers of the Mediterranean, since the Moslem conquest of the country. Merchants of Venice, Genoa or Aragon sheltered as much as they might behind the prestige or diplomatic skill of their states, and for the rest must put up with whatever oppression or extortion was meted out to them by the Moslem Sultans. It was worth the merchant's while to endure. The spice trade, calculated to supply the demands of medieval trans-Alpine cookery, was great not only in volume but in value; it has been assessed as worth, at the very least, a million ducats annually; a single big Venetian galeasse returning from Alexandria with her holds full of spice-sacks would carry cargo to the value of 200,000 ducats, and even a mixed freight of cinnamon, indigo, Brazil-wood, incense and Indian gum lac, gone to the bottom off Sicily, meant a loss of 35,000 ducats.[2]

It was the Atlantic nations of Southern Europe, the Spaniards and Portuguese, who, refusing to accept the situation, had set themselves with diligence and secrecy to find another sea route, which would bring them, as Friar Felix had imagined them being brought by the broken and sand-choked canal of the Pharaohs, to the spice lands of the far east. The results of enterprises of such magnitude and moment, and continued over so many years, though carefully hushed up, could not be altogether concealed. Felix Fabri himself noted the efforts "of a certain King of Spain of our time to discover ways of reaching, from the western ocean . . . beyond the Straits of Hercules, the Sea of India. But," he added, "he has tried in vain, though it is said that he has found some islands previously unknown, and very rich."[3]

That long period of effort was to end in 1498, when the Portuguese galleons which had weathered the Cape of Storms came to anchor in the harbour of Calcutta. But at the time when Friar Felix made his pilgrimage, and for nearly a quarter of a century more, Egypt, "the boundary of Africa and Asia," continued to hold the central and governing position in a great two-way movement of trade, so that the Alexandria at which the Friar and his friends had arrived was, as William of Tyre three hundred years before had called her, "the public market of both worlds."

The route by which the spices and other Eastern imports reached Egypt varied from time to time during the Middle Ages,[4] but the shoals and rocks of the Red Sea never allowed the ocean-going ships of India, or the big Chinese junks, to land their cargoes direct at any Egyptian port. During the fifteenth century trans-shipment took place on the Arabian coast. The merchants of India or China landed their goods twice a year, but in greater quantities at the autumn season, at Jiddah, the port for Mecca, to be met at the holy Moslem city by the traders of Syria and Egypt, by the customs officers of the Sultan, and, incidentally, when the seasons coincided, by the huge concourse of the Hajj pilgrimage.[5]

From Mecca the Egyptian or Syrian merchants, or those Indians who chose to sell in Cairo or Damascus,[6] had a choice of route. Those who dealt in the least heavy and most costly spices would make the journey by land, travelling with their camel caravans along the Hajj route and often with the returning Hajj pilgrims.[7]

But the bulk of the spices was loaded at Jiddah into small coastal craft which, sailing always in company, by day only, and close inshore,[8] made their way to the port of Tor on the west coast of the Sinai Peninsula, a tiny town of reed-built, mud-plastered houses, among the palm-groves of the monks of St. Katherine's monastery.[9] This was the end of their sea-journey. The prevailing wind in the Gulf of Suez is northerly, and whereas the southerly run can be accomplished in a matter of hours, for a boat going north it may be lengthened out to eight or ten days.[10] For this reason it was better to pay the higher cost of land transport from Tor, and the great spice sacks were transferred to the backs of camels brought in by the Arabs of the peninsula, two sacks to each camel, and so set off upon the last stage of their journey to Cairo by that same road upon which our pilgrims had entered when they left the mountains behind them, and by which they also reached Egypt.

Felix Fabri and his companions missed the sight of the great merchant caravan, but another pilgrim, the Spaniard Tafur, if we may believe him,* travelled with it, a caravan of "so many camels ... that I cannot," said he, "give an account of them as I do not wish to speak extravagantly," and laden with "spices, pearls, precious stones and gold, perfumes and linen and parrots and cats from India."[11] In the company of merchants went one, who though his packs were full of the rich and strange commodities of the Far East, was himself a Venetian born; this was Niccolo Conti, a man of many travels, experiences and sorrows, who entertained Tafur with stories—some very tall—of Malabar, India, Sumatra and Java; who showed him "a ruby of great worth," "and also a round hat of grass as delicate as the finest silk," and gave him some pellets of earth from the tomb of St. Thomas the Apostle.[12]

At Cairo the spices were warehoused outside the walls of the city, and no western Christian merchant was allowed to buy.[13] The last stage of the long journey of these precious products of the East, prior to their shipment in the western galleys, was that which Felix and his companions had shared as they sailed down the Nile, and at Alexandria the pilgrims happened to witness the very moment of their transference to the waiting ships. During one of their expeditions through the city they came out by the *Douane* gate upon the shore of the New Harbour, where the western merchantmen were at anchor, to find a crowded and tumultuous scene. There were seamen who had just come ashore, and others loading up boats which would ferry their cargo of spices out to the galleys. Everywhere the sacks, five foot in breadth by fifteen or more in length, lay about the waterside. " ... And though all the sacks had just been filled and weighed at the *fondaco* in the presence of the Saracen officers, and examined at the gates, yet even now when they were just about to be taken on board, the whole contents were spilled out upon the ground so that they might see what was being taken away. And round about this place was a great press, and many hurrying thither, for (when) the sacks ... are emptied there comes hastening a crowd of poor folk, women and boys, Arabs and Africans, and whatever they can grab they steal, and they search in the sand for ginger and cloves, cinnamon and nutmegs."

Such pilfering could not always be carried on with impunity. If "these thieving beggars" grew too numerous, and there might be fifty or more of them round about the heaps of spilled spices, or too importunate, the merchants would have them driven off by a Mamluk, the blows of whose staff, unmerciful and impartial, would fall upon any of the fleeing crowd, whether old men, boys or pregnant women. Yet the risk was worth taking, for they would hang about at the gate, willing to sell their trove

* Tafur's estimate of the distance between Tor and Mount Sinai (p. 84) is so grotesquely wrong that it may be questioned if he ever visited the latter.

cheap, "and some of the merchants follow them, and buy what they have found or stolen."[14]

While from the east this great movement of trade was taking place, ships of the Christian west drew to the same port, that is to say ships of Southern Europe, for as Felix Fabri realised, "the merchants thus divided the world; all the men of the west beyond the Alps... trade in Italy... and go no further, but the Italians,"—and he might have added the Catalonians and men of Southern France and the Adriatic Coast—"compass the Mediterranean."[15]

To Alexandria then the merchant galleys came to trade the goods of the west against the far more costly commodities of the east, and in closing the gap left by this adverse balance of trade to pour "a fountain of gold and silver"[16] into the treasury of one of the two great military powers of the Moslem world. This result of the traffic did not leave the conscience of Christendom entirely at ease. Piloti, a merchant himself, but a man who had set his heart upon a new Crusade, could not but admit that those who thus ministered to the power of Mamluk Egypt were "slaves of their goods to the Sultan." During the Crusading era Pope after Pope had tried to prohibit the trade, or at least to ensure that such vital war materials as iron and timber should not be supplied by Christian merchants to the chief Moslem power.[17] But the insatiable appetite of man for gainful commerce broke through or circumvented all restrictions; more and more the Mediterranean trade with Alexandria was geared to supply, through Egypt, the demands of consumers in Abyssinia, India and the islands of the Indian Archipelago,[18] and Piloti regretfully, respectfully, but plainly, told the Pope that "it is not possible that Christians should obey Your Holiness and that they should not come to Alexandria."[19] Obedience, in fact, would have entailed the total collapse of the medieval European system of commerce.

Spices, and especially pepper, constituted the main body of Egyptian trade with the West, and Venice was by now the chief exporter. But apart from spices the chief value of the cargoes of the East consisted in such articles of luxury as those which Tafur recorded, and those "jewels, balas rubies, diamonds... and all manner of gems" which Piloti lists,[20] while from Egypt itself the Venetian merchants took home with them delicacies for rich men's tables at home; dates and sugar,[21] capers which the Arabs sold to the Egyptians and the Egyptians bottled and sold to the West; or the thin-skinned lemons of Alexandria, the best in the world, which, preserved in large jars "in a certain syrup," were afterwards exported at 3 or 4 ducats a bottle.[22]

Upon the other hand Europe was ransacked for goods to offer against the rich products of the East. Woollen cloth was their chief cargo, of Spain, of Lombardy, and from the looms of Venice itself; brass in various forms, copper and furs; from Flanders came fine cloth "in great quantity and of great value," amber, soap, saffron and tin; coral of Spain and Ragusa, honey of Corfu and the Greek dominions of Venice, with wax, and the olive oil which Egypt lacked,[23]–all these and many more were brought to the markets of Alexandria. Some of the commodities might seem homely and common enough, yet the merchants found it profitable to carry oak galls overseas to Egypt, and the pilgrims were amazed to see how high a price a cargo of those filbert nuts would fetch at Alexandria, nuts which in the West "are for sale to children for their games, and are rated ... like acorns."[24]

Yet, though in general the West exchanged goods of use for goods of luxury, wives of rich Mamluks would choose fine Rheims linen to wear next their skin, and their husbands bought the cloth of gold, and gold brocades of Venice.[25] By now, too, the glass-makers of Murano had learnt the skills long monopolised by the East, and exported to Egypt even the glass lamps upon which appeared among trails of coloured flowers, texts of the Koran, or the device of some Mamluk Emir, or the name of the Sultan himself, which pious Moslem benefactors hung up in their mosques.[26]

All this volume of trade was immensely profitable to both parties. At Mecca, at Tor, at Alexandria, the Sultan exacted a toll, now of 10 per cent., now of 18 per cent., and his officials, even to the most exalted, took their squeeze as well,[27] so that it was reckoned among Venetian merchants, that out of every two or three galleys which left the port of Alexandria with their holds full of spices, the profit of the cargo of one had been eaten up by customs duties; and still "the merchants always wish to return, because they gain cent per cent and more on merchandise which here is useless and of little value."[28] Besides, as Piloti understood, it was not the merchant, but the consumers in far-away Germany or Flanders who paid the Sultan's exorbitant customs dues upon the spices used in their kitchens.[29]

For this reason, and since "Interest never lies," in spite of the conscientious scruples of Christendom, in spite of the greed or tyrannous caprice, or more or less justifiable anger of the Mamluk Sultans, who took their revenge upon resident western merchants for such dire injuries as the sack of Alexandria, or for some semi-piratical exploit of the unbendingly hostile knights of St. John, the trade bond held.

The Sultan's interest in the foreign Christian merchants, at once predatory and protective, led him to supply them in Alexandria with facilities of various kinds. Numerous warehouses were provided, of which the western merchants held the keys; officially sponsored auctions were arranged for the disposal of their goods; their bargains, if witnessed by the Sultan's officers, were protected and the terms enforced, by the custom of the city.[30]

As well as all this, at Alexandria the Sultan fostered rather than permitted the foundation of a settled and domiciled colony of western merchants. Just as in Cairo he built his nobly planned *wekâlas* or *khans* for the accommodation of the traders of Turkey, the Yemen, Persia and India,[31] so at Alexandria he provided *fondachi* for those of the west. Here the merchant found living accommodation for himself and warehouse space for his merchandise, conveniently close to the harbour,[32] the cost of building and the running expenses being debited to the profits of the Sultan's *douane*.[33]

The fifteenth century, which saw the appropriation of so great a proportion of the spice trade by Venice, saw also, as a consequence, a reduction in the number of *fondachi* at Alexandria, so that in 1483 there remained only, two for the Venetians, and one each for the Genoese and Spaniards, apart from those allotted to the Moslem traders, Turks, "Moors," or Tartars.[34]

If, as would seem not improbable, the general plan of the *fondachi* of Alexandria was the same as that of the Venetian Fondaco dei Tedeschi, we can see in Jacopo Barbari's view of the latter, and to a certain extent in the larger building which, after the fire of 1502, replaced the one he pictured, the appearance of the *fondachi* at Alexandria. Rectangular buildings of at least two storeys, "like large fine houses"[35] they were built around one or more courtyards, with vaulted store-houses on the ground floor, and living quarters above, the rooms of which opened upon a wide vaulted walk, "like a cloister of Friars," with arched openings giving on the court.[36]* At the Fondaco dei Tedeschi the side of this walk towards the court is surrounded not by a balustrade or narrow parapet, but by a thick wall with its top sloping inwards, to provide perhaps a convenient space for the display of goods.

The courtyard below, which, at the time of the spice market, took the overflow of the merchandise, provided also space for a garden of rare plants, and a home for tame animals and birds: ostriches, gazelles, young lions, leopards or monkeys, "white parrots, very costly, parrots red all over or some red with black markings, and many of the common

---

* E. Lane (*The Modern Egyptians*, 1908, pp. 320-1) gives a similar description of the *wekâlehs* existing in Cairo in the nineteenth century.

green bird." At the larger of the two Venetian *fondachi* an unusual pet was kept; a huge pig wandered about in the courtyard, an animal which, having a perverse antipathy to the pork-eschewing Moslems, was the bane of any of these who came unawares into the court.[37] Here also were some ostriches, one of which accepted and swallowed "quite a large key, as big as a finger" which Friar Paul offered it, and looked to his hand for more.

As well as lodging and warehousing the Sultan thoughtfully endowed the western visitors with a bakery, to provide them with the sort of bread to which they were accustomed, and a bath for their exclusive use; they were allowed to import wine, though the customs officials saw to it that this import would cost them dear; and each *fondaco* had its own chapel and resident chaplain.[38] The merchant community decided its own hours of opening and closing, subject always to the proviso that the *fondaco* must close during the Moslem hours of prayer every Friday; they were free also to elect their own officers, the chief of these being the "Consul," who was responsible for order in the *fondaco*, and who received, at the Sultan's expense, not only a free residence but a salary of 200 ducats.

But some of the duties of the Consul took him far beyond the walls of the *fondaco*, since he was in fact a go-between for his fellows in any matter which necessitated an appeal to the Sultan.[39] Even in the earlier part of the century this was a charge which might call for as much courage as tact, and there was sometimes blunt speech on both sides, as when the Venetian consul, protesting against the tyranny of some of the Sultan's high officials, went so far as to threaten the withdrawal of all Venetian merchants from Alexandria, and received from the Sultan the reply that "as to the power of you Venetians, and after that of the rest of Christendom, I hold . . . it not so high as a pair of old shoes."[40] Sometimes the consul was unfortunate enough to find himself in his negotiations like corn between the upper and nether millstones. Thus the dignified and gentle Andrea de Cabriel, who showed such kindness in Cairo to Friar Felix and his companions, had come to the capital, so he told them, upon an awkward piece of business; for while their own German countrymen buying spices in Venice would accept only those which were "sorted, picked over and of the best quality" in Alexandria, when the Venetians bought in bulk, they must take the shipload, "without sorting and without picking over . . . as they come from India, nor," said he, ruefully, "do they let us see beforehand what we are going to buy."[41]

We should in fact be mistaken if we supposed that the Moslem ruler of Egypt was moved by altrusim in his foundation of, and relations with, the *fondachi*. For visiting merchants the institution was invaluable, but it served the Sultan's purposes too, and in other ways besides the mere attraction of trade to the city. When an occasion arose in which, to his mind, it was advisable to put pressure upon any of the western powers, the concentration of merchants in a few great communities, put them conveniently in his power. And for all their internal freedoms, the wealthy visitants of each *fondaco* were every night as strictly gated as the undergraduates of an Oxford college; for Moslem officials went the rounds, locking the doors and removing the keys, till the hour, early the following morning, when these were opened again for the day.[42]

Friar Felix and his companions, reaching Alexandria from Cairo, had passed around the eastern wall of the city to a gate on the southern or landward side. Many pilgrims, however, and almost all western merchants, approached the city by sea, and thus saw her at once for what she was, "a great sea-port, and a great place of loading and unloading for Christians."[43]

As the ships drew near to the mainland of Africa the first sign of their proximity to Egypt was not any glimpse of the flat alluvial coast, but the outflow of the great river, which, charged with its silt, might stain the bright sea for many miles out.[44] Only when within twenty miles of the shore would the shipmen make out the two artificial hills within the city, and, after 1472, the new fortification built by Qa'it Bey–a guard tower with a mosque, mill and bakehouse,[45] at the eastern seaward tip of the long and narrow tongue of land which thrust out beyond the northern city walls, and divided from each other the two harbours.

In the guard tower perpetual watch was kept for approaching ships, and at the first sight of a sail port officers would row out to intercept the vessel and to conduct an inquiry as to her home-port, cargo, passengers and crew. These officials always brought along with them a crate of the carrier pigeons, the activities of which so greatly interested western visitors, and by one of these birds reported back–in duplicate, a modern touch–to the Emir, who was the military governor of Alexandria, and to the Sultan.[46]* When permission had been given to proceed, the ship, dipping her mainsail in token of respect to the fortress of Qa'it Bey as she passed, entered the eastern of the two harbours, known in the Middle Ages as the New Port,† and anchored half-a-mile or so off shore.[47] Once she lay at her moorings rudder and sails must be handed over to the port authorities, to be returned only when the shipmaster had fulfilled all the necessary conditions for departure.[48]

* Frescobaldi (p. 75) says that nothing was written down, but this seems to be unusual.
† Actually the original port of Alexandria.

View of Alexandria, from Pierre Belon's *Portraits d'Oyseaux, Animaux, etc. . . . d'Arabie*, Paris, 1552.

ALEXANDRIA: "THE PUBLIC MARKET OF BOTH WORLDS"

The landing place for merchants and their goods was upon the curving strand or quay, close to the city walls, and to the most easterly of three gates. This, a smaller gate than the imposing "common gate" of the town, was opened three times a week, and by it all merchants and merchandise must enter, for this was the first of the two "gates of the *douane*," the second being beyond it and upon the inner fortification, which here, as in the south of the city, consisted of a double line of walls.[49]*

At the outer *douane* gate the merchant himself underwent examination by the port authorities before whom he must, with the help of the "Consul of the Franks" and other merchants of his own state, establish his nationality and identity, and having done so must pay a landing tax, which, by the end of the fifteenth century, had risen from 1 to 2 ducats,† and a tax of 2 per cent. upon any silver which he brought with him.[50]

Next came the examination by the customs officials of the incoming merchandise which had been carried by porters or beasts of burden to the inner *douane* in which stood the great scales after which the place was named *Dogana del Gabbano*.‡ Here the merchant had a choice of two alternatives. He might leave his stuff in bond, in one of the great warehouses which lay thirty in a row against the outer face of the second wall of the city, or he might at once pay duty on it, and have it carried within his *fondaco*.[51]

The severity, ingenuity and thoroughness of customs officials of Alexandria were known to all western travellers. "They had us searched," says one merchant, "to our very shirts, and it was the same for the merchandise; they opened and searched everything which was tied up."[52]

But one condition mitigated the rigour of this customs examination. Should a merchant be caught in the act of smuggling, no penalty would be exacted, "for they say, 'Hide it as well as you know how, and I will search you as well as I can.'"[53]

Western merchants did not fail to respond to this challenge, and as large a sum as 600 ducats might come, undiscovered, through the customs, securely hidden "in the lock of the little chest."[54]§ But if this was smuggling on a sufficiently grand scale, it pales before the exploit achieved

---

* This seems to be the most probable interpretation of the various notices of the lay-out of the seaward walls and gates, *fondachi* and *douanes*. Piloti's account of these, detailed and interesting as it is, contains various obscurities owing to the very curious French into which the treatise of the Cretan-born Italian is translated, possibly by the author himself (Piloti, p. 312 n.).

† Pilgrims paid 5 ducats unless they managed, like von Harff, to pass themselves off as merchants (von Harff, p. 93).

‡ Italianised from the Persian Kabban (Heyd II, 451 n.).

§ "... nel regolo del cassoncello." I am indebted to Dr. Barbara Reynolds for the suggestion that the above is the meaning, in this passage, of the word *regolo*.

by Emanuel Piloti, when, as Consul of the Genoese, he lived in their *fondaco*, which in those days stood near to the inner *douane* gate. Piloti, realising that a certain warehouse of the *fondaco* backed upon one of the *douane* stores in which the more delicate merchandise lay in bond, and that the wall between was but frail, "with my own hands, and with one of my servants, broke through . . . so that I got in, and brought away a quantity of stuff belonging to myself and others . . . velvets, silk, cloth of gold, amber, saffron. . . ."[55]

CHAPTER XIV

The pilgrims at Alexandria

Friar Felix and his companions, enclosed between the inner and outer walls of the city, and therefore under restraint but also insulated from undesired interference, enjoyed a sleep so sound that it compensated for the painful watches of the two previous nights. At once on wakening, however, they must bend their minds to the problem of how best to dispose of their goods in preparation for the formidable customs examination. At day-break they were already busied about the concealment of those costly or forbidden exports which they hoped might escape the piercing glances of the officials;[1] the money, the balm, the precious stones, the lengths of silk, the works of Cairene gold- or silver-smiths[2] which the rich knights had bought.

Friar Felix was involved in this anxious activity, for he collaborated with some of his wealthy companions by hiding more than 100 of their ducats in his water jar. Others, he tells us, concealed their contraband among the biscuits, or dropped ducats or gems into jars of oil or sank them into the butter or cheese; yet here the reader begins to doubt whether the Friar is not enriching his narrative by suggestions culled from the writings or conversation of other pilgrims, since he has previously so tragically insisted upon the starving condition of his own party. Yet we may perhaps believe that he himself hid in a bag of flour a purseful of those rings and chains belonging to friends at home, which at the Monastery of St. Katherine he had laid upon the Saint's tomb.[3]

However heightened the Friar's account may be, it is yet not difficult to believe that the pilgrims were instant to hide what they might where they could, and that their chagrin was therefore considerable when the wretched Halliu told them that it would be far wiser to leave bags and baskets uncorded, and everything easily accessible, since all that was made fast would be slashed open and rigorously searched by the customs officers. When the pilgrims objected the protection of the Sultan's letter, which had cost them so dear, Halliu's advice was that they had better hide that too. With what feelings of distress and indignation we may easily imagine, the pilgrims re-packed, putting what was dutiable on top, and only persisting in keeping hidden their money and jewels.

Meanwhile a growing commotion from beyond the outer walls had announced the presence of a concourse of merchants with their laden camels, impatiently waiting for the gate to be opened in order themselves to pass the Sultan's customs, for this gate, named both then and now "the Gate of the Column" from the proximity of "Pompey's Column" a little way outside the walls, was in the Middle Ages and to Western travellers known as Pepper Gate, since through it must pass all cargoes of spice brought by road or river from Cairo to the market of Alexandria.[4]

The pilgrims, confident of their favourable position at the head of the queue, were sadly disappointed when, after opening the inner gate, the customs officials swept them and their stuff out of the fairway, and admitted the merchant-men with their camels. As there were, according to Friar Felix, close on a hundred of these, and as each beast was made to couch while the load was examined, and each man stripped and searched, there was plenty of time for the pilgrims' hearts to sink to the level of their boots.

But now they were approached by Shadbak* the Dragoman of Alexandria, " . . . a handsome man and swarthy (*niger*), big, well-built and with a choleric look, a mighty Mamluk, who knowing Italian greeted us gently and welcomed each one of us after their custom by a kiss."[5] No wonder, after all that the pilgrims had suffered from the moody and avaricious Taghribirdi and the supine, indifferent Halliu that, as Felix says, "thereby he broke the cords of our hearts and we put our whole trust in him."[6] At once the pilgrims asked his advice about the Sultan's letter. Certainly, he told them, they should show it to the officials, though he confirmed Halliu's warning of the infallible skill with which these men would ferret out even the most cunningly hidden jewels. Having next exhorted them to patience during the search, this cultivated and erudite Dragoman quoted to them similar examinations to which "the ancient city of Athens" subjected strangers. Finally, urging them above all to avoid showing any impatience during the scrutiny, for that would only make the search the more rigorous, he told them that "he intended to be present among the officials, so that they should not treat us badly."[7]

After a long period of waiting the turn of the pilgrims came. Shadbak led away to the officials, who sat "in the inner gateway under the gate-tower itself," the chief persons among the pilgrims' company, for even at the *douane* social precedence was observed.[8] The rest of the pilgrims

---

* "*Schambeck.*" But it seems probable that Fabri was trying to render the above name. There was at this time an Emir Shadbak (Ibn Iyas, p. 175).

looked on while the Sultan's letter was presented, received with signs of the greatest reverence, kissed, opened and read.

After all Fabri's strictures upon the Chief Interpreter of Cairo he might here have admitted that perhaps the letter which Taghribirdi had obtained for the pilgrims was worth its price. For now, when at last the dreaded customs' officials began their examination, "One by one," says the Friar, "they lifted the bags and baskets assessing their weight, and then searched them, but rather casually than carefully, not unfastening all that were closed, but doing it all in a hurry. When the stuff had been examined they stood in the gateway and, calling us one by one, searched our clothes and purses, and set aside separately each man's gold and silver, but did not strip us. And when I came to them, and they saw that I was a priest, they did nothing at all to me; they did not open the purse which I carried openly at my belt, but passed me through as a poor man, which in fact I was. . . . And so," Felix concludes, as if even in the recollection he drew a breath of relief, "And so, harmlessly, that storm passed over. Indeed it seemed to me that they were as loath to search as we to be searched." When all but the priests had paid 8 medines each the dreaded encounter was over.[9]*

They were now free to enter the city, and Shadbak, having fetched camels and donkeys, led the procession, presumably along the great thoroughfare of Pepper Street, upon which the Pepper Gate opened. He did not at once bring them to their lodging, but instead to the house of the Emir, the military Governor of Alexandria for the Sultan. This visit, which all pilgrims must pay, was sometimes, as for Frescobaldi and his companions, deferred for several days after their arrival, and might be an affair of great ceremony;[10] conducted through one of those splendid Alexandrian interiors, "paved with mosaic of marble, porphyry and other precious stones, the doors inlaid with ebony and ivory . . . each worth a well-full of gold,"[11] the Florentine merchants, in their stocking feet, had approached the Emir, kneeling three times before they drew near to the high dais upon which he sat cross-legged among a respectful crowd of Moslems, there to be closely questioned as to the purpose of their journey.[12]

This time, however, the interview was far less ceremonious. The Emir, "an old man, comely and venerable," himself came out to meet them, and after looking long and keenly at each one, and thus, Felix believed, in a single glance sizing up the strangers, he gave them their *permis de séjour*.

* Breydenbach, 121s, and Walther, p. 240, speak of a very thorough search both of persons and baggage, and payment of duty on some articles.

During the centuries Christian pilgrims arriving at Alexandria were lodged now here, now there, but not, it seems, at the house of the Chief Dragoman as at Cairo, since here it was easy and convenient to provide for them at one or other of the *fondachi*. At the end of the fourteenth century a French pilgrim stayed at the *fondaco* of Narbonne, not because he was a Frenchman, but because the "Consul" in charge of that *fondaco* held also from the Sultan the appointment of "Consul of the Pilgrims," and had the right to their fees.[13] A quarter of a century later another Frenchman found that pilgrims were lodged at the Venetian *fondaco* and was impressed by the lavish hospitality shown there to travellers of whatever Christian nation.[14]

In 1483 pilgrims put up at the Aragonese or, as Felix calls it, the Catalan *fondaco*, and thither, accordingly, Shadbak led his charges. Even as they entered the courtyard the Consul himself met them with a friendly greeting, servants ran out to help with the baggage, "and glad indeed we were," says the Friar, "to come once more into a Christian house . . . it made us feel that we were again in our own country."[15]

While the Consul hurried away to order a much-needed meal for his guests, the pilgrims had the satisfaction of giving Halliu his discharge, who filled to the brim his cup of iniquity by one last piece of ingenious knavery. Before the customs' examination had taken place, one of the knights, wrought upon by all that he had heard of the exactions of the officials, entrusted to Halliu a golden image of St. Christopher. Now he would only surrender it for a sum far larger than the heaviest possible duty. The unfortunate owner yielded; Halliu departed, and with him went also the Dragoman of Alexandria, having first warned the pilgrims that until he returned next day, none must go beyond the *fondaco*.

With what must have been a feeling of holiday gaiety the pilgrims now followed the Consul to the living rooms above, where the Consul's lady waited to welcome them; she "though a Greek" was a woman of great piety and was to prove herself a very good friend to Friar Felix.[16] Here, in a handsome apartment, the hungry travellers sat down to a "sumptuous dinner, and we drank wine from gold and silver cups and felt much better for it."[17] The pilgrims in fact were to fare well at Alexandria. All, as was customary, occupied unfurnished rooms,[18] but while the first of the three companies, that of von Breydenbach, young Solms and his tutor, preferred to board themselves, the other two sampled for the first time since leaving Jerusalem, food which was bought, cooked and served for residents in the country, and the Aragonese *fondaco* was chosen thirty years later as the place where an ambassador of France might be lodged and banqueted upon a regale of "many good fish, sweetmeats, fruit, and good wine."[19] Indeed the quality and variety of the food supplies of Alexandria roused the enthusiasm of more than one visitor. There was an abundance of all kinds of vegetables, "and fruit the best in the world, especially oranges . . . sweet as sugar . . . pears, apples, plums . . . the hugest of water-melons, yellow inside and with seeds between red and yellow, and truly the tongue of man cannot express the delicate flavour of them."[20] At the Consul's table the pilgrims will probably have enjoyed all these; will have been served with the boned meat which was customary, so that a man must ask if he wished to get a bone upon his plate; and, among the inevitably frequent dishes of poultry, will have sampled the little fat quails which a buyer would inspect alive in their small cages, "and you choose the fattest as you please."[21]

When the meal was over the new arrivals, turning their attention to the business of settling in, went down into the courtyard to collect their baggage. It was in this humdrum occupation that Friar Felix came as near as he had perhaps ever been to a sudden and painful death.

"I," he explains, "was standing by the baggage and thought I would separate the things belonging to our company, because everything lay mixed up in one heap. Now, we had a big basket in which were the heavier utensils, and it was so heavy that I could not lift it off the ground, so I laid hold of the basket and dragged it out of the heap, stooping and going backwards, and because it was heavy I did it with a heave, running backwards as fast as possible, and I could not look behind to see where I was going. But while I dragged the basket after me, dear me! what a shout was raised by those looking on from above–'Friar! Friar! get away! get away!' and my companions below, too, shouted to me to look out and get away quick!"

When he did look behind him to learn the reason for the excitement, he found that the rear of his stooping figure was within reach of the claws of a chained and savage leopard. Hastily altering his course, he got himself out of danger; and how grave that danger had been he must have realised a few days later when the same leopard tore off at a blow the wing of one of the tame ostriches which wandered about the courtyard, and which was as imprudent as he in coming within the leopard's range, and not so lucky.[22]

The day which, beginning among so many anxieties and apprehensions, had brought the pilgrims to the comfort and friendliness of the Aragonese *fondaco*, had still more pleasures in store. News of the arrival of a party of pilgrims had spread to the ships in the harbour, and now came ashore the hospitable Venetian sea-captains, not only to welcome but also to entertain the new arrivals, for they brought their own wine with them, and the whole company sat down to a conviviality which reminded Felix of the drinking clubs at home in Ulm.[23] These friendly visitors also led the pilgrims to the roof of the *fondaco*, from which they found themselves looking across the bright water of the harbour to the anchored ships, a sight beautiful in itself but to the pilgrims something more, for their hearts leapt at it, "as if we had caught a glimpse of the city to which we belonged." For Friar Felix there was yet another happy event. When he turned away from the view of the sea and the crowded ships he saw standing below in the courtyard two Dominican Friars. The sight of that familiar habit, after so long and coming so unexpectedly, caused a joy great enough to be almost painful; he hurried down and was welcomed by the two Italian brothers "honorary chaplains to the merchants," one of them, a Sicilian, attached to the Aragonese *fondaco*, and the other, a Genoese, at the *fondaco* of that city. They were to be good friends to him while he was in Alexandria, and began their kind offices at once by showing him where the key of the *fondaco's* chapel was hidden.

The visit of the two Friars was the last event of a full day. "Since it was now evening we sat down to dine by lamplight with the Consul with great good cheer, and at last went off to our rooms and lay down in those beds which we had brought from Jerusalem."[24]

Before the pilgrims could make any expedition of pleasure, piety or business in Alexandria it was necessary that they should pay their fees to the Shadbak, and that he should introduce them to the port officials. After dinner on the day following their arrival he returned to the *fondaco*, and having called them together read his rules and stated his terms; for dues, safe-conduct, and liberty to go about the city, he demanded of each the sum of 13 ducats.

At the mention of such a sum the pilgrims may well have gasped. When they spoke it was to object that "in the little books of pilgrims who had been here before, we find no more than 6 ducats a head, and why did he want to charge us more?"*

"To which, 'I care not for your books,' said he. 'I stick to the terms of my rules.'" Then, having advised them to "'take thought and pay without dispute,'" and warned them not to go beyond the *fondaco*, "'until I first have brought you out; if you go out by yourselves you will fare

---

* Von Harff (p. 93) gives 5 ducats as the amount paid by pilgrims at Alexandria. But the list given by Suriano (p. 35) which includes fees to a number of officials, reaches a total of 19 ducats per pilgrim, with a lump sum payment of 6 ducats from all the pilgrims. It is possible that some of these fees were included in Shadbak's total, which would then seem to be not so exorbitant after all.

badly,'" this "man of few words, no wrangler, but resolute," left them to turn over in their minds his demands and his counsel.

Shadbak stated his terms to the pilgrims on Saturday afternoon. They saw nothing of him on Sunday, and judging it wise to heed his warning they remained in the *fondaco*, which, however, with its cool, shaded rooms, though within hearing of all the bustle and excitement of the port, was not such an ill place of confinement after all the fatigues of their journey down the Nile.

Yet to be in a strange city for so long and without opportunity for exploration may well have irked Friar Felix. Certainly on Monday morning he disregarded the Dragoman's words, and, as a consequence, experienced one of his embarrassing, but in the upshot, lucky adventures.

He had come down early to read his Office, and had found a quiet and cool seat under the gateway arch. The doors were still closed but while he sat there the Saracen official, who each morning opened them from the outside, turned his key in the lock, swung the doors back and passed on, leaving the Friar confronted with all the stir and variety of a busy street. Perhaps Felix had already finished his prayers; certainly he now closed his book, "got up and stood under the gateway watching the people go by, amazed to see passing men of so many different nations. . . . Christians, both Eastern and Western, Jews, Samaritans, Saracens and Mamluks of both sexes."

Suddenly among the throng of strangers his eye was caught by a familiar face, that of a young man, a barber whom he remembered to have seen in Venice.

"'O'." Felix hailed him "in Italian," "'*Barbarero veza*.'" In what tongue the conversation was continued he does not say, but writes it down for his untravelled ecclesiastical readers in Latin.

"'If only, my good friend,' said I, 'I were in your lodging so that you could wash my head and trim my beard and tonsure. But alas! I am a prisoner, kept here with the rest till we have paid our dues to the Dragoman.'

"To which the young man answered, 'It's early yet and the Saracens aren't up. Come with me, and before the Dragoman leaves his house you shall be back in your place, shaved and washed and your hair done.' And when I was still afraid he said, 'What are you frightened of? You made no promise. So come along.'" Felix went.

But as he returned, spruce, clean and refreshed by all the washing, combing and cutting, he saw coming towards him in the crowd the last man in Alexandria whom he desired to meet. At once he attempted to evade the Dragoman by dodging down a side street.

Shadbak had, however, seen him, "and he called me back in the Saracen tongue.

" 'Thali, ihali, Christiane,' " (so the Friar renders the Arabic 'Ta 'ala') "that is to say, 'Come here, come here Christian.' "

Felix obeyed "trembling," but Shadbak, speaking gently in Italian, merely bade him go back to the *fondaco* and deliver a message to the rest of the pilgrims. The message was stern: he would come after dinner for his money, and if any refused to pay they would be sent to the public jail till they had changed their minds. But the voice and manner of the Dragoman were quite without anger, and Felix took heart.

" 'See, Sir,' I answered him, 'I will tell my lords the pilgrims what you say, but I swear to you by my crucified God that I am a poor friar and priest, and I have no money of my own, and what I had I have long ago used up, and I am supported by the generosity of the lords and am returning at their charges to my own country, which is far from here across seas and mountains.' "

Friar Felix in making this appeal had not mistaken his man. Here once more he had encountered a Moslem, austere yet clement, with that reverence for the manifestations of a rival religion which the Christian pilgrims had often to remark. "He listened to me kindly and said, '*Startu praeto non paga ingenti*,' that is to say, 'You are a priest, you shall pay nothing,' " and turned away, leaving the Friar to return to the *fondaco* and to waken his still sleeping companions with his own good tidings and the Dragoman's ultimatum.

In this curious and polyglot anecdote, with its garbled phrases and dramatic form, the admiration which Felix felt for the impressive personality of Shadbak is clearly to be seen. The reader might suspect that this admiration, and the consistently good Press which Felix gives the Dragoman, were due to Shadbak's liberal treatment of him, were it not clear that the deep impression made upon the Friar by the stern and lofty Moslem was shared by others. For when certain of the knights, smarting under his harsh demands, talked of appealing to the Emir, the Aragonese Consul dissuaded them, saying that, "they would have no chance against Shadbak because all loved him and counted him a true man, and if we fell foul of him we should fare badly in Alexandria."[25]

And, in fact, once the Dragoman had got his own way, he became that efficient and considerate guide, protector and counsellor, which the pilgrims had so sadly lacked since they parted with old Elphahallo at Cairo. He began his duties at once. On horseback, and followed by the pilgrims on foot, he brought them to the *douane* gate, and there pointed them out to the "guards, tax officers, customs' officials and searchers," as having paid their dues, and therefore free to go and come as they chose, though this freedom had certain qualifications. Before he parted with them that afternoon, at the door of the *fondaco*, the Dragoman gave his charges advice for their unattended expeditions. They might now go about the streets, enter the *fondachi* of the merchants, and shop in the markets, and at the cook-houses; but they must not go out of the city by any gate other than that of the *douane*, and must on no account approach the two artificial heights within the walls; they would be wise also to avoid the little lonely alleys among the ruinous parts of Alexandria.[26]

There were many of these last, for the city, though still the greatest commercial centre of the Levant, had never entirely recovered from the terrible devastation caused during the sack of 1365. "Every day," says Felix, "one house falls upon another, and the grand walls enclose miserable ruins."[27] The process of dereliction was assisted by housebreakers who removed marbles and mosaics from the deserted palaces and mosques for use at Cairo.[28]

In spite of this state of partial decay Alexandria still offered, as well as "merchandise of every sort and kind," sights of pleasure and interest to visitors. Outside the walls her delightful groves of fruit trees, within her water system, were remarked by many pilgrims. Built on a waterless site the city depended upon the Nile flood and its own not inconsiderable rainfall for water supply. The first was brought to it by the Nasiri Canal, and passing through the walls by an opening barred by an iron grating, was led through vaulted conduits to the subterranean cisterns of the town, which in fact was "hollow everywhere underneath all the streets and the houses." Every house had its underground tanks, in which was stored this flood water, and, as well, the winter rainfall. In addition to all these private storage tanks there were besides ten great cisterns, "caverns borne up by pillars, which are called the Sultan's Cisterns," the water in which was for use "at need."[29] As to the quality of this carefully hoarded water-supply opinions differed; Piloti believed that the waters of the river by their peculiar property cleaned and refreshed that in the cisterns, but Friar Felix put down the prevalence of fever among the galley-crews to their thirsty drinking in the hot weather of this long-stored water.[30]

There were besides, places of religious and historical interest in Alexandria, which our pilgrims did not intend to neglect. At their request the Dragoman conducted them upon a tour of these, guiding them with professional impartiality to the magnificent relics of the ancient world, and the reputed sites of Christian martyrdom. The pilgrims gazed, as tourists still gaze, at the "Column of Pompey" outside the city walls, and were also able to look with amazement upon a "beautiful and most remarkable column, actually of one stone, yet of marvellous height and bulk, of red marble. . . . The top of it is pointed . . . it is four-sided, and on the four sides are carved figures of animals, birds and people, walking, and pictures of tools of the mechanic arts from the top to the bottom; nor can any now know what these images mean."

Thus, Felix, confronted probably with "Cleopatra's Needle," and upon it the words of an unknown language in a forgotten script. But though it was all a mystery he could quote from his studies a passage in which Eusebius spoke of a similar method of writing, used "formerly" by the people of Ethiopia, in which "pictures signified, not letters, but the meaning and idea, as a hawk speed, a crocodile evil, and an eye watchfulness." And as well as this erudite reminiscence the Friar, following his engaging habit, gives us one much nearer home. He had known, he says, a Dominican lay-brother, who, though totally illiterate, "drew in images every word he heard, and so read, as though his signs were letters."[31]

The Christian traditions of Alexandria in the fifteenth century centred round St. Katherine, Felix Fabri's particular patroness. St. Mark had previously shared the honours with her, but though the pilgrims dutifully sought out the church where, it was said, his preaching had converted to Christianity all Alexandria, and where he had been consecrated and buried, "everything," as Felix said, "was now lacking, his body had been carried to Venice and the Catholic faith is extinct." It was therefore with greater enthusiasm that the party visited the "curious little building" known as the prison of St. Katherine, her church, the place of her martyrdom, and other churches and sites connected by tradition with her legend and those of other Saints. The last church they entered was that of St. Michael the Archangel, belonging to the Jacobite Christians, in which, according to custom, any Latin Christian dying in Alexandria was buried. The little crowd of German pilgrims did not guess that they were to leave one of their number in the vault which rang hollow under their feet as they moved about the building.[32]

But that very night the young Count of Solms began to suffer from dysentery, though for three days none thought gravely of his sickness, and the pilgrims occupied their time in expeditions about the city, viewing the *fondachi* of the Western merchants, watching the sad traffic of the slave market, and the animated scenes along the waterside, after which, having hired a boat, they had themselves rowed round about the anchored galleys, inspecting them with the keen and practical interest of intending passengers.[33]

It was at the hour of Vespers on the Eve of All Hallows that the young

Count's sickness suddenly grew serious; a doctor, hastily sent for from the Venetian ships, arrived, but could only tell the lad's friends that the end was near. In the small hours Friar Paul who was the sick boy's confessor gave him absolution, after which he seemed to mend a little, for the Franciscan, returning later, found him feeling better, and von Breydenbach and Philip von Bicken eating a cheerful meal together. But by nine o'clock it was clear that his condition had altered for the worse. Soon he could no longer speak; they put a candle into his hand; he moved his head to show that he understood and assented to the words of the priest. "Then at once," says Friar Paul, "I began to say the psalm "*In te domine speravi* . . . and . . . happily, without any disquiet, his holy spirit passed. . . ."[34]

That morning the body lay, wrapped in linen cloths, on a bier in the chapel of the *fondaco*, while the Consul made arrangements for the burial. With all the solemnity possible in a Moslem country this was performed; at the head of the procession went the Latin priests; Christians of other communities followed after the coffin; on either side marched a Saracen guard to keep off the unwelcome attentions of the crowd; the wealthy and generous Canon of Mainz had provided each of the boy's pilgrim companions with a candle, as well as "other great candles of white wax to set about the bier" during the Requiem Mass. Yet it grieved the pilgrims that not they, but Moslem bearers, had carried the boy to his resting place, and when the vault had received the body, and the stone again closed it, Friar Felix could only wish, in vain, "that instead of in heathen Alexandria, he lay today in the tomb of his fathers, or had been committed to the holy waters of the sea."[35]

Even before the boy's death the thoughts of the pilgrims had been earnestly bent upon the arrangements for their homeward voyage, although until October 30 nothing could be done in the matter, for until the arrival of the "*Traffico*," that is the two or three Venetian galleys which traded along the Northern coasts of Africa, no ship of Venice might leave the port of Alexandria, and no ships' captain would make any contract with would-be passengers. But at dawn upon that morning sounds from the direction of the harbour made the pilgrims aware of the arrival of ships. When Mass was over they rushed to the water-side, and found to their joy that it was indeed as they had hoped, and that the galleys of the "*Traffico*" now lay at anchor with the rest.

Over the dinner table they held a conference with the consul of the *fondaco*, which must a little have clouded their spirits. For when they asked him if they might hope to be able to travel all together in one galley, or whether each of the three companies should arrange to sail separately, he answered that there was no hope of the first, and little even of the second, so heavily laden were the ships with merchandise. Each man, he said, would have to make his own bargain, and he prophesied that they would find the noble captains "tough."

At the Venetian *fondaco*, crowded with captains and their servants and piled with bales of merchandise, the pilgrims soon proved the truth of this saying. These rich Venetians were "harsher and more unreasonable in the price they asked than Saracens or Arabs, for some demanded from every pilgrim 50 ducats, and when we stuck at paying this, another proud captain said that he would not accept less than 100 a man."

Whether or not in ordinary circumstances the pilgrims would have held out for easier terms, they did not so now. Back at the Aragonese *fondaco* the sick lad cried ceaselessly to be taken on board ship, where, he was sure, he would recover. Bernhard von Breydenbach therefore would not haggle, but accepted the terms of Sebastian Contarini, brother of the notorious Agostino "del Zaffo," that old and hardened subject who had carried Felix upon his first pilgrimage to Jerusalem. Sebastian's galley, the flag-ship of the Venetian fleet, in which the Venetian Consul and other nobles would return to Venice, obviously offered the best quarters for a sick man.[36]

Breydenbach had plenty of money, and on this occasion very good reason for spending it, but his surrender to the exorbitant demands of the captains put his companions at a disadvantage, a fact which caused some resentment. All the laymen at last, however, found accommodation, though not without some sharp passages between them, before the necessary adjustments could be made. The whole of the first company went, of course, with Breydenbach in the flag-ship. The knights of the second company were able to take passage together in Andrea da Loredano's galley, and those of the third in Bernardo Contarini's.[37]*

The arrangements of the penniless Friars necessarily followed another pattern, and here we must look back for a moment upon the proceedings of Friar Paul Walther. From one Order of Religious to another, from Germany to Jerusalem, he had pressed in search of that peace and contentment which his temperament set always at a distance. In Jerusalem von Breydenbach had suggested that he should join the party bound for Mount Sinai, and promised a benefice when they reached home. The Friar had leapt at the chance of leaving the Holy City to which he had once yearned, and gladly set off upon the further pilgrimage, acting

* Fabri speaks of Andrea de "Jordano." Paul Walther (pp. 249, 259) of Marco de "Lordano," or "Lardano."

meanwhile as confessor not only to the young Count, but also to several of the knights.[38] Yet when the pilgrims arrived at Alexandria Friar Paul separated himself from companions of whom he had wearied, and who, perhaps, had grown no less weary of him. With the Franciscan lay-brother, John of Cracow, he had gone straight to Andrea de Cabriel, the Venetian Consul who had dealt so generously with the pilgrims at Cairo, and had at once been given hospitality and promised a passage home by that kind-hearted and generous patrician. Now therefore, separated from the rest of their companions, the two Franciscans were to sail in the galley of Marco de Loredano, who, he assures us, assigned him excellent quarters, in spite of the fact that the galley was more over-crowded than any other with merchants and their stuff.[39]

Friar Felix also had fallen on his feet. Hearing that Breydenbach was intending to row out to the flag-ship so that he might prepare for the young Count's removal thither, "I," says Felix, "asked if I could go with him. So we two went by boat to the galley, and looked over it, and chose the accommodation. Now I liked that galley, and thought I had never seen a fairer, for it was new and roomy, and very well arranged and decorated, and the officers in it friendly, and the captain of the fleet, who was on board, a good man and experienced. Considering all this I began to sigh, for the longing that I had of remaining in that galley with the lords of the first company, and I told Lord Bernard ... what I longed for, but lamented that I lacked the fare."

With his usual open-handed liberality the rich Canon set about obtaining for Felix his desire. Back to the *fondaco* they went, and there Breydenbach spoke with the Venetian Captain, "interceding for me as a poor man, and arranged that I should travel in that galley." Nor was this all for " ... he took out 12 ducats and gave them to me for my expenses," asking only that the Friar would serve him and his party, and especially the sick lad, as their priest;[40] it is not to be wondered at if he thought that the company and influence of the cheerful Dominican would be more salutary for an invalid than that of Friar Paul. Felix, having so amply succeeded, did not forget his friend the Hungarian Archdeacon, who, from Venice onwards, had never been separated from him. Bringing Archdeacon John in his turn to Sebastian Contarini, and using what eloquent persuasion we are not told, he managed to obtain a passage for him in the same galley.[41]

The death of the young Count made vain Breydenbach's first pre-occupation in taking the berths, and turned the thoughts of the pilgrims to more solemn matters. But no sooner was the funeral over, and dinner eaten, than their minds reverted to two urgent concerns. They must buy what was necessary for the sea-voyage, and make any other final purchases; and they must, unless they were to resign themselves and their possessions to the full rigour of the customs examination, set about the business of smuggling out of the city as much as possible of their illicit or dutiable acquisitions.

Friar Felix himself started out alone to do a bit of shopping which he had long intended, but up to now had failed to accomplish. He wished to take back with him a supply of palm leaves for the Palm Sunday processions at Ulm, but common though these objects were, they had proved difficult to acquire, for though in the bazaars there were plenty of baskets made of plaited palm leaves nowhere could he find leaves offered for sale. At last, however, he contrived by signs to explain to one of the Saracen basket-makers what was his need.

"When he understood he left his work and his shop, and took me with him up a long street. But I began to be suspicious, fearing lest the Saracen was leading me astray, and I made a sign to him that I wished to return, and moved away from him. When the man saw this he was grieved and troubled, and spoke to me solemnly in Saracen, which I did not understand, looking up to the sky, as if swearing by God that I was safe, and he took me by the arm, keeping hold of me, and leading me so that I should not run away from him. After going a long way amongst the streets we came to his house, which was a fair house and spacious, with a marble pavement, smooth and polished, and walls faced with marble, and I was astonished that a basket-maker should own such a palace."

The Friar, who by now seems to have decided that he had nothing to fear, was led into a large upper room full of palm leaves, and left to make his choice, attentively observed from behind a curtain by the wives of the basket-maker. He selected sixty or more leaves, paid for them and departed, the sheaf of palm leaves carried proudly on his shoulder.

The obliging Moslem had made as if to accompany him, but Felix, so sure he was that he could find his own way back, would not allow it. For a while he walked stoutly on, but at last was unwillingly convinced that he was hopelessly lost, and, what was worse, in one of those deserted parts of the city against the dangers of which the pilgrims had been warned. Eventually—

" . . . I met a young Saracen, to whom I could only say, 'Oh, Saracen, Catalan *fondaco.*' But at once this lad understood that I was lost and that I was looking for the Catalan *fondaco*. He took hold of the front of my scapula, and shouting, singing and laughing . . . led me through the streets . . . I had to put up with being made great fun of on the way, though without any harm or injury, nor did I care, but gladly and gratefully accepted my rescue."⁴² —sentiments which prove, if any proof were needed, that Friar Felix was a truly good-humoured man.

Those palm-leaves, the pebbles which he had gathered in and around Jerusalem, the pretty shining stones from the valleys of the Sinai Peninsula, the oyster shells and coral from the shore of the Red Sea, besides some pieces of silk, and "a beautiful Turkish hanging," bought respectively at Jerusalem and Alexandria, and destined for the Church of the Dominicans,⁴³ these were the treasures which the Friar must see through the customs, and among them only the last two would possibly be dutiable.

But many of the acquisitions of the knights and noblemen were a very different matter, and must have occasioned much serious thought. As well as the balm, the jewels, the silks which they had brought with them from Cairo, they had been adding to their luggage by purchases at Alexandria. Some of these were doubtless such harmless devotional novelties as the "silk coverlets made to the measure of the Sepulchre to lay over women in childbirth,"⁴⁴ which the commercial enterprise of the Moslems offered to Christian visitors. But there were other objects which some of the fighting men of the party were determined to take home with them. In the bazaars of Alexandria they saw swords of the Damascus or Indian temper: they saw the short but superbly strong Turkish or Saracen bow, made with subtle art of a thin core of wood to which were glued strips of flexible horn and sinew, that on the inner curve from the horn of buffalo or antelope, that on the outer from the large neck tendons of ox or stag, and made malleable in hot water.⁴⁵ These magnificent weapons were not indeed dutiable; the export of them was forbidden.

Von Breydenbach took a rich man's way of solving all problems of the customs, and gave the Dragoman a handsome present to ensure that all his baggage should pass through unexamined.⁴⁶ The rest of the pilgrims set themselves to smuggle out piecemeal, hidden in their clothes, such of their purchases as would either have paid heavy duty or have been confiscated at the *douane*.⁴⁷ Friar Felix was much in demand in these proceedings, since his temperament, obliging and adventurous, and his Dominican habit with its voluminous folds, made him an excellent assistant, so that, as he says, "I carried down under my gown many things entrusted to me by the noblemen, in such a way that even if I had been searched they would hardly have been found on me."⁴⁸

Among these articles was a Turkish sword, entrusted to him by one of the young knights who had already had his first purchase confiscated by the *douane*, but who had persuaded a Saracen to buy him a second weapon. Friar Felix, undaunted, "took the sword, and went down to the sea, through all the gates, as though I had nothing on me." Perhaps this success went to his head; at the water-side he imprudently handed the weapon over to its owner; the transaction was observed by a Saracen who tried to snatch the sword away, but the knight tore it free and "ran with the sword to where the boats lay, and jumped into one of them, and escaping the Saracen, was rowed out to the ships.[49]

On Sunday, November 2, the Feast of All Souls, Mass in the chapel of the Aragonese *fondaco* was crowded with officers from the flag-ship, and with sailors from the rest of the fleet, and the total amount of the offertory, Felix notes, was proportionately high. When the Office was over the visitors advised the pilgrims to come on board without delay, seeing that now the ships might sail at any time.

Before their departure the usual settlement of accounts must take place. The knights paid the Consul's bill of 6 ducats a head; then came the turn of the Friar. But he had made his dispositions, enlisting on his behalf the kind offices of the Consul's wife who promised to persuade her husband, reputed to be "a man without mercy," to accept a lower fee. Now the Friar began his request, "For the love of God..." at which the Consul flew into a rage, and shouted " 'Roch, Roch,' that is 'Get out.' "* For a moment Felix was at a loss, but catching the eye of the lady, and seeing her nod, he took himself off, reflecting upon the surly generosity of the man, and the virtue and piety of the wife, as well as upon the strength of her influence over her husband since, "after that he saw me often, but did not ask me for anything."[50]

Once the pilgrims' bill was settled there was nothing to detain them. The luggage was collected from their rooms, and loaded upon donkeys which Shadbak had produced. Then, after farewells and the usual round of tipping, they set out on foot, behind the mounted Dragoman and the donkeys, to their final encounter with the Alexandrian customs.

At the out-set it seemed as though this would pass off easily. When, at the first gate, the officers barred the way and made as if to unload and open the stuff, Shadbak intervened, "swearing '*Walla halla*' that is," Felix explains, " 'By the true God' that we had no merchandise with us." This assurance, and a few coppers handed over, sufficed to pass them through. At the second gate they expected more trouble; but after Shadbak had spoken long with the officials, these made no attempt to search the baggage, though they carefully handled each bag and basket to test the weight.

This, however, brought Friar Felix under fire, for the basket containing

---

* We are never told the nationality of the Consul. Why he should speak in Arabic to a Western pilgrim is equally unexplained.

his collection of pebbles from Jerusalem "was very heavy and most carefully fastened. Surprised at its weight they took this from the donkey's back and began to open it, but I protested, begging them not to, because of the difficulty I should have to tie it up again, and I swore to them by the Cross, that there was nothing in the basket but ordinary stones picked up from the ground. They were surprised at that and laughed, asking if we had no stones in the West that we must carry them home from the East." When the Friar explained that "stones indeed we have, but not hallowed by the foot-steps of God . . . and his Saints," the basket was at once restored to him.

But it had unfortunately drawn the attention of the officers to his luggage, and they now turned to the basket containing palm-leaves. " 'What,' they asked, when the Friar had told them its contents, 'What did I want with those leaves?' " Felix eagerly explained the lack of palm trees in Germany, and the ritual significance of the branches, at which "they were amazed . . . for they thought that I wanted to make baskets, as they themselves do with the leaves and bark. So they passed my basket untouched."

At that even the courageous and enterprising Friar must have drawn his breath more easily, "For I was very frightened lest they should search among the leaves, because one of the knights had hidden a Saracen bow and arrows, and a Turkish sword among (them) . . . and if they had found these we should have got into a pretty bad scrape."[51]

The pilgrims, exultant as they realised that they had passed both sets of customs officials at the price of a moderate tip, passed on to the water's edge. The baggage was unloaded; Shadbak, having warned them, that since their safe-conduct now expired, it would be unwise for them to enter Alexandria again, took his leave, and turned back into the city. He had done well by them, and they were very soon to feel the lack of his guidance and protection. They had already hired a boat to take them out to the galleys, and were preparing to put their stuff on board, when some Saracens rushed up, seized the bundles and announced that there had still to pass "the closest search yet."

During the stunned pause which followed, Friar Felix alone took action. He was responsible both for his own luggage and for that of the Archdeacon who had already gone on board the galley; therefore, before the arrival of the customs officers, "I pulled out of the common heap" all the bags and baskets which the pair of them possessed, "and having made a separate pile I sat on them." From this perch he watched his companions endure a rigorous search of their effects, and pay a heavy duty.

And now the officers were approaching him and in a moment would begin to open and search his stuff. "But," says he, "I plucked up courage and stoutly resisted, not suffering anyone to touch my luggage, so that they stood astonished and laughing, thinking me not right in the head because I opposed all their efforts. Many Saracens and Christians came running up, surprised at the unusual dispute, and a Venetian standing near by asked, 'Why did I so resist the officers?'

"Said I, 'Because I am a priest and a Religious, and I do not carry things to sell, but religious articles and necessities, on which the Egyptians charge no duty. And knowing this I do resist and will not yield unless they use force, and if they do I shall go back into the city and show myself to the governors, as a priest exempt from the customs dues of the common crowd of lay folk and merchants.'"

This was to carry things with a high hand indeed, but the Friar's instinct was sound; the officials did not press the matter and turned away leaving his baggage untouched.

It was a triumph, and though the pilgrims were forced to cool their heels upon the shore for some time longer, and though Friar Felix had to repel the attentions of several who made as if to handle his stuff, he repeated his tactics with growing confidence, pointing to his tonsure, his breviary, and his scapular, and claiming benefit of clergy. It is more than probable that he was by now enjoying himself, and certain that he met one challenge in a playful spirit. For some boys began to play "Tom Tiddler's Ground" with him, "coming up behind as though they wanted to run off with something belonging to me. So I pretended to be very angry with them, but angry I was not, only I defended myself... against their childish behaviour lest worse should befall me."[52]

The sun had set by the time the pilgrims were at last able to leave the shore behind them. When the sailors had pushed off, and the boats began to make their way across the darkening water to where the galleys lay at their moorings, Felix and his companions raised their voices in that hymn which they had sung many months ago, as Venice fell away astern of the eastward-bound pilgrim galley. Now as they chanted to the dip of the oars, they were leaving a heathen city behind them, and their faces were set towards home. It was a joyful occasion, but for none so joyful as for Felix Fabri, who could reflect that the final examination by the Alexandrian Customs Officers had cost him nothing, whereas, "if they had made me pay duty... two ducats would hardly have covered it, and on that I could live for many days."[53]

Part Six

ALEXANDRIA TO VENICE

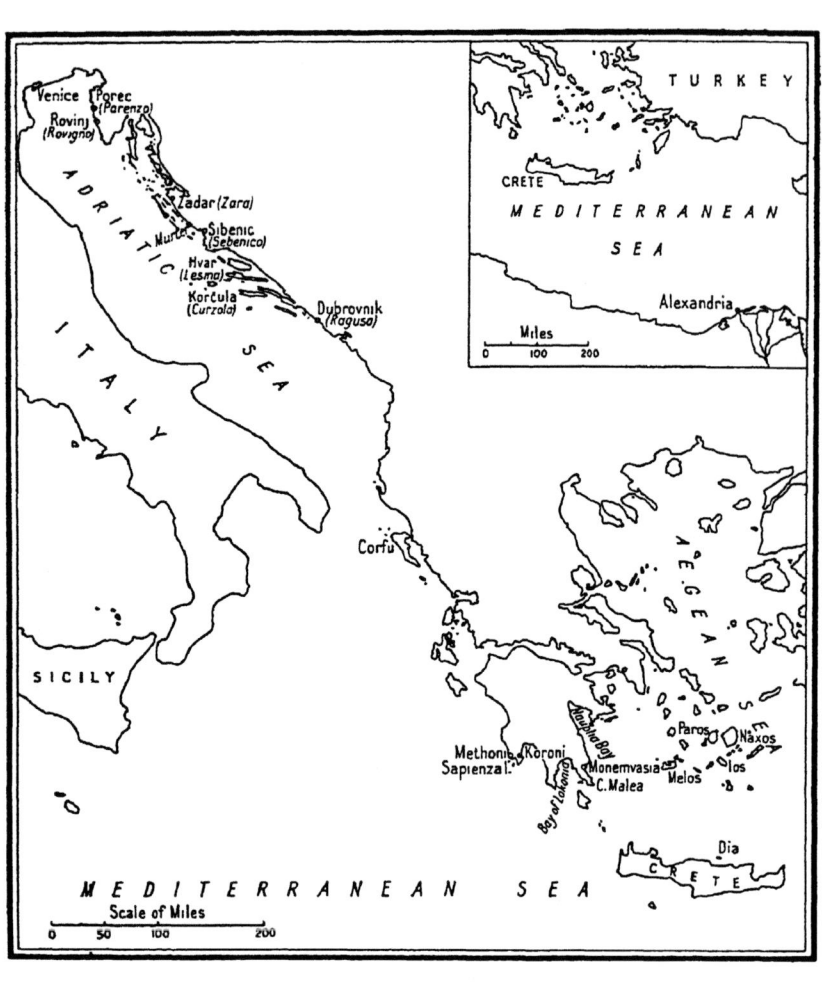

CHAPTER XV

On board the spice ships

Once on board, while von Breydenbach and his party went to their berths, Friar Felix and the Archdeacon made their way with due humility to "the place for poor men," that is to say the small compartment in the bows occupied by the crew of the forecastle. Here, though kindly received by the mate of the forecastle (*gubernator prorae*) and his men, the two priests spent a night of little repose, sitting on their baggage for want of space to lie down. And yet, because conscious that after so many miles across heathen lands, they trod the deck of a Christian ship, Felix and his friend thought themselves "in Paradise among the angels." Even the oaths of the rough men round about struck sweetly on their ears, for though the rowers swore shockingly by the cross or limbs of Christ such oaths bore, as if in reverse, the hallmark of the Christian faith.[1]

Next morning, accompanied by the friendly mate of the forecastle, they waited upon the Noble Captain to ask him to allot them some place for their berths. Sebastian Contarini, after consultation with the ship's clerk, the boatswain, and two mates of the hold* sent the whole party off to inspect, by lantern light, any odd corners left among the cargo below deck.

The ship in which Felix and the Archdeacon were to make the winter voyage back to Europe was one of the great trading galleys which Venice built for the distant voyages of her merchants, to Flanders or England, to Beirut or to Alexandria.

The sharp, rising forecastle, with its ram, the high poop where the Noble Captain slept in his gilded bed,[2] and where the Venetian merchant lords also berthed–these were similar to those which Felix had come to know in his voyages between Venice and Jaffa; but whereas in the pilgrim galleys of that route the whole waist of the ship below deck was occupied by a single large cabin for the passengers, in these great vessels of burthen

---

* " . . . *Vocato . . . custodibus carinae, quos guardianos vocant.* . . ." (*Evag.* III, p. 207). I have used the word "mate" loosely here, as also above, and for Felix's "*guardiani*" among the rowers.

all the space amidships was occupied by a hold able to accommodate 250 tons of cargo.³

Three-masted ships, and relying chiefly upon sail, both the merchant and pilgrim galley used oars for such emergencies as were caused by calms or adverse currents, or for entering and leaving port.⁴ Consequently, out of a crew of 200, the arbalestiers and bombard-men, the mariners and ship's officers, would account for no more than 30, and the rest would be rowers.⁵ These lived, ate, and slept during the voyage upon the benches along the upper deck. Wretched creatures enough, they were not the condemned and enslaved criminals of a later period, chained for ever to the oar, though some, indeed, were slaves, owned by the Captain. The rest were down-and-outs who had taken to this way of life; many were thieves and gamblers, but among them were better men, who scraped a living by peddling goods at the ports along the route, or who earned a little by sewing shirts or making shoes. Probably it was from such more respectable characters that a number of men were chosen to act as rowers' mates (*guardiani*) and it was with these that the two priests were to associate during the voyage.⁶

With the officers and mariners proper the Friar had little to do. The Captain stood high over all, one of the merchant princes of Venice. Under him a Master at Arms commanded the arbalestiers and bombard-men. The "*Caliph*" was responsible for the whole fabric and furnishing of the ship; the pilot, drawn from a corps of men, under the supervision of the "*cattaveri*" of Venice, individually qualified as pilot for one or other of the stages of the Mediterranean voyage,* exercised his skills in the steerage chamber on the poop. Of the ship's officers the "*Comite*" was chief: in the flagship of Sebastian Contarini he was a most efficient sea-officer, but a hardened and brutal man. Under him were the boatswain and his mate (*parono* and *subparono*), the former carrying the traditional whistle slung about his neck. Less than a dozen "companions" (*compani*), young and daring men, who, says Felix, ran about the rigging "like cats," acted as first class seamen, and with an unspecified number of mariners, or able seamen (*marinarii*) worked the ship when under sail. All these, from the *Comite* down, berthed on the upper deck. With two or three apprentices, a couple of barber surgeons, the ship's clerk, a few trumpeters, and the important Captain's Steward (*scalius, schalk*) who was in charge of all the commissariat of the vessel, and had under him a store-keeper (cellerarius), and cooks, the tale of the ship's company was complete.⁷

The place which the two priests chose for their berth, was below deck abaft the main-mast.⁸ It was, according to Friar Felix's considered

* See below, p. 239.

opinion, "wonderful," though it did not at first seem to deserve that enthusiastic adjective. Daylight never reached it; it was so low that there was room only to kneel upright upon the big spice sacks which half filled it; since in order to leave they must crawl fifteen paces or so, in the event of a sudden disaster they would undoubtedly be trapped without any hope of escape.

Only by experience were they to learn that "there was no better place in all the galley." For, to begin with, they enjoyed between the two of them space enough for six; the place was quiet; even in storms it was dry, and its temperature was such that though they might come down from the deck with chattering teeth they soon "warmed up again as if in a hot bath." Nor was this all. While they were settling into their new quarters, spreading their mattresses upon the hard spice sacks, and hanging up Felix's long basket of palm leaves on the side of the ship next to his berth, they discovered that they were next door to the ship's store-room. The store-keeper had been watching them through the cracks in the intervening partition; now, "he greeted us friendly and promised to look after us." A couple of nails were removed, and an opening made through which, with a little manipulation, the two priests could draw into their berth, "the extra food and drink and lights to burn" which the store-keeper promised to them.

Lights by which to read their office, whether by day or night, for a lamp burned always in the store-room, and snacks to vary or supplement the tedious sameness of the sea-diet, were excellent things; and there was, besides all other advantages, one which Felix evidently found important, for he expounds it at length. "Whatever went on in the galley, in the poop or in the prow, we heard . . . and whether the lords in the poop were accord, and how the officers were, and whether the wind was fair or not. . . ." All these subjects were ventilated in the gossip which went on in the store-room, "and every secret was told to us, and if not to us, yet to the store-keeper in our hearing." Among news of greater importance, since "the way down from the kitchen was into the store-room . . . before we were called to table we knew what we would be having to eat."⁹

The arrangement which they were able to make with regard to their meals was of a piece with the rest of their good fortune. They were still busy arranging their stuff when the trumpets blew for dinner at the Captain's table, at which all the Venetian merchant princes also ate. The store-keeper insisted that the two priests should answer the summons, but when they found "the tables indeed laid, but no other pilgrim, nor any other man of humble station" preparing to sit down, their hearts failed them; they retreated, and after consultation with the store-keeper, the steward, the cooks, it was arranged that they should eat below deck with the mates of the hold. By this they forfeited nothing but the exalted company of the poop, for " . . . they brought us the food and drink of the lords both at dinner and supper."[10] Here was a case where it was as good to be lucky as rich.

When the pilgrims left the *fondaco* to go on board the galleys, they believed that the fleet was about to sail, but for almost another fortnight the ships still lay in port. Going ashore on October 4 Friar Felix and the Archdeacon narrowly escaped being involved in a nasty riot. At one of the Venetian *fondachi*, a Captain of the *Traffico* galleys having in a dispute struck a Moslem, fled, was caught by an angry mob in the very gateway to the port, badly mauled, and thrown into prison. Since the Venetian Signory decreed that the Spice Fleet must never leave Alexandria till every galley was ready to sail, this held up all the ships, and resulted, on the one hand in difficult negotiations with the Moslem authorities, and on the other in hot debate among the Venetian Captains, some clamouring to break the rule, some to appoint a new Captain to command the prisoner's galley, and so be enabled to leave.[11]

During this period of tension the pilgrims were forbidden to land and found themselves condemned to a fortnight of "the longest hours and the most utter boredom."[12] Even a trivial episode was to be welcomed; one evening as it was growing dusk Friar Felix and his friend stood on the deck of the flagship as she lay at her moorings close to the Sultan's newly fortified castle,[13] and looked towards Alexandria across the harbour water. A boat-load of young Saracens approached the galley and quietly made fast alongside; it appeared that they had friends among the galley's crew, for now these went over the side "with flasks and jars and drinking bowls and glasses," to sit carousing in the boat with their Moslem acquaintances. The two priests watched the proceedings, enjoying, as the fumes of wine mounted to the heads of the young Saracens, the two-fold superiority of the sober over the tipsy, and the habitual over the inexperienced drinker. By the time the party broke up and the young men pushed off for the shore, these were, as Felix says, "full up," and he adds, speaking there for all unregenerate human nature which laughs at the clownish disasters of its fellows—"I stood waiting for someone to fall in, and to this day I believe that they can hardly have reached land without catching a baptism."[14]

But apart from such chance alleviations of the tedium Friar Felix at least found means of whiling away the time. Parrots, "vulgarly known as

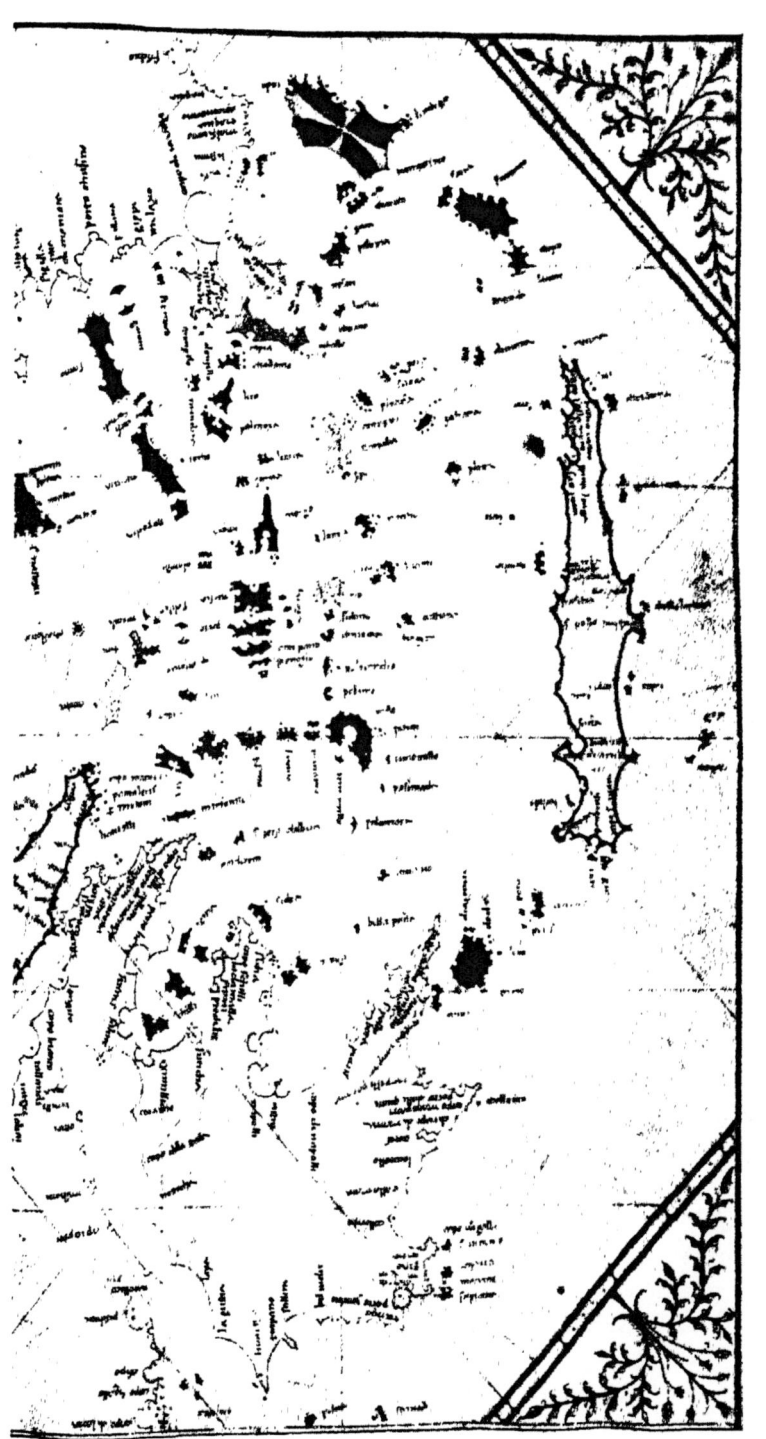

5. GREECE AND THE AEGEAN SEA IN THE FIFTEENTH CENTURY
Crete is seen in the centre; Rhodes with the cross of The Knights of St. John on the right

popingays (*papagogi*)" had, by their uncanny gift of speech, captured the imagination of the West, and in Sebastian Contarini's galley many were being carried homeward by Italian merchants or German pilgrims.

Friar Felix had, in the course of his reading, assimilated a quantity of information concerning this "noble and royal" bird. He knew that Psittacus, son of Deucalion and Pirrha, a contemporary of Moses, had, by permission of the gods, become the first of the species; he knew that every parrot was endowed by nature with the knowledge of, and the power to utter both in Greek and Latin, the correct word of salutation to be addressed to emperors, while its vocabulary could be extended by a rigorous training which included chastisement with an iron rod. He knew, perhaps from books, perhaps also from experiment, as, surely, our own John Skelton knew, that parrots were extremely susceptible to the effect of wine.[15]

In addition to the parrots of literature he had already encountered the real bird; in the house of the Chief Dragoman at Cairo there were green parrots with red ruffs about their necks; at the greater of the two Venetian *fondachi* in Alexandria rarer varieties, white, red, and red with black markings.[16]

Never before, however, had the Friar met these birds upon familiar terms, but now, since two of them lived next door in the store-keeper's office, he was able to study them at leisure. He listened, fascinated: "You would think, if you did not see it, that a human being spoke, but in a womanish voice." He watched, too, noticing the thick tongue, and the way the creature "feeds itself with its foot as a man with his hand." But he did more than watch and listen. He became "most friendly" with the birds, and in particular with a large white parrot, belonging to the Canon of Mainz, "a wonderful creature, bought for a great price."* There was, the Friar explains, a hole in the partition which separated the priests' berth from the store-keeper's office, "and when the bird knew that I was in my berth, it put its little hand through the hole, making a tapping with its fingers to make me come and play with it. Sometimes, if it was asleep, I made a noise with my fingers on the partition, inciting it to be pleased or angry as I wished."

Of the second parrot the Friar also made a pet, but in this case the intercourse of bird and man was chequered, and came to an abrupt end. "... On one occasion," says Felix, "it showed by signs that it wanted me to kiss it, but when I put my face close, it caught my nose in its curved

---

* Perhaps one of those white Javanese parrots, so admired by travellers, birds "the size of hens," which excelled in talking, "imitating human speech in a wonderful manner, and even answering questions" (*India in the fifteenth century*, III, p. 17).

beak and hurt me severely." He set himself to teach it a phrase; "... I used to say to it, '*Bubli*,* *kum hir zu mir*,'' so the bird, when I came, would say, '*Kum hir zu mir*.' " The Friar must have been gratified by the success of his tuition, but the owner took it amiss that the bird's conversation had been "corrupted" by the admixture of German, and he removed the parrot from Felix's neighbourhood.[17]

As well as in this "Pastyme with good company" among the parrots, Felix found occupation during the empty hours in port in writing up a new section of his *Evagatorium*. He had always expected, he explains with creditable candour, that he would, on this return voyage, as on that of his first pilgrimage, touch at the three great islands of the eastern Mediterranean-Cyprus, Rhodes and Crete, and had therefore refrained from giving an account of these places. Now he learnt that though pilgrim galleys from Jaffa called at the islands, the merchantmen would, after leaving Alexandria, bear "to the left," and that it was not their practice, even if they drew near to Crete, to call there.[18]

The Friar was not going to waste the carefully hoarded results of his reading and experience, and therefore inserted at this point of his narrative the account of an imaginary voyage, in which the three islands were visited, at the end of which, said he, "I shall return to the galley of the noble merchant Sebastian Contarini,"[19] somewhere off the coast of Crete.

We shall not follow him in this rehearsal. But since, in his account of his actual voyage, he shows us, casually after his fashion, and in haphazard glimpses, the Venetian colonial Empire as it was in the lull which succeeded their treaty of 1479 with the Turks, the successful defence of Rhodes of 1480, and the death of Mahomet II the Conqueror, it is necessary to recall the situation of these three islands, which formed the embattled eastern outwork of Christian Europe. Rhodes of the Knights was-and was recognised by the Ottoman Turks to be-the spear-point of the Christian defence. Cyprus, the "furthest east" of Latin Christendom, was already *de facto* and was soon to become *de jure* one of the Venetian possessions; Crete had been hers since it fell to her share in the division of the loot of the 4th Crusade, nearly 300 years earlier.

Little enough was left of that loot, except what lay in the hands of Venice, or of a few small dynasties of Italian origin, who by the favour and protection of the Signory maintained their island principalities among the Greek Archipelago. On the Greek mainland Venice herself had lost Negroponte to the Turks; she had gained Monemvasia upon its impregnable rock; Koroni and Methoni, with their complex of defences at the

* *Bubli*="little boy" in the Schwitze-deutsch of Felix's childhood.

south-western tip of the Morea, were focal points in both her military system and that of her merchant marine. Corfu was her naval base for the Levant. Along the east coast of the Adriatic the cities and islands, Ragusa only excepted, were now hers.

"Although," said Felix, "the Venetians desire peace, yet daily they prepare for war by land and sea."[20] Their Empire, founded upon commerce and maritime strength, must, in fact, like that of Britain in the eighteenth and nineteenth centuries, be ready to accept the challenge of any other naval power. In small matters, too, English readers catch a resemblance. "If a man be in any territory of theirs," the Spanish Tafur remarks, "although at the ends of the earth, it seems as if he were in Venice itself."[21]

Contemporaries, and especially those from beyond the Alps, marvelled at the "exquisite justice" of Venice, and in her overseas dependencies the Republic, though quelling resistance with an iron hand, ensured to the governed her own order and equity, by her unceasing vigilance over her colonial administrators. Spies, euphemistically known as "Inquisitors of the Levant," were despatched at intervals to look into the behaviour of the colonial governors, and such an inquisition was no matter of empty form; Venetian officials were unlikely to forget the execution of the *podestà* of Crete, which took place as a result of one of these investigations.[22] The colonial Governor, though many miles of sea might lie between him and Venice, was never allowed to feel himself anything but a servant of the Republic. Pilgrims travelling homeward from Syria or Egypt in Venetian ships would from time to time witness the arrival on board of one of these officers. Sometimes there would be little parade; Felix saw the Governor of Koroni come on board for his voyage home, from a solitary boat rowed out to the flagship as the fleet passed.[23] Sometimes the embarkation was an affair of considerable formality; old Canon Casola at Candia watched the ceremonies attendant upon the departure for home of the Governor and another official. The two were given their send-off by the magistrates and by many gentlemen of the island. Trumpeters and pipers accompanied them down to the quay, "very honourably and also with great dust." The Governor's wife and her ladies were "so adorned and so magnificent" that the travelled man of the world who watched them could find nothing inferior in their array to the splendours of ladies attending a festival at Venice itself.[24] Yet the Governor who came off-shore in a row-boat, and the officials who arrived on board with such state, were alike about to make their annual obligatory visit to Venice in order to render an account of their stewardship.[25] And in addition to this close supervision by the Republic, her colonial subjects possessed the right, often exercised and hardly ever in vain, of appeal by deputation to the Signory.[26]

Venetian state-craft, whose ruling principle was an enlightened self interest, protected also the religious freedom of subjects of alien faith. In its colonial territories priests of the Greek Orthodox Church had "liberty to preach and teach the holy word, provided only that they say nothing about the Republic or against the Latin religion,"[27] while the proselytising efforts of the Papacy were consistently rebuffed. In Crete, under this system, long years of propinquity and intermarriage between Catholics and Orthodox had produced an atmosphere in which intolerance was impossible.[28] Latin pilgrims saw processions of the Orthodox pass in state through the streets, their repeated cry of "Kyrie Elieson" sounding unpleasingly in western ears.[29] In Corfu relations between the two Churches were such that on the Feast of the Greek St. Spiridion, Catholics and Orthodox walked shoulder to shoulder in procession, and Venetian gunners touched off their cannon in honour of the Saint, while upon the Feast of the Catholic St. Arsenius the Orthodox crowded into the Church of the patrician hermit for joint celebrations in which, as the modern historian remarks, "the discordant chanting of Greeks and Latins represented their theological concord."[30] The Venetian colonial government extended the same tolerant and commonsense treatment to the hated Jew; he must wear a yellow hat, but on the other hand Christians must cease to pelt him with stones, a habit to which authorities objected, because it "did so much damage to the houses."[31] Both tolerance and worldly wisdom prompted the protection which the Venetians extended go Turkish merchants and traders in their possessions; pilgrims, to their disgust, discovered that they must not jeer at these enemies of the faith.[32]

CHAPTER XVI

Winter voyage

While Friar Felix made his disembodied voyage to the islands of Cyprus, Rhodes and Crete, the Spice Fleet lay immobilised in the harbour at Alexandria. Early in the morning of November 14, however,* so early that it was still dark, the hubbub which always preceded departure arose among the ships, officers shouting orders, sailors hailing and singing their chanties as they raised the anchors or hauled aloft the yards, all the time trampling heavily along the decks over the heads of Friar Felix and Father John.[1] So light a breeze blew from the west that they left the harbour under oars, dipping the useless mainsail as they passed the Sultan's Castle, in the required signal of respect. Next morning, however, they picked up a strong and favourable breeze, which drove them so fast upon their course that they sighted Crete at evening upon the fifth day out. This first glimpse of Christian land on which for many months their eyes had rested filled the hearts of the pilgrims with joyful emotion.[2]

Thus, in calm weather and an atmosphere of exhilaration, began the homeward voyage which was to lengthen out to close on two months, was to subject the pilgrims to a series of winter gales, and to drive them for shelter to the shores of more than one of the islands of the Greek Archipelago. All these experiences, together with details of the daily life of passengers travelling in the merchant ships of Venice, their discomforts, amusements, expeditions ashore, rare nights of calm and conversation on deck, are poured out in the incoherent pages of Friar Felix.

Already when the coast of Crete came in sight the wind was freshening. And now Sebastian Contarini shortened sail, and having signalled to the rest of the fleet to lie to, sent off a boat to fetch a doctor from another galley, for Andrea Cabriel, Venetian Consul, lay desperately ill in the flagship. The doctor's diagnosis left little hope, but to give the sick man relief he advised that the galley should seek calmer water than that of the open sea under a rising gale. Six of the ships therefore followed Contarini's

---

* According to Walther (p. 249). Fabri has November 5, but it seems certain that he had altered the date to give more verisimilitude to his imaginary voyage.

into the narrow strait between Candia and the little island of Dia, where as darkness fell they lay so close alongside under the cliffs of Crete that men could shout to each other from ship to ship.

Yet even here the storm fell on them, driving them out and to the north. All next day and the following night the tempest blew, and passengers and crew were perhaps equally wretched. The decks were swept by the waves, the kitchen was awash and the fire out; not that the pilgrims cared for that; they were too far gone to think of food; the din and shock of the waves was increased by the rumble of the stone bombard balls which, as the ship pitched, rolled back and forth from the prow to the mainmast. Even the snug berth of Friar Felix and his friend was penetrated by water which leaked through the seams of the labouring ship. Still the wind and sea rose higher and there were heavy squalls of rain. In the darkness the German pilgrim nobles from their berth below the forecastle, and some officers, though not the noble Captain, came down to the hold; a handful of wretched and fever-stricken rowers followed, begging to be allowed below lest they should die of cold on the benches; during that terrible night two of the poor fellows did die, "and were thrown overboard naked, for the sea beasts to devour."[3]

Daylight, however, brought relief; though the wind was still high, the seas were less, and the storm-beaten flagship was able to reach port in Ios, one of the most southerly islands of the Cyclades, and a part of the Duchy of Naxos; here, in a friendly harbour, for the Dukes were allies and almost dependents of the Venetian Republic, the flagship anchored, to be joined at intervals during the day by the rest of the fleet.

As usual in port most of those on board the ships went ashore, and Felix among them, to spend the afternoon in various pursuits, the galley slaves laundering the officers' linen in a spring of fresh water, the pilgrims meeting and conversing with their friends from other galleys, and all climbing up to the neighbouring fortified town to buy food and firing. Here Felix and his party suffered disappointment; when they reached the place there was "neither bread nor eggs nor fruit"; all had been bought up; they must resign themselves to a further course of ship's biscuit and the salt sturgeon of the Danube, with which, to their surprise, they had been served on board.[4] Felix very likely found some compensation in the wide view of sea and islands which the height afforded, and in an inspection of the tiny fortifications in which there was one good house only, that of the castellan, surrounded by a huddle of such miserable dwellings that they seemed like cells in a honeycomb. Yet these poor hovels were the homes of a race of which "the men were comely, the women very beautiful, and the children"–it is Friar Paul who noted them–"the children most lovely."[5]

The sun had set before the boats returned to the ships. But the hours which had passed pleasantly for the shore-going party were almost the last of the Venetian Consul's life. The sheltered anchorage had only given Andrea Cabriel a quiet space of time in which to die, and before the next day dawned the pilgrims heard the sound of a boy's weeping, and knew that a soul had departed, whose passing "not his son alone, but all who knew him, mourned."[6]

So, when daylight had come once more, the boats put off for the shore, bearing the ships' captains and the noble Venetian merchants to a Requiem Mass in the little chapel close to the sea's edge. When Mass was over, and the lad, who had thrown himself upon his father's body as it lay before the Altar, had been led away, the doctors and barber-surgeons of the fleet were left to do their grim work, for the body was now to be embalmed. With the doctors remained also Friar Felix, presumably by arrangement with "the physician and surgeon of the whole fleet," a man of character and parts, with whom he had struck up one of his many friendships.[7]*

The Friar, with his omnivorous appetite for experience, watched with unremitting interest the whole proceeding, in which the well-beloved Consul was, in Felix's pungent phrase, "gutted like a fish."[8] He records the various stages of the operation: the making of a long incision in the body, the extraction of the intestines, the cleansing of the cavity with sea water, the treatment with preservative ointments, the stuffing with dry straw and salt, the final stitching up of the orifice. He even, with the *aplomb* which would not disgrace a seasoned medical student, comments upon the quantity–remarkable, he thought, for so spare a man–and the whiteness of the fat enclosing the kidneys.

When all this had been accomplished the swathed body was put into a coffin, which had been dressed inside and out with pitch, and was now carefully sealed with the same. For it was the intention of the Captains to carry the body home with them to Venice for burial; and the coffin was now taken back to the flagship and with great secrecy laid deep in the sand ballast. There was secrecy, that is to say, as to its position, but the fact could not be hidden that there was a corpse on board the flagship.[9] As yet the seamen did not dare to question the will of the Captains, but

---

* This man, with whom the Friar enjoyed many serious and confidential talks during the days spent in harbour in the Greek islands, told Felix that he intended to become a Carthusian at the Venetian house of the Order; but he was killed by lightning off Methoni (Modon) a few weeks after the events related above (*Evag.* III, p. 334).

the pilgrims among themselves discussed with mingled alarm and indignation the well-known belief that "the sea will nowise endure dead bodies in ships." As Friar Paul remarked bitterly the saying was true when it concerned poor men, for two sailors died on the same day as the Consul, and were buried out of hand.[10] Another dying man troubled the hearts and disturbed the sleep of Felix and the Archdeacon in their berth below deck, as he raved, laughed and wept in his delirium, while his mates, candle in hand, stood round about waiting for the passage of his soul. Yet it seemed he could not die. At last a Greek sailor, noticing that the sack upon which the sick man lay contained pigeons' feathers, insisted that it should be removed; "'... Unless you take it away, the bed on which he lies, he cannot die.'" They took it away, and laid him instead upon the sack of ginger below, "and then–he died at once." The ancient and wide-spread superstition which the Greek quoted was, curiously enough, strange to Friar Felix.[11]

The voyage which had begun so prosperously had, in fact, entered upon a darker phase. For the next fortnight the fleet was to suffer violent storms, or contrary winds varied by calms, every kind of weather to balk the seamens' efforts to reach and pass Cape Malea, that "Cape of Storms" at the south-easterly extremity of the Greek mainland, where, simple folk believed, the winds were raised by the beating of the wings of its heavenly guardian, Michael the Archangel.[12] In point of fact, though sailors and pilgrims might lay the blame either on the Angel or the presence of the dead body in the bilges, strong south-westerly gales commonly prevail in these waters during the winter.[13]

Yet the next day dawned calm over Ios, and the fleet left harbour with the first light, while the dead Consul's parrot called on his master "in a clear and ringing voice, '*Miserlo Consulo*,' that is," Felix explains, "'My lord Consul'," and the dead man's son wept to hear the words which the bird had learnt at home in Alexandria.[14] Once clear of the island the hopes of the seamen faded; first the ship was caught by a current so strong that the rowers were helpless, and when the wind rose and the sails could be set, the gale blew from the south once more, driving them up the narrow strait between Paros and Naxos, where there was no good harbour;[15] as they ran beside the coast of Paros Friar Felix thought of the Parian marble which went to build churches and palaces in Venice, while, strangely enough, Friar Paul remembered that "lovely Helen" had been born there.[16]

The best that the captains could now do was to make for a harbour. They managed to round the north-easterly coast of Paros and came to anchor in the wide but sheltered bay of Naousa.* Here the ships were to remain, weather-bound for the best part of five days, so that the sailors began to recall the ill-fortune of last year's spice fleet, which had been forced to lie "in this prison" for a month.[17]

Yet, for Felix, even "the long hours in that barren and unprofitable place" had their compensations. The day after their arrival was Sunday: after Mass he "passed several hours playing with the parrot birds," before settling down to bringing his *Evagatorium* up to date.[18] November 25 was the festival of St. Katherine of Alexandria; no doubt his thoughts went back to her shrine below Mount Sinai and the lofty mountain where her body had laid; but he did not spend her Festival solely in meditation. "I designed," he says, "to pass the day in honest mirth," and to that end set off in a hired boat to visit his friends of the old "third company" who sailed in the galley of Bernardo Contarini. Here he found Heinrich von Schonberg suffering from fever, but so overjoyed was the knight at the sudden arrival of this companion of the desert journey that he declared himself quite restored; it is easy to believe that as a visitor the Friar would have just such a tonic effect.[19]

At last, on the evening of November 26, the wind shifted, and they left the harbour in the twilight. But at sunrise next morning the "unprofitable wind" returned, carrying them this time clear of the Cyclades, northwesterly towards Negroponte, that lost possession of Venice, whose tragedy was still a blood-stained memory in the minds of Christians. Lest they should fall on this now hostile shore they anchored in the Gulf of Aegina,[20] and there lay all night, "weltering and wallowing in the sea"–to borrow the words which an English pilgrim used to describe a similar situation.

For the next two days they were driven hither and thither by gales; once at least they were carried close enough to Cape Malea to see "the rocky height, smooth stone rising out of the deep sea."[21] After a storm which scattered the fleet some at least of the ships lay to under the lee of the great castellated rock of Monemvasia.[22]

* Fabri (*Evag.* III, p. 299) says that the ships "passed Naxos and left Paros behind," Walther (p. 251) that the fleet anchored off Paros. It seems clear that the latter is correct. Fabri here calls the island "Scefanus" but gives an account (*Evag.* III, p. 301) of a visit to "the town of Scheffanum," by which he almost certainly means Kephalos, the castle recently built by the Dukes of Naxos on the east coast of Paros (Miller, *Latins in the Levant*, p. 617; cf. Rubensohn in Pauli-Wissowa, *Real-Encyclopädie*, s.v. Paros). The "uninhabited" harbour which Felix describes can hardly have been the small bay below Kephalos, and he probably took this as the name of the island when he wrote his account of December 22, on the wet Sunday morning of December 23, and did not trouble to correct his mistake when on December 24 he visited the town.

On November 29 there seemed to be some hope of passing Cape Malea. "When evening had come we approached the Cape . . . but when we should have reached the point, out burst the wind in our teeth, with a great rushing noise, from the open sea, and swinging the ship about carried her far into the bay of Lakonia.* As we bore away, the other galleys met us, going towards Cape Malea at great speed, one after another, a marvellous sight to see. . . . For the galleys which were making for Cape Malea came full sail on the wind, but now also came the galleys which had been driven back, like them, full sail."[23] Here von Breydenbach, speaking in his own voice, makes one of his sudden interjections. "We traced a circle with the ships," says he, "as dancers go round in a ring."[24]

The night that followed, at anchor somewhere off the coast of the Morea, was, Friar Felix says, "dreadful." Next day the Captains decided to accept defeat, and running once more before the wind among the rock-strewn seas of the Cyclades, made for the island of Melos.[25]

As they passed through the narrow entrance of the harbour the great roadstead spread out majestically before them. It was "wide, roomy, deep, calm and sheltered, shut in on every side by very high cliffs. This harbour is of such a size that it would hold a hundred great ships. I never," says Felix, "saw any such harbour among the seas," and in his heart he thanked God, the Merciful, who had "from the beginning made it to be a refuge and place of safety for ships."

The pilgrims, however, were to experience not only the sight of this magnificent anchorage–one of the best in the whole Mediterranean–they were also to witness here the meeting of two Venetian merchant fleets. For when the four ships from the Alexandrian fleet and the two of the *Traffico* sailed into the harbour, there was a moment of alarm, as they sighted four great galleys at anchor under the lee of the shore.† But these were no Turkish enemies, nor even ships of those pirates in grain, the Sicilians or Spaniards; they carried the lion banner of St. Mark, being in fact those galleys of Venice which twice every year sailed to Beirut to bring home the merchandise of Damascus,[26] and which had come to port here to shelter from the late storm.

The encounter was not allowed to pass without a demonstration. As the ships of Alexandria and of the *Traffico* were recognised the sailors of the Beirut fleet crowded to the upper decks, the trumpeters blew, while the crash of the bombards re-echoed from the surrounding cliffs, and

---

* A mistake. The Gulf of Lakonia lies to the west of Cape Malea.

† Walther (p. 253) says that there was "one great galley from Beirut." Breydenbach (127a) agrees with Fabri. Three or four was the usual number according to Heyd (*Histoire du Commerce*, II, 460).

hid with smoke each ship from the next. Such, Friar Felix explains to his readers, was the custom when ships met together in friendship.[27]

When the galleys had anchored, the Captains having met in council resolved to remain in harbour till the weather improved. That night a great gale raged over the island, and next day there could be no thought of leaving port. But after sunrise the weather was considered good enough for an impromptu outdoor entertainment. Those watching from the ships, and it would seem a safe guess to suppose that Friar Felix was one, saw men row ashore to cut down trees, and with these to rig up a makeshift kitchen. Soon provisions of all sorts began to arrive from inland, with supplies of eggs, poultry, calves and pigs. When dinner time came the boats began to go back and forth between shore and ships, taking off the invited guests; the other two Commodores, and the Captains of the ten galleys, each attended by his trumpeters and accompanied by his Chief Officer. After them followed "those who were not invited . . . and the fleet was emptied of men."

The pilgrims were among those not invited to this Venetian festival, but they were prepared to enjoy themselves nevertheless. They landed, carrying a picnic meal, and climbed to a cave in the steep hillside behind the harbour. From this they commanded a view of the green space between cliffs and shore, upon which the stately Venetian merchantmen were congregated for their entertainment, "and it was astonishing to see the magnificent display of those lords in their coming together and their feasting, and such a multitude of men, and such a bustle. . . . After the banquet it was pleasant to watch the young men at their games . . . , while the old men and men of mark strolled on the shore."[28]

When the pilgrims tired of this spectacle they left their cave and began to explore. There was a small chapel near the shore; they entered it to pray; then wandered down to the water's edge to watch–as those who are at the seaside do watch"–the sea beating against the rocks;" they noticed the remains of ancient ashlar work which ran out from the shore, and on the opposite side of the harbour an old and ruinous tower. Poking about among the rock pools they found bits of pumice stone, not the white variety, "commonly called Bims, which the scriveners use to make the parchment smooth," but the grey. Friar Felix picked up and took home with him to Ulm some little bits of pumice for use in his bath.

Leaving the shore once more for the cliffs they soon found themselves looking down into a deep and narrow cleft between steep walls of rock, where the sea "made a sound in the depths like a bell," as it flooded the caves at the foot of the cliff, or was flung back from the rocks in clouds of spray; at this majestic and fascinating sight they stared for some time until Felix began to dread the collapse of the overhanging cliff, hollowed out as it was below, by the waves. They next explored some of the many caves in the cliffs above, in one of which they came upon the master gunner of the Syrian galleys, hacking out pieces of saltpetre from the walls. Here they noted and discussed the fossils of oysters which were visible in the sides and roof of the cave, deducing from these that the level of the sea must have been much higher. Friar Felix turned this over in his mind; there was always the Flood to account for so great a rise, and he recalled how, high up in the mountains of the Tyrol, there were great iron rings set in the rocks, which, he was told, had been fixed there for the convenience of ships during that great emergency. But, as he chewed on these things, he was puzzled to know how, in a bare six weeks, shell-fish should find time to grow into the rocks, and men to forge and install the iron rings. The problem defeated him. "Let who will solve these doubts," he concludes, "I will proceed with the ramble," and he brings himself and the other pilgrims back to a pleasant spot near the landing place where they sat down under some bushes, which, refreshed by the late rain, were beginning to flower.[29]

It had been an expedition after his own heart, and next morning, since there was no question of the fleet putting to sea, the Friar hired a boat and, having first paid a social call on "my friends in the other galley," had himself rowed ashore in order to repeat, in a luxury of solitude, the whole perambulation of yesterday, "satisfying my curiosity and examining and taking better notice of everything."[30]

A calm night set all the seamen making ready to sail, but in the morning the wind rose and blew fiercely from the south-west. Yet the sailors set their hopes on fair weather for the next day, because it was the Festival of St. Barbara. During the three weeks between November 22 and December 13 a whole cluster of Saints, held to be peculiarly well-disposed towards sailors, are commemorated by the Church, and the seamen had already petitioned in turn St. Cecilia, St. Clement, St. Katherine and St. Andrew. After the failure or inattention of the first two, the crews had drooped and desponded, but when neither St. Katherine nor St. Andrew answered the prayers of their suppliants, the sailors, who were losing patience, expressed their resentment openly. Now it was St. Barbara's turn, but she produced only heavy cloud, wind, thunder and lightning, with such torrents of rain that all hatches were battened down, and the pilgrims sat, bored and miserable, in the dark, while the sailors abused the Saint, "and refused with contumely to do her honour." They might still, however, try to secure the intervention of other celestial patrons; St. Nicholas, of old the helper of those in peril on the sea, ruled

December 6; the Blessed Virgin Mary herself, *Stella Maris*, held one of her festivals two days later. Should all these fail to control the elements, there was one more hope: St. Lucy. If she proved unpropitious, no ship, the seamen said, would pass Cape Malea that winter.³¹

Next day, December 5,* though not appropriated to any Saint of consideration to sailormen, there were signs of a change in the weather; the wind dropped, the sun shone, and the seas were less. As the fleet under full sail drew out of the harbour Father John Lazinus, to the admiration and delight of his friend, celebrated the occasion with one of his impromptu Latin couplets, which Felix took down in writing. But the rest of the day belied the hopes of its early hours, for the wind settled on the beam so that there was no possibility of passing the Cape.

Worse was to follow. After sunset a storm blew up; the sea rose and swept the decks; even the steersmen in the poop were wading in the water; while the sailors battled with the storm on deck the pilgrims below clung to anything stationary as the ship pitched and tossed. At some time during the night one of the galleys fouled the flagship, and smashed to fragments the longboat which was slung on the port side of the poop; another ship lost her kitchen which was swept away by the waves.³² In the darkness many of the galleys parted company; next morning Friar Paul in Marco Loredano's galley could see only three sail, and they were scattered far apart. These and three other ships were to spend the next couple of days beating about the Gulf of Nauplia, and the whole fleet would not be reunited till the galleys met in the port of Methoni.³³

As that night wore on, those in the flagship began to hope that the gale was blowing itself out, and that the Feast of St. Nicholas would dawn in calmer weather. The sailors, taking heart, prayed and even fasted. But the day brought black racing cloud with a raging wind, and at last the Captains of the ships which still remained in company gave up the struggle and ran for Melos again.³⁴

Their second sojourn in the island took on a gloomier tone than the first. Tempers were rising as hopes faded. The seamen ceased for a while to blame the Saints, and began to look for the root of their ill-fortune in the fleet itself. "Thus throughout the ships there were secret mutterings about the corpse of the Consul . . . and horrid oaths and imprecations against the dead man. If," says Felix, with some rancour, "it had been one of the great men among the pilgrims, they would hardly have suffered it, but because he was a senator of Venice no one dared to say or do anything."

* Walther (p. 253) gives the night of December 5–6 as the time of departure, and says that the storm began "about the 10th hour of the night."

Seeking for another and more accessible scapegoat the seamen began to accuse the pilgrims of being the cause of all the ill-luck of the voyage; perhaps they had visited the Holy Places with insufficient devotion, or they had with them on board bottles of Jordan water, or stolen relics. A suggestion was made that their baggage should be searched for such articles of religious contraband, but the pilgrims firmly rejected this, declaring that no search should take place until the corpse had been removed from the flagship.

The Eve of the Feast of the Conception of Our Lady dawned with the usual gale; but after dinner the wind began to drop. With one accord Captains, crews and pilgrims decided to make another bid for supernatural assistance. "Practically all," says Felix, rowed ashore and crowded into the little chapel, where "it was beautiful to see their sobriety, gravity, and faith." The Friar took a notable part in the service, chanting, solo, one of the hymns to the Virgin, particularly designed for use at sea.

> Placa mare, maris stella
> Ne involvat nos procella
> Et tempestas obvia.

That very evening the wind shifted and blew fair. Before nightfall the fleet put out to sea, and by brilliant moonlight and in calm weather sailed south-west. The pilgrims, full of hope and excitement, hardly went to bed at all, but instead sat up on deck, "talking with the rowers of this and that." Among the subjects touched on during the happy night of idleness was that of the mermaid and her dangerous *penchant* for sailors. According to one of the rowers the mariner who actually heard mermaids singing had little hope of escape, for the sound of their voices sapped all his power of resistance; only if these "great marvels of the sea" happened to be silent was it possible sometimes to divert their attention by throwing empty bottles overboard, "with which they play until the ship has passed."[35]

Next morning the fair wind still blew, strong and merry; by afternoon Cape Malea was in sight; in the evening they came abreast of the dreaded point; the wind was dropping, but a light breeze carried them past.[36]

CHAPTER XVII

Up the Adriatic

At eight o'clock on the morning of December 9, with a fair wind, the flagship and those galleys which had kept in touch reached the port of Methoni (Modon), and found already lying in harbour the six ships separated from them by the storm of a few nights earlier.

Methoni, with its satellite Koroni (Coron) on the Gulf of Messinia, and a small slice of surrounding territory, was a place of great military and maritime, and of some commercial, importance, in the Venetian overseas empire. "The chief eyes of the Republic"[1] they called these two coastal fortresses, buttressed by several small castles and fortified points, so strategically situated near the tip of the most south-westerly promontory of the Morea as to form at once a strong point and a look-out over the sea-ways leading to and from the Levant. Before the Turkish conquest of the mainland Methoni and Koroni had been "ports of discharge for Greece and the Black Sea, for all classes of merchandise,"[2] and the district was still famous for its siege engines, siege engineers and cochineal.[3] A provisioning station at which any Venetian ship could obtain a month's supplies, at Methoni, too, every Venetian Captain must stop to exchange the official pilot he had taken on board either at Poreč (Parenzo) on the outward run, or in the Levant, for the pilot qualified to direct the ship during the remainder of his voyage.[4] For this reason, and because the port was roughly half way between Venice and the Levant it was, in the words of a Venetian, "the receptacle and special rest of all our galleys, ships and vessels,"[5] a harbour where you might hope to find a ship for any Mediterranean port. While Felix Fabri was here a party of Breton pilgrims arrived and began to inquire about sailings for Sicily and Rome; they also had been to Jerusalem but by the long land route round the Black Sea, usually followed by Jews.[6]

This was the fourth time that the Friar had stopped at Methoni, and he both knew the place and was known there. He had already, on previous visits, walked the complete circuit of the magnificent walls of the town, the "inexpugnable fortifications" which yet were to fall to the Turks less than twenty years later. Built upon a rocky promontory of no great height the base of the seaward walls was lapped by the waves, though a fringe of outlying rocks formed a breakwater. On its landward side the town ran part way up a hillside, and was here defended by walls and towers of greater strength, and by a moat cut deep in the solid rock. Beyond the fortifications straggled a suburb of wretched huts, of mud plastered over reeds and withies, full of bad smells and dirty people of gypsy blood. But here also dwelt a colony of Jews who carried on a thriving silk industry.[7]

Felix thought it wiser to sleep with the rest of the pilgrims at the hospice of the Teutonic Knights, lest elsewhere he should miss some sudden nocturnal recall to the departing fleet. But his days he spent at the Convent with his fellow Dominicans. Among these was one, Brother John of Naples, "a very great friend of mine" said Felix, who had met him in Jerusalem, "a man of very pleasant conversation, who could talk well on many subjects, theological, philosophical and historical." A good linguist, Brother John taught Latin to the Greek boys of Methoni, and his occupation in fact provides a rare example of the scanty care which the Venetian Republic took in the matter of education among its colonial subjects.[8] The Neapolitan evidently knew Friar Felix's tastes. He took him out one afternoon, and from the top of a hill outside the town pointed out to him places of interest, connected, so he said, with the hero Hercules. Another day the two went for a walk along the seashore, and Felix listened to "wonderful things" concerning a river which from nearby ran beneath the sea to Sicily.[9]

While Felix and the other pilgrims passed the time in pursuits suitable to tourists, the Venetian Captains went about the serious business of commerce. Deep in lading as the galleys already were the patrician merchantmen could still find room for profitable cargo which offered along the homeward route. The Turkish country-folk inland, neighbours to the busy port, were accustomed on the arrival of a Venetian fleet to drive down to the outer suburbs of the town huge herds of swine from those which they bred, in order to meet the Christian taste for pork and bacon. Here the pursers of the ships met them, and did their marketing, after which followed a great to-do. The beasts were slaughtered, the hair singed off, heads and intestines removed, the meat cut up and boned, and only the fat retained. "Then," says Felix, who we may be sure watched the whole proceeding, "they stow into the empty body of one pig all the fat of two or three others, and with a needle firmly sew up the belly." He reckoned, in his usual care-free statistical style, that in this way, the fat of three or four pigs being contained in the hide of one, the product of more than 6,000 porkers was carried on board the galleys. This number,

6. VENETIANS ENJOYING A SPECTACLE
(*Detail from Mansueti's 'Miracole della Croce'*)

he admits, is large; but in Venice "they make an enormous number of sausages..." which, he notes, were sold by the ell.[10]

Oranges, another product of the district, too perishable for purposes of trade and little esteemed by the inhabitants, were therefore attractively cheap, as indeed were all food-stuffs at Methoni.[11] You could buy them by the hamper for five or six Venetian shillings.* Since even the pilgrims were allowed to bring these hampers on board, between them and the pigs the galleys must have been handsomely cluttered up.[12]

But Methoni produced something better than either fat pigs or fruit. "What," cries Felix, "shall I say of the wine that grows there, when even the thought of it is delicious on my tongue; for here grows a muscatel, whose reputation and noble name is stolen by a certain wine growing in the Trentino near the village of Tramin, which is water by comparison." Here was the real Malmsey, plenty of it, cheap, and better even than that of Crete; though both these wines–the reader will be glad to hear it for Felix's sake–could be bought at Ulm.[13] As for the despised Trammingers, there had been a time when the Friar counted them "noble wines."[14]

After no less than three false alarms, which brought the pilgrims at speed back to the galleys, the fleet at last, towards evening on December 16, stood out of the harbour, and anchored for the night in the narrow, sheltered channel between the mainland and a chain of small islands, the nearest and most northerly of which was that known as Sapienza. At this anchorage, next day, the Captains decided to remain, since the wind, though favourable, was too high for navigation, and sailors and pilgrims therefore went ashore on the neighbouring island, to spend one of those bye days in which Friar Felix took such pleasure.

The boats put in at the seaward point of the island and at the foot of Cape Sapienza, which rose above them to an imposing height; the sailors remained near the sea to disport themselves in a pleasant grassy plain, but the pilgrims preferred to climb to the crest of the Cape, from the top of which they were able to look "far and wide over the sea." After spending an hour or so here, they began to go down, but the Friar, who had been seized by one of his sudden fancies, separated himself unostentatiously from his companions, and climbed the hill once more. For he had realised that this was the day known in the Calendar as "O Sapientia," and where could he say his vespers more fitly than upon this, the brow of Cape Sapienza? So, in a delicious solitude, "I sang the whole of Vespers by myself... even the antiphon I sang joyfully in the loudest

---

* I.e. the *marchetto*. Walther (p. 255) who here calls the coin, as Felix usually does, "*marcellus*," says there are 12 to the ducat. (Cf. Walther, p. 81, n. 2.)

voice I could, yet for the height of the hill no one could hear me carolling. . . ." Vespers finished he made no haste to be gone, for this was a place after his own heart. There was a sailing-mark, to indicate the safe anchorage below; there were ruins,[15] probably of the look-out post which had stood here a hundred years earlier, and from which the watch had signalled in code with white flags upon a mast, to report passing shipping to the authorities at Modon.[16] Charmed with his surroundings, the Friar sat at the edge of the cliff for so long, "writing down about the place," that he all but missed the last boat off from shore.[17]

Two days sailing, one of which the pilgrims spent miserably under hatches while a storm raged, brought them to Corfu, the prosperous fertile island which reflected the dual character of the Venetian empire-wealth and strength. Corfu produced grain, "wines in perfection . . . and every kind of fruit, cotton and silk. . . ." These were country matters, but the towns were rich too. Those very Jews who, in their walks abroad were condemned to wear the yellow hat, made a brave show at home among themselves; an English country parson, looking on at one of their weddings, remarked how richly the women dressed, in damask, satin or velvet, with chains of fine gold about their necks, and many costly jewelled rings on their fingers, while the bride herself wore a crown of gold.[18]

But as well as being a prosperous island with a delightful climate, Corfu, lying at the very entrance to the Adriatic, and off a now hostile coast, was one of the key-points of the naval power of the Republic. The Venetians called it "their door, although Venice is . . . 800 miles away,"[19] and here in time of war was the regular station of the Venetian war galleys.[20] On Felix's first voyage out to the Holy Land the harbour at Corfu had been crowded with warships, for then the Turks were besieging Rhodes, and all the Mediterranean powers were awaiting with apprehension the outcome of that heroic struggle. Now once more, because of the state of war between Venice and Ferrara, the naval ships of the Republic under the command of the Captain of the Sea, filled the port, a circumstance which was to prove highly inconvenient both for the merchant captains and the pilgrims.

From the very outset things went wrong. "By some negligence of the sailors" the galley of Sebastian Contarini, in which sailed the Captain of the combined merchant fleets, came last, instead of first, into port. Stung by this insult to his dignity the Captain General began to rate the officers of the galley; his son joined in with all the heat of youth, and flung an ugly gibe at the chief officer; as the warships in harbour saluted the flagship with trumpets and shouting, with the crash of bombards and the clanging of bells, the seaman stabbed the young Venetian between the shoulders and jumped overboard, to cling undiscovered to the stern post till his friends rescued him and smuggled him away in a row-boat to one of the other galleys.[21]

As soon as the pilgrims landed they discovered the disadvantages which resulted from the presence of so great a concourse of men and ships in Corfu. Soldiers from the war fleet were everywhere, and for themselves there was "neither resting-place nor food." It was not, at this stage, that they could not have found, at a heightened price, a good dinner, for "in the public cook-shops we saw fire under the cauldrons, and sausages and roast meat. . . ." But the pilgrims, or at least those among them who wrote the account of this distressful occasion, were keeping the Advent fast and might not eat flesh. Hungry, and the hungrier for the seductive smells of cooking, they continued to search through the town, "like dogs, for bread." A friendly German soldier at last took pity on them, and led them to a poor sort of inn, where they were able to make a plain but pious meal of bread, wine and radishes.[22]

They had hoped that the galleys would sail that evening, but they were disappointed. Next day therefore they came ashore to another "starvation dinner," and to a bout of sight-seeing. Up they went through the steep and narrow streets, so narrow that even in summer the sun hardly shone there, and a lonely stranger might feel nervous among their sombre shadows.[23] They visited first the Cathedral, then the Churches of the Augustinians and Franciscans, the latter "a complete ruin," but worth the pilgrims' notice for the sake of the coats of arms of noble travellers hung on the walls or carved on the choir stalls.[24] Their tour was confined to the Latin Churches; as Felix remarked at Modon, "with the Greek Churches we did not bother;" but even so they were interrupted by the trumpets sounding the recall to the ships. They made haste to return, but, to their disgust, before ever they came on board, all stir of departure had ceased.

The Venetian Captain of the Sea was as eager to see the last of the merchant galleys as the pilgrims were to be once more on their way. He knew that the island could not long continue to supply so great a concourse of men and ships, and resented the fact that the Captains of the Spice Fleet had ever seen fit to call at Corfu. He let this sentiment be known; the only result was that the merchant Captains defiantly stayed where they were.

Amour propre was not the only motive which caused them to delay their departure. Before the flagship could sail it was necessary to patch up the quarrel between the young Venetian nobleman, whose wound was fortunately not serious, and the First Officer, who, as a most efficient seaman, was essential to the well-being of the galley. The Captains were also once more occupied with taking in cargo; this time it was a line in "Hungarian blankets," which the Venetian called "*Schiavini*" and the Germans "*Sclevs.*" More than three hundred were carried on board the flagship alone, and, though in general the passengers must have regretted the overcrowding which resulted from these repeated accessions of cargo, Friar Felix and Father John had here only cause for thankfulness. Till now they had laid their beds on "the bare and very hard sacks of spices"; bundles of woollen blankets made a much more cosy foundation for the thin cotton mattresses, and one for which they were to be very grateful as the weather grew increasingly cold.[25]

At last, when the merchant Captains has been three days in port at Corfu, the Captain of the Sea sent off a messenger urgently desiring them to leave; this time they did not refuse, and before dawn the fleet sailed.[26]

But now it was only two days before Christmas, and Friar Felix was convinced that the devil himself had had a hand in the transactions which had resulted in their leaving Corfu too early to celebrate the Feast there, and too late to celebrate it in any other port.[27] They kept their Christmas, he and Father John, as best they could, with the galley becalmed off the coast of Albania. Before midnight on Christmas Eve they borrowed a light from the friendly store-keeper next door, and rigged up an altar, laying over a chest "the lovely Turkish carpet" which the Friar had bought in Alexandria, spreading out the silks from Jerusalem, and setting up the sacred pictures which he and his friend carried with them. Then, with lights burning, they began to chant the psalms for Matins of Christmas Day.

The sound brought down to them something of a congregation, and they followed up Matins by reading the Mass of the Holy Night. But this was the only peaceful and happy time which they enjoyed that day, for though they repeated Mass at dawn and again later, the Chief Officer of the galley, a man "turbulent, evil spoken, blasphemous, without faith or conscience," saw to it that they should not do so undisturbed. "He came down into the hold, and calling all the rowers and sailors set them to hard labour. He altered the arrangement of the whole galley, moving and turning great heavy sacks of spices, and having them shifted from one side to another, with much shouting, cursing and swearing. He moved jars and chests full of merchandise, he shortened beams with axes and saws, and . . . ordered everything to be moved which had lain untouched since Alexandria . . . I never," says Felix, "saw men work harder, nor heard worse oaths and swearing, nor saw such an upset in all the sea voyage, as on that Holy Night and Day." Reflecting on the irreligious zeal of the Chief Officer, and sadly recollecting that, had not Venice surrendered to the Turks the town and territory of Scutari on the Albanian coast, they might have kept a joyful Christmas there, Friar Felix concludes with a sudden and startling bitterness: "It made me hate the Jerusalem pilgrimage."[28]

From now on, however, their course was to lie between Christian lands; though on the Dalmatian shore of the Adriatic the line of defence was very thin, yet it held, and was to hold, against all Turkish pressure. First in riches and fame of all the cities of that coast was Dubrovnik (Ragusa), small, even for the period, already past in the late fifteenth century, in which small principalities had held up their heads as proudly as the great nations, yet so rich and so strong as to survive as long as Venice itself, and to submit to no lesser conqueror than Napoleon.

The city had maintained its independence throughout the Middle Ages, partly by military strength, partly by such payments of tribute out of the almost fabulous wealth which her sea-trade brought her, as sweetened relations with her dangerous neighbours, whether Turk or Hungarian. But she did not depend upon her gold alone; her mighty fortifications also gave the measure of her determination to remain free. No pilgrim, secular or ecclesiastical, could ignore the tremendous walls which guarded the city on all but the seaward side. Friar Felix, doing the sights with young lord George Stein on his first pilgrimage, inspected "the wonderful defences . . . the towers, the very deep moat," which, in those days of alarm and suspense, men were cutting yet deeper.[29] Another Churchman, old Canon Casola, took the trouble to measure the thickness of the fortifications, and found them twenty feet, instead of the twenty-four he had been told. He was impressed, as well he might be, by the magnificent drum tower with its machicolated crown, recently engineered by Michelezzo, a work as beautiful as mighty, which still guards the landward corner of the fortifications towards the north. He climbed to the top of it, and from there saw, as visitors today see, the whole miniature city folded in its huge walls, in the midst the broad Stradone, then recently paved after the Venetian fashion,[30] running from gate to gate, and on either side the tilted planes of the site; the outer lifting to a sheer cliff edge with the sea at its base; the inner running up towards the impending rocky hills inland. The houses, built of the superb stone of Dalmatia, "white like marble" crowded close within the restricting walls. But if the Ragusan noble found himself cramped in the city he had only to go out a few miles to his pleasant country palace and vine-trellised garden on the shore of what is modern Dubrovnik's harbour, or along the green, calm waters of the lower Ombla.

Large as the sums were by which Ragusa continued to buy its peace, there was enough left in the coffers of the citizens to make the city beautiful as well as strong, and healthful as well as beautiful. Finest of all the secular buildings within the city was the Palace of the Rectors. Here, by a constitution so planned to make a ruling caste supreme, so prudently suspicious of the motives of individual rulers that it might have resulted from the collaboration of Plato with Diogenes, each Rector bore office for the brief term of one month, though in great and solemn state. The loggia by which the Palace is entered is tiny compared with that which runs the length of the Venetian Palazzo Ducale, but the sculptor's work on doorway and capital is exquisite. Within, the cultured Casola could liken the Council Hall, with its ceiling of gold and costly blue, to the Hall of the Great Council at Venice, "except that the seats are not gilded."

The churches of the city showed at once the piety and wealth of the merchants, and the craftsmanship of the silversmiths of Ragusa. In the Franciscan church was to be seen a *Maiestà* "of silver-gilt . . . two rows of large figures with twelve figures in a row . . . and . . . everything of silver," while the jewels were so large that Casola, seeing them quite unguarded, found it hard to believe that they were real. Here the sacristy, as to this day the treasury of the Cathedral, housed a magnificent collection of gold and silvergilt reliquaries; while as to the Friars' Psalters, the Milanese thought that "there are none more beautiful among Christian people."[31]

Charitable institutions and works of public utility were not neglected. A *Domus Dei* for the aged poor, a home for foundling children, and, in the Franciscan Convent, one of the earliest public dispensaries in Europe, all displayed the enlightenment and humanity of their founders. Enormous silos were sunk deep into the solid rock of the city's seaward side, for grain to feed the community during siege or times of dearth. The water supply of the city, after having turned the wheels of nine flour mills, was brought within the walls by an aqueduct, and flowed out at two fountains, one at each end of the Stradone. Both these were by the hand of Onofrio della Cava; one, small, aptly decorated with bas-reliefs of a limpid simplicity, showing naked boys carrying water-skins; the other, a huge rounded well head, below which twenty-three jets of water sprang from pipes set in two ranges, one above the other, the whole "so well built and adorned that it is not possible," an Italian pilgrim decided, "to describe it in writing."[32]

Pilgrims found the population very polite and pleasant to foreigners.

Country folk, poor enough, came crowding in at weekends to make a little money by selling to the visitors, who were impressed by the stature and comeliness of the men. The women were considered to be less handsome, but on the credit side it was observed that the noble ladies of Dubrovnik, with their notable horned head-dresses, were very modest in their behaviour, and in their apparel most magnificent, being "well adorned with jewels . . . and resplendent with gold, silver and pearls."[33]

Friar Felix was not, on this occasion, to have an opportunity of visiting those friends of his in the Dominican house, who had dealt so hospitably with him and young George Stein, supplying them in their need with a meal of "good food and first rate Slav wine," and, we may suppose, displaying, at least to the Friar, their new and beautiful cloister, and their gardens of pomegranate and orange trees.[34] For this time the Captain, unwilling to waste a favourable wind, after the delay at Corfu and the day spent becalmed off the Albanian coast, sailed on without coming to harbour at Dubrovnik. At Korčula (Curzola) the flagship stopped only a few hours in the little port which looks towards the sunset between the long flank of Mount Pelješac and the coast of the island. Friar Felix had been here on the outward voyage of his first pilgrimage,[35] but it is not to him but to Casola, the Milanese Canon, with his lively aesthetic sense, that we must look for a glimpse of this minute Venetian fortress town in the days of its prosperity. Built upon a ridged promontory which runs out into the channel, with the bright sea on three sides of it, its streets, narrow and cool, run up steeply the spine of the ridge at whose highest point the Cathedral stands. "As bright and clear as a beautiful jewel," the town was in Casola's eyes, and looking about at the miniature palaces, with their arched and sculptured windows, he found it "a marvel to see so many beautiful houses in one place."[36]

Hvar (Lesina) too they passed by, but here again Felix could look back upon a pleasant day on shore three years ago, when as well as visiting the convents of the Dominicans and Franciscans close to the little harbour, they had gone wandering up into the hills, among the deliciously scented, half-wild trees and shrubs. Vine, fig and olive grew here abundantly, but the Friar was more struck by the thickets of rosemary—a herb so common here that it was used for fuel.[37]

The Dalmatian coast was always "much affected by sailors on account of the excellent shelter and anchorages."[38] Nevertheless, in winter storms, it was a tickle business sailing the network of narrow canals, among clustered islands, sometimes large enough to accommodate several townships, sometimes occupied by no more than a shepherd's hut, sometimes merely a rock covered with scanty salt-drenched vegetation. There was plenty of occasion for accident, and more for the sort of discomfort which the pilgrims endured the night after leaving Korčula, when the darkness came down before the ships found anchorage for the night. When soundings were taken no bottom could at first be found. The big anchor was dropped, but dragged. A second attempt was no more successful; "the anchor followed the ship as a plow after oxen." When at last the flukes held on rock the ship must lie to in a shelterless channel, where all night it plunged "like a mad dog on a chain."[39] A few days later, with the ship wind-bound in a rocky deserted cove, heavy rain prevented the pilgrims landing, and reduced them to a state of exasperated boredom, against which Friar Felix contended by "writing, and asking about places." The rowers were the only people who positively welcomed the idle hours in shelter, for they spent it gambling over cards.[40] Next day, for the first time, to all their discomforts was added the nip of a cold so intense, and by now to the pilgrims so unaccustomed, that it drove the German lords down below to share the comfortable fug which the two priests enjoyed in their berth.[41] Worst of all, supplies were beginning to run short; not even Friar Felix and Father John in their favoured position near the store-house did very well in these days.

Yet, let the Friar but have the chance of going ashore, and he would find material for interest and enjoyment. Once landed it was almost certain he would make for the highest neighbouring hill, from the top of which he might receive such a joyful surprise as when, having left the ship anchored off a featureless shore among many small deserted islands, he found himself looking across the wide, almost completely landlocked harbour, at Šibenic (Sebenico) "the fair city," and saw below him a hillside rich in gardens and vineyards, with houses which when he explored and found empty, he guessed to be the summer residences of the nobles and wealthy merchants of Šibenic;[42] there were small chapels too, at one of which Felix attended Mass and listened with some disapproval to the incomprehensible Slav tongue, permitted in the churches of these independent-minded Catholics.

The habit of climbing hills, because "I wanted to see what, in fact, was on the other side," was, as the reader by now knows, ingrained in Friar Felix. Sometimes he was able to infect others with his own enthusiasm, or at least goad them into sharing in an expedition. A couple of days after he had caught that astonishing glimpse of Šibenic, a contrary wind forced the galleys once more to take shelter on the Dalmatian coast. One of the Venetian sailing marks, on the heights above, promised safe anchorage; the ships put in towards the land, and "passing through the cliffs by a narrow strait, we came to a delightful harbour. I have hardly ever," says Felix, "seen an uninhabited place so delightful as this, for the sea there was deep and quite surrounded, like a fish pond, by lofty rock walls, except for the narrow entrance . . . and the circular harbourage was fashioned as if by the art of man, and much better, for the maker of the world had formed that port . . ." so that there was a way up by natural steps to the summit of the cape; "it was marvellous to see such huge blocks as if disposed by hand for a stairway. . . ."[43]*

Friar Felix, on fire to make use of so tempting an opportunity, invited, teased and wheedled the Archdeacon into accompanying him. The cliff was high but the way not dangerous. God had made the place for such comrades as they to climb. "Perhaps, who knows, on top there will be something rare or strange. . . ." The Archdeacon, "the venerable man" yielded; the two had themselves rowed ashore, and from the foot of the rocks "went up, climbing like goats to the lofty summit."

Though what they found was perhaps neither "rare nor strange" yet the time which they spent on the headland must have been memorable for both men. For having first knelt in prayer before the wooden cross, they stood and looked about at the wide prospect of sea and mountain. " . . . And there Master John showed me the boundaries and mountains of Hungary. . . . But when we turned towards the west and I looked into the far distance I exulted, for in that direction appeared snowy mountain peaks faintly visible, and when I saw them I knew for certain that they were our Alps, which divide Italy from Germany. . . . And to my friend I said, 'Look, Master John, now I see the threshold of my land and my country, for those mountains which we, here on the sea's edge, behold, my brothers in the Convent at Ulm also see when they look out of the dormitory windows if the weather is clear.' "[44] However far out the two were in their conception of geographical fact, they shared in those moments a true emotion; for each it had been as if he opened to his friend the doors of home.

On January 8 a fair wind brought the fleet to Zara (Zadar), and at once everyone went ashore, to make his way, "whither he chose, either to the taverns or the churches." Next day, being Sunday, the pilgrims began

* The Friar calls the place "Larmolum," and refers shortly after to the village of "Muters" (Murter) as being close by. There seems to be now no such steep-sided anchorage as he describes, the coast here being low. But of the peculiarities he mentions, the narrow entrance into a wide harbour exists near by at Sibenic, and the step-like stone formation is to be seen in various parts of this coast; is it possible that many years of quarrying may account for the disappearance of the harbour?

with Mass and after dinner occupied themselves in visiting Zadar's holy relics, of which the body of St. Simeon was the most notable. It was enclosed in a magnificent silver shrine, in a chapel to the left of the altar of his church; over the choir the high, isolated Dalmatian rood-beam bore a crucifix in the midst of an array of "fourteen large figures all covered in gold . . . beautiful and very natural."[45] Apart from such rareties Zadar, a small town, "bright and clean," but paved with "little hard pebbles" which were very trying to gouty feet,[46] possessed various Roman remains—columns, arches and sculptured inscriptions, which Felix at least did not omit to notice.[47]

At once, upon his arrival at Zadar, the Friar had repaired to the Dominican Convent with a request that he might spend as much time as possible in the company of the Brothers. On the first night he returned to the galley after the excursion ashore; but next day, as well as eating his Sunday dinner at the Convent, he returned there after sight-seeing with the pilgrims, intending to sup and sleep. "But when we were sitting down to supper I heard the trumpets, recalling us to the ships, and dropping everything I rushed in the dark to the city gate, and found it shut. But there came running with me many others, and another small gate was opened for us, and we got out and took boat for the ship."[48]

The fleet did not after all sail that night, but Felix Fabri might have taken warning by so close a call. Instead, after hanging about for a while next morning trying to hear what a group of pilots thought about the weather, he made up his mind that another windless day would keep the ships in port, and went off once more to hear his Mass at the Dominican Convent. When he returned to the quay it was to see the whole fleet, with the exception of one galley, just clearing the port; a fair wind filled all the sails, and the flagship was far in the van.

"When I saw that," says Felix, "I was frightened, and opening my purse I threw a shilling* into a boat and jumped in after, making signs that I belonged to the fleet and to the galley of the Captain of Alexandria, for I could not speak to the boatman who was a Slav. . . ."

In a similar predicament Friar Paul, a few days earlier at Curzola, had found great difficulty in persuading a boatman to attempt to follow the ships. Perhaps the dash and vigour of Felix Fabri's approach, perhaps the shilling, paid cash down, carried the day. At once, "with all possible haste," the boatman pushed off and rowed the Friar out to the one galley whose sail had not yet filled; "for my galley drew always further away, and it was impossible to catch up with it."[49]

Thus pitchforked by chance into a strange ship's company, the Friar's

* "*Marcellus*," i.e. the Venetian *marchetto*.

luck served him well. Having explained his hard case successively to the forecastle men, the Second Officer and the ship's clerk, "how not from carelessness but for the sake of Mass I had happened to be late," he found himself made welcome by all. So far good, but better was to follow. The trumpets blew for dinner; the Friar, uncertain of his position, remained where he was. Suddenly he saw "Lord Caspar von Bulach, coming up from the berth under the forecastle, to fetch food from the kitchen... I shouted to him in German and called his name. . . ." Felix had in fact happened upon the very galley in which sailed the knights of the second company.

At Jerusalem and in the desert there had been friction between this and the third company, of which Felix was a member. But either all that was now forgotten, or the Friar had never been included in the quarrel. In a few minutes he was brought down to share the dinner and berth of the knights; they even assured him that they had been wishing that he could have been with them for a few days; as they were men after his own heart, "well behaved and conversible," time passed pleasantly in their society; " . . . we talked that day about many things."[50]

It was well for Felix that he had fallen among friends. During the night a storm blew up; even below deck they sat huddled together, drenched by the water which broke in through the seams, and crowded with the sails and ropes which the sailors flung in among them. Yet with all their discomfort the gale was a thing "delightful, and there was no man in the fleet would have wished it away, for it drove us on our journey at a great rate."

So well did the wind serve them that the galley reached Rovinj (Rovigno) next evening, and first out of the whole fleet dropped anchor in the harbour. St. Euphemia's bells were ringing for evensong from the magnificent white cliff on which her church stands among grass and pines, overlooking on the one side the sea far below, on the other the steep little town climbing up towards the shrine of its Saint. Fabri and his friends hastened to attend the service and thus it was that when the Captain and pilgrims from the flagship entered the church a little later, they saw to their astonishment Friar Felix, left behind at Zara, cheerfully singing vespers in St. Euphemia's choir. The reunion after the service was joyful, and when the Friar returned once more to his own berth there was jubilation "as over a brother who was lost and is found."[51]

After all the storms with which they had been vexed, their voyage was to end in calm and fair weather. Before dawn next morning, with the moon shining bright, the fleet left Rovinj. It was still early in the day when they entered the harbour of Poreč (Parenzo), and anchored between the town wall and the chain of islands which protects the small port. Upon one of these islands, as well as a small cell of Benedictine monks, their rich olive groves, and ancient watch tower, stood the Chapel of St. Nicholas, built with the offerings of sailors, and dedicated to the sailor's Saint, who has given his name to the island.[52]

Poreč was the last port before Venice on the homeward voyage, and it was in this small but beautiful chapel that according to old custom, all Venetian seamen, before setting foot in the town on their homeward voyage, must do honour to the Saint and pay such vows as had been wrung from those "hardened and desperate men" by the perils of the sea. In some great crisis, Friar Felix tells us, every soul on board a galley might have bound themselves by a common vow, and seeing the unanimity with which officers and crew now crossed over to the island he judged that they had done so during the late voyage.[53] He may have been right. But there is some reason to think that such transactions between sailor and saint were regulated and modified by a certain convention, for during a storm Canon Casola was called upon to draw out of a hat what would, one supposes, be considered the winning vow.[54]

Of the churches of Poreč, even of the holy relics which they contained, Friar Felix has remarkably little to say; he makes less of the pilgrims' visit to these than of a pleasant solitary ramble which he took along the shore, during which he spent some time sitting down to watch the boys who were gathering oysters among the rocks.[55] He has not a word to say of the ancient Cathedral, contemporary with that of Ravenna, with its apse, at once cool and glorious in mosaic of the sea's own colours–green, blue and gold–its delicately austere ranges of marble pillars and sculptured Byzantine capitals, its fine tesselated pavement. Nor does he mention the noble atrium from which the Cathedral is entered.* Yet he certainly came there, for he relates how, in the baptistery which faces the Cathedral across the atrium, he lifted the cover of the font, to find that "all the rim right round was full of scorpions, and they began to run when the cover was removed, and many, indeed most, fell into the baptismal water; others fell to the ground . . . I dropped the lid and fled."[56]

The galleys lay for a short time only in the harbour of Poreč, and the very evening of their arrival the trumpets sounded the recall through the streets. That was a joyful sound. Though the distance between this port and Venice was short the navigation was a matter of such difficulty that ships changed their pilots here for the last stage of their journey, and anything but a light breeze might keep them lying at Poreč for days.[57]

---

* Even Casola (p. 163) only remarks of the mosaics that they were in bad repair, and that long grass grew in the atrium.

That night on board was therefore both cheerful and sleepless. Supper was "very merry, with flesh and fish," and included an enormous crab which the friendly store-keeper had bought at Poreč, and which provided ample helpings for a large number, among whom Felix would surely be one. But after supper, when the pilgrims had gone to rest, they found it impossible to sleep. Cargo was being shifted, lights burned all night, and the sailors when not at work shouted and sang over their carousals. Yet as Felix waked and watched, as if to console him, he saw across the calm sea the snow-topped peaks of the Alps under the moonlight.[58]

Daylight came and they knew that they were almost in sight of Venice; but before those in the ships caught the first glint of sunshine on the gilded roof of the Campanile they heard the great bell of that most magnificent of all Venetian sailing marks begin to ring, and then all the deep-mouthed bells of Venice, to let its citizens know that their Spice Fleet had been sighted.[59] Now, according to custom, the sailors with shouting and singing began to throw overboard all the torn and ragged clothing which they had worn at sea; the Captain's servants came out with banners and hangings and "royally dressed the ships," which swept on in the morning light, as Felix says, "a beautiful sight to see."[60] When the fleet was abreast of the two forts of the Lido the anchors were dropped, and as the cables ran out of the hawse-holes, the voyage was at an end.

A swarm of small boats now pushed off from the quays of Venice, bringing men who wished to welcome a kinsman, or merchants anxious about a freight, or customs officers. With none of these, however, were the pilgrims concerned. Friar Paul and his fellow Franciscan, in Marco Loredano's galley, did indeed remain long enough to eat the excellent dinner to which the Captain treated them before he set them ashore at San Francesco della Vigna.[61] But in the flagship the pilgrims hastened their departure. "When we had paid our fare, and the charges," says Felix, "and tipped the servants who had looked after us, and said goodbye to everyone in our galley, both noblemen and servants, we put all our things into one boat and climbed down into it.... And though we were glad of our enlargement from that uneasy prison, yet, because of the companionship which had grown up between us and the rowers and others, sadness mingled with our joy...."

Their attention was soon to be diverted from the parting. First they were held up by a boatload of Venetian Customs officials, but the inquisition was brief and painless. Then as they passed the island of St. Andrea they determined to take a short cut, and, instead of making for the Bacino and the entrance to the Grand Canal, to keep to the northern side of the

Arsenal, and so enter the city from the lagoons. "But we ran into trouble, for, so cold it was, the canals by which we went in were frozen, and the ice had to be broken by the oars to make way for the boat."

At last, however, they reached their Inn, returning, as Friar Paul returned to the Franciscan Convent, to Peter Ugelheimer's Inn of St. George, or of the Flute.[62]* For Felix, who had stayed here upon his three previous visits to Venice, this was almost to come home. "Out ran all in the house who knew us, and welcomed and congratulated us, and our host gave us a good room apart." There had been no host at the Flute when the pilgrims left last summer, for Master John had died during their stay at the Inn; but since then his widow, Mistress Margaret, had married one of the head servants, Nicolas Frig; Felix thought this an excellent arrangement, for Nicolas was "a good fellow and a merry."[63]

* Approached from the Grand Canal the hostelry was reached by way of the Rio del Fontego upon the left bank of which stood the Fondaco dei Tedeschi (*Evag.* I, 83). The owner of the Inn of St. George, or of the Flute, was not the "Master John" of Fabri's narrative, but Peter Ugelheimer, a native of Frankfurt (Simonsfeld, *Fondaco dei Tedeschi*, II, pp. 69, 284; Röhricht and Meisner, p. 11). Ugelheimer was a man of varied occupations, who would be likely to have a manager to run the Inn for him. He traded as a merchant in Venice in association, after 1476, with Nicolas Jenson (E. Motta, *Pamphilio Castaldi . . . Pietro Uggleimer ed il vescovo d'Aleria, Rivista storica italiana*, 1884, pp. 260–3). Jenson had set up as a printer in Venice in 1469 (Garrison, *Introduction to the History of Medicine*, 1917, p. 179) and Ugelheimer before his death in 1487 had a printing press and bookselling business in Milan, which he left to his wife, Margaret (Motta, *loc. cit.*). It would seem likely that Fabri's "Mistress Margaret" was the daughter of these two, and that she and her husband ran the Inn for Ugelheimer. He himself may have lived elsewhere; Felix does not mention him, and may not have come across him; Breydenbach (f. 8a) on the outward journey found him helpful in negotiations with the Captain of the galley in which he sailed, but Fabri would not be involved in these as he travelled in another ship.

Part Seven

VENICE TO ULM

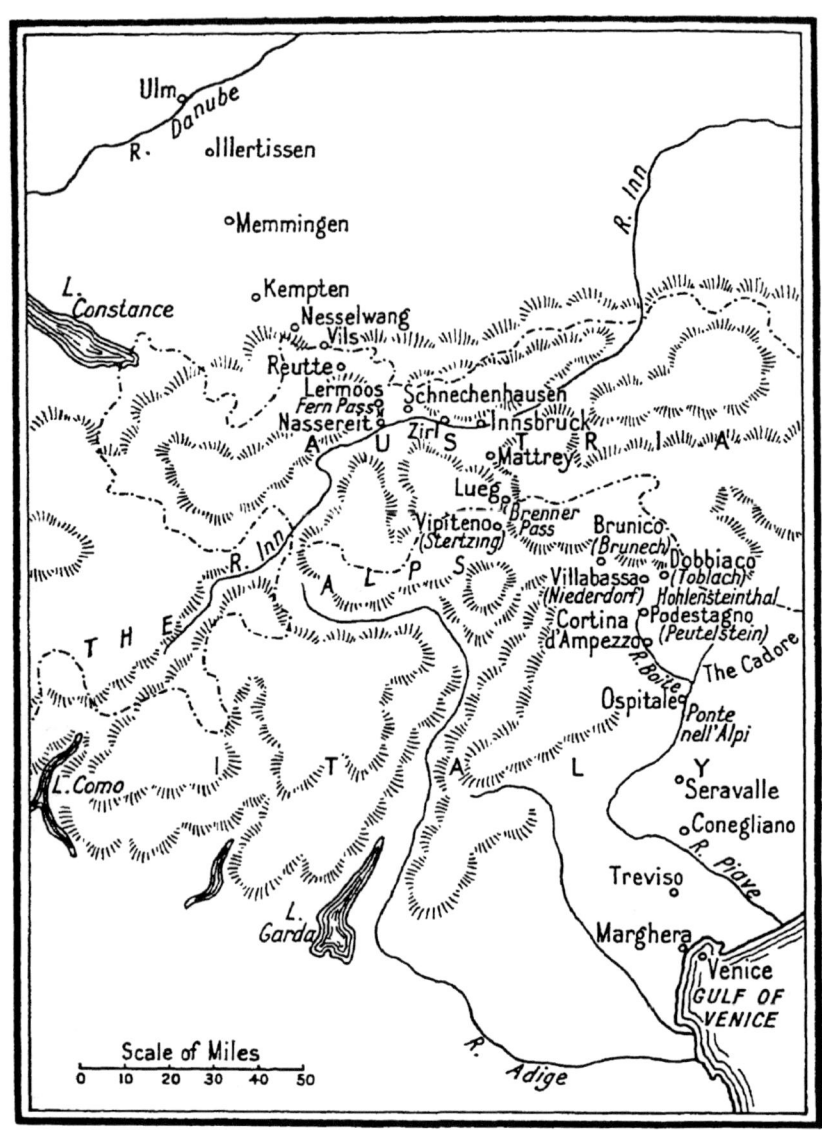

CHAPTER XVIII

Venice of the merchants

"The Sign of the Flute" had given Friar Felix a warm welcome; Father John was with him, and probably also those others of the Sinai party who had stayed at the Flute on the outward journey.[1] But Felix now felt the pull of an affection greater and of longer standing than any which was due to his companions in pilgrimage. So, "... before I tasted a crumb I rushed to the German *fondaco* to find out news of my country, and the city of Ulm, and our Convent."

Just as the Venetian galleys timed their voyage to Alexandria to meet the Indian spices there, so German merchants made their journey across the Alps in the dead of winter, to meet those same galleys when they arrived at Venice with their precious cargoes. It was therefore not surprising that as soon as the Friar entered the *fondaco* he recognised a group of Ulm merchants who, just arrived, stood talking together. For a moment they must have stared at him, for they told him after, that at first sight they had not known him, so pale he was and haggard, and as voluminously bearded as any Greek priest.[2] Then he was welcomed, congratulated on his safe return, and, what was more, invited to stay at the *fondaco* by "young, kind-hearted" Eitel Rentz,* already a man of note among the burghers of Ulm, who would not hear of him remaining at the hostelry. Such an invitation, which carried with it the certainty of finding company for the journey home, was irresistibly attractive. The Friar went back to "The Sign of the Flute", collected his baggage and settled down to enjoy the hospitality of the *fondaco*.

He thus parted abruptly, and with an alacrity which seems almost callous, from those who had shared with him so many and arduous experiences. Yet his indifference was apparent rather than real. On the second day after their arrival in Venice † he went round to the Inn. Some of the pilgrims had already left; others, and the Archdeacon among them, were to leave next day. Friar Felix remained with them till nightfall, and

---

* Fabri (*Evag.* III, 388) says that Rentz was "*procurator illius magnae societatis, quam nominant Rottengetter.*" Elsewhere (*Tractatus de Civitate Ulmensi*, p. 122), he speaks of a family called Rottengatter (cf. Simonsfeld II, 361, no. 653). This would appear to have given its name to one of the Ulm guilds.

† He does not assign this visit to any date, but in his narrative it immediately

when the time came to say goodbye, "we did not part without tears, but especially John Lazinus... parted from me with great weeping, and I left him with no less sorrow and regret."³ The two friends must have known that there was little likelihood of meeting again in this life; Lazinus was Archdeacon of Transylvania, or Siebenburgen as the Germans called it, a land where every church was a fortress, for it lay right in the track of the advancing Turkish power. Father John was going home to a country desperately near to the Iron Curtain of those days.

Even after the departure of his especial friend, Felix Fabri saw something of his late companions, sharing with them an expedition to Padua, and spending a day with Bernard of Breydenbach, who vainly tried to persuade him to collaborate over an account of their pilgrimage. Had the Friar consented, his narrative, with the illustrations of Erhard Rewich, would have formed one of the most remarkable travel books of the Middle Ages.

But apart from these contacts the Friar was left to employ himself in Venice according to his own taste, and to enjoy a sojourn which differed in many ways from his previous visits. Alone, he was free to spend as much time as he chose in visiting the Friars of his own order. Having already done his duty by the sights, both ecclesiastical and secular, which Venice offered to pilgrims, he could now pick and choose, take more time here, repeat a visit there, observe the whole tenor of the city's life, or notice a detail which had escaped him before. Now, as never before, he looked about at Venice with the eyes of a man able to compare the life he watched with that of one of the Moslem capitals of the near East. Now, too, he saw Venice, not as a station upon a pilgrim route, but as the port to which were brought at last the spices, whose distant sea-route he had first beheld from the top of Gebel Katerina; as the mart from which his own countrymen carried these same spices home to Germany.

For congenial society during his stay in Venice Felix went to the Black Friars of San Domenico.* The Convent "small, but very trimly built," stood at the eastern extremity of the main island of Venice, with "a large and lovely garden stretching out into the sea, and surrounded every way by the waters." Such a place was much to Friar Felix's taste, and the hours must have been happy which he spent walking there with the sober and devout inhabitants, one of whom was commonly reputed to be a Saint, and whose conversation Felix found "full of sweetness and piety."⁴

* Near the modern Giardini Pubblici. Practically nothing remains of the Priory (G. Lorenzetti, *Venezia e il suo estuario*, p. 290).

Very different from this small House of quiet and unworldly men was the other Dominican Convent of Venice. The towering roof of the great Church of San Giovanni e Paolo was one of the landmarks which first caught the traveller's eye as he approached the city; within the walls were lined with the princely tombs of many Doges, enriched with marble, silver and gold, and a profusion of sculpture. Friar Felix admired but could not approve these monuments. There was in them a lack of theological discrimination; Christ, Our Lady, apostles and martyrs appeared indeed, but surrounded by a mixed company of ancient gods, monsters and heroes. Especially he deplored the handsome tomb of the Doge Paolo Mocenigo, to the south of the great west door; here Hercules appeared, "wearing the skin of the lion he had killed, for a cloak"; the hydra was here too, short of one of its heads, and, more reprehensibly, naked warriors and boys; so many pagan stories, in fact, mixed up with those of Christianity, that Felix feared lest the ignorant should be confused, and render the honour due to Samson and the Magdalen to Hercules and Venus.

The hundred or so Friars and Doctors of the Order who inhabited the fine conventual buildings, also incurred Felix Fabri's censure. These Mendicants lived "in a glory of worldly pomp" which betrayed itself even in their devotions; on high festivals, when the Friars displayed their musical virtuosity, singing in parts in the new "figurate" style, their church, with its two organs (*orgona duplicata*), was crowded at Vespers and Compline by a fashionable congregation of young men and women; yet these came "not for the sake of the divine service, but for the music and to hear the descants sung."[5]

And here Friar Felix cannot refrain from inserting in the narrative of his pilgrimage an account of the splendours which he saw displayed at this same Convent, during the meeting of the General Chapter of the Order four years later. When, on that great occasion, the Doge himself arrived as guest, disembarking from his gilded and adorned barge at the garden of the Convent,* he was followed by a multitude of notabilities, whose gondolas crowded all the canals round about. Within the walls of refectory, offices and chambers, were covered with rich hangings of tapestry, and even of cloth of gold. There was profusion of meat and drink for all, but for the principal members of the Chapter "exquisite dishes and abundance of superb wine," so that "sugar and comfits of Sicily" were hardly regarded. All this, to a friend of the reforming Friar Fuchs at home, seemed reprehensibly worldly. But what most offended Felix Fabri was a circumstance over which, to be just, the Friars of San

*At this date the garden reached the lagoon. See the map of Iacopo Barbari (first state).

Giovanni e Paolo had no control. In addition to the male guests at this festivity there arrived a horde of Venetian ladies, who came, "with the permission of their husbands, so gorgeously dressed that you would have thought that Venus and her crew . . . had been despatched by the devil to our own Chapter." The resentment which Felix felt at this intrusion was at least partially justified; the ladies treated the privacy of the bachelor establishment with small respect; "they were not so much in Church, but wandered about . . . the whole Convent, explored all the dorters and cells, entered the living quarters of the brethren . . . and nosed their way into every nook and cranny of the monastery."[6]

What sight-seeing was done by Friar Felix upon this visit to Venice was limited both by time (his stay lasted only eight days), and by his previous thorough dispatch of the duty of a tourist. He did, however, on this occasion make a more careful inspection of the Palazzo Ducale, observing everywhere within it the utmost splendour of colour and gilding, penetrating even to the bedchamber of the Doge; and finding, high on the roof, a garden of fruit trees and sweet-smelling bushes.[7] It will surprise none of his readers that he also climbed the great Campanile, including the ladder which led to "the place of the watch, from which there is a view far and wide, over land and sea;" though he was convinced that the tower was slightly but alarmingly out of the perpendicular, "I," says he, "was often on top."[8]

But for the rest, having recovered from the stunning impact which visitors to the unique city at first experience, Friar Felix could now, as he says himself, "be silent of great things and speak about the small." In the market which took place in the Piazza of St. Mark, among the fish, the poultry, the meat, the fruit (fruit from abroad, fresh and cheap a Spaniard observed, as in his own country)[9] he recorded the astonishing quantities of herbs and of sausages which the culinary tastes of the Venetians demanded.[10] Passing here and there by boat among the canals (did Eitel Rentz supply him with pocket-money for boat-hire as well as hospitality?) he decided that "unless one kept one's eyes shut" one must notice that many houses, like the Campanile, looked to be in danger of falling. Now, on his wanderings, his ear would appreciate the peculiar sonority of the bells of Venice, or his attention be caught by an instance of the frugal prudence of the Venetians, who, setting lamps at dark corners in their tortuous and narrow streets "on the wall behind the lamp . . . put some image of the Blessed Virgin, so that the lamps burn both in honour of Our Lady and for the convenience of passers-by."[11]

The Friar himself was conscious of that change in himself which experience of lands beyond Christendom had brought. "I reckon," he says, "that I have seen the whole world in a two-fold mirror," reflected, that is to say, in the cities of Cairo and Venice. For him Cairo meant confusion, Venice order. It was not only that "people from every nation upon earth live there in such myriads that it is marvellous to see," so that churches, streets, *piazze* and canals swarmed with life, yet all without disorder. He, who so rarely was conscious of the abstract and the general, realised and extolled something of the essential quality of the Venetian constitution, in which power was held subject to checks upon power; praising also the exactitude of Venetian justice; the clemency to prisoners; the regard for the rights of the common people; the habits of discipline which were impressed upon the sons of the merchant-princes by careful education and apprenticeship in the harsh school of the sea.[12]

But as well as his new knowledge of other politics, Felix, who had made his bed during the long voyage upon the sacks of spices in the hold of a merchantman, possessed a new interest in, and understanding of, the sea trade of Venice. "Here," he says, under the ninth head of his "Praise" of the city, "here is a mighty port to which are brought all the goods of the East and West. ... It is astonishing to see the crowds of merchant ships that come and go."[13] This is what Venice meant to him now, and he could guess what rare and costly cargoes lay in the holds of the ships that he watched from the Campanile, or from the long Riva below the Palazzo Ducale – as well as the sacks of spices, "gold ... garments of purple, and perfumes, precious stones and ivory ... balsam and outlandish birds, woods unknown in our forests, gums and other resins, and roots not native to all soils, from which for sick men and sound are extracted things medicinal and delicious."[14]

If a stroll along the quays of Venice showed the volume of her maritime trade, the heart of the commercial city was in the Rialto. The wealth of Venice, said von Harff, lay in that small square, and the roads which radiated from it;[15] to this place, said Felix, "are brought all the goods of East and West; hence flow out the goods of the East into the West, and of the West into the East.[16] Business began here at the decent hour of ten o'clock, and was conducted with the utmost decorum, voices being kept so low that from the throng of merchants there rose no more than a gentle humming sound.[17] So varied and so great a volume of trade, and a mercantile system of such long standing had not failed to develop a mature commercial technique.* In the streets which led off the

---

* Marine insurance could be arranged. A document (Museo del Mare, Trieste, Case 9, no. 4) gives the conditions as agreed between the owner of a ship and other merchants in 1395. The ship was insured, at 3 per cent. premium, against "the sea, people, fire, and every chance accident. ..."

Rialto stood the Banks, which already fulfilled a triple rôle–changing foreign money, offering a safe place for the deposit of cash, and arranging credit for customers. For much of the business transacted at Venice bank credit was used, and bills of exchange could be obtained by travellers. Felix Fabri, travelling in his hand-to-mouth way, and depending upon the piety and generosity of his companions, naturally has nothing to say of such conveniences, but von Harff made use of them and found it easy, being sponsored by his friends among the German merchants, to obtain, from a Venetian, bills upon correspondents in Alexandria, Damietta, Damascus, Beirut, Antioch, Constantinople, "and other towns."[18] Venetian probity in business was known to be absolute; "if any man is minded to break faith in money matters they would rather pay his bills of exchange for him than suffer him to default."[19] The only difficulties which von Harff encountered when he tried to cash his bills abroad were linguistic, and as such not insuperable. "When I came to a heathen town, and presented these bills to the person to whom they were made out, although I could not speak with him I nodded my head at him and kissed my fingers to show my respect, and gave him the bills. Whereupon he would stare at me and disappear into the back of his house, returning at once and paying me my money, indicating with his fingers that I should write down how much I had received."[20]

To the merchants of Germany Venice did not only offer a school of commerce to which they sent their sons, "to learn our language and accounting" as a Venetian document puts it;[21] now that she had practically monopolised the spice trade of Egypt, she had become as important in the German mercantile economy as was Alexandria in her own. With the growing wealth of the great German cities, the demand for spices, among other luxuries, had increased; it is significant that at Ulm the "first and largest guild" was now no longer that of the wool merchants, but the guild which included "all who sell, in shops or booths, aromatic spices, drugs, powders. . . ."[22]

And if trade with Venice was of prime importance to Germany, that trade was extremely lucrative to the Republic. To what extent was variously computed; according to one, the total profit amounted annually to a million ducats;[23] a German merchant calculated that the inhabitants of the *fondaco* bought goods in Venice at the rate of 100 ducats a day, exclusive of customs duties.[24] Friar Felix believed that these duties themselves accounted for twenty thousand ducats a year; he adds that there were as well goods which paid no duty: small but precious objects, that passed the customs hidden among other merchandise, or consignments of stuff which were got out of Venice secretly by night.[25]

It is not surprising that in view of the great volume of German trade, the far-sighted Venetian senate, following perhaps the example of the Mamluk Sultan,[26] provided a *fondaco* for German merchants similar to those whose comforts and conveniences they themselves enjoyed at Alexandria, and like him, found their *fondaco*, the Fondaco dei Tedeschi, at once a source of profit and a means of controlling the foreign traders.

Two pilgrims, whose narratives we have used, knew the *fondaco* from the inside, each having stayed there as the guest of friendly merchants. But, regrettably, von Harff says nothing, and Felix Fabri next to nothing, of the life of the community. Only if we take the Friar's scanty references to the *fondaco*, and supplement and illuminate them by reference to the abundant supply of Venetian official documents, can we form a picture of the arrangements made for the convenience of the visiting merchants, and the regulations which governed their every transaction while in Venice.

The *fondaco* which Felix Fabri knew, but which was burnt down at the beginning of the next century, stood, as its successor still stands, at the angle formed by the Grand Canal and the Rio del Fontego, a few yards only from the wooden bridge which led to the Rialto. As the Friar says, and as we may see for ourselves in the first state of Jacopo Barbari's map, it was "double, with a pair of courtyards,"[27] and in fact followed, both in its general plan and the accommodation it provided, its prototypes at Alexandria, with rooms for the merchants above, and storehouses below.[28] Thus when Felix accepted the invitation of Eitel Rentz, his host "led me to his chamber ... (and) gave me the key of his strong-room so that I could put my baggage there, and sleep there ... ,"[29] by which we must suppose that the Friar dossed down once more among bales of stuff from the far East, and, as well, among the delicate manufactures of Venice.

There were fifty-six bed-chambers at the *fondaco*,[30] some of which seem to have been held in common by merchants of a town or guild,[31] the rest being let to individuals or at least to families. The annual fee for every merchant—the Club subscription as it were—was 4 ducats a year;[32] in addition there was a charge of 12 *piccoli* per night during residence. These sums were for the ordinary temporary occupation of a room, but certain merchants succeeded in establishing a right to retain "rooms of their own"* in which they left their account books and clothes whether in residence or not. A Nuremberg family claimed to have occupied the chamber known as "Paradise" for eighty years at least, and, not un-

---

* "*Chamere proprie*" (Capitolar. Cap. 277, p. 167)

naturally, were loth to be put into one less attractive. One merchant spent money upon installing a stove "for comfort and health especially in winter;" another–he was a Fugger-repaired and embellished his chamber; the Senate, when approached, might well decide that such an outlay gave a right to continued tenancy.[33]

What the wealthy obtained by such means, other merchants tried to compass by a less costly method. Pained reproaches were from time to time directed by the Venetian Senate at the inhabitants of the *fondaco*, on account of their habit of taking away with them at their departure, or handing over to a fellow merchant, the keys of chamber and strong-room. As a result, at one time only eighteen rooms were available for the accommodation of new-comers,[34] and the passages of the *fondaco* were crowded with the merchandise of those for whom there was no store-room available. The keys must, the Senate enjoined, be handed over to their officer, the seneschal; if he cannot be found they must be put through the hole in his door.[35]

Eitel Rentz, as well as giving Friar Felix his key, invited him to make use of the common refectory of the *fondaco*.[36] Here the merchants sat at their various tables; the Suabians, and therefore Friar Felix with his hosts the Ulm merchants, ate at the table which ranked as the first.[37]* The Senate supplied kitchen equipment, but the merchants catered for themselves,[38] and a Bohemian visitor found that they did themselves well.[39] But though the Senate wisely left the Ultramontanes to order their huge meals of highly spiced meat, it did provide for their use, and for the use of those with whom they did business, a tavern in the *fondaco* at which wine was sold at a low rate; as well as the merchants certain of the employees – the seneschal himself, the cook and his assistant, those who baled the goods, the messenger boys and the porters[40] – were permitted to take advantage of this convenience. But the tavern was all too popular; unauthorised and undesirable persons found their way in; it was probably on occasion a rowdy place, for it was thought advisable by the Senate to vest the chief officer of the *fondaco* with the right if necessary to resort to arms to restore order there.[41]

Such were the domestic arrangements of the *fondaco*, in which the

* In the *fondaco* there were then two kitchen fires and two cooks, one of whom cooked for the merchants of the Free Cities, the other for those who were subjects of the Princes (*Archivio Veneto*, t. XXXV, Venezia, 1888, p. 229). Geographically the division lay between Low Germany and High. The merchants of Cologne claimed not only precedence in the first of these, but also the right to eat in their own rooms, but the Signory discouraged the habit as sternly as our own Tudor sovereigns a similar tendency among the courtiers (*v.* Simonsfeld, I, 357, pp. 189–190).

VENICE OF THE MERCHANTS 265

Venetian Senate gave the German merchant considerable advantages and adequate freedom, while still maintaining a certain supervision over the conduct of its guests: the Germans were almost as strictly gated as the inhabitants of the Alexandrian *fondachi*; after the "third bell" had been rung at night and the door shut, no merchant, except a new arrival, might enter the *fondaco*.[42] In their commercial transactions the merchants were subjected to a rigorous supervision of every phase of their business, more pervasive and efficient than any exercised by the Sultan's officers in Egypt. The organising genius of the Venetians laid its hand upon the newly arrived German merchant as he hired a boat to cross the lagoon, for the boatmen were under oath to deliver him and his merchandise nowhere but at the *fondaco*.[43] Arrived there the merchant was received by the house-master (*fondicarius*), who, having showed him to his room, and received from him any weapons he carried, brought him to one of the three wardens (*vicedomini*), each of them a nobleman of Venice, to whom he must display the contents of his boxes and bales—[44] crude metal from Austria, furs from north Germany or Russia, leather goods, linen or hornwork,[45] or if, like Felix's friends, he came from Ulm, grey woollen cloth, or perhaps those two articles of commerce so strangely juxtaposed in the Friar's account of the manufactures of that city: sacrificial bread for the Mass, and playing cards;[46] on all or any of these he must pay customs duty, and declare upon oath that he carried with him nothing else of value. Moreover, during the whole of his stay in Venice, every transaction in which he disposed of his merchandise must take place in the *fondaco*, and in the presence of one of the chief officers, the seneschal (*meseta*).[47]

But the German merchant came not only to sell, but to buy. And while he bought, as while he sold, every bargain was subject to the supervision of the seneschal of the *fondaco*.[48] Spices were the chief German export, but the merchant would also make a selection from among other products of the far East or the Levant: the exquisite muslins of India, sugar from Egypt, wines of Crete and Corfu; or from among the hardly less coveted manufactures of Venice; silks, velvets, brocades or the glass of Murano.

A few days before Friar Felix left Venice he accompanied some of his merchant friends in an expedition up the lagoon in order to lay in a store of that glass which was so wonderful to the eyes of Ultramontanes,[49] vessels of rich blue, green or purple; or imitating the colours and veining of onyx, agate or chalcedony; or sometimes made to order with the armorial bearings of a noble German family.[50] Here again, though Felix does not mention his presence, the seneschal of the *fondaco* must have made one of the party which visited the furnaces and show-rooms of the glass-workers.

Felix spent the remainder of the day helping his friends to wrap up the fragile merchandise. This was only a preliminary packing; on the eve of their departure, after all customs dues on the exports had been paid, the final baling, boxing and roping was accomplished by the official "binders" (*ligadori*) of the *fondaco*, Germans all of them, but resident in Venice and members of a guild recognised by the Signory. After this the packages were sealed by other appropriate officials, and when the merchants left, would be carried to the boats by the appointed porters of the *fondaco*.[51]

Along with the merchants' purchases, Friar Felix's own luggage was packed–"the basket with palm-leaves, which I bought in Alexandria, and the basket with the stones collected from the Holy Places, and the bed which I bought at Jerusalem, and used across the desert and at sea, and everything else which I did not want to take with me on horseback."[52]

After this the Friar was for once at a loose end; with no heart for sight-seeing, "even though the city of Venice is lovely and wonderful," he fidgeted and fretted to be off during a day which "seemed longer than any other, just because we were due to set off next morning."[63]

Before it was light on January 17 Johann Müller, merchant of Ulm, came to knock him up. Together they, and some merchants of Augsburg who were to be of the party, having breakfasted, said goodbye to comrades in the *fondaco*, and to those friends who came to see them off, among whom may well have been some of Felix's companions of the Sinai pilgrimage still remaining in Venice. Then they went on board their boat, "and so, in the name of God passing through the canal, we left Venice behind us."[54]

As usual the party landed at Marghera, and when Friar Felix stepped out of the boat he realised that here was one of the turning points of his pilgrimage; here he was leaving the sea behind him, and his pilgrimage had taught him the part which the sea played in the life of mankind. It was the sea which brought together men of all nations, to exchange not only the riches of the earth but the knowledge of lands and peoples. Marvellous in his eyes was his own share in that communication. "Who, I ask you," he cries, "would ever have dreamed that F.F.F. would be the friend of heathens, and hob-nob with renegades; that he would perforce flatter the Turk, trust and collaborate with Saracens, agree with Tartars, be civil to Arabs and Egyptians, show respect to Mahomet, and walk humbly with the barbarian?" Who indeed! But, "the sea brings all together."

Looking back across the lagoon, while he thanked God for deliverance from the perils of the deep, he blessed the sea. And now, "I wished," says he, "that the sea had reached to the walls of Ulm city, because now that I was accustomed to sea-travel I loathed travel by land, and I was more frightened of riding a horse than of putting off in a ship."[55]

CHAPTER XIX

The way home

Rarely does any pilgrim writer continue the narrative of his return journey beyond a notice of his arrival in Venice; if he does, his account will almost invariably be limited to a bald recital of the distance between townships and castles along his homeward route. Here, as in so much else, Felix Fabri is in a class apart; from Venice to the foot of the Alps, across the great mountain barrier, down to the lowlands of the Danube, the gates of Ulm, the Dominican House itself, he continues his travel diary with unabated zest. His interest, and ours, is primarily that it was the record of his own keenly felt personal experience; but while we read of the laborious days of travel in snow, frost and thaw, we may remember that this is an account of a journey which was the common experience of many a merchant who made that winter passage of the Alps as he went upon his ordinary lawful and commercial occasions.

From Marghera the first day's journey through the rich plain brought them to Treviso; here the merchants provided Felix with a horse which would not fail him on the difficult roads ahead.[1]* Next day was Sunday, but after early Mass they set their faces towards the mountains, now rising before them; the country was beautiful and still fertile, but the flooded Piave held them up for an hour at one place, till a country lad heard their shouts and ferried them over the river in a horse-barge. They slept at Conegliano,†

---

* Treviso, still possessed of an important horse-fair, was the place where pilgrims usually bought or sold horses, before or after the crossing of the Alps (cf. *Evag.*, I, 81).

† "*Cunianum vulgariter, Hadober,*" cf. *Evag.*, III, p. 444. "Caniano." The route followed by Fabri is pretty clear: from Treviso, by Conegliano, Seravalle, and the valley of the Piave as far as the junction of that river with the Boite; thence up the Boite to Podestagno (Peutelstein), and so by the Hohlensteinthal to Dobbiaco (Toblach), Brunico (Brunech), Vipiteno (Sterzing) and the Brenner Pass. But the stages which he gives appear to be very uneven in length. From Treviso to Conegliano and from Conegliano to Ponte nel'Alpi (supposing that this is Felix's Plassprugg) give two approximately equal stages of about 31 kilometres each. But from here to Brunico (Brunech) the distance is 136 kilometres which would make his next two stages most improbably long. It is not difficult to account for inaccuracies in this part of his narrative. He would be unlikely to keep his diary with great care over this familiar part of the route, and, when, perhaps some years later, he came to write up the last stages of his pilgrimage it would be easy to confuse this with his other trans-Alpine journeys.

set among steep hills and olive groves, near to, though not yet among the mountains.

From Conegliano, after a breakfast eaten by candle-light, they rode all the short winter day upon the ice-covered roads, passing through Seravalle and now going always upwards, and always among steeper and more monstrous slopes, yet still among villages and habitations of men. Far down below, as they climbed through frozen snow, they saw a series of small lakes, one of which still retains the name by which Felix knew it: Lago Morte, the Lake of Death. At one point, scrambling among boulders and shattered and uprooted trees they had to cross the track of a landslip; but for the iron frost of the night before the deep snow would have made the way impassible.[2]

At one point they had to pass a Venetian toll house set strategically at that point where the road crossed a deep ravine; just beyond was a narrow passage between rocks through which "riders and laden waggons pass with all the merchandise from Venice;" the span of this opening determined the measure to which the official packers at the *fondaco* adjusted the merchants' bundles.[3]

Even if such a limitation of size was chiefly designed for the benefit of the Customs, it was further justified by the experience of next day, when, soon after starting, the whole party came to a halt at the crest of a hill from which the ice-covered road dropped steeply. A crowd of waggons was drawn up here, while the drivers roughed the shoes of the beasts; Felix's party did the same with theirs, and, even so, had to dismount and lead their horses by the bridle with anxious care. When evening drew on they were still among the prodigious shoulders of the hills, which rose, steep almost as walls, and breaking out here and there above into blocks or spires of bare rock; far below the Piave roared among its boulders; then they crossed it by a bridge and came to a village and to an inn, perhaps Capo di Ponte, now Ponte nel'Alpi.*

They had found shelter for the night, but that was all. "We could," says Felix, "get neither food nor drink, nor furnishing for the table nor proper fodder for the horses, because that very day the inn-keeper had gamed away everything movable in the house except his wife and children. The wife sat weeping and carrying on as one desperate for sorrow and dismay, and all the household was plunged into tribulation and hardly dared to be seen by the guests."[4]

Next morning rising early from the benches upon which they had spent a cheerless night, Felix and his companions, having waited a while for the tardy dawn, pushed on as soon as it was light, leaving behind them

* *"Pons Plabis. nostris Plassvruoo."*

that unhappy house, and the little world of disaster into which they had obtained the travellers' fleeting glimpse.

After a fasting ride, and a good breakfast at Ospitale,* they reached a point where they turned eastward from the Piave valley into the Cadore† district. On their way they had more than once to turn off the road so that waggons and heavily laden horses bringing Italian wines to Germany might pass by; as one step aside might send their own horses floundering among snow-drifts, Felix came to dread the sight of these overtaking wine-carts.‡ It was evening when they reached (perhaps) Campo,§ near Cortina d'Ampezzo, but even after the toils of the day Felix was not too tired to pay a visit to the church, where he was entranced by the spectacle of three uncorrupted corpses. He paid them more than one visit, and took pains to collect local gossip and tradition upon the subject.[5]

Another breakfast eaten before dawn followed by a painful ride at a foot's pace, and with frequent falls into deep, freshly fallen snow, and they reached and passed through the frontier fortress of Podestagno or Peutelstein‖ among the tremendous rock faces of the high Dolomites. As they came out of the further gate of the mountain fortress the Venetian guard on the wall gave the war-cry of the Republic—"Marco! Marco!" to which one of the younger members of the party replied with a jeering word—an indiscretion which caused his companions alarm, but fortunately brought no reprisals from the soldiers.

And now the small party of Germans knew that they had left behind them the territory of Venice, and the land of Italy, a land of strangers and of a strange language. At the end of a gruelling climb with the waters of a temporary thaw rushing down the road towards them, they came to a lonely inn, known as *"zum Holenstein,"* on account, so Felix believed, of a rock cavern near by, but probably so called after the Hohlensteinthal itself. Here they turned in for refreshment, and found, to the joyful wonder of Friar Felix, that every soul in the house spoke German, and, moreover, though so near to the frontier, were innocent of any knowledge

---

* " . . . *Qui hospitiolum dicitur.* . . ." † *"Cadubrium."*

‡ It is obvious that the merchants rode upon horseback, but not clear whether their merchandise was carried upon waggons or pack-horses. From Felix's references to "the other carts" bringing wine from Italy (*Evag.* III, p. 447, cf. *ibid.*, 446) the former would seem probable (cf. also *Evag.* III, p. 455 and p. 272 below). Felix says that these carts came *"obviam,"* but cannot mean that they met the northward travelling party.

§ *"Pratinum, vulgariter Haiden, id est ad Prata."* The name, and Fabri's description (*Evag.*, III, p. 447) of the place where they stopped—"a delightful place among the mountains, where there are many fields and pastures for cattle, and in the midst a big village . . ." seems to suggest some place near Cortina, if not that town itself.

‖ *"Butelstein," "Putasten."*

of Italian. "With delight," says he, "I talked to the children, for I was so glad to speak German," and he breaks forth in a song of praise upon the subject of that language, "in my opinion the noblest, most famous, most rational," which is unappreciated by other races by reason of its very virtues, "because our language is the most terse among languages, so that with a few words and syllables much is expressed, and those pregnant and brief words are difficult for the unaccustomed to . . . pronounce. . . . Enough," he concludes, "of these matters. Let them have their languages and leave us ours. . . ."[6]

The German-speaking inn stood at a water-shed,* and having passed it they had passed the highest point of their Alpine journey, but not the worst part of it, for following the valley down, "we came to a very bad place, where we sank to the belly of the horses in the snow, and if anyone dismounted he soon was stuck, waistdeep. For the snow was slightly frozen on top, so that now one of the horse's feet sank in, now the front legs, now the hinder, and the beasts were so tried that we could only expect that they would go lame. . . ." Even when they reached Dobbiaco (Toblach)† and a well-trodden road, conditions were hardly better; a bitter wind blew in their faces, half blinding them with the snow which it whipped up from the ground. That struggle with the elements daunted even Friar Felix. "Oh wretched F.F.F.!" he cried to himself, and remembered Brennus who had perished in the snows of the Alps, overwhelmed by the "white virgins" in the prophecy of "the Delphic Apollo."[7]

Yet they struggled on, and came, just before sundown, to a good inn and "the very pleasant pretty town" which Brunico (Brunech)‡ is to this day, and a very creditable essay in urban development by Bishop Bruno of Brixen, who had, in modern fashion, converted a village into a new, planned town. Here the Friar once more rejoiced to hear no word of Italian spoken, "but all things, manners and speech, are German."[8]

Beyond Brunico too the worst of their trials were over and as they followed the descending and widening valley the air seemed to have in it a touch of spring. After leaving Vipiteno (Sterzing), a busy town of bronze workers, whose great hammers were driven by the water power of the mountain streams, the party divided. The Augsburg merchants went their way; Johann Müller and Friar Felix set their faces to the long southern ascent of the Brenner. Here even the new road of the great road builder, the Archduke Sigismund, completed within the past year, was hardly passable for the melted snow which ran down it, while the old

---

* This would place it at or near the site of the modern Albergo Cimabanche.
† "*Tobel.*" Felix wrongly places Villabassa (Niederdorf) on the way to Dobbiaco. He must have passed it on the following day.   ‡ "*Brunegg.*"

road was no better than a rushing noisy torrent. As on his other newly improved route, between Brixen and Bolsano, the Archduke had here set up a Customs post, to compensate himself for his outlay in the public interest; at Lueg* beyond the watershed of the pass, stood a weighing machine so large and with chains so strong that the merchants' waggons were weighed together with their loads. Here Johann Müller had to pay a stiff duty on all his Italian imports.[9]

Down plunged the road now, between the huge flanks of snow-covered mountains. The reduced party spent the night at Mattrey, and at noon next day came upon that sudden and surprising view of the whole of Innsbruck, as the city is disclosed below in its wide valley, ramparted by dark mountains on the North, and divided by the pale and rapid waters of the Inn.

That day Innsbruck was crammed with a huge concourse of nobles and their servants who had come to the wedding of Duke Sigismund himself, so that in the city which Felix proudly describes as "of no great size but mighty in worth and nobility" the Friar and his company "could hardly find room to breathe." Perhaps because of this, the travellers made no stay but pushed on at once.

As a result they made a lucky encounter. The bridge across the Inn was packed close to the point of danger with the men and horses of one of the noble wedding guests, and among these they saw and hailed a man of Ulm, who told them of three horsemen on the road ahead, who, like themselves, were making for that city.[10] It was well to travel in company, and Johann Müller and Felix hurried on, to find at Zirl, a few miles up the river, no strangers, but friends and even a kinsman. For of the three horsemen one was the parish priest of Reutlingen, another Conrad Kraft, citizen and Mayor of Ulm, "related to me," says Felix, "and a very good friend;" and their servant was also a man of Ulm, by name Hans Schichenberger. So it was well met, and a cheerful company which rode on and up, and halted for the night at Schnechenhausen. Nor was that the last of their good fortune. " . . . When it was already dark, by chance there came . . . lord Wilhelm von Rappelstein . . . brother of lord Maximilian von Rappelstein," that knight of the second pilgrim company who had bought the young crocodile at Fua, and whom Felix had left behind in Venice. Lord Wilhelm naturally wished to hear news of his brother; and it is not surprising to hear that, "we hardly slept that night what with talking and what with the noise, for there are many strange folk in the house, and so, little quiet."[11]

From Schnechenhausen, by Nassereit to the Fern Pass, their way led

* "*Im Lug.*"

7. VENICE, 1500

A view of the old wooden Rialto bridge at Venice and of mediaeval Fondaco dei Tedeschi shortly before its destruction by fire. The Fondaco is the building in front of that marked 'Fontico dalaman'

next day once more among towering mountain slopes, and past little mountain lakes, peacock blue and green in summer, but now dulled over with ice, and on an island in the midst of one of these the gay toy castle built by Duke Sigismund for relaxation and pleasure, rather than for war. At last, through widening valleys, by Lermoos and Reutte, Vils and Nesselwang, they came to Kempten "where there was an end of the mountains," although for a while yet, if the traveller looks back, the awful presences may still be seen, a wall of peaks against the southern horizon.

But at Memmingen they were indeed in the lowlands, and also among friends; for here they stayed at no travellers' inn, but in the house of Johann Müller's sister and her husband. Besides, Memmingen turned out to be as crowded as Innsbruck, though for a tourney instead of a wedding; and among all the knights and nobles were many from Ulm, who as soon as they heard of Friar Felix's arrival, came to visit him. It is likely that he would have been pleased to go about visiting on his own account, for he knew, and was known to the whole population as a preacher, but two considerations kept him within doors. He was unwilling to appear to take a light-minded interest in all the shows, the music and the drinking that was going on throughout the town; and he was also a little shy of being seen with his face muffled in the superb beard, which was the badge of his pilgrim status, and at once an embarrassment and a source of pride.

One visit however he did pay, even though it kept him in Memmingen for another twenty-four hours; for there arrived for the tourney one of those in whose company Friar Felix had gone out to Jerusalem last spring, and whose generosity had made it possible for him to undertake the further Sinai journey. This was the knight, Johann Truchsess von Waldburg. Felix hurried off to meet him, to reassure himself that this man of delicate constitution had not suffered in health from the sea voyage home,[12] and to spend the whole day in his company. It must have been a great affection which could hold back Friar Felix, so near now to Ulm.

The last day of Felix Fabri's long journey now arrived. On the morning of January 29 "Johann Müller and I, having eaten and mounted our horses, left Memmingen, and hurried on." For now Felix was on fire to be home. It was perhaps this fever of impatience which made him so vulnerable to the discomforts of a heavy fall of rain which caught the travellers at Illertissen, "so that we were soaked almost to our skin . . . never in the whole of my pilgrimage was I so upset as I was by that downpour, for a man who is wet becomes woeful, cowardly, shrunken with cold and all to pieces; not to mention the irritation which he feels, and the anxiety for the things he has with him which will not stand rain, such as books and things of that kind."

But the rain passed over; they rode on, and towards evening "came within sight of the sweet city of Ulm."[13]

If we look, in the narratives of other pilgrims, for an account to match that which Felix Fabri gives us of his return to the Convent at Ulm, we shall not find it. One tells us the date of his home-coming; "on St. Martin's Eve ... 1399,"[14] and another adds to a similar statement of fact a remark curiously suggestive: " ... we got back to Anglure at dinner-time. ..."[15] Canon Casola gives us a little more; he slipped into Milan "in pilgrim dress and alone, though many of my friends had come to meet me at an earlier hour."[16] Another Milanese, the young man Sancto Brasca, who had been in the pilgrim company in 1480 when Felix first went to the Holy Land, does make quite a story of his arrival. When he reached Cassano he found himself involved in quarantine regulations and was refused admittance to the town. But his arrival had become known; out came two gentlemen of Milan, at Cassano on some business of the vintage; careless of quarantine they embraced him with brotherly affection, and having ordered out of the city "enough food and drink for twenty men" sat down with him to a picnic on the banks of the Adda, "with the greatest good cheer." Two days later he was allowed to enter Milan, "accompanied by his friends, in good health as in good heart."[17]

Very different from this sprightly narrative of a gay though devout young man, and the only one which in intensity of feeling comes near to Felix Fabri's story, is that in which the notary, Martoni, records his home-coming to the small town of Carinola in Southern Italy. Small, shortsighted, timid and unable to swim, during gales at sea Martoni would hide himself somewhere in the ship where he could cry unobserved.[18] Yet he had a kind of abject courage which, joined with dogged determination drove him on. Through it all, as in the ascent of St. Katherine's Mount,* faith and his resolution carried him through, and brought him back to Carinola one day late in May. As he approached the little town he found to his surprise that his friends and fellow-townsmen were crowding out along the road to meet him. "Most joyfully" he went along with them, his heart set upon reaching home, and Constance, the devout and charitable woman, his "comfort," his "dearest wife." But when he came to his house she was not there. Six weeks before that

* See above, p. 86.

day which should have been so happy, she had died, of grief, so they told him, at his long absence.[19]

There was nothing sad about the return of Friar Felix, but in his narrative, as in that of Martoni, we can feel the authentic stir of emotion beneath the words. He tells us how his first sight of the city came with a shock not only of joy but of surprise. The walls and towers of Ulm had been renewed along this the river side of the city during his absence, and now seemed to glow before his eyes, so greatly and grandly built that "I would hardly have recognised the look of the city . . . if the surroundings, which could not be changed, had not proved that it was the old Ulm."[20]

He and Johann Müller crossed the bridge over the Danube; the Dominican House, a ruin now, stood at the south-eastern corner of the city; here the merchant left him. The Convent gate was shut, and the sound of the brethren's voices chanting their vespers came from the church; when Friar Felix began to beat upon the doors they did not at once hear him. " . . . But I had hardly knocked for the first time when the Convent dog was there, who knew me through the gate, and not with angry barking, but with a strange joyful howling and whining scratched and bit at the planks as though he would tear the gate down, in such a hurry he was to get out to me. . . . And when the gate was opened, before I could cross the threshold, the dog jumped up almost to my chest, rejoicing with extraordinary leaping and whimpering, and much tail-wagging; then off he rushed through the Convent, making a squeaking through his nose as if he were announcing the coming of his friend." That was, says Felix, "the best welcome so far, from the best beast."

But now Prior Ludwig Fuchs, who had left from Vespers at the news, "forgetting his age and dignity," came running, "as if to put out a fire." Soon the sub-prior and the rest of the Brethren, having somehow got through their Evensong, were crowding round him. Together they repaired to the church, and there before the high altar and the tabernacle of the Host, as all knelt, Felix received from the Prior "the blessing of a brother returned from a journey."[21] After that glad, solemn and moving ceremony the Convent, as one man, made for the guest parlour, where, says Felix, "we began to talk more freely."

The sympathy and wisdom of Prior Fuchs extended this indulgence over the whole of the following week, during which the Convent was allowed to keep holiday in honour of their returned pilgrim. The house was thronged with visitors; the magistrates and officers of the city were the first; next, Felix's Benedictine friends came in from Elchingen,

Wiblingen and Blaubüren. Then the lay companions of his pilgrimage to Jerusalem arrived—Johann Werner von Cymbern, Heinrich von Stoffel and young Bär von Rechberg—each with his train of servants. Amongst all these moved Felix Fabri in his pilgrim gown, which, fresh from the Convent's wash tub, still bore the red pilgrim crosses.

But at last the holiday period came to an end, and the Friar must revert to the habit proper to a Dominican. Yet, obstinately, he continued to wear the pilgrim cross, though unseen beneath his clothing, and, for how long we do not know, preserved in his cell "as a relic of my holy pilgrimage," the cotton mattress made in Jerusalem and used by him in the desert and at sea.

Another concession he was obliged to make, and with even more regret, to Dominican propriety. Black Friars were clean shaven, and therefore, "when the days of recreation were over, I had my beard shaved off, which hitherto I had worn, and for eleven months had encouraged to grow in length and breadth. Unwillingly, I must say, I had it off, because it seemed to me that in it I looked bolder, more considerable, more robust, comely and reverend, and if I might rightly have kept it, I would rather not have parted from it, as it is a natural ornament embellishing a man's face, and makes him appear strong and formidable."[22]

CHAPTER XX

Valedictory

Felix Fabri had come back to the Dominican House where the Danube ran green just beyond the city walls, and the old Schützenthor, with its prison cells and torture chamber, overlooked the Friars' garden. Part and parcel of the city, responsible, like other citizen bodies, for the repair of its own length of that same wall,[1] the Convent was closely involved in the life of Ulm, and it is no wonder that Friar Felix, when he had finished the two large volumes of his *Evagatorium*, sharpened his pen once more to describe, in his "Treatise upon the City of Ulm,"* this Imperial Free City which had become his home.

It was a busy and a thriving place. Its merchants, as he had good cause to know, dealt in commodities of the furthest East; the work of its craftsmen was exported far beyond Europe to the cities of the Levant.[2] Its Saturday market was as busy as a yearly fair; Friar Felix characteristically notes that on some days there might be three hundred wine carts drawn up in the wine market, near the fishermen's houses – and yet every drop would be sold before noon.[3] The citizens' Rathaus was "large and fair, with a bell-tower all gilt... and a great bell that chimes the hours...." The Cathedral – though, Felix confesses, "I have seen many churches more beautiful in craftsmanship and material" – he found remarkable for the amount of light which floods every chapel, every corner within its walls. From its tower watchmen sounded their trumpets morning and evening, and there hung the great bell that was struck when that in the Rathaus had rung the hour.[4] The town had a water system which, having raised the water from the river Blau by wheels, distributed it to every quarter of the town; there were no less than twenty-three fountains;[5] one of these, the Fischkasten, remains as and where Felix knew it, to show how gay and fine the others may well have been.

Yet the city, with all its prosperity and crowded life, was a countrified place. As the Friar takes his readers upon a tour of the walls, upon the greater part of which it is still possible to follow him, he directs their attention at one point to where, in the meadows across the Danube, the

* *Tractatus de Civitate Ulmensi.*

citizens' flocks and herds are at pasture; the bridge by which they crossed is still named after them.⁶* There were fields too just outside the north-eastern part of the walls which in summer, so the saying went, were a prettier rose-garden than that of any other city of Germany, for here the ground was spread with the white flowers of the Ulm linen, bleaching in the sun.⁷ Not all the effects of this half-countrified economy were so pleasant as this; the streets, preserved from domestic pollution by an efficient system of drainage, were not so clean as they should have been, for the citizens would drive their swine through the town, and Felix complains that "there is nothing which so dirties the streets . . . as great herds of pigs."⁸

When, six years or so after his return,⁹ the Friar wrote the first words of his "Treatise on the City of Ulm," he claimed in them that this work was no other than the conclusion of his *Evagatorium*, since Ulm "is the place from which my wandering began, and at which it came to an end." That claim is just, and is so in a wider sense than, we may suppose, Felix himself realised. For not only in the *Treatise* does he show us the yardstick by which he had measured all the strange world of his pilgrimage, from the splendours of Venice to the most squalid and ruinous *banlieu* of Cairo, but in the *Evagatorium* he makes it clear that he had never for long forgotten Ulm or the Germany of which it was a part. Again and again in the course of his narrative he will make some comparison, shrewd or naïve, between unfamiliar and homely things. Moses, he says, lived in the wilderness with the sheep of Jethro, "just as those who herd oxen and cows on the alps stay with them."¹⁰ When he writes of the labyrinth of Crete he is reminded of those dark underground passages in the hillside above Blaubüren, through which, more than once, he had wriggled his way, accompanied by "the religious Fathers of the Order of St. Benedict."¹¹ The sweet and salt water which seeps up from pits in the desert recalls to him the waters which, at the Spa at Nassau, spring hot and cold, salt and fresh, from the same rock.¹² At Venice, having ridiculed the night fears of those strangers, who hearing the waves flop and work against the foundations of the house, cannot sleep for fear the whole fabric should collapse, he caps this with a curious anecdote concerning a country servant of his uncle who, the first time he was brought to a walled town and knew, at night, that the gates were shut upon him, suffered acutely from claustrophobia.¹³

But as well as these sudden and vivid juxtapositions of near things and far, the Friar will not infrequently reveal, though it may be only indirectly

* Pons gregis, the Herdbrücke.

8. VIEW AND PLAN OF ULM IN 1493

or casually, or in some brief aside, something of the tone and temper of society in the Germany of his day. His companions in the desert journey were for the most part men of the haughty, country- and castle-dwelling, exclusive German nobility, and though Felix got on well with all, and loved and even revered a few, yet in his narrative, in spite of his discretion, he allows us to see them as irresponsible, undisciplined and irascible.

It was indeed not with the feudal Germany, rising to its splendid apex in that House of Austria to which, the Friar proudly claims, "the kings and princes of the whole world pay homage . . ."[14] that he was most fully in sympathy. It was rather with the Germany of the great commercial cities, in which urbanised noble, merchant, artificer, monk, man-of-law and doctor of medicine formed a living and cohesive society. It was the industrious, inventive, studious Germany of the printing press and the quickening interest in new sciences; it was, too, the serious-minded and troubled Germany which was already fumbling its way towards a reformation of the Church.

This Germany Felix Fabri shows us, both in his *Evagatorium* and in his *Treatise*. When he writes of Ulm he reveals himself the same inveterate explorer of, and singer in caves that he was in his travels, knowing from experience precisely which cavern in the neighbourhood produced the most satisfying echo.[15] In the narrative of his pilgrimage he himself acts as a mirror or exemplar of the ideas and bent of the urban Germany of his day; medical science, horticulture, geography and the classics are the secular subjects which chiefly engage his attention, and it is just these subjects which his contemporaries of Ulm and Germany had much in mind.

There is plenty to show the Friar's interest in medicine, an interest which he shared with so many of his countrymen that in the twenty years between 1457 and 1477, the German printing presses turned out half a dozen popular treatises on the subject.[16] The Convent still-room in the Schützenthor was, we may guess, a place of frequent resort for Friar Felix; certainly it is the only part of the Dominican House whose position he fixes in his description of the city.[17] The same traveller who attended the operation of eviscerating and embalming the body of the Venetian Consul, remarks more than once in his narrative upon the manipulative surgery and massage of the East, as upon the medicinal waters and herbs of Germany. On his return voyage the Friar made friends with the Fleet Surgeon; at Ulm he was intimate with a whole company of "learned, noble and famous... doctors," with Johann Wirker, Heinrich Steinhöwel, Nicholas Stocker and his son Johann Stocker, Johann Minsinger, Johann

Jung, Johann Kyfer, and Ulrich Ulmer.* For their sakes, as the ship came within sight of Cos, the birthplace of Hippocrates, he looked narrowly at the island, "so that I could tell (them) about it."[18]

Felix's interest in botany is significantly appropriate for a man born in Zurich and brought up on Basel, though it was not until the next century that the former gave birth to Conrad Gesner and the latter produced, among an almost unrivalled output of magnificent printed books, the *Historia Stirpium* of Leonhard Fuchs. But already in Germany, Peter Schöffer of Mainz, who in 1486 was to print von Breydenbach's pilgrimage narrative,† published in 1485‡ the German *Herbarius*, or *Herbarius zu Teutsch*, with its lively plates, the production of "a painter of ready wit and cunning and subtle hand" who, like Rewich, had accompanied his rich patron upon the Jerusalem and Sinai pilgrimages, in order to portray to the life those plants which did not grow in Germany.[19]

The fifteenth-century interest in botany went hand in hand with an energetic practice of horticulture. Enterprising gardeners, attracted, as Felix was, by the incense scent, and the "lovely little flowers" of rosemary, were trying to grow this Mediterranean shrub in Germany. It proved not altogether hardy, "so in winter they put it away in cooking pots in a warm cellar."[20] Felix himself was in favour of a yet higher flight of experimental horticulture; he declared that efforts should be made by German gardeners to grow the *opobalsamum* of Matharea.[21] Apart, however, from such pioneering attempts, German townsfolk at this time had been bitten by a gardening craze not altogether unlike that of our own day. Nüremburg and Augsburg were famous for their flower gardens, and the country round a smaller town in Western Germany was said to be "like one field of almond trees."[22] The citizens of Ulm took to gardening among the rest; when Felix was wandering round the environs of Istrian Poreč, he noted a number of "little chapels," or perhaps "stone tombs ... but it is not a grave-yard," which reminded him of "the small buildings in each garden outside Ulm, where the rakes and shovels are kept."[23]

In 1482, the year which lay between Felix's first and second pilgrimages, the inland city of Ulm published one of the first printed editions of

* While highly approving of these male practitioners, the Friar rebukes "those ignorant women" the Béguines, who "take upon themselves to administer medicine" (*Evag.*, III, p. 268).

† Or perhaps only to lend the type for this purpose (v. Davies, *Breydenbach* . . . . pp. xxix–xxx; cf. E. Gordon Duff, *Early Printed Books*, London, 1903, p. 33).

‡ Arber (Herbals. p. 25) gives this date, Garrison (p. 185), 1484.

Claudius Ptolemy's *Geographia*, and the first of all in which the results of recent geographical discoveries appeared in the maps. It would have been strange if the Friar had not studied this handsome folio, with its hand-coloured wood-cut initial on the first page. But we may take it that he did in fact know it, and referred his readers to this "modern" book, as well as to the older examples, when he tells them, if they wish to know how long a voyage the Argonauts took, to look at "the first plate . . . and the eighth of Europe," the first being a map of the world, and the other of eastern Europe, with the territory of Colchis marked beyond the Black Sea.[24]

For Felix, and no doubt also for his home-keeping fellow-citizens, the Great Geographer remained the founder, almost the patron-saint of the study, and among the superb company of saints, patriarchs, sybils and philosophers, with which Jörg Syrlin peopled the choir of Ulm Cathedral, stands a representation of this Egyptian-born Greek himself, holding his astrolabe, in dress like any prosperous townsman of the day, in face so individualised that it is easy to believe that here is a portrait of one of the studious and cultivated citizens of Ulm.

The conversation of these laymen, whether noble or merchant, would be very different from that which Felix Fabri found so tedious when on pilgrimage with a company of country-bred young nobles. At Ulm, the family of Neithart, producing, in its various branches and through several generations, men of learning and ability, had endowed the city with what was perhaps the first public library in Germany, to be housed in the family chapel on the north side of the Cathedral choir.[25] Johann Neithart, a contemporary of the Friar, though "a layman . . . and without any university degree," read for his pleasure the works of Virgil, Seneca and Ovid, besides history, rhetoric and drama.[26]

This ancient and admired literature had of course always been fundamental to all medieval education, filtering through from clerks to laymen in greater or less degree of purity. Those "Baedekers" of the period, the "little books" which the knights took with them on pilgrimage, were full of topographical reminiscences of its tales.[27] Even the springs of popular poetry might rise in its territory. Felix alludes, with some scorn, to the song sung by German peasants, which told the story of the Suabian noble Danhuser "of Danhusen . . . near Dünchelspüchel" who lived in bliss with the Goddess Venus, within her secret mountain. Repentant, he sought absolution at the hands of the Pope, but in vain, and so returned to enjoy the delights of that unholy association until the Judgement Day. Nor, according to Felix, did the country-folk content themselves with minstrelsy, but would make a sort of infernal pilgrimage to the Tuscan hills, until Pope Nicholas V was obliged to refuse access to these valleys, and to emphasise his embargo by strategic posting of fierce ban-dogs.[28]

Though the Friar in relating all this registers disapproval of plebeian taste and behaviour, he yet takes pride in adorning his own work with flowers culled from the stories of the ancient gods. Even in his narrative of the desert journey he will find some pretext for scattering these about his pages; when he voyages among the Greek islands they naturally fall more freely from his pen, but it is in his account of Cyprus that they fill the foreground of his picture, so that the Apostle Paul yields place to the Cytherean, and it almost seems as if this devout, cheerful, Bible-reading celibate has become subject to the enchantment of the Queen of Love herself. Certainly the Friar could never forget that Cyprus was the birthplace of her who, in the jumble of grotesque tales which he reports, is now the daughter of Saturn, now a mortal, "dead and certainly damned," yet always the foam-born; though what was dark and ugly in the medieval monastic imagination added blood to the foam.[29] She might be half-devil, but she was still "a most beautiful virgin," and the Friar could no more ignore than he could approve that creature "of unequalled loveliness." While in the island he visited the places associated with her name as assiduously as if they were legitimate objects of pilgrimage. From Nicosia he went out all the way to Dali, the old Idalia, where he climbed the solitary hill which "the shameless Venus had made dedicate to herself." He visited both Old and New Paphos: he sat upon the Venus Rocks, the great cliffs which thrust themselves out into the glitter of the bright sea near Kouklia. "All these," he says, "I explored and inspected pretty thoroughly and carefully."[30]

Even in the cathedral of Nicosia he was able to discover a memorial of the wanton goddess which made such an impression as to cause him to ignore the existence, in the same church, of one of the water-pots from the Marriage at Cana.[31] In the Chapel of St. Dominic, in the second bay from the west on the south side of the church,[32] having first studied the frescoes of the Saint's life around the walls, and admired his golden altar, Felix turned his attention to a great tomb which stood in the centre of the chapel. He measured it by the outstretched span of his fingers, and found it to be 12 by 7 by 5, "cut all of one stone." There was a lid, with a "ridged back," as the lids of tombs often used to have," and the whole was of green jasper beautifully flecked and marbled with rose colour and red "as if it was sprinkled with little drops of blood." The bell was ringing for Vespers, and some of the canons were walking up and down in the cathedral waiting for its last note; the Friar approached them and asked for information upon the "incomparable tomb." The canons obligingly accompanied him to the chapel and standing there told him "a long and very pleasing story" of how Mars, who figured in it as the injured husband of Venus, in despite of the gryphons which guarded it, had procured this great block of jasper, a stone much conducive to the virtue of chastity, and had presented it to his wife for her bed. "And," the Friar concludes, "though I never read that story in any book, nor heard it elsewhere, yet I believe the words and put down what I was told ... and if the truth is not as I write, yet it is what I heard, and as I heard in innocence, so I have written in innocence, and in innocence it may be read, and without any damage to the faith may be believed by the devout."[33]

But for all the zest with which Friar Felix undertook these excursions into the dense undergrowth of medieval tales which had grown up around the fallen images of pagan worship, they were for him in the nature of a holiday and diversion only. Below this level the ground of his thought and emotion was that of the sober, religious Germany of his day, the Germany whose new presses had, by the end of the century, produced editions of the Vulgate by the score, as well as printing the first translation of the Bible into any European vulgar tongue.

It was in this atmosphere of religious concern and devotion that an attempt was being made in Germany to reform the houses of Religious. That Felix Fabri's sympathies were closely involved in this, we know not only from all he says upon the subject in the *Treatise*, but also from those frequent comments which he makes upon the state of the Religious Orders as he saw it in his travels. The reformed Benedictines of Padua, with their holy life, the sober Friars of the small Dominican Convent at Venice, receive his enthusiastic praise; equally we are left in no doubt as to his opinion of the secularised and worldly behaviour of the Black Friars of the greater Venetian House, or of those of Nicosia. It was the back-slidings of the representatives of the Latin Church in Cyprus which he most earnestly deplores. Set, as that Church was, among Greek and Syrian Christians, and visiting Moslem traders, it was in his eyes almost in *partibus infidelium*, and here, he declares, "sobriety is more necessary than, in Rome, sanctity...."[34]

At home he was close to the centre of the movement for monastic reform in Suabia. Ludwig Fuchs, his Prior and dear friend, having first peacefully reformed the Dominican House at Ulm, had gone on to take a foremost part in the reform both of men and women Religious in the neighbourhood.[35] Another of Felix's friends was equally ardent in the cause. Elizabeth Krelin, the Cistercian Prioress of Hegbach, whose death during Felix's first pilgrimage was so deep a sorrow to him,[36] had effected the reform of her own House with such astute and gentle diplomacy that the whole business went through without a hitch from the moment when she set out, one summer season, in her chariot, "as if to travel for pleasure and to take the waters," but in reality to investigate the ways of reformed nunneries, to the triumphant conclusion when even the elderly nuns of Hegbach voluntarily submitted themselves to the enclosed life enjoined by the Rule, already enthusiastically adopted by their younger sisters.[37]

But not always could the inhabitants of monastery or nunnery be persuaded into amendment. One reforming Abbot believed himself to be in such danger from his own monks that he wore a breastplate "concealed under his gown in choir, chapter and refectory."[38] If monks were suspected of murderous intentions, the nuns of more than one undisciplined house came out in open resistance to the agents of reform. Prior Fuchs, with nobles, ecclesiastics and guildsmen of Ulm, "armed and in their liveries . . . as if to do battle for the glory of God," set out to reform the Poor Clares of Soflingen, supported by Count Eberhart of Würtemberg, since they were aware that the matter was "difficult, hard and dangerous." They carried through the deposition of one Abbess and the installation of another, but to the accompaniment of "insults, clamour, wailing, roaring, crying, curses and blasphemies. . . ."[39] The disturbances at the Benedictine House of Urspring were still more violent. Here a reforming Abbess was faced by an opposition of high-born, unruly nuns. When no less a personage than a Dowager Archduchess of Austria arrived, with her knights, to support the Abbess, the rebels occupied the Convent infirmary; having locked the doors and barricaded them with "tables, benches, tree trunks, rocks . . ." and anything else they could find, they rushed to the upper windows of the building, and thence, having armed themselves with a variety of weapons, from sticks and stones to distaffs and spits, defied their besiegers.[40]

Such then was the Germany to which Friar Felix returned from his second pilgrimage. Strong currents, both secular and religious, were stirring in it, of which he was conscious, and in the exhilaration of whose new and hopeful energy he shared. But in that which was nearest his heart, the reform of the Monastic Orders, he looked back rather than forward. This, which had been the medieval panacea for the ills of every age, was still his greatest hope; he lacked altogether the clear vision which enabled Paul Scriptoris, the Franciscan Professor of Tübingen, to prophesy the imminence of a reformation in which the Church would turn its back upon the whole scholastic philosophy and return to a primitive simplicity of belief.

He was not, fortunately for himself, to live long enough to see that reformation shatter the unity of Western Christendom—to see, too, his beloved Ulm, exercising the option to which as a Free City it had the right, choose as its faith one which he, with his devout but conservative mind, must have judged heretical.

During the years which remained to him he may well have been as happy as industrious. He completed his great *Evagatorium*. He wrote his history of Suabia and the "Treatise on the City of Ulm." He visited Italy several times; he also made the pilgrimage to St. James of Compostella, and wrote an account of it,* which cannot, however, compare for interest with his other work.

Early in March, 1502, as he lay dying in the Dominican House which had by this time been his home for at least the past twenty-two years, it was to the great experience of his pilgrimage to the lands of the Bible that his thoughts turned. Obstinate sentimentalist that he was, he had kept by him all those years the pilgrim habit in which he had gone to Jerusalem. He asked, and was granted permission to wear it, and so, clothed in that garment of many memories, "fell asleep in the Lord."

The same hand which thus records the death of Friar Felix upon a page of his history of Suabia, adds also words which were probably meant and may be taken as his fitting epitaph. ". . . May his soul, after various disquietings, rest in peace eternal. Now he rejoices in Jerusalem which is above. . . ."[41]

---

* *V.* Konrad Häbler, *Das Wallfahrtsbuch des Hermannus Künig von Vach*, Strassburg, 1899, pp. 51-2; cf. Rohricht and Meisner, *Deutsche Pilgereisen nach dem heiligen Lande*, Berlin, 1880, p. 278. See Acknowledgments.

Bibliography

TEXTS

ANGLURE, OGIER, SEIGNEUR D'. *Le Saint Voyage de Jherusalem du* . . . Eds. Bonnardot et Lognon. Société des Anciens Textes Français. Paris, 1878.
BRASCA, SANTO. (Viaggio alla Sanctissima cita di Ierusalem.) Begin. "Ad Magnificum Dom. Antonium Landrianum . . . " Milan, 1481.
BREYDENBACH, BERNHARD VON. *Peregrinatio in Terram Sanctam.* Mainz, 1486.
CONTI, NICOLÒ DE. *The Travels of Nicolò Conti in the East . . . India in the Fifteenth Century* . . . Ed. R. H. Major. Hakluyt Society. 1857.
FABRI, FELIX. *Fratris Felicis Fabri Evagatorium in Terrae Sanctae Arabiae et Egypti Peregrinationem.* Ed. C. D. Hassler. Stuttgart, 1843-1849. 3 vols.
— *Fratris Felicis Fabri Tractatus de Civitate Ulmensi.* Ed. G. Veesenmeyer. Tubingen, 1889.
— *The Wanderings of Felix Fabri.* Trans. A. Stewart. Palestine Pilgrims' Text Society. Vols. VII-X. London, 1892-97.
Frescobaldi, Lionardo di Niccolò, *Viaggio di Lionardo di Niccolò Frescobaldi Fiorentino in Egitto ed in Terra santa.* . . . Ed. (G. Manzi). Rome, 1818.
GEMNICENSIS, GEORGIUS. Georgii Gemnicensis. *Ephemeris. Thesaurus Anecdotorum Novissimum.* B. Pezio. Pp. 455-639. Augsburg, 1721.
GUYLFORDE, RICHARD. *The Pylgrymage of Sir Richard Guylforde to the Holy Land.* Ed. H. Ellis. Camden Society. N.S. No. 51. London, 1851.
HARFF, ARNOLD VON. *The Pilgrimage of Arnold von Harff, Knight.* Trans. M. Letts. Hakluyt Society. 2nd Ser., No. XCIV. London, 1946.
IBN IYAS. *Histoire des Mamlouks Circassiens.* Vol. II. Trans. G. Wiet. Cairo, 1945.
Informaĉon for Pylgrymes into the Holy Londe. Ed. G. H. Freeling. Roxburgh Club. London, 1824.
JOINVILLE, JEAN DE. *Histoire de Saint Louis.* Ed. N. de Wailly. Paris, 1906.
KHITROVO, B. DE. Trans. *Itineraires russes en Orient C. 12-16.* Societé de l'Orient Latin I, i. Geneva, 1889.
LA BROCQUIÈRE, BERTRANDON DE. *Le Voyage d'outremer de La Broquière.* Ed. Ch. Schefer. Recueil des Voyages et de Documents pour Servir a l'Histoire de la Geographie. Vol. XII. Paris, 1892.
LANNOY, GUILLEBERT DE. *Oeuvres.* Ed. Potvin. Louvain, 1878.
LUDOLPHUS DE SUCHEN. *Ludolph von Suchem's Description of the Holy Land.* Trans. A. Stewart. Palestine Pilgrims' Text Society. Vol. XII. London, 1895.
MACHAUT, GUILLAUME DE. *La prise d'Alexandrie.* Ed. L. de Mas Latrie. Societé de l'Orient Latin. serie historique, t. 1. Geneva, 1877.
MAKRIZI. *Description historique et topographique de l'Egypte.* Trans. Paul Casanova. Mémoires publiées par . . . l'Institut Francais d'Archeologie Orientale du Cairo, t. IV. Cairo, 1920.
MARTONI, NICOLÒ DE. *Nicolai de Marthono Liber Peregrinationis ad Loca Sancta.* Ed. Leon le Grand. Revue de l'Orient Latin. III. 1895, pp. 566-669.

NEWETT, M. N. *Canon Pietro Casola's Pilgrimage to Jerusalem.* . . . Manchester University Press, 1907.
NOE BIANCHI v. *Viazo da venesia.* . . .
Pélerinage v. *Un Pélerinage.* . . .
PILOTI, E. *Traité d'Emmanuel Piloti, sur le Passage dans la Terre-Sainte.* Ed. de Reissenberg. Monuments pour servir a l'Histoire des Provinces de Namur, de Hainaut et de Luxembourg, Vol. IV. Brussels, 1846, pp. 312–419.
PIRI REIS, *Kitabi Bahriye* Türk Tarihi Arastirma Kurumu Yayinlarindan No. 2. Istanbul, 1935.
POCOCKE, R. *Description of the East.* . . . London, 1743–45. 2 vols.
PTOLEMAEUS, CLAUDIUS. *Geographia.* Ulm, 1482.
ROTZMITAL, LEO OF. *Travels.* . . . Trans. M. Letts. Hakluyt Society. 2nd ser. No. CVIII. London, 1957.
SANUTO, LIVIO. *Geographia distinta in XII libri.* . . . Venice, 1588.
SCHILTBERGER, JOHANN. *Bondage and Travels of Johann Schiltberger.* . . . Trans. J. B. Telfer. Hakluyt Society. 1st ser. 58. 1878.
SIGOLI, SIMONE. *Viaggio in Terra Santa ed al Monte Sinai.* Ed. B. Puoti. Naples, 1831.
SIMONSFELD, H. *Der Fondaco dei Tedeschi in Venedig.* Vol. I. Stuttgart, 1887.
SURIANO, FRANCESCO. *Treatise on the Holy Land.* Trans. T. Bellorini and E. Hoade. Jerusalem, 1949.
TAFUR, PERO. *Travels and Adventures, 1435–1439.* Trans. and ed. M. Letts. Broadway Travellers. London, 1908.
THENAUD, J. *Le Voyage d'Outremer de Jean Thenaud, siuvi de La Relation de l'Ambassade de Domenico Trevisan auprés du Soudan d'Egypte.* 1512. Ed. Ch. Schefer. Rec. de Voyages et de Documents pour servis a l'histoire de la Geographire. V. Paris, 1884.
THOMAS, G. M. *Capitolare dei Visdomini del Fontego dei Todeschi in Venezia. Capitular des deutschen Hauses in Venedig.* . . . Ed. G. M. Thomas. Berlin, 1874.
TORKINGTON, RICHARD. *Ye Oldest Diarie of Englisshe Travell.* Ed. W. J. Loftie. London, 1884.
TRÉVISANO, DOMENICO. v. Thenaud. J.
Un Pélerinage en Terre Sainte et au Sinai au XVe siècle, Bibliothéque de l'Eocle des Chartes. Vol. LXVI. Paris, 1905.
Viazo da Venesia al Sancto ikerusalez et al monte sinai. . . . (By Noe Bianchi.) Bologna, 1500.
WALTHER, PAUL. *Fratris Pauli Waltheri Guglingenis Itinerarium in Terram Sanctam et ed Sanctam Catharinam.* Ed. M. Sollweck. Stuttgart. 1892.
WRIGHT, T. *Early Travels in Palestine.* . . . London, 1848.
YOUSSOUF, KAMAL. *Monumenta Cartographica Africale et Egypti.* t. 4. fasc. 1. Cairo, 1926.

LATER WORKS

ALLEN, P. S. *The Age of Erasmus.* Oxford, 1914.
ARBER, AGNES. *Herbals, Their Origin and Evolution.* . . . Cambridge, 1912.
AYALON, D. *L'esclavage du mamelouk.* Oriental Notes and Studies, publ. by the Israel Oriental Society No. 1. Jerusalem, 1951.
— *Studies in the Structure of the Mamluk Army,* Bulletin of the London School of

BIBLIOGRAPHY

Oriental and African Studies, XV, 1953, p. 203; XV, 1953, p. 448; XIV, 1954, p. 57.
— *The Circassians in the Mamluk Kingdom.* Journal of the American Oriental Society, LXIX, 1949, pp. 135-147.
BAEDEKER, K. *Egypt.* Part First. Lower Egypt and the Peninsula of Sinai. London, 1895.
BENT, J. T. *The Cyclades.* London, 1885.
BRIGGS, M. S. *Muhammadan Architecture in Egypt and Palestine.* Oxford, 1924.
BURCHHARDT, J. *The Civilisation of the Renaissance.* Trans. S. G. C. Middlemore. London, 1898.
CASANOVA, P. *Histoire et description de la citadelle du Caire.* Mémoires publiés par les membres de la Mission Archéologique française du Caire. t. 6. 1897, pp. 509-781.
DAVIES, H. W. *Bernhard von Breydenbach and His Journey to the Holy Land, 1483-84. A Bibliography.* London, 1911.
DOBSON, A. M. R. *Mount Sinai. A modern pilgrimage.* London, 1925.
DRAKE, C. F. T. *Literary Remains.* Ed. W. Beraut. London, 1877.
Encyclopædia of Islam. Leyden, etc. 1954.
FREEMAN, E. *Sketches from the subject and neighbour lands of Venice.* London, 1881.
GARRISON, F. H. *An Introduction to the History of Medicine.* Philadelphia and London, 1917.
Geographical Handbook Series. Naval Intelligence Division. Greece v. III, 1944-5.
GUNNIS, R. *Historic Cyprus.* London, 1936.
HART, H. C. *Some Account of the Fauna and Flora of Sinai, Petra, and Wâdy Araba.* Palestine Exploration Fund. 1891.
HEYD, W. *Das Haus der deutschen Kaufleute in Venedig.* Historische Zeitschrift, 32, 1874, pp. 193-221.
— *Histoire du commerce du Levant au moyen-âge.* Edition française refondue et ... augmentée par l'auteur, publiée ... par F. Raynaud. Leipzig, 1923. 2 vols.
HILL, GEORGE. *A History of Cyprus.* Cambridge, 1940-1948. 3 vols.
HONEY, W. B. *Glass. A Handbook ... to the Museum Collection.* London, 1946.
HULL, EDWARD. *Mount Seir, Sinai and Western Palestine.* Palestine Exploration Fund. London, 1885.
JAL, A. *Glossaire nautique. Repertoire Polyglotte de termes de marine anciens et modernes.* Paris, 1848-50.
JANSSEN, J. *History of the German People at the Close of the Middle Ages.* Trans. M. A. Mitchell and A. M. Christie. London, 1896. 2 vols.
JARVIS, C. S. *Three Deserts.* London, 1936.
— *Sinai Past and Present.*
KAHLE, P. *Die Katastrophe des Mittelalterlichen Alexandria.* Mélanges Maspero. III. Orient Islamique. Mémoires publiés par ... l'Institut Français d'Archéologie Orientale du Caire, t. 68, pp. 138-154. Cairo, 1935.
— *Zur Geschichte des mittelalterlichen Alexandria.* Der Islam. Vol. XII, 1922, pp. 29-83.
LABORDE, L. E. S. J. DE. *Journey through Arabia Petræa to Mount Sinai. ...* London, 1836.
LANE, E. W. *Cairo Fifty Years Ago.* Ed. S. Lane-Poole. London, 1896.
— *The Modern Egyptians.* Ed. London, 1908.

LANE, F. C. *Venetian Ships and Shipbuilders of the Renaissance*. Baltimore, 1934.
LORENZETTI, G. *Venezie e il suo estuario*. Venezia [1926].
MAS LATRIE, J. N. J. L. DE. *Histoire de l'île de Chypre sous le règne des Princes de la maison de Lusignan*. 3 vols. Paris, 1861–1865.
MAYER, L. A. *Mamluk Costume. A Survey*. Geneva, 1952.
MILLER, W. *Essays on the Latin Orient*. Cambridge, 1921.
— *The Latins in the Levant*. London, 1908.
MOTTA, E. *Pamphilio Castaldi . . . Pietro Uggleimer ed il vescovo d'Aleria*, Rivista storica italiana, 1884.
MUIR, W. *The Mameluke or Slave Dynasty of Egypt* (1260–1517). London, 1896.
PALMER, E. H. *The Desert of the Exodus*. 2 vols. Cambridge, 1871.
— *Journey through the Desert of the Tîh*. Palestine Exploration Fund. Quarterly Statement No. IV. London, 1869.
PALMER, H. S. *Sinai from the Fourth Egyptian Dynasty to the present day*. London, 1892.
PAYNE-GALLWEY, R. *The Crossbow*. . . . London, 1903.
PERTILE, *If Fondaco dei Tedeschi in Venezia . . . del dott: Enrico Simonsfeld*. . . . Archivio Veneto, Vol. XXXV. Venice, 1888, pp. 226–236.
PETRIE, W. M. F. *Researches in Sinai*. London. 1906.
POOLE, S. LANE. *A History of Egypt in theMiddle Ages*. London, 1901.
— *Cairo. Sketches of its History,Monuments and Social Life*. London, 1892.
— *The Art of the Saracens in Egypt*. London, 1896.
— *The Story of Cairo*. Medieval Towns Series. London, 1906.
RABINO, M. H. L. *Le Monastère de Sainte-Catherine du Mont Sinai*. Royal Automobile Club d'Egypt. Cairo, 1938.
RUNCIMAN, S. *A History of the Crusades*. Vol. III. Cambridge, 1954.
SIMONSFELD, H. *Der Fondaco dei Tedeschi in Venedig*. Vol. II. Stuttgart, 1887.
STANLEY, A. P. *Sinai and Palestine*, London, 1889.
STUBBS, W. *Germany in the Later Middle Ages*. London, 1908.
VOINOVITCH, L. DE. *Histoire de Dalmatie*. Paris, 1934. 2 vols.
WOLLEY, C. L. AND LAWRENCE, T. E. *The Wilderness of Zin*. Palestine Exploration Fund, 1914.

Notes

Part One

JERUSALEM TO GAZA

Introductory

1. Evag., II, 495.
2. Walther, 178, n. 2.
3. Evag., II, 107. Walther, 186. Breydenbach (104b).
4. Evag., III, 375.
5. Ibid., I, 85; II, 108. Cf. III, 3–4. Breydenbach (104b).
6. Evag., II, 108, 500–501; III, 325. Breydenbach (115a).
7. Evag., II, 526, 528.
8. Ibid., 108, 500. Walther, pp. 180, 187 and n.
9. Ibid., 261–262.
10. Evag., II, 109.
11. Ibid., 436.
12. Ibid., II, 475.
13. Ibid., III, 326.

The last of the Holy Land

1. Evag., II, 199. Walther, 188–189.
2. Evag. II, 113.
3. Ibid., 179.
4. Ibid., 330–331.
5. Walther, 188.
6. Evag., II, 331.
7. Ibid., 330–331.
8. Harff, 134–135. Thenaud, 37.
9. Pèlerinage, 84–85.
10. Evag., II, 405.
11. Doughty, Arabia Deserta, I, 98.
12. La Brocquière, 20.
13. Evag., II, 331–332. Tyrwhitt-Drake, Lit. Rem., 261.
14. Evag., II, 332–333. Walther, 189.
15. Evag., II, 98–101. Breydenbach (103b–104a).
16. Evag., II, 373.
17. Pèlerinage, 84–86.
18. Harff, 134.
19. Pèlerinage, 86.
20. Harff, 134–135.
21. Evag., II, 335–337, 338–339.
22. Ibid., 360, 379. Walther, 190.
23. Evag., II, 361, 379.
24. Pèlerinage, 86, 87. Anglure, 44. La Brocquière, 20.
25. Evag., II, 362–363.
26. Ibid., 360, 379. Cf. Ibid., I, 186. Walther, 190.
27. Evag., II, 361–362.
28. Harff, 185–186.
29. Evag., II, 365. Walther, 190–191.
30. Evag., II, 366–368.
31. Ibid., I, 218.
32. Ibid., II, 368–369.
33. Harff, 114.
34. Evag., II, 368–369.
35. Walther, 192.
36. Ibid., 193.
37. Evag., II, 372–373. Cf. Harff, 122.
38. Evag., II, 371.
39. Pèlerinage, 87.
40. Evag., II, 372.
41. Ibid., 371–372.
42. Ibid., 374.
43. Doughty, Arabia Deserta, I, 110.
44. Pèlerinage, 86.
45. Evag., 375–376. Breydenbach (105a). Walther, 191.
46. Evag., II, 376–377.
47. Ibid., 377.

292 NOTES

Part Two

GAZA TO MOUNT SINAI

The school of the desert

1. Evag., II, 405–406. ct. Walther, 193.
2. Evag., II, 405. Walther, loc. cit.
3. Evag., II, 405–406. Pèlerinage, 81.
4. Evag., II, 405, 409.
5. Ibid., 380–381, 385, 407
6. Ibid., 405.
7. Baedeker, Lower Egypt, 1895, p. 234.
8. Evag., II, 379.
9. Petrie, Researches . . . 4.
10. Evag., II, 382–384.
11. Ibid., 381.
12. Ibid., 382.
13. Ibid., 384. Cf. Harff, 136. Frescobaldi, 113.
14. Doughty, loc. cit., I, 262, 618.
15. Pelerinage, 86.
16. Evag., II, 384.
17. Ibid., 356, 406. Cf. Frescobaldi, 112. Petrie, Researches, 9. ct. Pèlerinage, 96.
18. Petrie, loc. cit., 4.
19. Evag., II, 407, 420.
20. Petrie, loc. cit., 6.
21. Evag., II, 337, 361.
22. Ibid., 338. Walther, 193.
23. Evag., II, 408–409.
24. Ibid., 420.
25. Petrie, loc. cit., 2.
26. Evag., II, 398.
27. Walther, 199.
28. Pèlerinage, 88–89. Evag., II, 399.
29. Evag., II, 402.
30. Pèlerinage, 88.
31. Thenaud, 78.
32. Ibid., 77–78.
33. Evag., II, 440, 339.
34. Ibid., 402.
35. Palmer, Desert of the Exodus, II, 297, 299.
36 Pèlerinage, 89.
37. Thenaud, 37.
38. Suriano, 209. Evag., II, 445.
39. Frescobaldi, 114. Cf. Suriano, 209.
40. Evag., II, 398.
41. Ibid., 398–399. Frescobaldi, loc. cit. Cf. E. H. Palmer, Palestine Exploration Fund Quarterly, 1869–1870, 319.
42. Evag., II, 443–444.
43. Ibid., 300.
44. Suriano, 209.
45. Doughty, Arabia Deserta, II, 394.
46. Frescobaldi, 132–134.
47. E. H. Palmer, Palestine Exploration Fund, 1870, I, 319.
48. Thenaud, 66–68, 74.
49. Harff, 135.
50. La Brocquière, 21–23.
51. Harff, 138; Suriano, 187.
52. Thenaud, 58.
53. Frescobaldi, 115.
54. Martoni, 605.
55. Viaza (f. between m IV and n. 1).
56. Evag., II, 393. Pèlerinage, 87.
57. Evag., II, 425.
58. Ibid., 416.
59. Walther, 196.
60. Pèlerinage, 87–88.
61. Harff, 137.
62. Doughty, Arabia Deserta, I, 367.
63. Evag., II, 413.
64. Ibid., 418–419.
65. Ibid., 413. Cf. E. Hull, Mount Seir, Sinai and Western Palestine, 56.
66. Evag., II, 392. Petrie, 235.
67. Evag., II, 431.
68. H. S. Palmer, Sinai . . . 15.
69. Evag., II, 433. Cf. Woolley and Laurence, Wilderness of Zin, 40.
70. Evag., II, 393.
71. Ibid., 392.
72. Frescobaldi, 112–113.
73. Evag., II, p. 411. Cf. E. H. Palmer, Desert . . . I, 33.
74. Evag., II, 412.
75. Evag., III, 163.
76. Pèlerinage, 87–88.
77. Evag., II, 413.
78. Ibid., 440. III, 27.
79. Doughty, loc. cit., I, 173.
80. Evag., II, 417.
81. Ibid., 418.
82. Ibid., 415. Cf. E. H. Palmer, II, 287. H. S. Palmer, 48.
83. Huc and Gabet, 141. Evag., II, 427.
84. Evag., II, 436.
85. Ibid., 406–407, 419–420.
86. Ibid., 407. Cf. Drake, 266.

NOTES

87. *Evag.*, II, 408.
88. *Ibid.*, III, 177.
89. *Ibid.*, II, 537.
90. *Ibid.*, 424.

91. *Ibid.*, 433, 427, 431.
92. *Ibid.*, 437.
93. *Ibid.*, 424.

The desert journey

1. *Evag.*, II, 429.
2. *Ibid.*, I, 198.
3. *Ibid.*, III, 449.
4. *Ibid.*, II, 429.
5. *Pèlerinage*, 90. Anglure, 45–46.
6. *Pèlerinage*, 90–91.
7. *Evag.*, II, 425. Cf. *Ibid.*, 418.
8. Suriano, 186. Harff, 140 and n.
9. *Evag.*, II, 411–412. Jarvis, *Three Deserts*, 130.
10. *Evag.*, II, 414.
11. *Ibid.*
12. *Ibid.*, 415–416.
13. *Ibid.*, 419.
14. *Ibid.*, 420–423.
15. *Ibid.*, 424.
16. *Ibid.*, 425.
17. *Ibid.*
18. *Pèlerinage*, 89.
19. *Evag.*, II, 426–7.
20. *Ibid.*, 427.
21. Walther, 198. *Evag.*, II, 434.
22. *Ibid.*
23. *Ibid.*
24. *Evag.*, II, 435–436.
25. *Ibid.*, 437. Walther, 197–198.
26. *Evag.*, II, 432–433.
27. *Ibid.*, 437–438.
28. *Ibid.*, 438–439. Walther, 198.

29. *Evag.*, II, 440.
30. H. S. Palmer, 23.
31. *Ibid.*, 24. Cf. E. H. Palmer, *Desert* . . . I, 21, 27.
32. H. S. Palmer, 25–26.
33. Walther, 199.
34. *Evag.*, II, 441.
35. *Ibid.*, 442.
36. Thenaud, 70.
37. *Evag.*, II, 440.
38. Breydenbach (106a).
39. *Evag.*, *loc. cit.*
40. *Ibid.*, 441–442.
41. *Ibid.*, 442.
42. *Ibid.*, 443–444. Walther, 199.
43. *Evag.*, II, 444. Walther, 200.
44. *Evag.*, *loc. cit.*, 446.
45. Doughty, II, 561.
46. H. S. Palmer, 47. E. H. Palmer, *loc. cit.*, 81.
47. Hart, 22.
48. Suriano, 144, n.b.
49. *Evag.*, II, 448.
50. Breydenbach (111a). Cf. Harff, 140–141. Thenaud, 70.
51. Suriano, 144, n.b.
52. *Evag.*, II, 448, 449.
53. *Ibid.*, 449. Walther, 201.

Part Three

MOUNT SINAI AND THE MONASTERY OF ST. KATHERINE

The monks of St. Katherine

1. *Evag.*, II, 451.
2. Suriano, 187–188.
3. *Ibid.*, 189.
4. Harff, 140. Cf. Jarvis, *Sinai* . . . 225
5. Thenaud, 71. Laborde, *Journey* . . . 230.
6. *Evag.*, II, 476. Rabino, *Le Monastère de Ste Catherine* . . . 51.
7. *Evag.*, II, 505.

8. Suriano, 189.
9. E. H. Palmer, *Desert* . . . I, 61.
10. Harff, 140. Suriano, 186, 188.
11. *Evag.*, II, 492.
12. Thenaud, 74.
13. *Evag.*, II, 505. Suriano, 189. Ct. Harff, 141.
14. *Evag.*, II, 470, 505.
15. Rabino, *loc. cit.*

16. Ibid., p. 2.
17. Harff, 141, but Cf. Rabino, 45 n.
18. Evag., II, 501. Breydenbach (110b).
19. Evag., II, 503.
20. Frescobaldi, 118.
21. Harff, 140. Cf. Pococke, I, 152.
22. Frescobaldi, 119. Evag., II, 503.
23. Evag., II, 508. Frescobaldi, 121. Anglure, 48–49.
24. Harff, 146. Frescobaldi, 122. Evag., II, 486, 476.
25. Frescobaldi, 120.
26. Evag., II, 504.
27. Ibid., 505, 507. Ct. Thenaud, 72.
28. Walther, 202. Evag., II, 504. Suriano, 189.
29. Suriano, 187–188.
30. Harff, 140.
31. Evag., II, 489.
32. Rabino, 85.
33. Evag., II, 509.
34. Ibid., 542–543. Walther, 210.
35. Evag., II, 450, 451.
36. Martoni, 608.
37. Thenaud, 72–74.

The monastery, the mountains and the shrines

1. Lannoy, 69.
2. Anglure, 46.
3. Evag., II, 499. Cf. Frescobaldi, 119. Pococke, I, 149.
4. Harff, 140.
5. Evag., II, 450. Rabine, 35. Pococke, Plan. I, 150.
6. Rabino, 34.
7. Evag., II, 500.
8. Ibid., 451. Laborde, 230. E. H. Palmer, I, 63. Rabino, 16.
9. Evag., II, 501. Rabino, 40.
10. Rabino, 24. Suriano, 188.
11. Harff, 141.
12. Suriano, loc. cit. Rabino, 22.
13. Harff, loc. cit. Evag., II, 500.
14. Martoni, 607.
15. Evag., II, 499–500.
16. Rabino, 4–5.
17. Evag., II, 475.
18. Martoni, 608.
19. Evag., II, 457–458. Cf. E. H. Palmer, I, 105–107.
20. Evag., II, 458–459.
21. Ibid., 459.
22. Ibid., 476, 509. Breydenbach (111a).
23. Martoni, 607–608.
24. Ibid., 609.
25. Evag., II, 476. Walther, 206–207.
26. Evag., II, 461.
27. Ibid., 461–462.
28. Ibid., 467.
29. Anglure, 52.
30. Evag., II, 462–463.
31. Ibid., 463. Walther, 207–208.
32. Evag., II, 463. Walther, 208.
33. Evag., II, 463–464.
34. E. H. Palmer, I, 131. Evag., II, 466.
35. Ibid., 465–466.
36. Ibid., 466–467.
37. E. H. Palmer, I, 132–135. Cf. Baedeker, Lower Egypt, 271.
38. Frescobaldi, 129–130.
39. Ibid., 129. Evag., II, 531. Cf. A. P. Stanley, Sinai and Palestine, 5 and n.
40. Evag., II, 474.
41. Walther, 209. Pèlerinage, 93.
42. Evag., II, 492. Harff, 142. Pococke, 150.
43. Evag., II, 490.
44. Frescobaldi, 130–131.
45. Pococke, 152.
46. Evag., II, 491.
47. Rabino, 26, n.
48. Evag., II, 491.
49. Suriano, 188.
50. Ibid., 496.
51. Ibid., 491, 492.
52. Ibid. 497–498.
53. Tafur, 87. Rabino, 56. Jervis, Sinai... 223.
54. Evag., II, 500–501.
55. Tafur, 87.
56. Frescobaldi, 118.
57. Evag., II, 498.
58. Ibid., 499.
59. E. H. Palmer, I, 67.
60. Evag., II, 451.
61. Ibid., 508.
62. Ibid., 508–509.
63. Ibid., 510.

NOTES

Part Four

MOUNT SINAI TO EGYPT

More of the desert

1. E. H. Palmer, I, 42-43.
2. Evag., II, 510.
3. Ibid., 511.
4. Ibid., 512-513.
5. Harff, 148-149.
6. Breydenbach (111b).
7. Evag., II, 513.
8. Cf. Anglure, 53.
9. Evag., II, 514-515. Walther, 211. Cf. Petrie, 224.
10. Evag., II, 516. Walther, 212.
11. E. H. Palmer, I, 19.
12. Evag., II, 519.
13. Ibid.
14. Breydenbach (111b).
15. Evag., II, 519-520. Walther, 212-213.
16. Evag., II, 519-521. Walther, 213.
17. Evag., II, 521-522. Breydenbach (111b).
18. Sigoli, 44.
19. Evag., II, 524, 529.
20. Ibid., 526.
21. Ibid.
22. Evag., II, 523-530. Walther, 213-214.
23. Breydenbach (112a). Cf. Thenaud, 66.
24. Breydenbach, ibid.
25. Viazo (f. between n. iv and n. i).
26. Thenaud, 65.
27. Suriano, 187.
28. Evag., II, 531-533. Breydenbach (112a).
29. Ibid., 533.
30. Ibid., 521.
31. Ibid.
32. Evag., II, 415. Harff, 138.
33. Harff, 138. Suriano, 187.
34. Evag., II, 534.
35. Thenaud, 62, 65.
36. Frescobaldi, 111.
37. Evag., II, 533. Harff, 137.
38. Evag., II, 535.
39. Ibid., 536-537.
40. Piloti, 356.
41. Ibn Iyas, 183, 194, etc.
42. Harff, 135. Piloti, loc. cit. Cf. la Brocquière, 24-25.
43. Evag., II, 542.
44. Ibid., 540-541.
45. Evag., II, 543-545. Walther, 216-217.
46. Evag., II, 543.
47. Ibid., 545.
48. Ibid, III, 1. Walther, 217.
49. Evag., III, 1-2.

Part Five

EGYPT

The Garden of Balm

1. Evag., III, 2.
2. Ibn Iyas, 149, 58.
3. Evag., loc. cit., 2, 8.
4. Piloti, 349, 350.
5. Anglure, 57. Cf. Pèlerinage, 97-98. Khitrovo, I, i, 250. Piloti, 348.
6. Evag., III, 14. Cf. Schiltberger, note 23.
7. Evag., III, 12, 4. Piloti, 348.
8. Evag., III, 2, 3-4. Breydenbach (113a).
9. Pèlerinage, 98.
10. Evag., III, 2-3.
11. Evag., II, 142-143.
12. Evag., III, 3. Breydenbach (112b).
13. Evag., loc. cit. Walther, 217. Breydenbach (112b).
14. Evag., III, 13. Breydenbach (113a). Walther, 217. Cf. Piloti, 350.
15. Evag., III, 3-4.
16. Ibid., 4.
17. Ibid., 5. Walther, 218. Tafur, 78. Pèlerinage, 97.
18. Evag., III, 7-8. Walther, 220.
19. Walther, 219.
20. Harff, 127.

21. Breydenbach (113b). Evag., III, 15. Tafur, 77.
22. Evag., III, loc. cit. Cf. Suriano, 195.
23. Frescobaldi, 109.
24. Walther, 220. Tafur, 77. Harff, 127 n. Piloti, 349–350. Ludolf, 70.
25. Suriano, 195. Schiltberger, note 232, p. 209.
26. Piloti, 349–350. Cf. Suriano, 195.
27. Evag., III, 16. Heyd, II, 579–580.
28. Evag., III, 14.
29. Ibn Iyas, 483.
30. Evag., III, 17–18.
31. Piloti, 349. Frescobaldi, 109. Ludolf, 69. Schiltberger, 60.
32. Piloti, loc. cit.
33. Frescobaldi, 109.
34. Evag., III, 16. Cf. Ludolf, 68.
35. Walther, 219.
36. Piloti, 349. Cf. Ibn Iyas, 483.
37. Piloti, 350.
38. Lannoy, 68. Cf. Martoni, 599.
39. Harff, 127.
40. Heyd, II, 576.
41. Evag., III, 17.
42. Schiltberger, 60.
43. Evag., loc. cit.
44. Ibn Iyas, 483.
45. Walther, 219.
46. Evag., III, 18.
47. Ibid., 17.
48. Schiltberger, 60.
49. Ludolf, 69.
50. Evag., III, 18, 14.
51. Ibid., 8.
52. Walther, 220.

Among the Mamluks

1. Evag., III, 32.
2. Ibid., 19.
3. Ibid.
4. Tafur, 72–73.
5. Sigoli, 17.
6. Evag., III, 20–21.
7. Ibid., 21. Sigoli, 17. Harff, 102.
8. Evag., III, 23–29.
9. Ibid., 32.
10. Ibid., 32–33, 296.
11. Piloti, 391, 392–393.
12. Piloti, 405. Lannoy, 118.
13. Harff, 121, 122. Evag., III, 37.
14. Suriano, 191. Harff, 103–105 and nn. Cf. Lannoy, 118–119. Muir, The Mameluke Dynasty . . . 219.
15. Piloti, 377.
16. Joinville, 117.
17. Ayalon, L'Esclavage . . . 3. 25–30.
18. Ibid., IV, V, 24, 29–30. Studies . . . XV, 206.
19. Tafur, 74. Encycl. of Islam, s.v. Mamluks.
20. Lannoy, 118.
21. Ibn Iyas, 366, but cf. Suriano, 126 and n.
22. Sigoli, 36.
23. Ibid., 34–35.
24. Ayalon, Studies . . . XV, 206. L'Esclavage . . . 3.
25. Piloti, 331, 338–340.
26. Heyd, II, 555–556.
27. Ibn Iyas, 1.
28. Encycl: of Islam, s.v. Ka'itbey.
29. Ibn Iyas, 1–2.
30. Piloti, 340. Harff, 106.
31. Joinville, 117–118.
32. Piloti, 340–341. Harff, 108.
33. Breydenbach (117a).
34. Harff, 106.
35. Evag., III, 93–94. Lannoy, 119–120.
36. Evag., loc. cit.
37. Ibid.
38. Lane Poole, Art of the Saracens . . . 229.
39. Evag., III, 34–35. Breydenbach (115a).
40. Evag., III, 93. Breydenbach, loc. cit.
41. Evag., III, 34. Walther, 236–237.
42. Evag., III, 33, 34.
43. Piloti, 404.
44. Thenaud, 63–64.
45. Evag., III, 26.
46. Ibid., 176. Walther, 248 and n.
47. Georgius Gemnicensis, 471.
48. Frescobaldi, 76.
49. Ibid., 89–90. Sigoli, 17.
50. Frescobaldi, 106.
51. Walther, 222. Cf. Breydenbach (115a).
52. Frescobaldi, 106.
53. Evag., III, 20. Walther, 221.
54. Gemnicensis, 482.

NOTES 297

55. *Evag.*, III, 20.
56. Walther, 221.
57. Torkington, 63–64. Harff, 81.
58. *Evag.*, III, 20. Walther, 221.
59. 1 Gemnicensis, 482.
60. Hill, *History of Cyprus*, III, 741 and n. Mas. Latrie, *Hist. de Chypre*, III, i, 477.
61. Hill, *loc. cit.*, 821, 823 and n. Mas. Latrie, *loc. cit.*, 478.
62. Suriano, 192.
63. Ibn Iyas, 374.
64. Harff, 102.
65. *Ibid.*, 106, n.
66. Thenaud, XLV–XLVI.
67. *Ibid.*, LIII.
68. Gemnicensis, 471.
69. *Ibid.*, 475–482.
70. *Ibid.*, 475. Cf. *ibid.*, 513.
71. Thenaud, LV–LVI, LIX.
72. *Evag.*, III, 22–25, 105–106. Walther, 222.

Seeing Cairo

1. Harff, 121. Mayer, *Mamluk Costume*, 24.
2. *Evag.*, III, 34. Walther, 231.
3. Breydenbach (115a).
4. *Evag.*, III, 35.
5. *Ibid.*, 43–44, 42–43. Walther, 234.
6. *Evag.*, III. 43. Walther, 234.
7. Tafur, 78.
8. Anglure, 65–66.
9. Suriano, 196.
10. *Evag.*, III, 43. Baedeker, *Lower Egypt*, 140.
11. Harff, 126.
12. Baedeker, *loc. cit.*, 145.
13. Anglure, 67.
14. Thenaud, 53.
15. Anglure, 68.
16. Suriano, 196–197.
17. Baedeker, *Lower Egypt*, 150–151.
18. *Evag.*, III, 44.
19. *Ibid.*, 46.
20. Suriano, 197.
21. Thenaud, Trevisan, 199.
22. *Evag.*, III, 37. Walther, 231.
23. E. Lane, *The ... Modern Egyptians* ... 144.
24. Walther, 231.
25. Walther, *ibid.*
26. *Evag.*, III, 40.
27. *Evag.*, III, 41.
28. Walther, 231.
29. *Evag.*, III, 42. Cf. Harff, 97.
30. Laborde, 302.
31. Walther, 232.
32. Piloti, 352.
33. Walther, 232.
34. *Evag.*, III, 58. Walther, *loc. cit.*
35. Walther, *loc. cit.*
36. Piloti, 352.
37. *Evag.*, III, 57–58. Walther, 232.
Harff, 110. Ludolf, 67. Cf. E. Lane, 317–318.
38. Piloti, 352–353.
39. Ludolf, *loc. cit.* Piloti, 353.
40. Harff, 110.
41. Suriano, 192. Cf. Piloti, 353.
42. Suriano, *loc. cit. Pèlerinage*, 99.
43. Ludolf, 67.
44. Piloti, 353.
45. *Evag.*, III, 59.
46. *Ibid.*, 49–50.
47. *Ibid.*, 51. Walther, 233.
48. *Evag.*, *loc. cit.*
49. *Ibid.*, 49.
50. *Ibid.*, 52–57. Walther, 234.
51. *Evag.*, III, 61–62.
52. Casanova, *Histoire . . . de la citadelle du Caire*, 596.
53. *Evag.*, III, 59–60, 62.
54. Schiltberger, 53.
55. *Evag.*, III, 66. Walther, 234.
56. Schiltberger, 69.
57. *Evag.*, III, 69.
58. *Evag.*, III, 70.
59. Tafur, 80. Ibn Iyas, 169.
60. Ibn Iyas, 61.
61. Tafur, 74–76.
62. Thenaud, 44–45.
63. Schiltberger, 52, 54.
64. Harff, 103, 108.
65. Casanova, 670.
66. Thenaud, LXXIX, n. 2. *Ibid.*, Trevisan, 188, 190, 203.
67. Walther, 225.
68. *Evag.*, III, 73.
69. Ibn Iyas, 72. Harff, 107.
70. *Evag.*, *loc. cit.* Harff, *loc. cit.* Ibn Iyas, 367.
71. *Evag.*, III, 73.

Cairo, the passing show

1. Walther, 230, 231.
2. Evag., III, 87–88, 47, 85–86. Cf. 103.
3. Ibid., 103–104.
4. Ibid., 112.
5. Piloti, 393.
6. Walther, 224.
7. Pèlerinage, 100.
8. Harff, 108.
9. Evag., III, 80–81.
10. Lannoy, 113.
11. Walther, 226
12. Ibid.
13. Evag., III, 103. Walther, 228. Harff, 115–116.
14. Harff, 124.
15. Anglure, 59.
16. Breydenbach (116a).
17. Pèlerinage, 100.
18. Walther, 224. Cf. Evag., III, 82.
19. Lannoy, 115.
20. Evag., III, 81–82. Harff, 109.
21. Harff, 109. Lannoy, 115. Makrizi, Description ... de l'Egypte, IV, i, 54.
22. Thenaud, Trevisan, 213. Cf. Evag., III, 83. Suriano, 191.
23. Evag., III, loc. cit.
24. Walther, 224.
25. Suriano, 191. Tafur, 68. Evag., III, 82. Cf. M. S. Briggs, Muhammadan Architecture in Egypt ... 146. Cf. E. Lane, 20.
26. Thenaud, Trevisan, 213. Harff,112.
27. Harff, 112. Cf. Trevisan, 213.
28. Evag., III, 19, 23–25.
29. Harff, 112.
30. Evag., III, 34.
31. Sigoli, 19. Cf. E. Lane, loc. cit., 481–482.
32. Evag., III, 82.
33. Thenaud, 46–47.
34. Thenaud, Trevisan, 211.
35. Thenaud, 46.
36. Ibid., 47.
37. Ibid., 46, Cf. Evag., III, 82. Breydenbach (115a). Thenaud, 46.
38. Evag., III, loc. cit.
39. Sigoli, 27. Cf. Frescobaldi, 104.
40. Evag., III, 23–29. Walther, 223. Breydenbach (114b).
41. Evag., III, 26. Harff, 95–96.
42. Evag., III, 24.
43. Evag., III, 27–28. Harff, 86.
44. Evag., III, 27–28.
45. Ibid., 30.
46. Piloti, 327.
47. Ibid., 409. Evag., III, 100. Sigoli, 30.
48. Evag., III, 39.
49. Harff, 113, 121–123. Anglure, 43.
50. Evag., III, 38–39. Cf. E. Lane, loc. cit., 142–144.
51. Tafur, 100. Thenaud, 47. Sanuto, 107, a. Evag., III, 101.
52. Evag., loc. cit.
53. Harff, 111.
54. Martoni, 601.
55. Thenaud, 47. Evag., III, 42. Harff, 111. Walther, 226. Makrizi, IV, 1, 54–55.
56. Tafur, 100.
57. Evag., 100–101. Harff, 109. Frescobaldi, 99.
58. Sigoli, 17. Harff, 102.
59. Evag., III, 21.
60. Evag., III, 21. Suriano, 191, n. 192.
61. Tafur, 70.
62. Ibid., 81.
63. Piloti, 327–328.
64. Sanuto, 106 a.
65. Harff, 119.
66. Evag., III, 132.
67. Piloti, 328. Evag., loc. cit.
68. Evag., III, 21.
69. Frescobaldi, 92.
70. Sigoli, 31.
71. Piloti, 347.
72. Suriano, 191, n. Frescobaldi, 104. Harff, 109.
73. Piloti, 327. Harff, 110–111.
74. Piloti, 347. Harff, loc. cit.
75. S. Lane-Poole, The Story of Cairo, 108.
76. Tafur, 100.
77. Evag., III, 137.
78. Ibid., 138.
79. Walther, 218.
80. Evag., III, 5–6.
81. Ibid., 101–102.
82. Thenaud, Trevisan, 212.
83. Piloti, 330.
84. Heyd, II, 434–435, 491.
85. Thenaud, 48.
86. Livio Sanuto, Geographia ... (106 a and b).
87. Ibid. (106b).
88. Evag., III, 136–137.

89. Sigoli, 42.
90. Piloti, 351.
91. Sigoli, 18. Piloti, 351. Thenaud, Trevisan, 211–212. Frescobaldi, 95–96. Harff, 124. Thenaud, 56. Cf. E. Lane, *loc. cit.*, 39–40.
92. *Evag.*, III, 36–37.
93. *Ibid.*, 40, 164.
94. *Ibid.*, 165–166.
95. *Ibid.*, 165–167.
96. *Ibid.*, 152.
97. *Ibid.*, 70–71.
98. Heyd, II, 561.
99. *Evag.*, III, 432.
100. Heyd, II, 561.
101. E. Motta, *Pamphilio Castaldi . . .* 261–262.
102. Heyd, *loc. cit.*, 562.
103. *Evag.*, III, 167–168.
104. *Ibid.*, 166.
105. *Evag.*, III, 125. Fabri, *Tractatus de Civitate Ulmensi*, 194.
106. *Evag.*, III, 129–130.
107. *Ibid.*, 130.
108. Lannoy, 126. Cf. Suriano, 194.
109. *Evag.*, III, 131.
110. Lane Poole, *Story of Cairo*, 44.
111. Piloti, 345. Lannoy, 127.
112. Piloti, *loc. cit.*
113. *Evag.*, III, 125.
114. *Ibid.*, 127.
115. *Ibid.*, 125–126. Piloti, 344.
116. *Evag.*, III, 126.
117. Piloti, 344–345. Harff, 97.
118. Piloti, 344.
119. *Ibid.*, 343.
120. Tafur, 79–80.
121. E. Lane, *loc. cit.*, 498–499.
122. Piloti, 343. Lannoy, 125. Cf. Tafur, 80.
123. Piloti, 343.
124. Suriano, 194. Thenaud, Trevisan, 207.
125. Piloti, 343–344.
126. Hakluyt, V, 336. *A description of the yearly voyage.* . . .
127. Makrizi, IV, i, 59.

Going down the Nile

1. *Evag.*, III, 74–76.
2. *Ibid.*, 73. Cf. Ibn Iyas, 226.
3. *Evag.*, III, 76.
4. *Ibid.*, 77–78.
5. *Ibid.*, 105.
6. *Ibid.*, 106–107. Walther, 238.
7. *Evag.*, III, 107–108. Walther, *loc. cit.*
8. *Evag.*, 107–108.
9. Anglure, 77. Frescobaldi, 84. See Kahle, *Die Katastrophie das . . . Alexandria, Islam*, 75–78. Heyd, II, 636.
10. *Evag.*, III, 113. Heyd, II, 428–429.
11. Heyd, II, 436. Kahle, *loc. cit.*, 79.
12. Thenaud, 29, n.
13. Lannoy, 127.
14. Piloti, 390.
15. *Evag.*, III, 108. Breydenbach (119b).
16. *Evag.*, *loc. cit.*
17. Martoni, 593–594.
18. Frescabaldi, 87–88.
19. *Evag.*, III, 133–134. Anglure, 76. Harff, 97–98. *Pélerinage*, 100. Tafur, 70. Suriano, 194.
20. *Evag.*, III, 135.
21. Tafur, 102–103.
22. *Evag.*, III, 134. Harff, 98–99.
23. Suriano, 194.
24. Lannoy, 127. E. Lane, 337.
25. *Evag.*, III, 109.
26. *Ibid.*, 110. Cf. Thenaud, 33 and n.
27. Sigoli, 8. Cf. Lane, *loc. cit.*, 97.
28. *Evag.*, III. 111. Walther, 238.
29. *Evag.*, *loc. cit.*
30. *Evag.*, III, 112.
31. *Ibid.*, *loc. cit.*
32. *Evag.*, III, 113.
33. *Ibid.*, 113–114. Walther, 238.
34. *Ibid.*, 114–115. Walther, *loc. cit.*
35. *Evag.*, III, 115.
36. *Ibid.*
37. *Ibid.*, 115–116.
38. *Ibid.*, 117–118.
39. *Ibid.*, 118–119, 138–139. Walther, 239.
40. *Evag.*, III, 139–141. Walther, *loc. cit.*
41. *Evag.*, III, 141–142.
42. Walther, 239–240.
43. Walsingham, *Ypodigma Neustriæ*, 309.

NOTES

44. Kahle, *Mélanges* . . . 138.
45. *Evag.*, III, 144. Lannoy, 105. *Pèlerinage*, 102. Cf. Pocoche, I, 3-4, v. Plan *ibid.*, p. 2.
46. *Evag.*, III, 145.
47. *Evag.*, III, 145-146.
48. *Ibid.*, 146.

Alexandria: "the public market of both worlds"

1. Piloti, 359.
2. Heyd, II, 453-454 and n.
3. *Evag.*, II, 536.
4. Heyd, I, 378-380.
5. Piloti, 354-355. Heyd, II, 446.
6. Heyd, I, 380; II, 457.
7. *Ibid.*, II, 457, Cf. Piloti, 356.
8. Piloti, 357.
9. *Evag.*, II, 469-470. Harff, 149.
10. Baedeker, *Lower Egypt*, 233.
11. Tafur, 83.
12. *Ibid.*, 90-91, 95. Cf. *India in the Fifteenth Century*, II, 4.
13. Heyd, II, 435. Piloti, 357-358.
14. *Evag.*, III, 170.
15. *Ibid.*, 177.
16. Piloti, 377. Cf. Heyd, II, 440.
17. Heyd, II, 23-35; I, 385-387.
18. Heyd, II, 442. Piloti, 358.
19. Piloti, 378.
20. *Ibid.*, 377.
21. *Ibid*, 346. Harff, 99.
22. Piloti, 352.
23. *Ibid.*, 358, 373-376.
24. *Evag.*, III, 153.
25. Heyd, II, 441-442.
26. Honey, *Glass* . . . 50-53.
27. Heyd, II, 25, 451-452, 490, 492.
28. Thenaud, 27.
29. Piloti, 378.
30. Heyd, II, 451-452.
31. Thenaud, 48. Cf. Heyd. I, 425. S. Lane. Poole, *Art of the Saracens* . . . 95-96.
32. Piloti, 389. *Evag.*, III, 151.
33. Heyd, I, 411.
34. *Ibid.*, II, 431-432. Harff, 95. *Evag.*, III, 162.
35. Lannoy, 109.
36. Frescobaldi, 76. Heyd, II, 430-431.
37. Walther, 241-242. *Evag.*, III, 163-164.
38. Heyd, I, 411; II, 433. *Evag.*, III, 151, 161-162, 201. Walther, 243.
39. Heyd, I, 411; II, 431-432.
40. Piloti, 394.
41. *Evag.*, III, 33.
42. Lannoy, 109-110. Harff, 93. *Evag.*, III, 154. Heyd, II, 431. Schiltberger, 62-63.
43. Tafur, 102.
44. Harff, 96.
45. Schiltberger, 216, n. *Evag.*, III, 176. Walther, 248. Ibn Iyas, 172.
46. *Pèlerinage*, 102. Harff, 92. Cf. Heyd, II, 429.
47. Lannoy, 101, 103-104.
48. Frescobaldi, 75. Heyd, II, 430.
49. Lannoy, 108. Piloti, 388. *Evag.*, III, 204. Machaut, 85. Kahle, *Mélanges*, 142.
50. Heyd, II, 430. Frescobaldi, 75-76.
51. Heyd, II, 451. Piloti, 388-389.
52. Frescobaldi, 75-76. Sigoli, 4-5. Walther, 240. *Evag.*, III, 149.
53. Sigoli, 4-5.
54. Frescobaldi, 75-76.
55. Piloti, 389.

The pilgrims at Alexandria

1. *Evag.*, III, 147.
2. *Ibid.*, 148.
3. *Ibid.*, 147.
4. Machaut, 98, 280, n. 19. Kahle, *Mélanges* . . . 143. Forster, E.M. 75.
5. *Evag.*, III, 147-148.
6. *Ibid.*, 148.
7. *Ibid.*
8. Breydenbach (121a).
9. *Evag.*, III, 148-149.
10. Sigoli, 10-11.
11. Thenaud, Trevisan, 173.
12. Sigoli, *loc. cit.*
13. Anglure, 78.

14. *Pèlerinage*, 101-102.
15. *Evag.*, III, 149.
16. *Ibid.*, 150. Cf. 203-204.
17. *Ibid.*, 150.
18. *Ibid.*, 151. Frescobaldi, 76.
19. Thenaud, 22.
20. Sigoli, 5.
21. *Ibid.*, 7-8.
22. *Evag.*, III, 150-151.
23. *Ibid.*, 151.
24. *Ibid.*
25. *Ibid.*, 154-156.
26. *Ibid.*, 158. Cf. Lannoy, 107.
27. *Evag.*, III, 178.
28. Piloti, 351. Harff, 93. Cf. Kahle, *Mélanges*... 138.
29. Piloti, 345-346. Lannoy, 105.
30. Piloti, 345. *Evag.*, 175.
31. *Evag.*, III, 159-160.
32. *Ibid.*, 160-161.
33. *Ibid.*, 162-171.
34. Walther, 244-246.
35. *Evag.*, III, 200-201. Walther, 246-247.
36. *Evag.*, III, 171-172.
37. *Ibid.*, 172-173.
38. Walther, 1-2, 11, 177, 245, 261.
39. *Ibid.*, 240-241, 249.
40. *Evag.*, III, 172-173.
41. *Ibid.*, 173.
42. *Ibid.*, 173-174.
43. *Ibid.*, 354.
44. Frescobaldi, 84.
45. Payne-Gallwey, *The Cross bow*, App. 4.
46. Breydenbach (123b).
47. *Ibid.* (123b.). *Evag.*, III, 201.
48. *Evag.*, *loc. cit.*
49. *Ibid.*, 201-202.
50. *Ibid.*, 203-204.
51. *Ibid.*, 205.
52. *Ibid.*, 205-206.
53. *Ibid.*, 206.

Part Six

ALEXANDRIA TO VENICE

On board the spice ships

1. *Evag.*, III, 207.
2. Harff, 73.
3. F. C. Lane, *Ships ... of the Renaissance*, 15.
4. E.g. *Evag.*, III, 369.
5. F. C. Lane, *loc. cit.*, 22, 24.
6. *Evag.*, I, 126. Cf. III, 295, 322.
7. *Evag.*, I, 122-127; III, 207-209. Cf. Felix Fabri, *Wanderings*... VII, 133-139. Jal, *Glossaire Nantique* s. vv. *Cometo. Parone.*
8. *Evag.*, III, 210.
9. *Ibid.*, 208-209.
10. *Ibid.*, 209.
11. Walther, 249-250. *Evag.*, III, 212. Breydenbach (124a).
12. Breydenbach, *loc. cit.*
13. *Ibid.*
14. *Evag.*, III, 213.
15. *Ibid.*, 28.
16. *Ibid.*, 163.
17. *Ibid.*, 28-29, 300-301.
18. *Ibid.*, 197, 269.
19. *Ibid.*, 197-198.
20. *Ibid.*, 413.
21. Tafur, 172.
22. *Ibid.*, Miller, *Essays* ... 205.
23. *Evag.*, III, 330.
24. Casola, 318.
25. Tafur, 50-51.
26. Miller, *Essays* ... 205-206.
27. *Ibid.*, 209.
28. *Ibid.*, 197.
29. Casola, 200.
30. Miller, *loc. cit.*, 197, 210.
31. *Ibid.*, 211.
32. *Evag.*, III, 285.

Winter voyage

1. *Evag.*, III, 213.
2. Walther, 250. Cf. Harff, 92. Breydenbach (124a).
3. *Evag.*, III, 290–291.
4. Breydenbach (124a).
5. *Ibid.*, 295. Walther, 251.
6. *Evag.*, III, 296.
7. *Ibid.*, 334.
8. *Ibid.*, 33.
9. *Ibid.*, 296. Walther, 250.
10. Walther, 251.
11. *Evag.*, III, 298.
12. *Ibid.*, 313.
13. *Geographical Handbook series. Naval Intelligence Division. Greece*, III, 409.
14. *Evag.*, 300.
15. *Ibid.*, 299.
16. *Ibid.*, Walther, 251.
17. *Evag.*, III, 301–302.
18. *Ibid.*, 300–301.
19. *Ibid.*, 302.
20. *Ibid.*, 302–303, 306.
21. *Evag.*, III, 314.
22. Walther, 252.
23. *Evag.*, III, 315.
24. Breydenbach (126b).
25. *Evag.*, III, 316. Breydenbach, *loc. cit.* Walther, 253.
26. Heyd, II, 460.
27. *Evag.*, III, 316–317. Walther, 253. Breydenbach, *loc. cit.*
28. *Evag.*, III, 318–319.
29. *Ibid.*, 319–322.
30. *Ibid.*, 322–323.
31. *Ibid.*, 298, 325.
32. *Ibid.*, 324.
33. Walther, 253. *Evag.*, III, 330.
34. *Evag.*, III, 325.
35. *Ibid.*, 327–328.
36. *Ibid.*, 329.

Up the Adriatic

1. Miller, *Latins in the Levant*, 152.
2. Tafur, 50. Cf. Brasca (10a).
3. Miller, *loc. cit.*, 340, 208, 24, 153.
4. Miller, *loc. cit.*, 39. Casola, 170, 372.
5. Miller, *loc. cit.*, 40.
6. *Evag.*, III, 343.
7. *Evag.*, III, 337–338. Casola, 192.
8. Miller, *Essays*, 211.
9. *Evag.*, III, 331–332.
10. *Ibid.*, 336–337.
11. Walther, 255.
12. *Evag.*, III, 337.
13. *Ibid.*
14. *Evag.*, I, 73.
15. *Evag.*, III, 343–344.
16. Frescobaldi, 73.
17. *Evag.*, III, 344.
18. Torkington, 63–64.
19. Tafur, 48.
20. Miller, *Essays*, 205.
21. *Evag.*, III, 347.
22. *Ibid.*, 348. Walther, 256.
23. Casola, 185, 186.
24. Walther, 77–78.
25. *Evag.*, III, 349.
26. *Ibid.*, 350, 352.
27. *Ibid.*, 349.
28. *Ibid.*, 354–355.
29. *Ibid.*, I, 35. Cf. Tafur, 153. *Informacon*, 13b.
30. Voinovitch, *Histoire de Dalmatie*, 817.
31. Casola, 172–176.
32. Brasca (8a).
33. Casola, 177–178. *Evag.*, III, 361.
34. *Evag.*, I, 35. Casola, 174.
35. *Evag.*, I, 34.
36. Casola, 327.
37. *Evag.*, III, 364.
38. Tafur, 154.
39. *Evag.*, III, 361–362.
40. *Ibid.*, 365.
41. *Ibid.*
42. *Ibid.*, 366.
43. *Ibid.*, 369–470.
44. *Ibid.*, 370–371.
45. Casola, 166.
46. *Ibid.*, 165.
47. *Evag.*, 372.
48. *Ibid.*, 373.
49. *Ibid.*
50. *Ibid.*, 373–374.
51. *Ibid.*, 377–378.
52. Casola, 164. *Evag.*, III, 379.
53. *Evag.*, *loc. cit.*
54. Casola, 324.

NOTES

55. Evag., III, 381-382.
56. Ibid., 384.
57. Evag., III, 385-386. Cf. Tafur, 156. Casola, 170, 377 n. 56.
58. Evag., III, 386.
59. Ibid., 387, 421. Tafur, 164.
60. Ibid., 387.
61. Walther, 261.
62. Evag., III, 387-388. Breydenbach, (8a), (130b).
63. Evag., I, 101, 111, 388.

Part Seven
VENICE TO ULM
Venice of the merchants

1. Evag., III, 389.
2. Ibid., 388-389, 390.
3. Ibid., 389.
4. Ibid., 426.
5. Ibid., 424-425. Cf. Janssen, *History of the German People*, I, 246, n. *Oxford Companion to Music*, s.v. musica figurata.
6. Evag. III, 435.
7. Ibid., 402.
8. Ibid., 421, 398.
9. Tafur, 166.
10. Evag., III, 431.
11. Ibid., 398, 420-421, 427.
12. Ibid., 403-404, 405, 408, 409, 410.
13. Ibid., 431-432. Cf. Tafur, 47.
14. Evag., III, 438.
15. Harff, 51.
16. Evag., III, 432.
17. Burkhardt, *Civilization of the Renaissance*, 63.
18. Harff, 71.
19. Tafur, 171.
20. Harff, *loc. cit.*
21. Simonsfeld, *Der Fondaco dei Tedeschi* . . . I, 525, no. 289-90.
22. Fabri, *Tractatus* . . . 134.
23. Heyd, *Das Haus der deutschen Kaufleute in Venedig*, 217.
24. Harff, 51.
25. Evag., III, 432.
26. Simonsfeld, II, 4-5.
27. Evag., *loc. cit.*
28. Heyd, *loc. cit.*, 201.
29. Evag., III, 388-389.
30. Heyd, *loc. cit.*, 200.
31. Simonsfeld, *loc. cit.*, II, 10. *Ibid.*, I, 309-310, no. 568.
32. Ibid., II, 11-12. Thomas, *Capitular des Deutschen Hauses* . . . 63, no. 149.
33. Simonsfeld, I, 184, no. 351; 193-194, no. 362; 298, no. 544; 315, no. 582.
34. Heyd, *loc. cit.*, 201.
35. Simonsfeld, II, 14. Thomas, *loc. cit.*, 166-167, no. 277.
36. Evag., III, 389.
37. Heyd, *loc. cit.*, 203-204.
38. Ibid., 207.
39. Rozmital, 161.
40. Heyd, *loc. cit.*, 201. Thomas, *loc. cit.*, XVII.
41. Heyd, *loc. cit.*, 201, 209-210.
42. Thomas, XVIII.
43. Heyd, *loc. cit.*, 200.
44. Ibid., 209-210, 212.
45. Ibid., 214.
46. Fabri, *Tractatus*, 135, 146.
47. Heyd, *loc. cit.*, 212-213.
48. Ibid., 216.
49. Evag., III, 395-396.
50. Honey, 57.
51. Simonsfeld, II, 19-20. Heyd, *loc. cit.*, 211.
52. Evag., III, 396.
53. Ibid., 397.
54. Ibid., 436.
55. Ibid., 439, 437.

The way home

1. Evag., III, 440.
2. Ibid., 444-445.
3. Ibid., 446.
4. Ibid.
5. Ibid., 447-448.
6. Ibid., 449-450.
7. Ibid., 452-453, 456.
8. Ibid., 454.
9. Ibid., 454-455. Cf. Ibid., I, 71.
10. Ibid., 457-458.
11. Ibid., 459-460.
12. Ibid., 462-463.
13. Ibid., 464-465.
14. Harff, 295.
15. Anglure, 102.
16. Casola, 345.
17. Brasca (47b-48a).
18. Martoni, 566-567.
19. Ibid., 667-668.
20. Evag., III, 465.
21. Ibid., 466.
22. Ibid., 467-468.

Valedictory

1. Tractatus de Civitate Ulmeusi, 45-46.
2. Heyd, Das Haus . . . 216.
3. Tractatus, 19, 52.
4. Ibid., 39, 52.
5. Ibid. 48, 51.
6. Ibid., 43.
7. Ibid., 47-48.
8. Ibid., 52.
9. Ibid., 148.
10. Evag., II, 446.
11. Ibid., III, 278-279.
12. Ibid., II, 516.
13. Ibid., III, 347.
14. Ibid., 458.
15. Tractatus, 189.
16. Garrison, History of Medicine, 181-182.
17. Tractatus, 46.
18. Evag., III, 266-267.
19. Arber, 21.
20. Evag., III, 364.
21. Ibid., 14-15.
22. Janssen, I, 339-340.
23. Evag., III, 383.
24. Ibid., 452. Ptolemy, Geographia, Ulm, 1482. Pl. 1 and Europa 8. Cf. idem Rome, 1478. R. V. Tooley, Maps and Map-makers, 8.
25. Janssen, I, 82. Tractatus, 94-95.
26. Tractatus, loc. cit.
27. E.g., Evag., III, 248.
28. Ibid., 221.
29. Ibid., 218.
30. Ibid., 222-223.
31. Brasca (43a).
32. Gunnis, Historic Cyprus, 51.
33. Evag., III, 230-233.
34. Ibid., 242.
35. Tractatus, 168-169.
36. Ibid., 182.
37. Ibid., 180-182.
38. Ibid., 177.
39. Ibid., 204-205.
40. Ibid., 183-185.
41. Ibid., 223.

Index

Aegean Islands, 19
Aegina, Gulf of, 233
Albertus Magnus, 177
Alexandria, 19, 57; arrangements for pilgrims at 204-9; customs regulations at, 188, 199-200, 202-3, 216-18; harbour regulations at, 197-9; sightseeing at, 209-10; smuggling at, 201, 215-18; water supply of, 209
Alexandria, military Governor of, 203
Anglure, Ogier d', 140-1, 158n.
Animals, in the desert, 54, 56, 72, 99; in Cairo, 160-1; in Alexandria, 195-6, 205
Arabs, 21, 42, 61, 65, 78, 81, 107, 108, 161, 182-3; customs and character of, 44-50, 94-5
Artus, Conrad, 20, 89, 117, 118
Augsburg, 280

Babylon New, (or Old Cairo), 146, 148-9
Balm, Garden of, at Matariya, 115-23
Barbari, Jacopo, 195
Barqūq, first of Circassian Mamluk Sultans, 138n., 140n.
Bars Bey, Sultan, 152
Baths, at Cairo, 32, 154; at Gaza, 30, 31-3; at Matariya, 115
Bethlehem, 29
Bicken, Philip von, 19, 211
Blau, the River, 170
Blaubüren, 276, 278
Blessed Virgin, 77, 86, 116, 118, 237, 238
Brasca, Sancto, 274
Brenner Pass, 271
Breydenbach, Bernhard von, Canon of Mainz, 17, 19-20, 22, 27, 35, 74, 100, 111, 138n., 140n., 146n., 157, 203n., 204, 211, 212, 213, 221, 225, 234 and n., 254n., 258, 280
Brunico (Brunech), 271

Bruno, Bishop of Brixen, 271
Bulach, Caspar von, 251
Bulak, 175
Burton, Richard, 57

Cabriel, Andrea de, Venetian Consul in Alexandria, 126, 196, 213, 229; death of, 231, 232, 237
Cairo, 18, 19, 57; arrangements for pilgrims in, 124-6; commerce in, 161-7; houses in, 137, 143, 153, 157-8; life in, 155; population of, 157; sightseeing in, 139-54; size of, 156-7
Calinus, The Greater, 23, 27, 29, 30, 31, 34, 36, 39, 42, 56; The Lesser, 21, 27, 29, 30, 34, 39, 46, 52, 55, 59, 60 and n., 61, 62, 64, 66, 67, 68, 69, 72, 73, 94, 95, 99, 101, 103, 104, 110, 111, 112, 116, 124, 126
Camel-men, 24, 28, 39, 40, 41-4, 69, 73, 96, 100, 103, 116-17, 186
Candia, 227, 230
Casola, Canon Pietro, 227, 245, 247, 252, 274
Cava, Onofrio della, 246
Chaucer, Geoffrey, 17, 141
Chawatha (probably Khalasa), 61
Chemnitz, George, Carthusian Prior of, 135, 136
Christians, Coptic, 121, 127, 149; Eastern, 40, 161, 207; Greek, 79, 81, 228; Jacobite, 121, 210; Latin, 81, 207, 228
Church of
St. Euphemia at Rovinj, 251
St. George at New Babylon, 149
St. Katherine, at Mount Sinai, 77, 84-5, 92-3
St. Michael, at Alexandria, 210
St. Sergius, at New Babylon, 148n.
St. Simeon, at Zadar, 250
San Giovanni e Paolo at Venice, 259
The Holy Sepulchre, at Jerusalem, 23

INDEX

The Nativity, at Bethlehem, 85
The Transfiguration. *See* - of St. Katherine
Clares, the Poor, of Soflingen, 284
"Cleopatra's Needle," 210
Column, Gate of the (Alexandria), 202
Conegliano, 268, 269
Consuls, Venetian. *See* Gabriel
Contarini, Bernardo, 233; Sebastian, 212, 213, 221, 225, 229, 242
Conti, Nicolò, 18, 132, 192
Corfu, 227, 228, 242; Greek churches of, 79; pilgrims ashore at, 243–4
Cortina d'Ampezzo, 270
Cos, 280
Cracow, Thomas of, 20, 213
Crete, 163, 226, 229, 230; Greek churches of, 79
Cyclades, the, 230, 233, 234
Cymbern, Johann Werner von, 276
Cyprus, 226, 282; Greek churches of, 79; Venetian policy in, 134

Damietta, 128; Governor of, 178
Darb el Hajj, 60, 66, 68n., 110, 111, 115, 191
Debbet-el-Ramla, 69
Desert, the, dangers of, 50–1, 61–6, 70, 104, 107, 112; hardships of, 51–3, 64–8, 100, 101, 103, 108–9, 110, 111; preparations and provisions for, 23–36; routes across, 29, 60, 64, 66, 67, 72, 99, 100, 108, 110, 115; routine of travel in, 40–1, 53, 55
Dia, Island of, 230
Dobbiaco (Toblach), 271
Dogana del Gabbano, 199
Donkey-men, 25, 39, 40, 69, 89, 92
Doughty, Charles, 25, 35, 41–2, 46, 52, 57, 70n., 73
Doves, tame, in Cairo, 159
Dragomans, 28, 46–7, 48, 132, 133. *See also* Calinus, Halliu, Shadbak, Taghribirdi
Dubrovnik (Ragusa), 245, 246

Eberhart, Count of Würtemberg, 284
Edku, lake of, 181
Egypt, climate of, 161; geographical importance of, 19, 190; imports of, 166–7, 193–4; population of, 127; produce of, 163–5; Sultans of, 19, 33, 128, 129, 130, 150, 166, 194–5, 196–7. *See also* Barquq, Bars Bey, Qa'it Bey; Trade, regulation of in, 190–7
Elchingen, 275
El-Dha'iqa, gorge of, 62
El Maadiyeh, 182n., 185n.
Elphahallo, The Lesser Calinus. *See* Calinus
El Watia, 73
Es Zawieh, 30
Evagatorium in Terram Sanctam, 17, 60n., 174, 226, 233, 278, 279, 285

Fern Pass, 272
Fondachi, at Alexandria, 192, 199–200, 212, 213, 225; general plan of, 195; organisation of, 196–7; consuls of, 196, 200, 206, 211, 216
Fondaco, Aragonese or Catalan, at Alexandria, 169, 204–12, 217
Fondaco dei Tedeschi, 195, 254n., 257, 262, 266; domestic arrangements of, 263–4; rules of, 265
Forty Saints, monastery of, 87, 90
France, Kings of, Charles VI, 79; Louis IX, 128; Louis XI, 79
Francis, a Christian merchant, 125, 126, 136
Frescobaldi, Lionardo, 18n., 46, 47, 50, 94, 125, 133, 197n., 203
Friars, Dominican, 17, 206, 240, 247, 250, 258, 259–60, 275–6, 283. *See also* Ulm, Dominican Convent at; Franciscan, 17, 23, 24, 26, 71, 78, 246, 247. *See also* Mount Sion, Franciscan Convent on
Frig, Nicholas, 254
Fua, 176, 178, 181n.
Fuchs, Leonhard, 280
Fuchs, Prior Ludwig, 275, 283, 284

Gaza, 29–36, 39, 40
Gazelus, the, 24
Gebel Hilal, 62; – Katerina, *see* Mount, St. Katherine's; – Minshera, 66; – Musa, *see* Mount Sinai
Germany, reform in, 279, 283–5; culture in, 279–81; trade in, 257, 262, 265

Gesner, Conrad, 280
Gharbiyeh, 163
Gucci, Giorgio, 46

Hajj Road. See Darb el Hajj
Hallicub (perhaps Wadi Khallal), 67
Halliu, 175, 180, 181, 182, 185, 186, 188, 201, 202, 204
Harff, Arnold von, 18n., 25, 28, 30, 49, 50, 78, 82, 110, 121n., 132n., 134n., 135, 138n., 141, 147, 156, 165n., 178n., 199n., 206n., 261, 262, 263
Hebron, 29
Herbarius zu Teutsch, 280
Historia Stirpium, 280
Holy Cross, Feast of the Exaltation of the, 63
Holy Family, the, 115-16, 148
Hvar (Lesina), 247

Illertissen, 273
Inn of St. George, or of the Flute, in Venice, 254, 257
Innsbruck, 272
Ios, Island of, 230, 232
Israelites, 66, 143
Itinerarium . . ., of Paul Walther, 17, 60n.
Iyas, Ibn, 134

Janus III of Cyprus, 152, 178
Jerusalem, 17, 19, 23-9
Jethro, 73; daughters of, 80
Jiddah, 191
John, "the cook," 20, 89, 104
Joinville, Jean de, 128, 130, 163n
Jung, Johann, 280
Justinian, 77; Church of, 84

Kempten, 273
Khalig, the, 172
Khanka, 115
Kom ed-Dik, at Alexandria, 187n.
Korčula (Curzola), 247
Koroni (Coron), 226, 227
Kraft, Conrad, Mayor of Ulm, 272

Krelin, Elizabeth, Cistercian Prioress of Hegbach, 283-4
Kyfer, Johann, 280

La Broquière, Bertrandon de, 18n., 25, 49-50
Lago Morto, 269
Lakonia, bay of, 234
Lane, Edward, 147, 172n.
Lannoy, Guillebert de, 18n., 127, 129, 138n., 156, 170, 179n., 187n.
Lawrence, T. E., 57
Lazinus, Archdeacon John of Transylvania, 20-1, 34, 89, 94, 131-2, 139, 213, 217, 232, 237, 244, 248, 249, 257-8
Lermoos, 273
Loredano, Andrea da, 212
Loredano, Marco de, 213, 237, 253
Lueg, 272

Mahomet II the Conqueror, 226; the Prophet, tomb of, 110
Malea, Cape, 232, 233, 234, 237, 238
Mallengart, Nicholas, 179
Mamluks, 103, 115, 121, 122, 139, 149, 150, 151, 152, 153-4, 157, 163, 166, 167, 171, 192, 193, 194; empire of 18, 46; social structure and power of, 33-4, 127-38
Manna, 73-4
Marghera, 266
Martoni, Nicolò, 86, 140n., 158n., 159 and n., 188, 274
Matariya, 115-23
Mattrey, 272
Mecca, 110, 191, 194
Megmar, 68 and n.
Melos, Island of, 234-6, 237
Memmingen, 273
Menkaura, tomb of, 142
Mernawe, Bernhard von, 20, 35, 186
Methoni (Modon), 226, 237, 239-41
Michelezzo, 245
Minsinger, Johann, 279
Misr-el-Fustat, 149
Mocenigo, Doge Paolo, 259
Monemvasia, 226, 233
Monks, Benedictine, 283; of St. Basil, 80, 81
Morea, the, 234, 239

Morspach, Sigismund of, 21, 89
Moses, 73, 77, 80, 86, 92; Well of (Ayun Musa), 108-9
Moslems, 21, 23, 27, 34, 103, 108, 110, 115, 121, 122, 124, 151, 155, 161, 162, 167, 175, 177, 187
Mount Horeb or "of the Law." See Mount Sinai
Mount Moqattam, 151, 157
Mount St. Katherine's, 57, 77, 85, 89-92
Mount Sinai, 1, 2, 57, 69, 73, 77, 84; ascent of, 85-7, 91
Mount Sion, Franciscan Convent on, 23, 24, 25, 26; Father Guardian of, 26, 27
Müller, Johann, 266, 271, 272, 273, 275

Nakhl, 60, 64
Naousa, bay of, 233
Naqb Rakna, 60, 69
Nasir Mahomet, canal of (Nasiri Canal), 176, 209
Nassau, Spa at, 278
Nassereit, 272
Nauplia, Gulf of, 237
Naxos, 232
Negroponte, 226, 233
Neithart, Johann, 281
Nesselwang, 273
Nicholas V, Pope, 282
Nicodemus, Brother, of St Katherine's Monastery, 86, 89, 90, 92
Nicopolis, battle of, 18
Nicopolis, ruins of, 186
Nicosia, Cathedral of, 282-3
Nile river, 18, 143; boats on, 146, 163, 176, 180-4; crocodiles in, 177; flooding of, 120, 170-2, 183, 209; source of, 170
Nuns, Benedictine, 284; Cistercian, 283-4. See Clares, the Poor
Nüremburg, 280

Oppenheim, a man of, 133

Palazzo Ducale (Venice), 260
Palmer, E. H., 47-8, 100n.
Parenzo. See Poreč

Paros, 232
Parrots, 195-6, 224-5
Peter, King of Cyprus, 187
Pigeons, carrier, 150, 197
Piloti, Emmanuele, 18n., 110, 120, 127, 128, 132, 138n., 147, 148, 156, 166, 172, 190, 193, 199n., 200, 209
Podestagno, (Peutelstein), 270
Pompey, Column of, 202, 209
Ponte nel' Alpi, 269
Poreč (Parenzo), 239, 251-2
Poultry, production and management of, in Egypt, 146-8
Ptolemy, Claudius, *Geographia of*, 281
Pyramids, 140-2, 151

Qa'it Bey, Sultan, 19, 115, 129, 131, 133, 134; tomb and mosque of, 151, 152, 153-4, 172, 180n., 197

Ragusa. See Dubrovnik
Rappelstein, Maximilian von, 179, 272; Wilhelm, 272
Rechberg, Bär von, 276
Red Sea, 18, 57, 66, 69, 80, 91, 108, 109
Rentz, Eitel, 257, 260, 263, 264
Reutte, 273
Rewich, Erhard, 17, 20, 258
Rhodes, 79, 226
Rialto, the, 261
Rôda, Island of, 171, 172
Rosetta, 176, 179, 180
Rosetta Gate (Sun Gate or Canopic Gate) at Alexandria, 187n.
Rovinj (Rovigno), 251

Sabathytanco, the Greater Calinus. See Calinus
Saint
  Benedict, Rule of, 80
  James of Compostella, 285
  Jerome, 41, 91
  Joseph, 148
  Katherine of Alexandria, 85, 87, 89-90; relics of, 92-3, 210, 233, 236
  Katherine, Monastery of, 70, 72, 74, 77-96, 201

INDEX 309

Katherine, Star of, 56, 73
Marina, 86
Mark, 210
Michael the Archangel, 232. *See*
    Church of, at Alexandria
Nicholas, chapel of, at Poreč, 252
Saba, monastery of, 81
Simeon, 250
Spiridion, 228
Thomas the Apostle, tomb of, 192
Saladin, 150
Samson, 31
Sanuto, Livio, 180n.
Sapienza, Cape and Island of, at, 241–2
Schambeck. *See* Shadbak
Schichenberger, Hans, 272
Schiltberger, Johann, 18, 132, 150, 152n.
Schnechenhausen, 272
Schöffer, Peter, of Mainz, 280
Schonberg (or Schauenberg), Heinrich von, 21, 89, 105, 167, 233
Scriptoris, Paul, 284
Seefogel, a German Mamluk, 132, 153
Serabit el-Khadim, 100
Seravalle, 269
Shadbak, Dragoman of Alexandria, 202, 203, 204, 206–9, 215, 216, 217
Šibenic (Sebenico), 248
Siculi, Caspar von, 21, 89
Sigismund, Archduke, 123, 271, 272, 273
Sigoli, Simone, 18n., 46, 124n., 166
Slavery, 143, 167–9
Solms, John Count of, 19, 89, 167, 204; death of, 210–11, 212, 213
Solms Liech, Cuno, Count of, 19, 89
Solomon, King, 116
Spain, Ferdinand and Isabella of, 135
Sphinx, the, 142
Steinhöwel, Heinrich, 279
Stocker, Nicholas and Johann, 279
Stoffel, Heinrich von, 276
Suabia, monastic reform in, 283; Fabri's *History of,* 285
Suchem, Ludolf von, 146n.
Sultan, Well of the, 60, 64, 109
Suriano, Francesco, 18n., 46, 60n., 78, 79, 81–2, 85, 138n., 141, 142, 172n.
Syrlin, Jörg (the Elder), 281

Tafur, Pero, 18n., 125, 131n., 138n., 152, 163, 178, 191–2, 227

Taghribirdi, Chief Dragoman of the Sultan, 117, 118, 119, 123, 124, 125, 126, 133–8, 139, 142, 153, 173, 174, 175, 176, 180, 202, 203, 225; house of, 158–9; menagerie of, 160; wives of, 134, 136–8
Tarfet el-Gidarein, 99
Thenaud, Jean, 45, 48–9, 78, 79, 82–3, 132, 162, 180n., 181n.
Tîh Desert, 18, 57, 60, 69, 91, 99, 100
Tor, 57, 79, 91, 99, 102, 103, 191, 194
Trade, 240–1, 244; routes, 18, 57, 91, 102, 190–1, 229–54; spice-, 190–5, 257, 262. *See also* Alexandria, Cairo, Egypt, Venice
"*Traffico*", galleys of the, 211, 224, 234
Treatise on the City of Ulm, 278, 279, 283, 285
Trevisano, Domenico, 153
Treviso, 268

Ugelheimer, Peter, 254
Ulm, city of, 275, 277–8; Dominican House at, 17, 19, 277
Ulmer, Ulrich, 280
Umm Rakna, pass of. *See* Naqb Rakna

Velsch, Peter, 21, 34, 35, 104, 167
Venice, citizens of, 259–60; galleys of, 211, 221–4, 234, 242–4; governors, colonial, 227; overseas possessions of, 19, 226–8, 239; Sea Officers, 205, 212, 221, 222, 235, 240, 242–4; Trade, regulation of, 261–6. *See also* Contarini; Bernardo and Sebastian; Loredano, Andrea and Marco
Vils, 273
Vipiteno (Sterzing), 271
Virgin, Well of the, 115, 116, 120

Wadi el-Akhdar, 72, 99
el Arish, 62, 64, 65
el Foqeia, 67
Gharandel, 108, 109
Hargus, 99
Homr, 100
Khamila, 71
Leja, 87
el Sheikh, 72, 74

Waldburg, Johann Truchsess von, 273
Walther, Friar Paul of Guglingen, 17, 20, 22, 24, 33, 35, 44, 60n., 68, 70n., 73, 177, 121, 123, 126n., 132, 134, 136, 140, 143n., 146n., 147, 149, 155, 156, 158, 164, 179n., 181n., 185, 186, 203n., 212–13, 231, 233n., 234n., 237, 256
Wiblingen, 276
Wirker, Johann, 279

Wittenberg, 19

Yashback, Emir, 115
Ysbech, Emir, 172

Zadar (Zara), 249–50
Zirl, 272
Zurich (Birthplace of Felix Fabri), 280

Lightning Source UK Ltd.
Milton Keynes UK
UKOW051439230712

196440UK00001B/116/A